C000104031

RELATIVE RACES

Brigitte
Fielder

Relative
Races

GENEALOGIES OF INTERRACIAL KINSHIP

IN NINETEENTH-CENTURY AMERICA

Duke University Press *Durham and London* 2020

© 2020 Duke University Press
All rights reserved
Printed and bound by CPI Group (UK) Ltd, Croydon, CR0 4YY
Designed by Aimee C. Harrison and Courtney Leigh Richardson
Typeset in Arno Pro and Univers LT Std
by Westchester Publishing Services

Library of Congress Cataloging-in-Publication Data
Names: Fielder, Brigitte, [date] author.
Title: Relative races : genealogies of interracial kinship in nineteenth-century
America / Brigitte Fielder.
Description: Durham : Duke University Press, 2020. | Includes bibliographical
references and index.
Identifiers: LCCN 2020008239 (print) | LCCN 2020008240 (ebook)
ISBN 9781478010104 (hardcover)
ISBN 9781478011156 (paperback)
ISBN 9781478012689 (ebook)
Subjects: LCSH: Race in literature. | American literature—History and criticism. |
Race relations in literature. | Literature and race—United States. | Race. | African
Americans—Race identity.
Classification: LCC PN56.R16 F545 2020 (print) | LCC PN56.R16 (ebook) |
DDC 810.9/3552—dc23
LC record available at https://lccn.loc.gov/2020008239
LC ebook record available at https://lccn.loc.gov/2020008240

Cover art: Craft, Emiline Kinloch. "William and Ellen Smith Craft Photo
Album," Lowcountry Digital Library, Avery Research Center at the College of
Charleston. Photographs of Charles Craft, Alfred Craft (adult), Alfred Craft
(baby), Aunt Ellen Craft, and Ellen Craft.

Duke University Press gratefully acknowledges The Office of the Vice Chancellor
for Research and Graduate Education at the University of Wisconsin–Madison,
which provided funds toward the publication of this book.

IN LOVING MEMORY OF

Ann Dorothy Summerford Fielder
(1918–2011)

&

Thelma Rhoda Richards Degon
(1922–2014)

AND IN HUMBLE DEDICATION TO MY PARENTS,

Sue Ann Fielder &
Stephan Howard Fielder,
who taught me to read.

CONTENTS

ACKNOWLEDGMENTS

Whenever I assign an academic monograph in a graduate course, I always ask my students to read the acknowledgments. I tell them that book acknowledgments sections are a reminder that even single-authored academic writing is not done in isolation, but in relation. I explain that reading this section carefully is as important as paying close attention to citational practices. I ask them to consider this genre of genuinely grateful and deeply loving writing as they find "their people" and work to build and sustain ethical communities of learning, colleagueship, camaraderie, and care. I ask them to remember how family—both biological and nonbiological—influences a writer's life and work and helps to shape it, hopefully for the better, whether or not these folks have read or ever will read the words written in their loved one's books. I read acknowledgments sections with fervor and have been composing this love letter to my colleagues and family and friends for years. What I have written here insufficiently represents the love and care I have received and my gratitude to the people mentioned. It also fails to express the extent to which I, personally, need to have actual conversations and contact with people in order to think and to write. Nevertheless, I want to register the fact that my life and work and learning and writing about any of the things I discuss in this book have always been done in—and will continue to be improved by—relation to others.

I owe special thanks to Shirley Samuels, Eric Cheyfitz, and Grant Farred for various kinds of encouragement and early support that included helping to convince me that this project could become a book. As I reframed and revised the project over these subsequent years, Monique Allewaert, Sarah Chinn, Peter Coviello, Elizabeth Freeman, Toni Wall Jaudon, Koritha Mitchell, Jonathan Senchyne, and Kyla Wazana Tompkins provided essential feedback on its larger structure and value. Each of these people helped me to develop my thoughts about this book and what it could do and also about my own potential as a writer. As I made final revisions to the manuscript, Koritha, Jonathan and also Derrick Spires patiently talked me through my evolving relationship to this project and the continuing evolution of my writing more generally. I am deeply grateful for their various reassurances as I worked through these ideas.

I presented early versions of chapters 5 and 1 at workshops at the Futures of American Studies Institute at Dartmouth College, and I am grateful, in particular, to Eric Lott, Donald Pease, and Elizabeth Maddock Dillon for their feedback and encouragement. I am grateful also to the editors and anonymous readers of *Studies in American Fiction* and *Theatre Annual* for the feedback I received on portions of chapters 2 and 1, respectively. Portions of this material were previously published in "'Almost Eliza': Reading Mary King as the Mixed-Race Heroine of William Allen's *The American Prejudice Against Color*," *Studies in American Fiction*, 40, no. 1 (2013), 1–25, © 2013 by the Johns Hopkins University Press; and in "Blackface Desdemona: Theorizing Race on the Nineteenth-Century American Stage," *Theatre Annual* 70 (2017), 39–59.

I would not have been able to complete this project without the amazing resources and knowledgeable staff of research libraries, including the Samuel J. Mays Antislavery Collection in Cornell University Library's Division of Rare and Manuscript Collections, the Library Company of Philadelphia's collection of African Americana (and the special help of Krystal Appiah), the research library at the Buffalo Historical Museum, and the Schomburg Center for Research in Black Culture. I am especially grateful to past and present staff of the American Antiquarian Society, at which I have benefited from innumerable acts of assistance from Paul Erickson, Marie Lamoreaux, Jaclyn Penny, Elizabeth Pope, and Laura Wasowicz.

This project has benefited immensely from a First Book Workshop sponsored by the University of Wisconsin–Madison Center for the Humanities, and from the excellent feedback I was therefore able to receive from Monique Allewaert, Cindy Cheng, Christy Clark-Pujara, Elizabeth Freeman, Sarah Guyer, Karen Sanchez-Eppler, and Timothy Yu. A Nellie Y. McKay research fellowship from the University of Wisconsin–Madison granted me the necessary time to complete my final round of revisions. Although I never had the privilege of meeting McKay, her work and legacy are well known to me and I am particularly honored to have held a fellowship named in her honor. Additional support for this research was provided by the University of Wisconsin–Madison Office of the Vice Chancellor for Research and Graduate Education with funding from the Wisconsin Alumni Research Foundation. It also bears mentioning that while working on this project I benefited from the parental leave that both my partner and I received from the University of Wisconsin–Madison. We recognize that we are privileged to have had access to leave policies and that many of our peers have not been afforded the same benefits. In order to best support academics with kinship responsibilities (biological or otherwise), US academic institutions must support parents and other caregivers with better leave polices.

I cannot begin to name all the people whose generosity and colleagueship have helped to make this project possible. Significant mentors have included Susannah Ashton, Robin Bernstein, Hester Blum, Sarah Chinn, Peter Coviello, Anna Mae Duane, Duncan Faherty, Robert Fanuzzi, Jonathan Beecher Field, Pier Gabrielle Foreman, Elizabeth Freeman, Eric Gardner, Susan Gillman, Glenn Hendler, Honorée Fanonne Jeffers, Eric Lott, Dana Luciano, Koritha Mitchell, Philip Nel, Meredith Neuman, Carla Peterson, Mark Rifkin, Karen Salt, Karen Sanchez-Eppler, Cristobal Silva, and Kyla Wazana Tompkins. At the University of Wisconsin–Madison, Cindy Cheng, Tom DuBois, and particularly Jordan Rosenblum have been exceptional mentors. During my time here, I have been extremely grateful for the colleagueship of Fenaba Addo, Johanna Almiron, Danielle Evans, Martin Foys, Christa Olson, Jen Plants, Carolina Sarmiento, Susannah Tahk, Steph Tai, Monica White, Timothy Yu, and Jordan Zweck. In Madison, Karma Chávez, Colin Gillis, and Dan Wang offered me new opportunities for writing and collaboration that have helped me to develop my writing beyond what can be conveyed in citations.

I remain permanently indebted to Alex W. Black, Jill Spivey Caddell, Melissa Gniadek, Toni Wall Jaudon, Jonathan Senchyne, and Xine Yao, who managed to sustain our graduate student camaraderie into professorial colleagueship. In addition to these, friends and colleagues from a variety of academic fields have provided key conversations and models for both my academic work and the nature of colleagueship itself. These include Sari Altschuler, Tara Bynum, Michael Cangemi, Rinku Chatterjee, Rachel Collins, Sarah Park Dahlen, Michael Dwyer, D. Berton Emerson, Hilary Emmett, Sarah Etlinger, Danielle Evans, Benjamin Fagan, Stephanie Farrar, Molly Farrell, Danielle Haque, Jameel Haque, Kamila Janiszewska Kehoe, Corinne Martin, Erich Nunn, Jason Payton, Daphna Ram, Britt Rusert, Gina Sipley, Tristan Sipley, Derrick Spires, Nafissa Thompson-Spires, Ebony Elizabeth Thomas, Harlan Weaver, and Nazera Wright. These friends have offered academic and non-academic conversations, archival finds and professional advice, foot-notes and shared meals, social media distractions and writing accountability, class visits and coffee dates, museum and sports outings, films and stories and poems, (real and virtual) cat encounters, and all forms of emotional support whether we were physically present or socially distant, all of which have been essential to my writing process and survival. The people named here contribute to the very manner of academic generosity that I hope to replicate in my own practices.

I am ever grateful to Duke University Press and the readers for this project. Kenneth Wissoker's encouragement and support has been invaluable as I have completed *Relative Races*. His ability to understand the shifts through which this project has moved over the last stages of its revision has helped me to enact what I could not yet write, but only describe in conversation. I am also grateful to the Press's careful copyeditors, Annie Lubinsky and Philip Thomas. As I completed this project, I responded to final editorial queries during a global pandemic and without physical access to some necessary library resources. People who provided key assistance accessing information during this time include Sarah Marty, Jen Plants, Kathryn Vomero Santos, Lynne Stahl, and Karen Woods Weierman. Thomas Massnick was an adept and immeasurably patient research assistant through this process. I am deeply grateful for his assistance as he tracked down information, walked me through his translation of a German text, and helped me to talk through some important citational decisions.

I am grateful to my extended family, and especially my plethora of cousins, for the love and encouragement they have offered over the years and across miles of distance between us. I continue also to count Bethel Willingham as family, and as such, she deserves special thanks for her unwavering friendship throughout each of my endeavors, academic and otherwise. My parents, Sue Ann Fielder and Stephan Fielder, have never questioned my ability to complete this or any other academic project. Their unconditional love and support has been a radical alternative to the various forces that would discourage a Black girl, a first-generation college student, a nonacademic worker, a mother, or someone in any other position of academic marginalization I have occupied. These were the first theorizers of race I encountered and it is, perhaps, from them that I learned the basic premise of this study: that race is often believed to work in certain ways, but that is not necessarily so. My parents are also the people who taught me to read and to love reading, and who first put African American literature into my hands while at the same time these works were being largely neglected during almost the first two decades of my formal education. This book is for them.

Jonathan Senchyne has been my first and last reader, my sometimes collaborator, and my companion through my best academic endeavors. I look forward to embarking on future projects with and alongside him. I owe special thanks to Ezra Fielder-Senchyne for each moment of joy he has produced and for ensuring a necessary respite from writing over the last four years. He does not yet know how much he contributed to this project.

Introduction

Genealogies of

Interracial Kinship

IN KATE CHOPIN'S 1893 STORY, "Désirée's Baby," race follows a queer genealogy. Désirée is a woman of unknown parentage, adopted as an infant and raised by white people. She marries a wealthy enslaver, Armand, and they have a child together. Three months pass, and other characters begin to exchange knowing looks about the child. Armand's temperament toward his family changes entirely as he turns from a proud father into an absent and avoidant one. Désirée herself finally notices what seems to be some resemblance between her child and an enslaved "quadroon" boy. She confronts Armand for an explanation, and he angrily replies, "It means that the child is not white . . . It means that you are not white."[1] Armand's logical shift from characterizing his child's race to making a statement about Désirée's illustrates the nonnormative directions in which racial inheritance sometimes flows.

"Désirée's Baby" represents what might best be called a "backward" genealogy of racial transfer, as Désirée is re-racialized by virtue not of her own parentage but via the racialization of her child. Coming to see the baby as visibly Black, Armand assumes that Désirée herself must therefore be racially mixed.[2] At the story's end, of course, we discover that Armand actually has Black ancestry, a fact that has been hidden from him by his white Creole father and mixed-race mother. Still, the racial refiguring of Désirée—a figuring dependent upon the emerging Blackness of her baby—has already taken effect. While we learn nothing of Désirée's biological parents over the course of the story, she effectively becomes a mixed-race heroine. She and her baby are both cast out of the husband/father's house because of their supposed, shared Blackness. "Désirée's Baby" narrates an effective reversal of racial transfer from child to mother rather than the other way around. This story shows how the production of "amalgamated" children has implications even for previously racially defined parents, particularly for mothers who are held responsible for (re)producing race.

While one might initially call this a story of racial misrecognition since we learn that Armand is the one—but not necessary the only one—who is "really" Black, the fact that both woman and child can be racially re-figured is illustrative of the slippery business of racialization: "white" women apparently have the potential to be racially marked—effectively re-racialized—by their children. Alys Eve Weinbaum argues that "Ultimately, *there are no white people in this text*, whose deepest meaning pivots on recognition of the pretense that neither the 'pure' origins of individuals nor those of nations can ever be discerned."[3] However, giving readers a genealogical racialization of Armand via a revealed mixed-race mother does not turn him into a Black man any more so than having a Black child turns any white nineteenth-century male character into someone who will acknowledge and care for that child. Armand's own embodiment does not give this racial genealogy away. And after he expels Désirée and their baby from his home, neither will his kinship relations suggest his Black ancestry. Although revealed to both Armand and the reader, we presume that his racial genealogy will remain a secret, thus preserving Armand's whiteness and status in his white supremacist community and the white supremacist nation, while Désirée effectively becomes a mixed-race heroine by the story's close.[4]

In Désirée's re-racialization we observe a trajectory of racial transfer that does not work according to normative models of the genealogical inheritance of race wherein race flows from biological parents to children. Chopin's story is one of many narratives in the long nineteenth century that explore how racial formation in the United States follows queer genealogical roots rather than normative ones. In the queer genealogy Chopin probes, it is possible for race to be transferred from child to mother. It is also possible for race to skip generations, to be reconstructed entirely between one generation and the next, as in Armand's case. Although racialization often depends upon factors such as individual identification and physical racial presentation, Chopin's story of racial (re)production shows us how race is also relative. It is produced not in individual bodies themselves, but, crucially, in the relationships between them—in kinship relations that are not simply direct genealogies of racial inheritance from one generation to the next, but which work in decidedly gendered and non-heteronormative ways.

Relative Races: Genealogies of Interracial Kinship in Nineteenth-Century America presents an alternative theory of how race is constructed. Rather than tracing "downward" genealogies by which race is transmitted from parents to children, my readings of nineteenth-century literature show how race can follow other directions. This theory of race turns to queer theorizations of time in order to describe the non-heteronormative, nonbiological models by which genealogies of interracial kinship (re)construct race. Contrary to notions of biological and cultural racial inheritance (understood as the genealogical transfer of racial materiality and identity from parents to children), I show how race is not simply constructed according to heteronormative trajectories. Rather, race follows different lineages in narratives of interracial kinship, which themselves defy neat boundaries between races and clear correlations of familial and racial identification. Reading race's queer genealogies shows us how race is not constructed according to mere biology or even within individual bodies, but in the relations between racialized bodies. This is the queer genealogy of racialization in which Désirée comes to function as a mixed-race Black woman by virtue of her child's visible Blackness.

In framing this project around how race is constructed via kinship relations, it bears mentioning that what I am *not* discussing is what Alisha Gaines describes as "temporary black individuals operating under the alibi of racial empathy."[5] While interracial kinship relations sometimes do and sometimes do not produce the kinds of (temporary or lasting) empathy that Gaines describes, I am concerned, rather, in instances of how such relationships produce race itself, though in unpredictable ways. My discussion of racialization extends beyond the notions of individual, racial identification with which it might conflict (as we see in the case of Désirée). While the history of antiblackness is central to US racial formation and therefore central to my project, my discussion also includes the racialization of Indigenous people in literary and cultural discourses. The continued conflation of indigeneity and race in popular and academic discussions of racialization has had lasting implications, as discussed by Kimberly Tall-Bear, J. Kēhaulani Kauanui, Jean M. O'Brien, and other Native scholars, and adds an additional problem to be unpacked in discussing US histories of racial formation.[6] I do not wish to conflate racialization and indigeneity, but instead mean to recognize what Jodi Byrd calls "the entanglement of colonization and racialization," by recognizing how racialization cannot be divorced from matters of land and sovereignty.[7] This point becomes clear in several of the texts I discuss.

The theory of race I present here therefore makes apparent how race (and racism) are made and matter beyond the bodily scale, in the domestic spaces of family and nation that reveal race's structures in their future-oriented trajectories of racial production and reproduction. I read texts that exhibit processes of race-making that are not necessarily heteronormative (even when they may follow heterosexual genealogies) and which are produced through interpersonal relations at multiple scales, in relations between racialized bodies and within racialized families and nations. Throughout, I show that race itself is relative, formed through genealogies of racial inheritance, relations of racialized domesticity, and in larger structures of racial belonging. To show how race is not individual but formed in relation, I turn to interracial kinship, reading narratives in which we can more clearly observe race's directional flow between people, across generational time, and through everexpanding spatial scales.

Unpacking the construction of race as relative is this book's main project. I mean the term "relative" to refer both to the production of race in relation—as constructed not within individual bodies but in the relationships between them—and to its production through kinship ties—though not necessarily in exclusively biological or heteronormative genealogies of racial descent. The process of race-making not only transfers race from a genealogical past to future descendants, but differently, through nonbiological relations of adoption, "horizontal" relations of sexual kinship, and "backward" genealogies of racial reflection from children to parents or "circular" relations by which race is constructed and reconstructed *ad infinitum*. These genealogies might best be understood as creating a "queer temporality" of racialization. Race is still relative in these alternative genealogies, as the figures I discuss form racial identifications that affect how they construe kinship relations and vice versa. This theory of racialization effectively reimagines the relationship between race and family. It also reimagines the spaces of racialization as happening not simply within the body and through racial self-articulation, but also through familial recognition. Race is produced—and reproduced—in relation, in the connections between bodies, in domestic spaces, through literary genre, and in practices of racialized reading and naming.

Relative Races describes a theory of racial formation that acknowledges both the understanding of race-making as a taxonomic project of comparison and the importance of kinship relations for assigning bodies to racialized groups. The term "racialization" appears throughout my project to refer to the various processes of race-making I discuss here. I use this term to distinguish the processes of race-making from their end product: race. Different processes of racialization may work in tandem with or even against one another, and their potential conflict reveals the nature of race as constructed—as historically comprehensible though not entirely predictable, as complex, as mythos, and as entirely real in its import and impact on racialized bodies and relations of kinship and power. Passed through genealogies of inheritance across generations of history, race is not essential to this inheritance but constructed by it. Here we see how race itself does not produce but is produced by societal relations in various historical settings. Race is constructed, though this fact does not make it any less real.

Expanding the scale of comprehending race beyond the individual shows how race is relational rather than generational. Race is relational, or "relative," in that it is not simply embodied by an individual but constructed as racialized bodies are placed into relation with or comparison to one another. Race is also relative in the sense that it is structured by and through kinship relations in the texts I discuss. Because race is not simply inherited, relatives may be assigned different races, mixed-race people are racialized in ways that ignore some relations and prioritize others, and nonbiological relatives may still inform one another's racialization. These differently directional genealogies might be understood as creating a "queer temporality" of racialization that refuses what Elizabeth Freeman calls chrononormativity, "the use of time to organize individual bodies toward maximum productivity."[8] My reading of racial genealogy as directional takes up this model of both nonnormative time and kinship. Wary of prioritizing biological kinship, I instead read kinship's different trajectories of inheritance. Unlike notions of genealogical nationalism, which Holly Jackson describes as "a symbolic property passed down the family line, a vertical inheritance from their fathers," racial belonging does not necessarily follow the same lines of inheritance.[9] Despite the predominance of heterosexuality in the texts I discuss here, characters' racial reproduction does not always follow chrononormative genealogies of descent. Rather, we can observe genealogies that resist what I call "downward" trajectories of racial inheritance in favor of differently directional genealogies, such as Désirée's apparent inheritance of race from her child.

My use of the term "queer" to describe race's genealogies of construction and reconstruction describes processes of racialization that cannot be explained by solely heteropatriarchal models of inheritance. Just as they do not follow normative chronologies, neither are genealogies of interracial kinship necessarily patrilineal. The notion of hypodescent—the "one drop rule" for designating someone with any amount of "Black" ancestry as Black, regardless of other racial genealogies—itself does not follow a patrilineal model. In this respect, hypodescent is, perhaps, the dominant framework in which race's queer genealogies operate in the United States. The notorious law of the Virginia colony, *partus sequitur ventrum*, tells us that the child follows the condition of the mother. Just as a mother's enslaved status alone determined her child's, only one parent's identification as Black is sufficient to racialize children as such. In its most ironic sense, we might regard hypodescent as a queer genealogy of race that oddly aligns with Black feminism in its resistance to patriarchal and even heterosexual notions of race's biological transfer. This understanding of hypodescent resists the antiblackness inherent in the assumption that inherited Blackness is only or necessarily oppressive. My Black feminist reading of hypodescent is clearest in chapter 4; here I discuss anti-passing literature, in which Black mothers are prioritized over white fathers. Even where we might purport to trace race through a biological mother and father, the genealogy of racialization refuses this heteronormative structure in US law and custom, prioritizing or excluding certain parental genealogies in favor of others. The result is not necessarily what Hortense Spillers calls "kinlessness" or the loss of the mother described by Saidiya Hartman, but sometimes results in a prioritization of Black and Native mothers over other kin in narratives of mixed-race women and mixed-race children whose racialization both uses and resists tropes of white womanhood in order to resist white supremacy.[10]

My discussion of the inherent queerness of racialization in interracial kinship follows recent work in Black queer feminist theory, whose readings of racial theory recognize the relations of race that I most want to discuss. Alexis Pauline Gumbs refers to the "queer" workings of racialization via hypodescent, writing that "[b]ecoming black is queer in that it is not based on purity, and it is not reproducing a narrative about what blackness itself is."[11] Darieck Scott similarly notes the "queerness of blackness," writing that "the term *queer* emphasizes a liberatory dissolution of fixed boundaries between genders, sexualities, and races."[12] Notions of racial biologism, on the other hand, are inherently heteronormative, prioritizing biological reproduction and futurity, and ignoring other forms of race-making and kinship-making. Even though race usually becomes visible via something like familial genealogies of racial resemblance, it does not always do so. That race is not necessarily visible (even while it usually is) reveals the ultimate nature of race as queerly unpredictable and sometimes queerly radical. In their explorations of race and family, nineteenth-century US texts often represent the differently queer genealogies through which relational race-making happens. Enabled by the concept of relative racialization, students and scholars are invited to take up the ways that the queerness of racialization calls into question heteronormative narratives about race and race-making more generally.

Like the genealogically queer notion of "hypodescent," racial temporalities do not necessarily make linear or logical sense. They operate in simultaneously competing ways. Resisting both essentialist notions of race's permanence and, to a lesser extent, ideas of racial movement and "fluidity," I want to suggest racialization as neither static nor as shifting between racial positions, but as necessarily contradictory in its construction. This understanding of race as contradictory is related to an understanding of race's temporalities as illogical. This illogic is inherent to white supremacy's ever-reaching effects on processes of racialization that sometimes but do not always follow predictable patterns. As Colin Dayan aptly explains, "Bad logic makes good racism."[13] I do not mean to argue that what I call queer temporalities are themselves necessarily illogical, but that illogic may follow from simultaneously operating and sometimes competing racializations, rendering them unpredictable. John Ernest writes that "to understand race it is useful to be guided by chaos theory, a theory devoted to the patterns created by complex and seemingly irregular systems."[14] My reading of racial formation similarly recognizes that race is complex and, at times, chaotically confusing. This said, the arguments I make here about racialization are not absolutist or even conditional, but occasional, as all arguments about how racialization happens in the United States must be, to some extent. As cultural construction rather than essentialist truth, race-making is not always logical. Though often—or even usually—predictable, race is not always so. Race does not always follow the same patterns; other linear paths, other genealogies are possible. Moreover, the moments of race-making and re-racialization I discuss here are not necessarily permanent; they are not all-encompassing or definitive. But they reveal something about the nature of race's construction in their potential transience and unpredictability. They show how other racial structures (and whiteness, in particular) are also precarious. As race is constructed, it must be continually reconstructed, remade and rearticulated, sometimes with a (not necessarily logical) difference.

Race's illogic and precariousness are not to be confused, however, with its impotence. Race is indeed a powerful and significant social construction. While race has often been called a myth or a fiction, this characterization risks masking the resonance of lived, racialized experience—particularly the experience of racism. Race is, indeed, real and powerful, even if fictional. In this, unpacking the literary metaphor becomes necessary. Like the literary genre with which race is compared when it is described as "fiction," its constructed or contrived nature has real, material effects on our understanding of and experiences in the world. And in this reality, race is experienced in relation—as narratives of othering and belonging, articulated against and alongside additional racial realities. Race is constructed in the spaces of relation to others' experiences of race, often in relations of kinship. In this dependence upon relation, racialization is very much like literary genre. Both are best "read" in context, in comparisons that become recognizable but may depart from a dominant pattern. Throughout this book, I "read" racialization's generic, relational underpinnings within their sociohistorical and literary contexts.

When we understand racialization as constructed rather than essential, we can understand race as cultural—we might even say literary or linguistic. Practices of ascribing human bodies to racialized groups are not unlike practices of arranging texts into literary genres. While both have something to do with the apparent content or appearance of bodies/texts themselves, they also have to do with relation, how bodies/texts fit in with larger collections of bodies/texts that are somehow "like" them. In both cases, there are sometimes compelling reasons to categorize bodies/texts otherwise. A body/text might bear features of multiple races/genres. Or, it might not fit well with the available categories at all, calling these categories themselves into question. When we see race constructed in nonnormative ways, this presents problems of genre—problems of narrating the genealogies by which race travels and the relationships that themselves become racialized. In dealing with these textual difficulties, I also address some of the problems of race-making itself. The compulsion for singular classifications of bodies/texts is compelling and useful. It allows for things like identification, coherency, and historicization. But to fully understand how race or genre work, we must understand them as constructed, not natural or necessary, but human-made, created within specific historical and cultural contexts and produced, in part, by the various texts that attempt to represent or explain them.

Literature has long been a site for theorizing race. Throughout this project, I attend to race's literary nature. In my first chapter, this point becomes clear, as US productions of *Othello* make the play an urtext for exploring particularly US American racist anxieties. I discuss racialization as it inheres differently in different literary genres (in chapters 2 and 5), as certain types of kinship that have been described as "fictive" (in chapter 4), and in the language we use to describe racialized relationships and the metaphors of race itself (in chapters 3 and 6, respectively). Just as discussions of who falls into which category of racial classification have always been in flux, so has the language we use to talk about race. In my movement between genre and language as different, simultaneously operating scales for writing about—and modes for theorizing—race, I also acknowledge the limitations of dominant, historical, essentialist racial discourse for discussing race's complexity, construction, and shifting terrain.

Race is constructed, in part, through the language we use to describe it. Richard Dyer notes the stability of the term "white" as a linguistic symbol, rather than as a descriptor of skin tone.[15] John Ernest similarly reminds us, "What is white about white people . . . is not the color of their skin (which is not, after all, white) but rather the historical situation that has made 'white' bodies such able predictors of experience, understanding, and access to privilege and cultural authority."[16] The seemingly benign terminology of race-as-color masks histories of racial privilege and racialized violence. The metaphorization of race as color has often coalesced around and thereby reinforced a black-white binary. The resonances of this binary become particularly clear, for example, in my discussions of blackface, and of mixed-race Black people. This binary also complicates readings of race and visuality in many of the images I discuss and that are reproduced in this book, which appear quite literally in black-and-white—a medium of racial representation that is inherently nonmimetic. Articulating race's significance beyond this surface-level euphemism, distancing oneself from historically racist language, reappropriating racial terms for redefined uses, and creating new terms to discuss racial phenomena are also some of the ways race is constructed. The relationship between language and race is essential to this project, evidenced by my discussion of some of the ways race-making happens through the very means we use to write and talk about race. Several of the texts I discuss here deal directly with these problems of discussing race—with naming it—as well as with the problems of naming and narrating the kinship relations through which racialization happens—for example, when our language system prioritizes certain kinds of genealogies and kinship relations, leaving us with inadequate words for naming others, a point I discuss at length in chapters 3 and 4.

While this book acknowledges and interrogates problems of racial essentialism, the language available to discuss race is often problematic, and problematically limiting. I recognize the fact that I cannot entirely escape these limitations of the language available for discussing race. In addition to the term "African American," I also use the term "Black" to refer to people of African descent more broadly. At times I also refer to "mixed-race Black people," using the former as a modifier of the latter in order to describe a specific and particular way of being Black. This registers the fact that such people more often than not in the nineteenth-century United States (and afterward) have identified as Black rather than as white and generally did not regard the category "mixed race" as a racial designation of its own.[17] The theory of racial hypodescent that I treat throughout this book explains why this is the case. I use the words "Indian" as well as "Native" to refer to Indigenous peoples of North America when I am not referring to people's or characters' specific tribal affiliations. Because nineteenth-century discourses often included "Indian" in literary, popular, scientific, and legal racial classifications, this category becomes important for understanding Native people's collective racialization in the United States, even while we must understand and acknowledge the more complex relations of kinship and sovereignty that are masked by this form of racialization, points to which I return in chapter 5. My emphasis on the treatment of white-Black and white-Native interracialism is in accordance with the dominant discourses of the century and the conversations around which race was constructed in this white-centered landscape of US racism.[18] At times I also use phrases like "nonwhite people" and "people of color" in my discussions of people of various racial identities who have been collectively racialized outside of (and in relation to) whiteness.

Race is constructed in a maelstrom of social convergences, but it is also experiential, lived. To be racialized is to experience, to be subjected to forms of racial privilege or oppression—to live in racial relation. In the nineteenth century, to be racialized as nonwhite was often to be harmed by settler colonialist and/or antiblack violence. Racial embodiment is a state of being in the world, not necessarily of having racial materiality or performing race, although these are also often involved in racial being. Race is identifying or being identified as a racialized being, but it is not only individual. Race is collective. It is not constructed in a personal vacuum, but, like language and literary genre, through a complex set of relations at various simultaneous scales. Race's comparative nature is one reason why Black/white racial dualism persists in US culture. This is a shorthand, a lazy but convenient compression of race from the complexities of racial relations into a white/nonwhite dichotomy that extracts only the position of racial supremacy and disregards the nuances of other "nonwhite" positions and relations. This dualism, however, also draws attention to the importance of antiblackness to US histories of structural racism. In a white supremacist society, racial dualism is also what structures power only in relation to its highest wielder. While this simplistically reduces various positions of nonwhiteness, it can sometimes be useful for understanding white supremacy and the spectrum of various relations of racialization to whiteness.

Defined by comparison, race is also imagined to be somehow perceptible—often via visualization. But what notions of "colorblind" racism elude in their reduction of race to color is that even in the midst of anxieties regarding racial ambiguity, race has continually been imagined as material—as biological. Scientists and others in the US have debated the nature of race as well as its location—in quanta of imagined "blood" according to the 1705 Virginia Colony or the Indian Reorganization Act of 1934, in the "scarf-skin," or even the "bile," as Thomas Jefferson posits in *Notes on the State of Virginia*, or in the size and shape of the skull as Samuel Morton argues in *Crania Americana* and *Crania Aegyptiaca*.[19] More recently, Henry Louis Gates's PBS series *Finding Your Roots* reads race into DNA—via genealogies of biological relations. Such understandings of race illustrate the racial logic of biologism, as defined by the *Oxford English Dictionary* as "the interpretation of human life from a strictly biological point of view," and as can be particularly found in the scientific racism that emerges as the dominant discourse of race in the nineteenth century.[20] The idea that race is simply a product of biological, genealogical descent also shows nineteenth-century discourses of kinship are dependent upon what Eric Cheyfitz refers to as a "bio-logic" of racial formation.[21] Kinship, however, is more complex than biological genealogy. As Judith Butler recognizes "it is not possible to separate questions of kinship from property relations (and conceiving persons as property), and from the fictions of 'bloodline' as well as the national and racial interests by which these lines are sustained."[22] To reduce race to biology is also to disregard its intersections with other social formations such as class and nation, as well as its relations to sexuality, kinship, legitimacy, sovereignty, and inheritance. The bio-logic of racial essentialism suggests race's trajectories as inevitable, wholly predictive of racial genealogies and their trajectory through expanding scales of body, family, and nation. This much is evident from twenty-first-century attention to DNA tracing, and all of its racialized implications for imagined places of a person's genealogical origin in some geographical-racial past. Kimberly TallBear shows how Native DNA is best understood as "co-constituted with U.S. race categories, which themselves are coproduced with Euro-American colonial practices, including eighteenth- through twentieth-century U.S. race laws, policy, and programs."[23] However, while race may be visible, visual, material, geographical, genealogical, and cultural, its biology is actually miniscule and suspect. The racialization of DNA shows us surprisingly little about how race "works" in historical contexts. However, such DNA tests are revelatory precisely because racialization is not an entirely predictable phenomenon.

Departing from strictly biologist understandings of race, Katy Chiles discusses a prior era of race-making in early America, in which racial difference was not imagined to be "fixed in nature" (as Jefferson held) but by its impermanence, its status as "transformable."[24] Chiles describes race as "potentially mutable" because "it was thought to be an exterior bodily trait, incrementally produced by environmental factors (such as climate, food, and mode of living) and continuously subject to change."[25] My own discussion of later racial formation—and, more particularly, the ongoing process I here term "racial (re)formation"—refers instead to race's changeability through different factors—relations. If race is a social construct, then it is a relational one. And as race cannot entirely escape its history of biological underpinnings, it has to do with kinship.

My theorization of race as relative also situates itself between the persistent notions—and legal imperatives—of race as inherited through genealogical lines of descent and theories of race's construction in various historical moments and social spaces. Kinship and racialization emerge not through monolithic ideologies but in structures of feeling. Both speak to the affective elements inherent in relations: who belongs with whom and how and with what responsibilities. Mark Rifkin describes these affective elements as "genealogies of sensation" in which "peoplehood inheres in forms of feeling."[26] By extending kinship beyond the biological, nuclear family nonwhite people have not always conformed to normative white models of feeling. White supremacists therefore represented African Americans and Native Americans as emotionally inappropriate in their feelings of kinship—as uncaring in the face of familial loss or improperly extending kinship beyond the heteronormative nuclear family. The connections between kinship and racialization also suggest conflicts of affect and political alignment. Christina Sharpe argues that for white people to show anti-racist solidarity, "One must refuse to repair a familial rift on the bodies cast out as not kin."[27] The connection between kinship recognition and racialization shows how racial construction often depends upon the articulation of relations—racial figuring not only within a sociohistorical context, but in terms of articulating (recognizing, denying, and re-forming) family relationships. Thus, individual and familial racial production and (re)production extend to the larger implications for and project of theorizing and retheorizing race, racial construction, and (re)construction. This project seeks to recognize the collapsed scale and recursive teleology of race-making at the respective levels of body, family, and nation, the connections between which become most visible in narratives of interracial kinship.

Interracial Kinship and Racial (Re)Production

During the 1858 political campaign season, Democrats in Indiana played-up concerns that Republicans were "amalgamationists" in a demonstration involving young white women in white dresses carrying banners that read "Fathers, save us from n[—] husbands!"[28] Apart from the assumption that white women are universally desirable and therefore the potential objects of sexual desire for Black men, this rhetoric also assumes that white women are not subjects capable of desiring Black men, and therefore must be "saved" from interracial sexual encounters that were categorized definitively as rapes. This understanding of white women designates whiteness, as Elise Lemire explains, as "an identity people can only claim if they have certain sexual race preferences."[29] A matter of sexual preference or "taste," then, also works to racialize these subjects. More simply put, interracial desire risks racializing white women because it does not seek to preserve racial segregation, separation, or "purity." It racializes them because it makes them (like Désirée) unable to reproduce white children.

My discussion of racialization is premised on the understanding that race-making has as much to do with the construction of whiteness as it does with other kinds of racial construction. Discussions of white womanhood, in particular, in the American nineteenth century have primarily emphasized the notions of essentialized biological, genealogically inherited race that I seek to critique. Because the figure of the white woman has become central to narratives of normative, genealogical racial reproduction, I give particular attention to texts that upset this rhetoric of white womanhood in nineteenth-century American literary culture. In relations of interracial kinship, the figure of the white woman ceases to be a supposed preserver of racial "purity," but becomes a racially malleable and precarious figure who might be re-racialized through interracial kinship relations. Racist anxieties like those expressed by anti-amalgamation discourses about white womanhood imagine race as something potentially transferrable to white women subjects. White women are thereby positioned as especially susceptible to "receiving" race (a point I will discuss at length in chapter 1) and (as we see in the power relations between Armand and Désirée) somehow hold more responsibility than white men for reproducing race. In short, genealogical notions of racial inheritance are upset when we look at white women figures in interracial relationships of sexual kinship or childbearing. This focus on white womanhood shows us how race is constructed by illustrating how whiteness is—and isn't—reproduced. The importance of racial reproduction becomes visible when white reproduction fails. While white supremacy is dependent upon exclusions that define "white" people only in relation to people who are not white, it is also dependent upon the ability of whiteness to reproduce itself. In her discussion of the devaluation of Black reproduction, Dorothy Roberts writes that "I have also noticed that America is obsessed with creating and preserving genetic ties between white parents and their children."[30] When whiteness fails (or refuses, as I discuss in later examples) to preserve or perpetuate white reproduction despite these genetic ties, race's queer genealogies become visible.

As we will see throughout this study, racialization does not always fall under the purview of white men. This fact works against the usual practices of scientific taxonomization by which white men have debated the nature of racial difference and the characteristics, relations between, and even the number of different "races of men." The converging branches of scientific inquiry in which race has been be parsed is, itself, a social structure of race-making. Based on white supremacist assumptions and what would later come to be understood as pseudoscientific methodologies, nineteenth-century racial science depended upon structures of white, patriarchal power as an origin point for scientific knowledge.[31] Racialization has, historically, been a gendered affair. Jennifer Morgan notes how "enslaved women experienced the explicit and implicit claims upon their wombs" in the forced reproduction of enslaved bodies.[32] Though not a comparable burden, the responsibility of white women to reproduce white people fold the same logics of racial reproduction and white supremacy. Chopin's story, for example, first appeared in *Vogue* with the title "The Father of Désirée's Baby," on January 14, 1893. The alternate title suggests a question about where the force of racialization comes from: does Désirée's baby re-racialize her, or does Armand? That white men are a force of power in race-making is clear and, insomuch as

Armand is the origin of crafting Désirée's race, he does so from his position of white male power. But, in the differences between Armand and Désirée, we see how white women, specifically, become racially precarious; they risk re-racialization precisely because it is mothers (and not fathers) who are held responsible for (re)producing race.

The "relative races" of the historical figures and literary characters I discuss here are therefore complexly organized around the power of interracial kinship relations to racialize white women in particular. My focus on white women takes up a thread of American Studies (exhibited by scholars such as Amy Kaplan, Linda Kerber, Karen Sanchez-Eppler, and Shirley Samuels) that positions the white woman as a definitive site for racial construction in nineteenth-century US popular and literary culture. As literal reproducers of whiteness, white women have most often been discussed as figures whose primary function is to keep the racial Other outside the domestic spaces of the home, family, and nation. *Relative Races* reads the rhetoric of white womanhood when interracial kinship relations come into play. In readings of personal narratives, novels, plays, stories, poems, and images, I show how the figure of the white woman is formed through readings of their relative racialization—that is, by reading how their race is re-formed in relation to their differently racialized relatives. In interracial kinship relations, white women do not simply reproduce whiteness, but instead construct race through kinship ties that depart from normative heterosexual genealogies. The kinds of kinship I discuss here are "queer" even when heterosexual, as they refuse heteronormative genealogies. As Roderick Ferguson describes, nonwhite kinship formations have often "violated a racialized ideal of heteropatriarchal nuclearity."[33] This is not to say that this kinship is not reproductive, but that this reproduction is differently reproductive than the reproduction of bio-logic. Race might be produced and reproduced across generations, but also within the same body. I am interested in this project not simply in the reproduction of bodies in kinship formation, but in the reproduction of race itself.

In this book's theorization of relative races, I turn especially toward the interventions of work in Black feminism, Native studies, and queer theory. These theoretical perspectives offer the critiques of kinship and genealogical time that are necessary for understanding ways of race-making that challenge settler colonialist, white supremacist, patriarchal, and heteronormative frameworks with which racialization has most often been imagined in the United States. The thread by which race and genealogy are linked is also fundamentally a matter of time. I therefore draw upon the work of theorists who reconceptualize time's lineage, particularly in queer theorizations of time by writers such as Lee Edelman, Dana Luciano, Peter Coviello, José Muñoz, Carla Freccero, Elizabeth Freeman, and Mark Rifkin. Scholarship by Katy Chiles, Alys Eve Weinbaum, Sharon Patricia Holland, Christina Sharpe, and Alexis Pauline Gumbs also deals with time, asking readers to reimagine race's trajectories, calling up race's past lives while looking toward contemporary understandings of race's meaning and efficacy. The most pressing critiques of race also dovetail with—and are inextricable from—critiques of kinship, as can be seen in the work of Hortense Spillers, Saidiya Hartman, Nancy Bentley, Elizabeth Maddock Dillon, and Holly Jackson.

The most foundational critique of kinship at the heart of this project involves recognizing a tendency away from white, patrilineal genealogies in the texts I read. Writing on mixed-race Black heroines in African American literature, P. Gabrielle Foreman has critiqued how some scholars' "over-emphasis on patrilineal descent and an identification with and projection of white desire ... continually revisits the paternal and the patriarchal, the phallic and juridical Law of the (white) Father."[34] Such readings fail to recognize the ways that nineteenth-century African American women writers, in particular, centered motherhood in their narratives and theorizations of racialization. My discussion of race's matrilineal and nonheteronormative genealogies builds upon the work of scholars of African American women writers such as P. Gabrielle Foreman, Frances Smith Foster, Carla Peterson, and Ann DuCille, who recognize the complex ways such writers theorized race, particularly with regard to mixed-race Black people. The importance of Black women to these theorizations of race—both as writers and thinkers who theorized the complex connections between race, sexuality, and kinship and as important reproducers of race—cannot be overstated.[35] Even where I read white women's inability or unwillingness to reproduce whiteness, Black women's racial reproduction looms as a counter to white racial reproduction and the reproduction of white supremacy. Black women's reproduction—even when forced under conditions of enslavement—has been met with Black feminist resistance to white norms. Such resistance is not unlike race's occasional resistance to normative genealogies for reproducing whiteness. The complex intertwining of race, sexuality, and kinship evident in the study of nineteenth-century African American women follows threads that become visible in work of Black queer studies, by scholars such as Roderick Ferguson, Cathy Cohen, Darieck Scott, and Robert Reid-Pharr. Ferguson explains that "African American culture has historically been deemed contrary to the norms of heterosexuality and patriarchy." [36] So too, I add, has non-white racialization.

Although this book is invested primarily in nineteenth-century American Studies, it relies heavily on critical race theory as well as nineteenth-century African American Studies and Native studies more specifically in its discussions of race and racialization, turning to anti-racist, anti-colonialist critiques that are not new, but forms of resistance that have been foundational to the history of race-making in the United States. Reading literary genres such as the frontier romance, abolitionist literature, and literatures of race, reunion, and Reconstruction, visual depictions of interracial families in book illustrations and political cartoons, and essays and legal rulings on interracial kinship relations, this project also extends beyond models of white womanhood. I explore the intersections of African American and Native American identities with whiteness as a means of theorizing how mixed- or ambiguously raced characters function in literary and cultural texts.

The queer futurity of racial reproduction becomes significant in another way when we understand that this differently directional genealogy of race upsets teleologies of racial mixture. Like abolitionists who would prioritize mixed-race heroines in garnering sympathy for enslaved people, later writers in Critical Mixed Race Studies would be critiqued for the seeming antiblackness inherent in the articulation of mixed-race identification, as well as for popular assumptions that the production of mixed-race bodies will someday render racism impossible. I return to these critiques of racial mixture as antiblack and as reconciliation in the conclusion. The field of Critical Mixed Race Studies is one of many fields of interdisciplinary intersection for this project. This field's overwhelmingly presentist focus, however, often relegates its discussions of interracial kinship to twentieth- and twenty-first-century contexts. I hope to add this project to the work of scholars such as Tavia Nyong'o, Werner Sollors, Elise Lemire, Karen Woods Weierman, Teresa Zackodnik, Cassandra Jackson, Martha Hodes, Eve Allegra Raimon, Peggy Pascoe, and Greg Carter, who extend their treatment of racial mixing into earlier periods of US history.

Antiblack racism is, of course, at the heart of these discourses of racialization. My project therefore focuses not on the racist origins of racialization via hypodescent, however, but on its anti-racist potential. Rather than "depoliticize blackness" or effect a "slippage ... between race and racism" that Nyong'o observes in histories of US racism, the anti-racist potential of race-making depends upon embracing, rather than rejecting nonwhite racialization.[37] This retooling of racialization away from its racist uses is perhaps most visible in the long nineteenth century in Native American theorizations of belonging and family that reject the problematic "bio-logic" of racial (racist) essentialism and in anti-passing literary responses to the "tragic mulatto/a" trope. While I discuss the settler colonialist production of race as well as Native understandings of nonbiological kinship relations, antiblackness looms throughout this project because normative models of racialization came to prioritize notions of black/white dualism in the nineteenth-century United States. This reification of racial dualism was accompanied by assimilationist projects of Native genocide and land theft. There is no neat separation of the ways racist ideologies build upon both stolen bodies and stolen land, which represent two scalar sites of race-making, a point I will discuss further in chapters 5 and 6. Still, inasmuch as Blackness becomes a touchstone for discourses of race-making, its resonance seeps even into the problematic racialization of the Indigenous people of North America. This becomes visible in the genealogy of captivity discourse and even in Mary Jemison's narrative. As Toni Morrison notes, American literature and Americanness—and I would argue, American models of racialization—have been overwhelmingly shaped by their relation to ideas about Black people.[38]

This project is, primarily, a study of how race is revealed to follow these unexpected constructions in the literary and visual culture of the nineteenth-century United States. My texts, correspondingly, come from this period, with some important exceptions. At various points, I turn to twentieth- and twenty-first-century adaptations and historical fictionalizations of earlier texts, periods, and events, reading these alongside the nineteenth-century literature that remains at the heart of this study. The most significant of these turns to later writing appears at the end of chapters 1 and 4, and in the conclusion, in readings of twenty-first-century adaptations and historical fiction by Toni Morrison. I read these later pieces of writing not simply as literature to put into useful conversation with the older texts I discuss (and particularly to the long history of African American women's fiction writing), but—in keeping with my earlier discussion of race as theorized through literature—as theorizations of race and kinship which reveal the continued resonances of the themes I discuss. As Barbara Christian has noted, people of color's theorizing has often appeared "in narrative forms."[39] In truth, African American creative writers theorized and continue to theorize race, sexuality, and kinship in ways that resonated and continue to resonate with contemporary discussions of race's importance. In this sense, Morrison's creative writing is in conversation with not only the various theorizations of race present in the nineteenth-century texts I discuss but also with the other Black feminist work that is central to this project, by scholars including Spillers, Hartman, Sharpe, Gumbs, Foreman, Patricia Hill Collins, Cathy Cohen, Joyce Green MacDonald, Kimberly Wallace-Sanders, and Ruha Benjamin.

These departures from the nineteenth century extend my theorization of race forward to the present, noting the continued resonance of the ways race was imagined in these earlier texts. Race's complexity, we can see from this, does not follow distinct periodizations demarking popular understandings of race, but trajectories that extend into (and sometimes compete with) new theorizations, confusingly overlapping with one another to form the larger web of race's complexities. The long history of theorizing what we call "race" extends from the eighteenth century through to the twenty-first. Like Critical Mixed-Race Studies, the broader field of Critical Race Studies, in its focus on its various contemporary moments for understanding the effects of race and racism, at times dismisses earlier instances of race-making and making sense of race. While presentist priorities are crucial for a world in which racism continues to create and sustain racial inequality at every scale, the short-sightedness of some contemporary race theory proves detrimental to understanding the sometimes archaic ways in which race continues to function. I do not reject this history of theorizing race, of course, but seek to build upon it by fleshing out yet another element of race's complexity. I take seriously the work of writers who chart race's social construction in particular. Writers such as Michael Omi, Howard Winant, David Roediger, Henry Louis Gates Jr., and Nell Irvin Painter have charted the specific historical and social moments in which race is formed. My own historicist project also takes up "the sociohistorical process[es] by which racial categories are created, inhabited, transformed, and destroyed."[40] My focus on kinship relations looks at just one avenue for racial construction, but a powerful one.

Romance, Reproduction, Residency

Relative Races's organization reflects what Mark Rifkin names as three elements of kinship: "residency, reproduction, and romance."[41] My trajectory follows these elements in reverse order, through three sections that will focus on sexual kinship, kinship's genealogies of reproduction, and the domestic spaces in which kinship inheres. This path simultaneously traces and challenges the arc of racialization from individual racialization and through sexual coupling, reproduction, and the racialization of family and nation. How race is made is also a matter of how race is read as residing in individual bodies, as following genealogies between bodies, and as dwelling within in domestic spaces. *Relative Races's* three sections therefore follows this pathway of racial construction, from its legibility upon and inside the body, through generational relations of race's varied directional movement, and toward its suffusion within the domestic, cultural, and national spaces in which race has become imbued.

The book is divided into three sections, each comprised of two chapters: "Romance: Sexual Kinship," "Reproduction: Genealogies of (Re)Racialization" and "Residency: Domestic Racial Relations." These sections trace the literary and cultural resonances of interracial kinship from relations of interracial sexual kinship to depictions of interracial motherhood and nonnormative genealogies of relatedness and, finally, through depictions of interracial families and their implications for narratives of national domesticity. Rather than taking a chronological approach to texts, the project moves through the teleology of sexuality, family, and nation showing how the texts I discuss—even as they appear in what are, on the surface, heteronormative structures of racialization—push against normative heterosexual and patrilineal genealogies that rely on biologically constructed notions of racialization at each of these expanding scales. In *Relative Races*, white womanhood is not necessarily inherited according to these structures of kinship, but kinship relations do often create relations of racial belonging in other, non-genealogical directions, having effects that extend beyond biological notions of race and from notions of race's location in individual bodies to racial production and reproduction in ever expanding nexuses of racialized relations.

The historical figures and literary characters I discuss here exhibit race's queer genealogies of kinship, following non-heteronormative trajectories of racial reproduction. The processes of race-making that each chapter takes up varies, representing possible genealogies of relational racial construction. In some texts, assumedly white women are re-racialized by a seeming metaphor of race's transferability, as Othello's blackface makeup rubs off on Desdemona, making her "begrimed and black." Much like Désirée, Mary King is "read" as a mixed-race heroine by virtue of her mixed-race family's fugitivity. Iola Leroy aligns herself with her Black mother's family, rejecting her history of unknowing passing. Roxy switches her baby for that of her enslaver, effectively re-racializing both children by virtue of her relationships to them. Mary Jemison, though born white, is adopted by a Seneca family and thereby becomes a Seneca woman. Literatures of national family race-drama illustrate the different scales in which race is made, simultaneously racializing at the level of body, home, and nation, and creating race's circular teleology of (re)production and (re)construction. These cases of race's different directionalities show how race might be constructed through kinship relationships, though not in the expected genealogical ways. Moreover, the expanding scale of romance, reproduction, and residency indicates race's ever-expanding stakes.

Relative Races shows, in part, how some nineteenth-century texts shifted the expectations of racialization away from the reproduction of whiteness and toward a model of white womanhood that was able to produce structures of multiracial family. This model of white womanhood and racial reproduction illustrates the possibilities of racial construction and reconstruction that white supremacists imagined to be most dangerous. The characters I discuss offer a counter-narrative of white women's relationship to race and racism that shows why depictions of white supremacist and separatist womanhood became so important to dominant cultural constructions of white supremacy and the nationalist exclusion of nonwhite people. Recognizing this anti-racist potential in white women's racial relations decenters white womanhood read only within the racist models that have dominated US literary culture from texts like Mary Rowlandson's captivity narrative to Kathryn Stockett's *The Help*. Attention to different models of white women's interracial relations allows us to see that white supremacist tropes of white womanhood are not the only ones available, even in a nineteenth-century context.

My first section shows how nineteenth-century discussions of interracial sexual relations evidence contradictory assumptions about white feminine "nature" in their readings of the effects of interracial desire on white women. In her *Appeal in Favor of Americans Called Africans*, Lydia Maria Child questions white racist assumptions about a general "repugnance between the two races, founded in the laws of *nature*," citing the existence of "interracial" desire as proof that such desire is not "unnatural," but dependent upon individual inclinations.[42] Characterizing interracial desire instead as a "matter of taste," Child individualizes the notion of desire in a way that this racist rhetoric cannot. My first two chapters take up white women in interracial kinship relationships from the iconic to the individual, showing how white women's interracial desire was imagined to change the nature of white womanhood itself. Both the "blackening" of Desdemona and the refiguring of Mary King as a mixed-race heroine work against this notion of racialization, positioning these stories' white women "beyond the pale" of whiteness itself.

The extent to which sexual relationships are racializing can be seen also in the reverse of imagining Desdemona and Mary King as marked by their relation to Blackness: in Ellen and William Craft's disguise and escape. Because

Ellen could "pass" for white and her husband could not, her relationship to him needed to be refigured in order to effect their passing. Specifically, Ellen's whiteness depends upon her distance from any assumption of sexual kinship with William. Here we see how race intersects not only with class and gender, and ability, but also with sexuality. Ellen's disguise as white becomes more effective if she presents herself as belonging to a certain class, and she is removed from having to write and to have too much conversation by virtue of her passing as disabled. Her gender passing upsets a possible search for a man and a woman traveling together. But also through this re-gendering, we see relations of heterosexuality refigured. By assuming the role of William's enslaver, Ellen performs a reimagined relationship to her husband—one in which her sexual relationship to him is not assumed. A white woman would seem out of place traveling with a Black man whom she did not own. But in a world of racial ambiguity, this out-of-placeness would also signal questions about this apparently "white" woman's race. The couple's disguise, then, is not only Ellen's dress and her class/ability/gender presentation, but Ellen and William's relationship to one another.

The relationship between Ellen and William Craft is visualized on the cover of this book, which features portraits of each, as well as portraits of some of their children.[43] Represented alone, Ellen Craft might easily be "read" as a white woman, but viewed in these relations to her more obviously, visibly Black family members, she becomes more legible as a mixed-race Black woman even though she was able to pass as white. The racializing effects of this relationship are such that Ellen can become white only as William's enslaver, not as his spouse. Although Blackness is not always visible, both Ellen's and William's race is relative; it is constructed in comparison and in the space of their interpersonal relationships. Even as these anxieties about how race might travel through interpersonal relationships reveals how race was imagined to work, narratives of interracial romance such as William Allen and Mary King's often focus on individual concerns and rights, displacing the more expansive logic of racist amalgamation anxieties. The narrow scope of "interracial" desire in such narratives indicates the limitations of these individualistic accounts for challenging the larger implications that lie at the foundation of racist discourse. Examining when interracial desire is permissible and when it is denied indicates the limits and potential of these stories to work against racist models of racial futurity. Addressing interracial desire only as a matter of taste serves as an insufficient response to the racist logic that attends to larger implications for the future of racial genealogies.

My second section treats racialization as intergenerational by reading how race's queer genealogies work upon mixed-race heroines and in their complex, "kinfull" relations of racialization.[44] Désirée's baby enacts a fear central to passing literature—that Blackness will become visible in future generations, thereby "outing" previous generations' Blackness and the fact that they are merely "passing" for white. This anxiety about race's future visibility depends on notions of racial essentialism—that passing people are "really" Black, by virtue of their Black "blood" or other essentially "Black" genetic material. It also recognizes that visual cues of race do not always follow clear lines of descent. This failure of race to follow clearly detectable lines in mixed-race people is representative of race's different possible constructions against its essentialist, biological definitions.

For the majority of nineteenth-century texts, interracial sexual desire is always framed as heterosexual desire, oriented toward biological reproductive futurity. It is therefore implicated in reproducing race; the anxieties that surround "interracial" desire are not only about racial integration, but racial mixture in "amalgamated" bodies. This overdetermined positioning of desire must be taken into account when examining white racist discourses against "amalgamation" and the limits of "pro-amalgamation" literatures if we are to fully understand the potential (or maybe the necessary) consequences of this desire: the reproduction of race. Race's relativity is tied to racial futurity, and race's relative futurity follows, in part, from the genealogical link between interracial sex and mixed-race people. Mixed-race people's identification with their racially oppressed kin is one example of the paradoxes of racial logic. In discourses of racial ambiguity, we can more clearly see the simultaneously operating modes of racialization—as paradoxical, atemporal, and representing queerly circular patterns.

My last two sections therefore deal not only with interracial kinship but with racially mixed figures of various kinds in order to illustrate the generational relations of race's queer temporalities. Race's relationship to embodiment—that is, race's visibility, detectability, and its corresponding supposed materiality and biology—is challenged when bodies are racially ambiguous. Nineteenth-century American literature abounds with instances in which the visual markers of race do not align with genealogies of hypodescent or racial identification or both. Departing from white woman figures, I discuss texts in which characters' connections to white womanhood are slippery or tenuous, denied by laws of racial hypodescent, and at times outright rejected by or denied to white(ish) women themselves.

Racial construction cannot be understood without turning to notions of racially reproductive futurity. Inasmuch as the figure of the child is, as Edelman puts it, "the emblem of the future's unquestioned value," the child—and particularly the racially mixed child—looms large in my project as the projected container of interracial desire and racial content.[45] When children are figured as decidedly not white, however, their signification varies significantly from the iconic child of Edelman's imaginings. Childhood studies scholars such as Julian Gill-Peterson, Rebekah Sheldon, and Kathryn Bond Stockton have critiqued framings of childhood's idealized projection into the future.[46] Black and brown childhood, in particular, has not been universally protected and sentimentalized, but perpetually threatened and even denied. Supposed childhood innocence and purity must therefore be reimagined if we are to seriously consider nonwhite children.[47] It becomes clear, then, that this discussion of racial reproduction and futurity cannot escape the specter of antiblackness. Throughout US history, the racial theory of hypodescent has focused on what Nyong'o calls "the biopolitical question of who counts as black in America."[48] My final section therefore explores the scalar implications of the interracial family for a racialized national "family," as interracial kinship queerly (and quite literally) reproduces the American nation.

Continuing the trajectory of queer racialization within bodies and families to nations, my final section extends my second section's discussions of interracial family to even more expansive notions of race's possible futures. This discussion takes up but also complicates readings of the domestic space of the home as a microcosm for the domestic space of the nation. Here I attend to ever-increasing scales for racialization (in racialized bodies to racialized domestic spaces to the racialized nation) as inherently intertwined. While Katherine McKittrick explains that "Black matters are spatial matters," I hold that this is true of racial matters more generally.[49] If we understand that "geography is always human and the human is always geographic," we might also acknowledge how space and race are socially produced in relation to one another.[50]

These last chapters move from a reading of Mary Jemison's racialization in a moment of national racial beginnings to fictional narratives of national-racial postwar shifts. This section therefore maps the scalar and temporal shift from readings of individual (re)racialization to those of national racial (re)construction. The most profound anxieties about amalgamation lie in larger implications for the racially construed nation. Here we see the nation both as a continued teleology of race's genealogical futures and as an expansionist space in which race is continually produced and reproduced. I introduce this discussion at the end of my project in order to avoid too heavily foregrounding essentialist arguments about race that such discussions of racial mixture and production cannot seem to avoid. Nevertheless, I mean here to acknowledge the spatiotemporal connections between race's social construction between individuals and within domestic spaces of various scales. In this comparison, we can see how race's queer genealogies shift from bodies to families to nations, transferred genealogically and generationally through both space and time, even while resisting racial essentialism.

I end my discussion with a turn to the alternative—and more common—phenomenon of white womanhood's steeling itself against the kinds of queer (re)racialization I have discussed throughout this project. The history of white feminism in the US has been marked by its continued refusal to build models of interracial sisterhood. This political failing runs in tandem with the rhetorical preservation of white womanhood against threats of re-racialization and participation in different kinds of queer racial (re)production. Reading the conclusion of Morrison's *A Mercy* in light of twenty-first century white feminist rejections of interracial political sisterhood, I show how the theory of race I present here has continued resonance for our current landscape.

I

Romance

SEXUAL KINSHIP

Blackface Desdemona, or,

the White Woman "Begrimed"

Her name, that was as fresh
As Dian's visage, is now begrimed and black
As mine own face.
—Shakespeare, *Othello*

ANNA CORA MOWATT RITCHIE'S 1855 story "Stella" describes a novice actress's first encounters with popular leading roles for young women. Stella Rosenvelt's early roles include Desdemona in a production of *Othello*, one of the most popular Shakespearean dramas in the mid-nineteenth century United States. Among its theatrical mishaps, "Stella" depicts the troubles of Othello's blackface makeup: "The reddish-black dye, which gave to Othello's visage its swarthy hue, could be removed by a touch."[1] As Mr. Tennant, the actor playing Othello, draws Stella close, their faces accidentally touch, and "Stella's forehead had largely received the somber impression."[2] Tennant describes the effect, telling her that her forehead is "as black as the ace of spades" and warns her not to turn her face to the audience lest she disrupt their impression of Desdemona, the iconic white woman figure.[3] Stella's attempts to wipe the blacking away only smear it further, and she risks marring her performance of Desdemona by failing to represent the character's iconic, unchangeable whiteness. The blacking makeup's "begriming touch to her own fair forehead" is not a unique mistake to the particular production, however, but a common occurrence in nineteenth-century US theatrical productions.[4] Desdemona became a site of anxiety and debate over how white womanhood could be undone or resignified by intimate or sexual relations with Black men, how her race could be inherited through kinship with her husband or children.

Unsurprisingly, nineteenth-century American productions of *Othello* emphasized Othello's Blackness.[5] Accordingly, the titular role was most often performed by white actors in some form of blackface makeup.[6] Blackface performances perpetuated derogatory stereotypes of African American people. They also gave form to popular racist anxieties in the literal "begriming" of the initially "white" Desdemona. Blackface makeup was messy and transferrable to costumes and other actors. Audience accounts convey that by the end of the play, Othello's "blacking" had inevitably rubbed off onto the "white" Desdemona. William Winter recounts Junius Brutus Booth's performances of Othello: "on one occasion, having no black stockings, he blackened his legs as well as his face and hands, and thereby, in the course of the performance, soiled the white dress of the fair Desdemona."[7] Another reviewer noted blacking makeup's "many disadvantages: particularly in coming off inconveniently and being transferable from hand to hand; oftentimes they were seen to touch nothing they did not soil; let it be *Desdemona's* dress or even her cheek."[8] Similarly, English actor Ellen Terry complained that Henry Irving, playing Othello to Terry's Desdemona in 1881, had left her "as black as he."[9]

The fact that Desdemona could become—quite literally—"begrimed and black" is more than a curiosity of this medium of performance. The begrimed and blackface Desdemonas discussed in this chapter are testaments to complex theorizations of race and the nonnormative genealogies by which race was imagined to be transferred. Simply put, the "begrimed" Desdemona literalizes white racist anxieties about interracial sex. Abigail Adams, for example, recalls her experience of seeing *Othello*: "my whole soul shuderd [*sic*] when ever I saw the sooty More [*sic*] touch fair Desdemona."[10] One must wonder, what is it about this "sooty" touch that was perceived to threaten white womanhood? While there is evidence that Desdemona wore white makeup to accentuate her skin's contrast with Othello's in some performances, anxieties about racial transfer seem unidirectional. Blackface performances of *Othello* presented only Desdemona's iconic whiteness as subject to racial marking.[11] This image of Desdemona "begrimed" illustrates how nineteenth-century American beliefs about interracial sex came to bear on understandings of white womanhood.[12]

While Shakespeare scholars have discussed *Othello*'s significance for early modern racial formation extensively, and many have recounted the play's American adaptation and performance history, a more specific discussion of nineteenth-century American interpretations and adaptations of *Othello* requires their contextualization within American racial formation and its stakes during that period.[13] Specifically, we can learn much about how race was constructed in nineteenth-century America by investigating how race was presented with regard to the period's most racially invested Shakespearean play. Celia Daileader describes the cultural work of *Othello* in her notion of "Othellophilia": "the critical and cultural fixation on Shakespeare's tragedy of interracial marriage to the exclusion of broader definitions, and more positive visions, of inter-racial eroticism."[14] This phenomenon illustrates the iconic resonance of Shakespeare's couple, making *Othello* a particularly fertile site for theorizing race in nineteenth-century America.[15]

In this sense, *Othello* becomes what we might call a very "American" play. It makes sense that Americans would interpret and reinterpret *Othello* as a way of processing the national-racial drama of "miscegenation." This construction of interracial heterosexuality has been reiterated in American social customs, anti-miscegenation law, state-sanctioned and extralegal racial violence, and the representation of interracial relations. Othello and Desdemona are icons, masking other combinations of interracial sexuality and reifying oppositional racial/gender difference in the dualism of white women and Black men. This particular relationship becomes hyper-visible by the mid-nineteenth century.[16] In *Playing in the Dark*, Toni Morrison writes of "the ways in which a nonwhite Africanlike (or Africanist) presence or persona was constructed in the United States, and the imaginative uses this fabricated presence served."[17] One such imaginative use of the "African" becomes visible in how the performance of Othello and Desdemona becomes an American urtext for interracial sexuality and kinship and, I will argue here, for theorizing racialization more broadly.

Discussions of blackface performance (in *Othello* and elsewhere) have focused largely on the failed mimesis of blackface caricatures of African American people and, as Eric Lott's discussion in *Love and Theft* illustrates, the complex significations of race, class, masculinity, and desire working in blackface performance.[18] In seeming contrast, most prominent nineteenth-century discussions of white womanhood insisted upon white women's biological, unchangeable whiteness, and its need for protection. In this chapter and the next, I turn to "horizontal" genealogies of what I call "sexual kinship" between Black men and white women to show how racialization has been imagined to flow from the former to the latter through sex.

This chapter is therefore invested in how blackface performance came to bear upon representations not of Othello, but of Desdemona. Examining the white woman within the realm of blackface performance, we see a theory of race that registers not only race's apparent materiality and gendered signification, but also literalizes anxieties about race's movement, in the possibility of blackface makeup rubbing off onto a white woman's skin. This spectacle of racial transfer illustrates how white womanhood was theorized via nineteenth-century representations of race-as-blacking-makeup, a marking that might not only be put on or removed, but also transferred from one body to another. Reading material representations of racial transfer in nineteenth-century images of Desdemona, this chapter attends to the queer temporalities of racialization—temporalities by which race does not follow normative genealogies of inheritance—at work in nineteenth-century ideas about interracial sexuality.

Additionally, some nineteenth-century minstrel adaptations took Desdemona's "begriming" one step further by recasting Desdemona in blackface. Blackface Desdemona appears always already "begrimed and black" in such productions, imagining race as both visible and material, but not biologically essential. While Angela C. Pao argues that "complex investigations into the politics of identity" were not possible until late twentieth-century performances and analyses of *Othello*, Robert Toll and Francesca T. Royster have acknowledged Shakespearean minstrel adaptations as distinctly American tools for theorizing race.[19] This chapter shows how nineteenth-century commentary on and adaptations of *Othello*—and of Desdemona, in particular—illustrate American constructions of race and gender. Sharing Daileader's assessment that both white and Black women are central to these narratives, I illustrate how depictions of begrimed and blackface Desdemonas offer theorizations of the connections between race, gender, and sexuality by pushing against popular notions of white womanhood while simultaneously commenting on constructions of Black womanhood to which Blackface Desdemona alludes.

First, I will discuss how nineteenth-century American tropes of white womanhood depended upon assumptions about the transfer of (biologically construed) race via heterosexual sex. The image of Desdemona "begrimed" offers a distinctly nineteenth-century American idea of interracial sexuality. Next, I examine notions of Desdemona's whiteness via nineteenth-century American readings of her potential re-racialization,

showing how this theory of begrimed Desdemona works against normative ideologies of genealogically inherited race. Moving to a discussion of
minstrel adaptations in which Desdemona's whiteness is literally refigured
in blackface performance, I read Blackface Desdemona's representation as
further complicating this linearity of gendered racialization. Blackface Desdemona simultaneously reimagines notions of this iconic white woman
as racially/sexually "pure" while also recalling the "Africanist presence" of
actual Black women, whose oppression is inherently linked to popular images of Desdemona. I conclude with a brief discussion of Toni Morrison's
2011 play, *Desdemona*, and its potential for rethinking interracial kinship beyond Desdemona's relation to Othello—that is, beyond interracial heterosexuality. *Desdemona* revises this character's relation to Blackness through
Black womanhood and thereby toward a more progressive dialectic of interracial kinship. Ultimately, examining how Desdemona is "blackened," both
in metaphors of interracial sexual kinship and more literally on the minstrel
stage, reveals the implications of Desdemona's racialization for rethinking
American racial theories beyond normative genealogies of race that continue to dominate racial discourse.

"Tupping Your White Ewe": White Women and Sexual Kinship

In the last act of Shakespeare's play, Othello laments Desdemona's name:
"Her name, that was as fresh/As Dian's visage, is now begrimed and black/
As mine own face."[20] This comparison with Othello's "begrimed" self signified both sexually and racially for interpreters reading racial Blackness into
Othello's "complexion." While Lois Potter argues, "So long as Othello was
played by a white actor, sexual propriety was likely to be more important
than the possibility of racial scandal," this was not the case in nineteenth-
century America.[21] Rather, notions of sexual propriety were informed
by—and inextricable from—racial scandal for a text most often read as
an "anti-miscegenation" play.[22] John Quincy Adams wrote that "the great
moral lesson of the tragedy of *Othello*, is that Black and white blood cannot be intermingled in marriage without a gross outrage upon the law of
Nature; and that, in such violations, Nature will vindicate her laws."[23] For
racist readers and audiences, Desdemona is not "begrimed" by any false
charge of adultery, but by the fact of her marriage to Othello—a marriage that would have been prohibited by many states in which *Othello*
was performed throughout the nineteenth and into the mid-twentieth
century.[24] Although Virginia Mason Vaughan indicates that "Shakespeare

did not necessarily accept his society's fears about miscegenation," most nineteenth-century white Americans probably did hold them, as is evident in their interpretations of the play.[25]

American discussions of *Othello* were sometimes invested in early modern perceptions of race, but these discussions tell us much more about American racial construction. In some American productions, lines with racial connotations were excised. Other omissions centered around images of Othello and Desdemona having sex: "Even now, now, very now, an old black ram/Is tupping your white ewe"; "you'll have your daughter cover'd with a Barbary horse"; and "Your daughter and the Moor are now . . . making the beast with two backs."[26] As Virginia Mason Vaughan and James Shapiro have argued, American appropriations reworked Shakespearean racial discourse for their own devises.[27] I share Shapiro's view that "Spectators throughout antebellum America, a nation hurtling toward civil war over the question of race, certainly saw *Othello* through a different lens than British audiences at the time," and American interpretations had national implications.[28] American national discourses of interracial sexuality, in particular, were being worked out through American interpretations of *Othello*.

Here, race was not only a social category of identification, but also a legal one, upon which issues such as enslavement, citizenship, suffrage, and marital and filial legitimacy were dependent. The fact of race as a legal category demanded a supposed understanding of what, exactly, race was even in the absence of agreement on the matter. Although the nature of race was under popular debate throughout the nineteenth century, notions of biological racial essentialism often stood in the foreground of national conversations. Despite the complex and contradictory racial logics available to nineteenth-century Americans in various literary and cultural interpretations of race's fluidity and malleability, the Black/white racial dichotomy persisted in national discourse. That false dichotomy was compounded by the prevalence of the male/female heterosexual relations of imagined racial-sexual threat/victim that Othello and Desdemona represented.

The possibility of sexual relations between Black men and white women was not unthinkable in nineteenth-century America. On the contrary, it was reiterated to the point of obsession in the national psyche (see figure 1.1). Documents from Edward William Clay's 1839 caricatures of racial mixture to David Croly and George Wakeman's 1864 pamphlet, *Miscegenation: The Theory of the Blending of the Races, Applied to the American White Man and Negro*, and the various responses it elicited—demonstrate that racial mixture

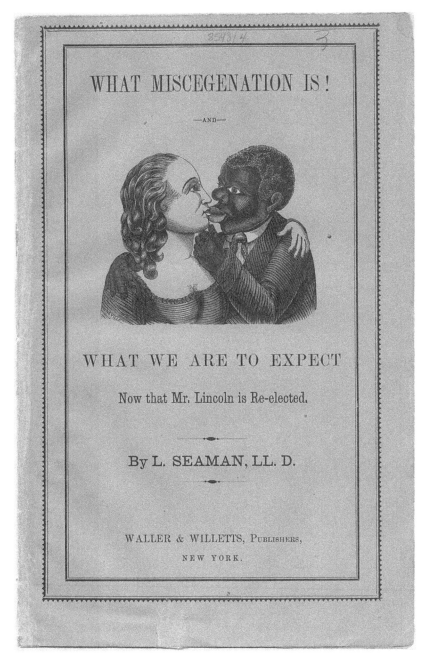

1.1 "WHAT MISCEGENATION IS! AND WHAT WE ARE TO EXPECT NOW THAT
MR. LINCOLN IS RE-ELECTED," 1864. COURTESY OF THE AMERICAN ANTIQUARIAN
SOCIETY.

1.2 EDWARD WILLIAM CLAY, "THE FRUITS OF AMALGAMATION," 1839. COURTESY OF THE AMERICAN ANTIQUARIAN SOCIETY.

1.3 "OTHELLO & DESDEMONA." DETAIL OF EDWARD WILLIAM CLAY, "THE FRUITS OF AMALGAMATION," 1839. COURTESY OF THE AMERICAN ANTIQUARIAN SOCIETY.

was widely viewed as a threat.[29] Othello and Desdemona appear as icons, literally in the background of Clay's "The Fruits of Amalgamation" (see figures 1.2 and 1.3). Because racial hierarchies depend upon articulating racial difference, sexual relations that might produce mixed-race people threaten white supremacist structures. Nineteenth-century American productions of *Othello* emphatically and deliberately presented demonized images of Black men, figuring them as threats not only to white women, but also to imagined white "purity" and therefore to American racial hegemony.

The stakes of this threat become remarkably clear in Josiah Nott's warning of "probable extermination of the two races if the Whites and Blacks are allowed to intermarry."[30] Women were particularly implicated in this danger, as the burden of reproducing the white nation lay in the impetus to bear white children. In "The Modern Othello," a newspaper cartoon from 1863, Othello is played by "the Everlastin' Darkey" and Desdemona by "Columbia" (see figure 1.4). Here the nation is identified as, and is meant to identify with, Desdemona/Columbia. As this illustration suggests, discourses of "miscegenation" became inextricable from suggestions of a racial/national threat by the mid-1860s. Given the poignancy of images like these, it is unsurprising that most discussions of *Othello* and race have (quite rightly) focused on portrayals of Othello and especially on *Othello*'s blackface performance history.[31] Blackface performance and its particular historical and cultural resonances are therefore necessary for understanding how this iconic "Black" character has been constructed. Desdemona's relationship to blackface performance has been decidedly different, as blackface has not become an essential part of this character's construction. A blackened Desdemona is an aberration, and therefore bears examination beyond usual readings of *Othello*.

Because women are susceptible to bearing children who may not be racialized like themselves, theories of race and heterosexuality joined interracial couples in kinship not only by the fact of their coupling, but also through their actual or potential progeny. I call the heterosexual relation on which I focus "sexual kinship," in part because of its potential to create interracial biological family relations, regardless of legal marital status. In this encounter, notions of fixed, biological racialization shift to the background in favor of a construction of white womanhood that is not dependent upon the linear temporality of genealogical parentage, but on what might be called the "horizontal" or "backward" temporalities of racialized kinship structures in sexuality and childbearing. This nonlinear genealogy produces a "queer temporality" of racialization which refuses to adhere to

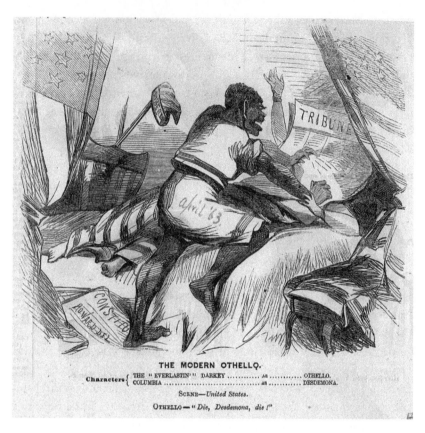

THE MODERN OTHELLO.

Characters { THE "EVERLASTIN'" DARKEY .... as .... OTHELLO.
COLUMBIA .... as .... DESDEMONA.

Scene—*United States.*

Othello—"*Die, Desdemona, die!*"

1.4 "THE MODERN OTHELLO," 1863. COURTESY OF THE AMERICAN ANTIQUARIAN SOCIETY.

what Freeman refers to as "the interlocking temporal schemes necessary for genealogies of descent."[32] Despite their heterosexuality, Othello and Desdemona's racialized relations do not follow chrononormative genealogies. Race is here imagined as not only transferring from past to future descendants, but also horizontally through sexual encounters between partners, or even backward from child to mother. Desdemona's racialization is thereby divorced from her parentage and linked instead to other kinship relations that racialize her: her sexual kinship with Othello and the possibility of bearing mixed-race children.

One must regard this imagined racial transfer in not only metaphorical but also literal terms, referring to the transfer of semen, understood as the origin of shared kinship and a potential origin for biologically construed race. The literal transfer of race—from Black and brown men (who "have" race) to white women (who "receive" and "reproduce" it)—thereby under-lies white anxieties about interracial sex.[33] This genealogy of race works not only in linearly "downward" trajectories of inheritance but also horizontally, as race is transferred not only from parents to children, but from nonwhite men to their white partners. A 1799 study by Benjamin Rush evidences such anxieties regarding the sexual transfer of race.[34] In one case study, he de-scribes "a white woman in North Carolina [who] not only acquired a dark color, but several of the features of a negro, by marrying and living with a black husband. A similar instance of a change in the color and features of a woman in Bucks county in Pennsylvania has been observed and from a similar cause. In both of these cases, the women bore children by their black husbands."[35] Rush's supposition about how the white wife of a Black hus-band might acquire dark skin herself calls us to take seriously beliefs about race that would today seem archaic. I do not, of course, mean to validate Rush's theories of scientific racism here, but offer this as an illustration of popular beliefs about not only race's biology but also its materiality, show-ing that white anxieties about race's possible transfer were seriously held, however misguided.

Rush's argument construes race (or, more specifically, Blackness) as contagion—and sexually transmitted contagion at that. Taking this account of white women who have become Black as a result of sex and reproduc-tion with Black men, we might imagine the transfer of race from Othello to Desdemona as not only metaphorical but literal—pointing to race as mate-rial content. Blackness becomes, in Rush's accounts, something contained by these white women and their offspring. Through the acts of conceiving and carrying mixed-race children, white women literally embody Blackness, con-taining the racial Other within their own bodies. According to this theory, white women capable of "receiving" race in this way also become racially malleable themselves. That is, a white woman can become Black as her prox-imity to (and perhaps, her inextricability from) her Black child (or potential children) renders her own whiteness precarious.

Blackface minstrelsy's location of race upon the skin simultaneously sug-gests and evades its location elsewhere—that is, in the womb, where it might be invisible. While blackface performance ensures the legibility of race on the bodies who perform it, in the context of this metaphorical understand-ing of racial transfer, Othello and Desdemona's final scene becomes an easily adopted metaphor that makes the "dangers" of racial mixture similarly visible. I turn next from the stakes of interracial sexual kinship to the significance of Desdemona's racial marking.

"Begrimed and Black as Mine Own Face": Desdemona's Racial Marking

Productions of *Othello* figured race as material (locatable as marking upon the body) and as transferrable (transmittable from one person to another). In *Notes on the State of Virginia*, Thomas Jefferson famously pondered where in the body race resides, staking an ultimate claim in racial essentialism. Jefferson attests that, "Whether the black of the negro resides in the reticular membrane between the skin and scarf-skin, or in the scarf-skin itself; whether it proceeds from the color of the blood, the color of the bile, or from that of some other secretion, the difference is fixed in nature, and is real as if its seat and cause were better known to us."[36] While most nineteenth-century Americans laid similar claims to race as "fixed in nature," others signified the mutability of race, registering the possibility of racial mixture through the genealogical transfer of race from one body to another, and the difficulty of discerning racial difference in racially mixed bodies. Blackface productions presented race as both essential and provisional, relocating the marker of racialization from somewhere *within* the body, as Jefferson posits, to *upon* it. These productions rendered race visible, while also producing racialization as a de-essentialized practice of performance that might therefore be adapted.

Because Blackness signifies race in specific ways, the question of how dark Othello ought to be became a contentious debate, sparking arguments about whether he should be represented as "black," "white," or "tawny." In her 1869 *Studies in Shakespeare*, Mary Preston notoriously asserted that "Othello *was a white* man!"[37] Conversely, Adams, in his 1835 "Misconceptions of Shakespeare on the stage," argued that Othello's Blackness is essential to Shakespeare's tragic plot.[38] The question of whether interracial romance was central to *Othello* became key to these arguments. This paired desexualization of the play's language and the whitening of Othello indicates the tension between American audiences' fascination with the coupling of sexual and racial themes and their investment in rhetorics of racism that present interracial marriage as a point of white racist anxiety. The extent to which Desdemona was marked by her interracial encounter mattered. James Dormon discusses the history of Othello appearing in blackface, noting that "by the end of the ante bellum [*sic*] period, Othello had to be played as near-white, or not at all" in the American South.[39] The spectacle of race in Othello's representation as "less black"(and perhaps "less Black"?) and in the layering of racialization in performances by white actors in blackface served to buffer implications of actual interracial sex.[40]

A 1997 production of *Othello* featured a "photonegative" casting in which Patrick Stewart—happily—did not appear in blackface and most other parts were played by Black actors.[41] In this example, I am less interested in Stewart as a white(washed) Othello, or even with this production's insistence on maintaining racial dualism, than I am with the portrayal of Desdemona as Black, played by the Jamaican-born actor, Patrice Johnson. In light of this character's historically iconic whiteness, one must ask: what does it mean to render Desdemona Black?[42] This question is broached, if not answered, on the nineteenth-century American stage. I present Johnson's portrayal of Desdemona as a point of differentiation, making clear the fact that—as with portrayals of Othello—the "Blackness" represented by white actors in blackface and that of Black actors is emphatically different. Patrice Johnson is most definitely *not* the same as a Blackface Desdemona. My reading of begrimed and blackface Desdemonas therefore differs from reading a Black Desdemona embodied by an actor like Johnson, even as actual Black women are evoked (though not represented) by this figure.[43]

Understanding Desdemona's racialization necessitates thinking about how actual Black women are implied by Desdemona's "begriming." As various scholars have argued, Black women do figure in *Othello*'s margins.[44] Desdemona is accompanied by an "Africanist presence." Racist readings of Desdemona's whiteness as sexual purity imply that Black women are impure, over-sexualized and sexually available, and therefore subject to a history of systematic sexual violation. Here race becomes a function of gender and sexuality, similar to Elise Lemire's understanding of racialization as an alignment with racially specific sexual "taste" or "preference."[45] To this effect, Mary Preston held Othello's Blackness as "a stage decoration which *my taste* discards."[46] Preston's taste cannot imagine interracial romance in what she describes as a "simple narrative" of courtship and "true love."[47] Othello's whitening on American stages functioned to preserve Desdemona's whiteness, as did certain characters' readings of Desdemona's sexual/racial victimization.

As Iago contends, "Even now, now, very now, an old black ram/Is tupping your white ewe," the urgency of his repetition places Othello, the "old black ram," as the active "tupper," hiding Desdemona's agency in the sentence's predicate. In this scene and in Brabantio's accusations of Othello having "enchanted" Desdemona with "foul charms,"[48] Desdemona's supposed passivity or enchantment positioned Othello as a sexual/racial threat to a potentially innocent victim, contributing to the horror of racist audiences. Similar to Lemire's alignment of whiteness with white supremacist "taste" or "preference," white supremacist beliefs also assumed Black people's sexual "preference" or desire for white people.[49] The confluence of these assumptions denied that white women might ever desire Black men, characterizing Black men as perpetual would-be rapists. The framing of Desdemona as victim is common to this set of racist assumptions. Accusations of her enchantment or passivity also brings to mind the relationship between captivity and assumptions of rape, a point to which I will return in chapter 2.

This duality of threat and victim is not the only popular reading of *Othello*, however, even in the nineteenth century. Writers also explained Desdemona's sexuality as immorality, theorizing her death as punishment rather than tragedy. In his assessment of interracial marriage as a "gross outrage upon the law of Nature," Adams does not regard Desdemona as a passive victim of interracial violence. Attending to the moments when a feminist reading might view Desdemona as most empowered, Adams notes her "elopement from her father's house" and "clandestine marriage," claiming that she "made the first advances" by giving undue attention to Othello's "braggart story" and that her defense of Cassio is similarly inappropriate, as "it is not for female delicacy to extenuate the crimes of drunkenness and bloodshed, even when performing the appropriate office of raising the soul-subduing voice for mercy."[50] Desdemona's sexuality, Adams holds, is "deficient in delicacy."[51]

Adams's fiercest critique of Desdemona focuses on the agency she demonstrates in her marriage choice. He acknowledges Desdemona's passion, but marks it as "*unnatural*, solely and exclusively because of [Othello's] color," and argues that, while not false to her husband, "she has been false to the purity and delicacy of her sex and condition when she married him."[52] Desdemona's transgression is not her elopement; she cannot be compared to Juliet or Miranda, who Adams argues are driven by "pure love." Rather, Desdemona's "unnatural passion; it cannot be named with delicacy," marks her name and her character by her relation to Othello.[53]

As Tilden Edelstein notes, "Only by seeing Desdemona as wanton and the play as a lesson against racial intermarriage could Adams accept the credibility of even a bleached Othello and a Desdemona who betrays her race and class."[54] *Mirror* editor and writer, George Pope Morris attaches a similar preference to women he refers to as "New York Desdemonas," white women theatergoers who he worries may become enamored of other blackface characters, like Jim Crow and Gumbo Cuff.[55] These readings of Desdemona locate the play's stakes in the relationship between Desdemona's racialization and her sexual kinship. That is, Desdemona's apparent racial difference from Othello should preclude her sexual passion and legal marriage. These theorizations of interracial sexuality as immorality also risk re-racializing the white woman who cannot here be understood within the bounds of racial/sexual "purity." Effectively, Desdemona is not sufficiently racist to represent white womanhood.

As these discussions of Desdemona have it, the effects of interracial sexuality come most emphatically to bear on white women who engage in them. T. D. Rice's minstrel adaptation, *Otello, A Burlesque Opera*, makes this point.[56] Rice's Otello is distinguished from the other characters, both through his unique minstrel dialect (mockingly parodied by Iago) and by other characters' references to his "black" appearance and use of the epithet "n[—]." Otello's difference from Desdemona is also emphasized, as Rice presents interracial marriage as the play's central problem. The chorus predicts, in the second scene, that "if a black shall wed a white,/And afterwards go free,/In a very pretty pickle then/Our daughters soon will be."[57] This "pickle" stems from Desdemona's original wish "That heaven had made her such a man," suggesting simultaneously that Desdemona both desired that such a man as Othello was made for her, and that she was such a man herself.[58] Rice reframes this wish in racialized terms, as Desdemona wishes that "Heaben hab made/Her sich a n[—]," an account by which we might also understand Desdemona to be wishing for her own re-racialization.[59] This sentiment quickly shifts, as Otello continues, "My story being done,/She only wished I had a son."[60] Thus Rice directly addresses Desdemona's sexual desire and alludes to her potential embodiment of Blackness. Answering a commonly debated question—whether the couple's marriage is ever consummated—Rice gives Otello and Desdemona a child.[61]

Sex is of obvious interest to audiences preoccupied with the play's interracial romance, and Rice places clear evidence of interracial sex onstage. Oddly, this child has no lines and seems to serve no purpose in the plot other than as proof of sex. When exactly the child is conceived is unclear, as neither the character's age nor how much time has passed since the couple's wedding is specified. W. T. Lhamon offers one possibility, however: as Desdemona recounts having swooned after hearing Otello's shocking tale, she comes to "sitting on his knee" and rises up "Greatful," that is, pregnant.[62] The moral of her story, "Never sit on young men's knees," is given despite Desdemona's marriage, "though I got a husband by it," suggesting that Desdemona's pregnancy partially explains the couple's hurry to wed.[63]

Whether Othello and Desdemona had intercourse before or only after their marriage is irrelevant, however, to racist "anti-miscegenation" interpretations. Their son's presence is sufficient to imply this taboo. He appears in the 1853 manuscript's stage directions simply as a "child" accompanying

Desdemona, is listed as "Young Otello" in an 1852 playbill, and appears even more interestingly in an 1846 playbill as "Master Lorenzo Otello (eldest son of Otello and that there may be no partiality, nature has colored him half and half)."[64] The child's racial mixture—literally drawing the line of racial demarcation down the center of his body—proves his paternity, visually linking Desdemona to Otello through his presence. This extraneous character thereby provides a spectacle of Desdemona's racial "begriming," as the sexual transfer of race from Otello to Desdemona is visualized in the dually marked body of their offspring.

Otello and Desdemona's child does not fully enact amalgamation, however, but maintains racial dualism as a marking upon—rather than in—his body. Young Otello is not simply a representation of racial mixture, but provides visual, material evidence of his genealogical past. Bearing race unmixed upon his skin, the child bears witness to Otello's and Desdemona's sexual encounter, and creates a reverse genealogy by which Desdemona's begriming might also be understood. Here audiences saw a character other than Otello represented in blackface: a character connected to—and having emerged from—the body of Desdemona. Rice's presentation of Desdemona's racially mixed child suggests, even as it does not depict, her literal embodiment of the racial Other in pregnancy. If Desdemona is able to contain Blackness in this way, the chorus's suggestion of a "black" Desdemona is not unthinkable. They argue in the play's final scene, "If his wife hab but been black,/Instead of white, all had been right."[65] While Rice did not go so far as to represent a Blackface Desdemona, other minstrel adaptations of *Othello* did. I turn to such representations in the next section.

Blackface Desdemona

Taking further liberties with *Othello* on the American minstrel stage, the play's usual paradigm of Black/white and male/female dualism was sometimes complicated by characters other than Othello appearing in blackface. These productions offer a theorization of race that performs white racist anxieties about white womanhood, making Desdemona's "begriming" more explicit than in the previously discussed blackface makeup mishaps. My discussion of Blackface Desdemona examines two anonymously penned texts: *Othello; A Burlesque,* performed by Griffin and Christy's Minstrels at their opera house in New York in 1866, and *Desdemonum, An Ethiopian Burlesque*, published by the Happy Hours Company in 1874—two productions that extended blackface performance beyond the title role.[66] Kris Collins argues that "The mainstage and blackface productions of Othello provided the alter-egos of both Othello and Desdemona—civilized, whitened, and innocent in the former; bawdy, blackened, and buffoonish in the latter."[67] However, these images of Blackface Desdemona are not simply buffoonish but more complex in their reframing of Desdemona's racialization.

Tavia Nyong'o imagines blackface performance as a display of the Bakhtinian carnivalesque—a hierarchical reversal in all of its "topsy-turveydom"—rather than as evidence of race as simply theatrical.[68] In this, he observes minstrelsy's "facility for inverting, burlesquing, and blackening anything"—even, as we see here, the "fair" Desdemona's iconic whiteness.[69] English illustrator Charles Hunt's depiction of *Othello's* final scene shows a version of Desdemona that might be best understood as Blackface Desdemona (see figure 1.5). Hunt's Desdemona is not represented as an actual Black woman, but—as in the minstrel "wench" stock character and in most nineteenth-century depictions of Black people—as a caricature of one. Just as this illustration is clearly not interested in any realistic representation of Black womanhood, neither are readings of begrimed or blackface Desdemona interested in realistic representations of white womanhood. This is not to say that Desdemona's representation is offensive to the same extent as blackface portrayals like Hunt's caricature. However, both the Black and the white caricature are similarly constructed, depending upon the same set of assumptions about race, gender, and sexuality. Reading Desdemona's sexual purity as inextricable from her whiteness (even whiteness that is impermanent, capable of "begriming" through interracial sexuality) demands similar assumptions about Black women as sexually promiscuous or "available."[70] Representations of Blackface Desdemona reveal the transferability of these similarly racist views of Black and white womanhood.

Griffin and Christy's burlesque draws upon a practice more common in post–Civil War minstrelsy, the depiction of white ethnics in blackface.[71] Historical commentary on minstrel shows has not been as carefully documented as commentary on traditional or "high" theatrical productions, such as Adams's musings on *Othello*. Nevertheless, reading the extant manuscripts of minstrel adaptations reveals their complex theorizations of Desdemona's race and sexuality. In this production, Iago is coded as Irish (singing an air entitled "Ireland the Place Is" in the third scene) and adopting an Irish accent in the textual rendition (dropping the *g* in words like darlin' and amazin'). Brabantio is represented as German, his dialog also marked by a distinct accent ("my" becomes "mine," "with" becomes "mit," "think" becomes "tink," and so on).[72] Even more interestingly, neither

1.5 CHARLES HUNT, PRINTMAKER, "OTHELLO ACT 5 SCENE 2," TREGEAR'S BLACK JOKES. G. S. TREGEAR. LONDON: C. 1828–32. COURTESY THE FOLGER SHAKESPEARE LIBRARY.

Othello's nor Desdemona's speech is marked by dialect. Their dialog appears in standard English, which here appears as the most "Shakespearean" of the play, much of which is written in rhymed iambic pentameter, sometimes spoken, sometimes sung. Strikingly, Desdemona's accent does not resemble her father's but Othello's. If marked language is an indication of racial or ethnic designation—as is often the case in the minstrel tradition—Othello and Desdemona are aligned.[73] Or, if we take the marked speech of Iago and Brabantio as designating national or geographic associations—as dialect often does—both Othello and Desdemona "belong" in the American South: their early love duet is sung to the tune of "Dixie," as the happy couple plan their future life together "Away, away, &c.," presumably in Dixieland, as the song goes.[74]

Although the nature of blackface performance often compels scholars to focus on visual rather than linguistic or aural representations of race, Desdemona's and Othello's shared blackface appearance is reinforced by this additional resemblance. Audiences would have easily perceived this alignment, if only in its difference from standard depictions of Desdemona's difference from Othello. This adaptation correlates dialect (here indicating something more akin to geographical origin than race), visual resemblance, and marital kinship in a way that standard presentations of *Othello* do not. Despite these complications of linguistic and visual representation, the interracial romance plot is still central to this adaptation. One wonders, then, what possibilities blackface might foreclose for Desdemona in its plot. The end of the tune of "Dixie" marks a point of racial difference despite visual and linguistic similarities, as Desdemona sings, "I'll love you dearly all my life,/Although you are a n[—]."[75] However, most dualistic black/white imagery of the play has been evacuated: there is no "white ewe" to Othello's "black ram." Another significant difference lies in the final scene, as Othello never realizes Desdemona's faithfulness. Thereby, the burlesque includes Desdemona's murder, but omits Othello's remorseful suicide.

This absence of remorse recalls Adams's unsympathetic reading of Desdemona's death, in which we see the full extent of his fear of interracial heterosexuality. Adams writes, "This character [Desdemona] takes from us so much of the sympathetic interest in her sufferings, that when Othello smothers her in bed, the terror and the pity subside immediately into the sentiment that she has her just deserts."[76] It is impossible, of course, to imagine how close Adams's sentiment might have been to that of Griffin and Christy's audiences, but the play's changed ending, with the unpunished murder of Desdemona, suggests a similar refusal to sympathize with Shakespeare's heroine, despite the minstrel play's ostensibly comic tone. Leaving Desdemona's devotion to Othello unrevealed de-emphasizes her virtue in marital fidelity, while retaining only the sexual desire with which Adams is so uncomfortable.

Desdemonum differs most obviously from Griffin and Christy's adaptation in its language. This play has no white-ethnic-coded characters; the entire cast (here portraying the roles of Desdemonum, Oteller, Iagum, Brabantium, and so on), speak in a similarly inflected minstrel dialect, all deriving from the town of "Wennice." While not distinguishing Othello's and Desdemona's dialect as unique unto themselves, this version resists what Rice's *Otello* accomplishes—Otello's linguistic segregation. Although the dialect of *Desdemonum* is clearly racialized, the absence of linguistic difference between Oteller and the other characters has something of an equalizing effect. Despite this shared dialect and blackface representation, however, Blackness still signifies racial difference. In Desdemonum's first duet with Oteller, she underscores the medium of blackface performance, proclaiming "since burnt-cork am de fashion, I'll not be behind—/I'll see

Oteller's wisage in his highfalutin' mind."[77] Desdemonum not only lauds Oteller's blackface as fashionable, but also "puts on" the "fashion" of burnt cork herself. Still, the text frames Blackness as undesirable, as Brabantio familiarly argues that Oteller has "bewitched her, dat's de matter; come de Hoodoo on de gal./ He's played de black art on her."[78] Later, he asks if Desdemonum truly devotes herself "To dat Jamaica nig? Why, gal you're blind," to which she replies again, "I see de feller's wisage in his mind;/Beauty's but skin deep anyhow you know."[79] This trivialization of appearance cannot, however, be taken as mere dismissal in the context of blackface minstrelsy, where appearance always signifies.

As *Desdemonum* presents the spectacle of Blackface Desdemona, "put on" in burnt-cork fashion, one wonders what to make of her whiteness.[80] Desdemonum, like the other characters, seems to have been meant as comical, but a more serious commentary on race underlies this complex intertwining of blackface and drag performance. Joyce Green MacDonald argues that, in this adaptation, "a minstrel in drag playing Shakespeare's heroine firmly muzzles the sexual and cross-racial horrors incited by Shakespeare's climax."[81] I contend, rather, that the "horrors" of Desdemona's racialization emerge in this medium. Oteller tells Desdemonum upon their elopement, "De hour am propitious—come, my darling flame!/Dey say dat in de dark, al cullers am de same."[82] This reference to the dark's homogenization of color immediately precedes an embrace that had to evoke popular cultural images of Othello and Desdemona despite their shared gender and blackface appearance. At first this seems like just a slightly bawdy joke (even evoking less vivid imagery than the original text), but herein lies a more complex theorization of amalgamation and a critique of racial dualism.

Blackface Desdemona is no white woman. As Dympna Callaghan notes, "if Othello was a white man, so was Desdemona."[83] Desdemona's appearance not only in blackface but also in drag further complicates these two adaptations' representations of race and gender. The cast of characters for Griffin and Christy's *Othello; A Burlesque* lists George Christy (well known for portraying stock "wench" characters) in the role of Desdemona, and Kenneth Gross confirms that Desdemonum would also have been played by a man.[84] While scholars have written extensively about all-male Shakespearean productions, in nineteenth-century America it had become standard to cast women in Shakespeare's female roles, and even some burlesque and minstrel adaptations—including Rice's—cast women as Desdemona.[85] On later, integrated productions, Sheila Rose Bland writes that "To see an actual black man kissing an actual white woman on stage is a powerful image—but one that misrepresents an even more powerful image on stage intended by Shakespeare: to see a white man in blackface kiss a white man in woman's clothing."[86] A white man in blackface kissing another white man in blackface and women's clothing might have been a different kind of powerful altogether.[87]

Bland calls the original *Othello* a "minstrel show" for its representation of Black masculinity, but race and gender are decidedly more complex when is becomes one literally.[88] Andrew Carlson notes how confusing the layers of identification and performance become in Griffin and Christy's Desdemona, who is "a white man in blackface playing a woman of German descent who differentiates her race from her black husband."[89] We can see this layering in the image of Rollin Howard playing a "wench" blackface character opposite Griffin (see figure 1.6). As Carlson suggests, this complexity—like the imagined absence of a real "threat" of miscegenation when Othello was played by a white man in blackface rather than by a real Black person—may serve to buffer the impropriety of actual pairings of Black men with white women.[90] Thus, the would-be miscegenation drama became a comedy, played out in burlesque form, between white men.[91] According to Carlson, these plays "simultaneously outline . . . the dangers of femininity and Blackness to reinforce a community of white masculinity."[92] Here we might revisit Desdemona's wish "that heaven had made her such a man" as Othello. In these minstrel productions, Desdemona does become "such a man"—a white man in blackface.[93]

Eric Lott discusses the particular brand of white masculinity at work here, describing the minstrel "wench" character as an "extravagant" display of the form's misogyny, stemming from anxieties about not only cultural shifts in racial power but in gendered power as well.[94] In this way, the minstrel "wench" bespeaks the threat of female power in the domestic sphere, even when actual women are absented from the minstrel spectacle. What Lott refers to as the "'phallic womanhood" that minstrel transvestitism implies is the potential masculinization of women in minstrel transvestitism, connoting not only the taboo of same-sex desire but also (male-threatening) feminine power.[95] Women's domestic power has particular implications for Black women. While "wench" acts may have been aimed at the emasculation of Black men, the stakes of Black women's power resonates not only for the heteronormative domestic spaces of Black homes, but also for white homes, given Black women's historical role as domestic servants. As Lott explains, "the 'wench' encompasses in her person male and female both; and the relationship between the two figures is foregrounded."[96] The desire for Blackness enacted in white men's minstrel performance was not a strictly homosocial desire. The relation of white masculine power to Black womanhood is

1.6 ROLLIN HOWARD ("WENCH") AND GEORGE W. H. GRIFFIN, C. 1855. COURTESY OF THE HARRY RANSOM RESEARCH CENTER, THE UNIVERSITY OF TEXAS AT AUSTIN.

also on display here. Though systematically oppressed by white patriarchy, Black women also enacted and articulated their own reclaimed power, in a wide variety of ways.

Beyond Sexual Kinship

Toni Morrison's play *Desdemona* offers a complex rethinking of Desdemona's whiteness, as well as her relation to Black women. Desdemona says, early on in the play, "I am not the meaning of a name I did not choose."[97] If Desdemona is not bound by the meaning of her name, we might reevaluate that name's being "begrimed and black" as Morrison takes up Shakespeare's detail that Desdemona was raised by an African nurse, Barbary.[98] Desdemona's critics have cited her mother's absence as contributing to her defiance of white womanly standards. Richard Grant Wright, for example, comments that "The lack of restraint of a mother's solicitude and cautions had developed in Desdemona an independence of character and a self-reliance to which otherwise she might not have attained."[99] It is not her mother who Desdemona recalls in the play's penultimate act, however, but Barbary.

Desdemona centers on an evolving dialog between these two women, set in the afterlife. Through this relationship, Morrison differently theorizes Desdemona's relation to Blackness. Their conversation juxtaposes the stories Othello told Desdemona during their courtship with the stories Barbary told Desdemona throughout her childhood. An announcement for the play's premiere explains Desdemona's enchantment with Othello through her familiarity with Barbary, and hence, Africa: "Othello wooed Desdemona with stories of his adventures. Raised by an African, Desdemona felt familiar and kindred with Othello."[100] Decentering the play's male characters, Morrison looks beyond heterosexual relations to explain Desdemona's feelings of interracial familiarity and kinship. Desdemona's connection to Africa therefore precedes her interracial sexuality. We might surmise that Desdemona fell in love with Othello because "Desdemona was brought up by an African maid who told her African stories."[101] Desdemona does not first enter into interracial kinship through Othello, then, but through this maternal figure.

Morrison's Desdemona exhibits the "mammy nostalgia" typical of nineteenth- and early-twentieth-century descriptions of white children's dependence upon, affection for, and ultimate misunderstanding of their Black "mammies." Barbary, however, transcends the "mammy" trope. Played by Mali-born singer-songwriter Rokia Traoré, Barbary is, indeed, given what one critic has called "equal staging—and equal voice—with Desdemona."[102]

Taking control of the event of her own naming, she revises the "mammy" role through self-articulation. Foreclosing Desdemona's false nostalgia of equality, Barbary reminds her of her enslavement. "You don't even know my name. Barbary? Barbary is what you call Africa . . . Barbary is the name of those without whom you could neither live nor prosper."[103] In this line, "Barbary" becomes Sa'ran, and the women's conversation continues. MacDonald notes the resonance of Black women throughout *Othello*, as Othello's mother first gave him the handkerchief, and "A foreign woman domesticated to the uses of Brabantio's household transmitted to his daughter the song's voicing of feminine mourning for lost love, lost integrity."[104] In Desdemona's exchanges with these Black women, MacDonald reads transmissions of "secret female power—if only the power to grieve," working against *Othello*'s underlying white patriarchy.[105]

Sa'ran, in this act of self-naming, also calls out her oppression within the play's white patriarchal system. Desdemona protests, "whatever your name, you were my best friend"; Sa'ran tells her, "I was your slave."[106] Asserting herself ("No, you listen"), Sa'ran answers Desdemona's question "You blame?" with "I clarify."[107] This conversation allows for a new understanding between these characters, eclipsing the relation between Black "mammy" and white child and approaching a feminist, anti-racist dialectic. Desdemona and Sa'ran are open to conversation, and hereby alter the American literary tropes within which they are both inscribed. Sa'ran's song is now hopeful, as she sings, "No more 'willow.' Afterlife is time and with time there is change. My song is new." Desdemona adopts this song, redefining herself as tied not only to Othello, but to Sa'ran, as they both proclaim that they "will never die again."[108]

Desdemona creates a space not only for white but also for Black womanhood, marginalized in Shakespeare's original and occluded by minstrel Blackface Desdemonas. Thus, *Desdemona* affirms a transracial feminism that is not only absent but unthinkable in either Shakespeare's original or blackface renditions, but which engages (though differently) the allusion to Black women that the racism of these minstrel plays evoke. Moreover, Morrison creates space for the play's women to function independently of Shakespeare's male characters, allowing Desdemona to re-create herself beyond boundaries of normative white womanhood and white kinship. Desdemona's recognition of her own participation in an oppressive system and Sa'ran's good faith that Desdemona does not mean to further contribute to that oppression sparks potential for interracial feminist understanding. For Desdemona, the elder woman has become a source of strength. In their shared refusal of the violent, white, male patriarchy of *Othello*, the women plant seeds of hope in the afterlife. Foreclosing the myth of kinship in structures of enslavement, *Desdemona* leaves open the possibility for interracial kinship—though not without acknowledging that this will necessitate a process of transformation from Desdemona's position of white privilege.

Morrison's Barbary/Sa'ran may be who Daileader calls "the black woman in Desdemona's shadow," but she is not, as Daileader claims, omitted but unconsciously evoked in the minstrel plays I have discussed.[109] Kim F. Hall has argued that "When white women bear the symbolic weight of the culture . . . attention is deflected from the equally vulnerable bodies of white men and the potentially threatening bodies of black women."[110] However, Morrison shows how these bodies are all evoked in the spectacle of *Othello* and, as I have shown here, they are also visible in the layering of white masculinity, white femininity, and Black femininity that converge in the figure of Blackface Desdemona.

Despite their differences from Morrison's adaptation, representations of Blackface Desdemona—like Morrison's cultural Africanization of Desdemona through her relationship with Sa'ran—also critique the standardization of blackface in productions of *Othello*. The Blackface Desdemona of minstrel plays appears much like Othello—neither an accurate representation of racial "whiteness" nor of "Blackness," but an indication of how race is constructed and theorized in these nineteenth-century representations. This is not to argue that the re-racialization of Desdemona in blackface holds the same weight as the racialization of Black women, but that it works within the same racial ideology that marks Blackness as material, visible, and sexual. Nevertheless, Blackface Desdemona evades rhetorics of essentialized white womanhood and normative genealogies of racial inheritance, taking up race's differently directional construction.

As Morrison's play indicates, however, the rhetorical blackening of Desdemona (here aligned by cultural rather than visual cues) need not present as ridiculous or necessarily derogatory, but might instead speak to the very serious need to refigure Desdemona's whiteness—and her relation to Blackness—through a Black feminist lens. Representations of Blackface Desdemona in the nineteenth-century social/cultural imaginary offer a theorization of white womanhood: one in which Desdemona's "whiteness" cannot be so neatly contrasted with Othello's "blackness," and in which American ideas of "white" and "black" are constructed through the performance of race and kinship.

In the midst of his racist critique of Desdemona, John Quincy Adams asks, "Who, in real life, would have her for his sister, daughter, or wife?"[111]

This rhetorical question makes the connection between Desdemona's sexuality and kinship relations. If we understand Desdemona's relationship with Othello as rendering her somehow unfit for white kinship, then this question is actually answered by the suggestion of her sexual kinship. Who claims kinship with women who have sexual relations with Black men? Black people. The relationship of Blackface minstrelsy to Blackness as a product of social construction is not the same as its relationship to Black people, although Black people's experience of race (and racism) has been informed by the many ways Blackness has been constructed historically. If racialization is, in part, a process of establishing kinship relations, Desdemona's blackening is not simply (or even necessarily) an articulation of her racial identification, but of her racialized kinship relations.

The metaphor of blacking makeup in the image of Blackface Desdemona indicates how race is imagined to move in "horizontal" relations of sexual kinship, with this flow of racialization answering John Quincy Adams's question of who would have Desdemona as kin by indicating how her kinship with Othello is prioritized and how it constructs race. This kind of queer genealogical movement is one of the bases of racist anxieties about interracial sexual relations. Blackface Desdemona provides an urtext not only for this movement, but for race's theorization as both material and "legible" upon the skin. Despite the presence of ambiguously raced people (to which I will return in chapters 3 and 4), racial construction has been largely dependent on race's legibility. Thus, Blackface Desdemona is one example of how race was "read" into the body. Morrison's intervention in Desdemona's relation to whiteness illustrates the limitations of sexual kinship relations for framing Black women, and both the limitations and possibilities of other interracial kinship relations. In the next chapter, I turn to another practice of reading race: via literary genre. In the case of William Allen and Mary King, we see a similarly horizontal flow of racialization through sexual kinship, as well as a backward racialization from (potential) child to mother, but also evidence of racialization's outward-originating directionality from audience/viewer/reader toward a racialized subject. Mary King, I show, is racialized both by these interracial kinship relations, as well as by the outward process of framing her within the particular literary genres in which she is "read."

"Almost Eliza"

Reading and

Racialization

Your flight is a flight for freedom, and I can almost call you *Eliza*.
—John Porter, letter to Mary King, March 27, 1853

THE PROPOSED MARRIAGE of William G. Allen, the "coloured professor" of the New York Central College at McGrawville, and Mary King, the white daughter of abolitionists, became a popular controversy in upstate New York in 1853.[1] The couple's engagement incited letters of family disapproval, newspaper commentary, and mob violence leading to their forced (though temporary) separation. According to Allen's personal narrative of their engagement and marriage in *The American Prejudice against Color*, the couple met when he was openly received as a guest in the Kings' abolitionist home and he and Mary's relationship developed at the racially integrated, coeducational school where Allen taught and King was a student. Allen recounts that King's father and sister originally supported the couple's engagement, but that Mr. King changed his opinion under pressure from his wife (Mary's stepmother) and sons, all Christian abolitionists who nevertheless vehemently opposed "amalgamation."

While King and Allen were visiting with friends in Fulton, New York, on Sunday, January 30, 1853, a white-supremacist mob descended on the couple, threatened Allen with physical violence unless he immediately left town, and forcibly escorted King to her parents' home. This mob (a group of white men) framed their interference as the benevolent "rescue" of a white "damsel" from supposed captivity. Following this separation, Allen and King eventually managed to correspond (at first under the surveillance of King's family and then through third parties) and ultimately eloped. They were married in New York City on March 30, 1853, and soon emigrated to England, never returning to the United States.

In a letter to Mary King during the week before she and Allen were married, the couple's friend, John Porter, wrote, "Your flight is a flight for freedom, and I can almost call you *Eliza*," referencing the well-known mixed-race heroine of Harriet Beecher Stowe's *Uncle Tom's Cabin*.[2] Porter's evocation of abolitionist literature is intriguing not only because it refuses to perform the more obvious slippage of relegating prejudice against the African American Allen (a man who was born to a free mixed-race woman and was never enslaved) to the discourse of slavery, but because it chooses the white woman as its subject and refigures her in one of abolitionism's most popular tropes of enslavement, the mixed-race heroine.[3] Not simply an equation of all race-related persecution with slavery, Porter's comparison of Mary King to Stowe's Eliza displaces the racist rhetoric of the couple's forced separation, which rendered King a "damsel" in need of the white male "protection" from interracial marriage that the mob purported to give her. Instead, Porter's "reading" of Mary King's position places her in the abolitionist literary tradition, where her and Allen's story reads as a narrative of African American fugitivity rather than white captivity. My use of the language of fugitivity in this chapter is deliberately not an evocation of the metaphorical or theoretical, but refers to the literal, material, and legal conditions of the historical people whose safety and liberty are threatened by antiblack violence. Beyond fugitivity, Porter's characterization of King as "almost . . . Eliza" emphasizes a close generic proximity to the figure of the mixed-race heroine, recognizing the interracial allegiance of King and Allen's proposed kinship, and a reracialization of the figure of the white woman along lines of her participation in interracial sexual relations and reproduction.[4]

Like Desdemona, Mary King harbors sentiments incompatible with dominant imaginings of white womanhood—her sexual desire for a Black man. This desire implies resistance to the white patriarchy into which she refuses to marry and also the breakdown of imagined biological racial barriers in its potential to produce racially mixed children—children who, like their father, would function as Black. By refiguring Mary King as "almost Eliza"—a mixed-race literary figure who is both aligned with the enslaved, and able to garner white sympathy—we can better gauge the content of King's "whiteness," an ideological construction that she resists despite public attempts to preserve the biologically and emotionally conceived notions of white womanhood to which she is attached. Similar to the material "begriming" of Desdemona, this literary re-racialization of Mary King depends upon "reading" race—here, via literary genre rather than on the racially marked body.

These two readings of Mary King—as either white captive or mixed-race fugitive—constitute alternative racializations, as the different genres within which she is figured are, essentially, alternative genealogies through which her race might be determined. Reading genre itself as a genealogy of race is consistent with theories of race's construction through social narrative. Mark Twain refers to the classification of his white-looking, though enslaved, protagonist, Roxy as Black according to "a fiction of law and custom."[5] I want to extend this understanding of race-as-fiction to literal and literary terms. If race itself might be understood as a fiction of social construction, the literary is an apt site for examining racial construction's inner workings. As countless scholars have shown, race literature both reflects and constitutes the surrounding cultures of racialization from which it emerges. We might therefore regard the racialized genres of captivity and fugitivity as literary genealogies of race. This is to say that the stories we tell about race are, themselves, processes of racialization. But looking further at the relationship between literary constructions and racial ones, we will also see how literary taxonomies and racial taxonomies align. That is, the kinds of stories we tell inform the kinds of racial construction involved therein.

This chapter takes up John Porter's comparison of Mary King to Eliza Harris and reads Mary King as the mixed-race heroine of William Allen's narrative. In the private and public discourse surrounding Allen's engagement and marriage to King, Mary King is figured according to different generic constructions of racialized womanhood in the two primary versions of the story—Allen's own version, and that in support of the racist mob that separated the couple. First, I discuss the racist rhetorics by which Mary King is read in the tradition of "anti-amalgamation" literature—a subgenre of the body of writing that emerges in response to abolitionist literature, which I argue has its roots in the American captivity narrative.[6] Understanding how Mary King functions generically in these versions of her and Allen's story helps us to understand accounts of King's ostensible "rescue" from interracial marriage. That is, the writing and rewriting of the Allen-King relationship demonstrates how the racialization of characters within specific literary genres structures how living people are "written" and "read" according to similar processes of racialization.

Reading Allen's narrative, I go on to illustrate how Mary King functions more closely to the mixed-race heroine of abolitionist literature than to the "damsel" of the captivity narrative. By refiguring Mary King in the terms by which an abolitionist reader compares her to the a mixed-race literary figure who is both aligned with the enslaved (and enslavable) and able to garner white sympathy, we can better gauge the content of King's whiteness as an ideological construction that she resists despite public attempts to preserve the notions of white womanhood to which the captivity narrative version of her story attaches her. Porter's reading of King as Eliza takes into account King's own version of events—close readings that are necessarily ignored by interpretations of King as captive. Finally, I turn to William Allen's 1852 commentary on *Uncle Tom's Cabin* in the *Frederick Douglass' Paper* and the significance of Allen's own critical focus on Stowe's character Cassy rather than Eliza. By reading Allen and King's story in relation to those of Stowe's "quadroon" heroines, Eliza and Cassy, it is possible to escape the underpinnings of the moderate—racial separatist—brand of abolitionism with which Stowe's novel concludes. When we take seriously the idea of King functioning in the generic role of the mixed-race heroine, we are open to the more radical possibilities of Allen's narrative—namely an alignment of King with more radical mixed-race heroines like Cassy, rather than moderate ones like Eliza.

Additionally, paying attention to the abolitionist rhetoric in Allen's narrative shows how William Allen, John Porter, and Mary King appropriate the concept of fugitivity for the cause against racial prejudice, rather than against enslavement alone. While slavery may very well have been a more hideous national problem than racial prejudice, the fact that racial prejudice cannot be legislated away—and could not even be erased through civil war—presents racism as the more insidious national problem. P. Gabrielle Foreman and others have noted the persistence of racism in the antebellum North, especially, and Black responses to racism that reached beyond antislavery efforts. Allen's focus on "prejudice" acknowledges this problem as more fundamental than enslavement by hinting that even the abolition of slavery will not correct the "American prejudice against color." While abolitionist discourse subsumes the condition of free African Americans in the nineteenth-century United States, Allen's narrative appropriation of abolitionist rhetoric repurposes abolitionist literature toward a more radical, anti-racist cause. In effect, reading Mary King as a mixed-race heroine challenges popular assumptions about white womanhood, illustrating how racializing this character becomes a practice of reading her story, and thereby challenges us to read characters across lines of race and genre, opening up new possibilities for understanding racialization's different directionalities.

The "Mary Rescue": Mary King and Anti-Amalgamation Literature

Mary King and William Allen's marriage was not illegal in New York State in 1853.[7] Nevertheless, the absence of laws preventing the marriage of white and Black people did not ensure that such marriages would be accepted equally by white Northerners. Allen's personal narrative acknowledges what writers such as Harriet Wilson and Frank Webb also depict in their narratives of mid-century race relations: the fact of Northern racism.[8] The title of Allen's narrative, *The American Prejudice against Color: An Authentic Narrative, Showing How Easily the Nation Got into an Uproar*, is clear in its emphasis on racism, rather than slavery, as its central problem. In it, Allen both tells his own version of the events surrounding his and King's engagement and marriage, and reproduces various newspaper accounts written in opposition to their marriage and even in support of the mob that threatened them. By this juxtaposition, the narrative reveals popular anxieties surrounding interracial marriage, or "amalgamation" in the nineteenth century, but further speaks to questions about how race works generically in the various retellings of the Allen-King story.

Reading these generic differences shows how the figure of the white woman is positioned at the center of white racial anxieties. As with my discussion of Desdemona in the previous chapter, my focus on the figure of the white woman in the Allen-King story seeks to acknowledge the significance of this positioning, while also acknowledging (and hopefully not reinforcing) problems that arise as a result of such a focus on the figure of the white woman: the false assumption that the category "white women" can be easily determined; the nonrepresentative universalizing of the white woman as a central, national figure; and the potential masking of women of color and their struggles. As in the previous chapter, my discussion of Mary King also shows how the figure of the white woman—and particularly white women's sexuality—became a site for racialization in nineteenth-century discourse.

Figuring Mary King as an embodiment of popular ideologies about white womanhood, most popular accounts of her story paint her as an innocent "victim" of an alleged racial "threat" posed by Allen. The nature of white violence in response to this supposed threat is implied, though not explicitly stated, as Allen invokes the "various torturings and mutilations

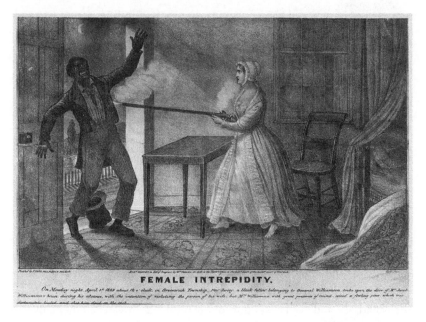

FEMALE INTREPIDITY.

2.1 EDWARD WILLIAMS CLAY, "FEMALE INTREPIDITY" [NEW YORK]: PRINTED BY
I. CHILDS, 160½ FULTON ST. NEW YORK, [C. 1839]. COURTESY OF THE AMERICAN
ANTIQUARIAN SOCIETY

of person . . . too shocking to be named in the pages of this book," which
he was intended to endure only if he and King had already been married at
the mob's arrival.[9] I would like to posit the mob and its supporters' response
to Allen and King as an attempt to write their story in light of an assumed
positioning of characters. In effect, this writing (or rewriting) attempts to
situate Allen and King generically, within a distinct and familiar narrative
framework. This framework is accompanied by a series of assumptions
about how the characters resemble recognizable tropes, and expectations
that they will function in predictable ways, thus anticipating how the story's
plot will progress.

Edward Clay's illustration of "Female Intrepidity" depicts a typical narrative of the supposed relation between white women and Black men. The text
below the image explains the situation clearly enough (see figure 2.1):

> On Monday night, April 1st, 1839 about 12 o'clock, in Greenwich Town-
> ship, New Jersey, a black fellow belonging to General Williamson, broke
> open the door of Mr. Jacob Williamson's house, during his absence, with
> the intention of violating the person of his wife, but Mrs. Williamson,

with great presence of mind, seized a fowling piece, which was fortunately loaded, and shot him dead on the spot.

The threat/victim relation is demarked along Black/white and male/female lines in this scenario, and the underlying sexual threat is accompanied by the imperative to protect the white woman from interracial sex—figured only as sexual violation—at all costs. The image itself is reminiscent of the 1773 title page to *A Narrative of the Captivity, Sufferings and Removes of Mrs. Mary Rowlandson*, in which Rowlandson holds a gun to ward off Indian intruders. As Michelle Burnham notes, this illustration is inconsistent with the content of Rowlandson's narrative (see figure 2.2).[10] The scene of Rowlandson staving off an Indian attack upon her home is not one that appears in her narrative, but a visualization of white racist anxieties about Native proximity to white domestic spaces. This is ironic, of course, as it is white settlers who first encroached upon Native land and homes, rather than the other way around. This reimagining of Native people as threat rather than victim is similar to the framing of Black men as threats to white women, while enslaved Black women were much more liable to be raped by white men. Like the captivity narrative, literature denouncing amalgamation traffics in racist anxieties that imagine a white need for protection from oppressed people as it also conflates the protection of white women and the protection of the nation. The threat of the male racial Other—a threat that carefully positions the figure of the white woman—is at the center of both the captivity narrative and the genre we might call "anti-amalgamation" literature.[11] Developing from a literary genre in which the racial Other is posed as somehow dangerous to normative models of whiteness, anti-amalgamation literature characteristically emphasizes its central threat as that supposed "fate worse than death": interracial sex.

These genres' similar positioning of the white woman at the center of their narratives, and their similar structuring of her kinship relations along lines of racial allegiance, develop her as a figure in need of white male protection from Black and Native men. In this, the absence of the white man in Clay's image does not mean that his rhetorical presence is not implied: Mr. Williamson, in his relation to the white woman (a legal relation, as well as a social one), is evoked as his wife's would-be protector, even though he does not appear in the image and is quickly glossed over in the narrative description.[12] The captivity narrative makes particular assumptions about the white woman. Perhaps most characteristic is the assumption that her familial and sexual allegiances are with white men rather than nonwhite men. Therefore, this

A
NARRATIVE
OF THE
CAPTIVITY, SUFFERINGS AND REMOVES
OF
Mrs. *Mary Rowlandſon,*

Who was taken Priſoner by the INDIANS with ſeveral others, and treated in the moſt barbarous and cruel Manner by thoſe vile Savages : With many other remarkable Events during her TRAVELS.

Written by her own Hand, for her private Uſe, and now made public at the earneſt Deſire of ſome Friends, and for the Benefit of the afflicted.

BOSTON :

Printed and Sold at JOHN BOYLE's Printing-Office, next Door to the *Three Doves* in Marlborough-Street. 1773.

1773

2.2 TITLE PAGE, *A NARRATIVE OF THE CAPTIVITY, SUFFERINGS AND REMOVES OF MRS. MARY ROWLANDSON* (BOSTON: JOHN BOYLE'S PRINTING-OFFICE, 1773). COURTESY OF THE AMERICAN ANTIQUARIAN SOCIETY.

genre has particular difficulty placing stories about women for whom this is not the case. As I will discuss further with regard to Mary Jemison in chapter 5, we see the particular difficulty of categorizing a white woman who does not meet the sexual/racial expectations of the captivity narrative.[13]

Anti-amalgamation literature, of course, depends upon similar assumptions about racial allegiance. The anti-amalgamation genre with which white racists describe the King-Allen engagement does not require King's acknowledgment of her alleged captivity, as the threat of the male racial Other is stipulated, even though evidence of this threat does not appear in Allen's account. Significantly, there is no account of Mary King confirming this narrative of a threatening interracial encounter. The mob's characterization of King's part in her proposed marriage to Allen not only reveals white anxiety about "amalgamation," but also defines the quickness with which the mob would explain King's actions, even at the risk of denying her all agency as a victim. Conceived as either an opponent to or a passive agent in the proposed interracial marriage, the mob assumes Mary King to be either, first, complicit in their action by sharing the mob's racial anxieties and having rejected Allen's unwelcome proposal, or second, an impressionable youth, corrupted by the teachings of her abolitionist family and/or her integrated college, and therefore unfit to make decisions regarding her marriage. Both cases assume that Mary King is in need of white male protection. Providing this "protection" is the mob's primary pretended purpose.

Newspaper accounts refer to the mob event as "The Fulton Rescue Case," "Another Rescue," and "The Mary Rescue," emphasizing the supposed threat that Allen poses and the necessity of rescuing King, while also making a blatant mockery of the local abolitionist movement.[14] The narrative in which Mary King is figured as a "damsel" in need of "rescue" shows how the structures of kinship at work in this genre would position the white woman in kinship with white men because of assumed ties of consanguinity and, because of the assumed absence of such ties, in an adversarial relationship with Black men. When relations between Black men and white women are the focus, however, mere "captivity" is no longer at the center of this story, but is replaced by the explicitly sexual threat that Black men supposedly pose.

Closely related to and overlapping with the genre of "anti-abolition" literature, anti-amalgamation literature depends upon the construction of both Black male sexuality and white female racism. Images such as Edward William Clay's "Female Intrepidity," as well as his *Practical Amalgamation* series of the same year, including "The Fruits of Amalgamation," "An Amalgamation Waltz," "The Wedding," and "Musical Soireé," illustrate the extent of overtly racist anti-amalgamationist rhetoric in such texts. While more radical writers such as Lydia Maria Child and David Walker wrote in support of interracial marriage as necessary for legal racial equality, the anxiety-laden interpretations of *Othello* discussed in chapter 1 illustrate the extent to which overtly racist anti-amalgamationist rhetoric had become prevalent by the mid-nineteenth century. The debate that coined the term "miscegenation" during the 1864 Lincoln reelection campaign brought this discourse into the realm of political campaigning, and "anti-amalgamation" literature became more highly visible following the Civil War, most emphatically in plantation nostalgia fiction, a genre whose popularity extended well into the twentieth century.[15]

Abolitionist attention to amalgamation tended to focus on the sexual exploitation and rape of enslaved women, citing amalgamation as another of the particular evils of the "peculiar institution" of slavery. This can be seen in popular texts such as Richard Hildreth's *The White Slave*, Stowe's *Uncle Tom's Cabin*, and William Wells Brown's *Clotel*. The genre of anti-amalgamation literature, in contrast, focuses most heavily on the supposed threat of sexual relations between Black men and white women. Such texts imagine the Black man's sexuality as explicitly directed at the white woman, whom he supposedly prefers to women of other races, including his own.[16] Determining the Black man as a threat to both white women, individually, and to an imagined white racial preservation, generally, is often at the center of these discussions.[17]

The similarities between captivity narrative and anti-amalgamation literature, and the trajectory from one genre to the other, are apparent in the uses of captivity rhetoric by authors of the racist counter-narratives to King and Allen. These racist counter-narratives frame the story around a basic assumption about King (i.e., that she does not desire Allen, or at the very least, that marrying him is not in her best interests). Such accounts of King and Allen's relationship foreclose other genres in which we might read their story, particularly the genres through which Allen, King, and their abolitionist friends recount their narrative. The conflicting discourses of "captivity" and "rescue" surrounding King are evidently at odds in Allen's narrative, as he positions anti-amalgamationist narratives against his own version of his and King's story.

"Almost Eliza": Mary King as a Mixed-Race Heroine

Foreclosing an anti-amalgamationist reading of the white woman, Mary King's letters never suggest Allen as a threat or that her relationship with him is anything but voluntary. Allen's inclusion of King's letters as he tells the story of their courtship and marriage is the one available record of King's commentary on these matters. Thus, his narrative includes her voice as well as his own, in a move that importantly reveals her agency against the racist accounts that would deny her either voice or agency in the matter of her own engagement and marriage. The disingenuousness of the supposed purpose of her "rescue" is evident in King's own accounts, as these assumptions are, of course, inconsistent with her eventual marriage to Allen and departure from her white family in the United States. The narrative Allen provides is of a different genre—and its heroine of a different kind—than the one implied in the story of mob action or the accompanying newspaper rhetoric of her "rescue." Allen gives King's voice a prominent place in his narrative, reproducing excerpts of King's personal letters, which emphasize the imprisonment to which she is subjected by her so-called "protectors."

These respective positionings of Mary King indicate two separate and competing genres in which she might function in the Allen-King story: the anti-amalgamationist literature of newspaper accounts and the body of abolitionist literature from which Allen is drawing and which contextualizes his narrative. Mary King is racialized differently in each of these genres. While in the former she appears as a white woman in need of white male protection from Black men, in the latter she functions in the role of a mixed-race heroine. Elise Lemire's discussion of whiteness as a position of sexual/racial desire is useful here, in that she describes "whites" as a group constructed around having "certain tastes." Lemire argues that "whiteness is an identity people can only claim if they have certain sexual race preferences."[18] Considering this racialization of sexual desire, King and Allen's engagement and the potential for interracial kinship relations that their desire implies suggest that we might read King as differently racialized here than when she is associated with more familiar tropes of white womanhood.

When we bracket the prominent model of white femininity (the "damsel" in need of white male "rescue") presented in the racist newspaper accounts and view it against her own letters, Mary King can be seen as actively struggling against white male domination in seeking marriage freedom (ironically, in a state in which interracial marriage was not illegal.) A closer examination of alternative representations of King illuminates how she works against the press's representation of her as adhering to popular nineteenth-century tropes of white womanhood—particularly that of the white woman who desires sexual racial segregation. Further, this racist version of white womanhood is not figured as the making of a mere choice of sexual relations here, but as regarding this version of nonnormative, interracial sexuality as a threat. Accordingly, the article "Another Rescue," which appeared in the anti-abolitionist *Syracuse Star* on February 1, registers this alleged "threat." Here, King is thrice referred to as "the damsel."[19] In Allen's representations, however, we find a character more proximate to the mixed-race heroine of abolitionist fiction than to the white "damsel" of anti-amalgamation rhetoric. King's proximity to Black kin (i.e., her intended marriage to Allen, which also implies the possibility of their future mixed-race children) distances her from the normative model of white womanhood contained in the captivity and anti-amalgamationist genres.

While reading King as a more normative white heroine suggests the privilege of whiteness in the supposed protection of white womanhood, the reality of her story is that the alleged "protection" of the white mob actually endangers both herself and her potential kin. This turns any assumption about the permanence of white privilege on its head, exposing how King is not fixed within, but can be removed from, this category of protected white womanhood.[20] By reading King's imprisonment at the hands of white men, her fugitivity in a society that seeks (legally or otherwise) to disallow interracial marriage, and her own declared interracial desire for Allen, we find someone who is better compared with the "quadroons" of Harriet Beecher Stowe's *Uncle Tom's Cabin* (published the year before the Allen-King controversy) than with the dominant, racist ideal.[21] It is with these models of alternatively raced and racialized womanhood, found most explicitly in the genre of abolitionist literature, that we might best contextualize Allen's narrative.

Discourses of abolition and amalgamation were tightly linked by the 1850s: because the two words were often conflated in pro-slavery rhetoric, some abolitionists found it necessary to promote "anti-amalgamationist" beliefs, while others (including Allen himself) argued that interracial marriage freedom was a necessary condition for, rather than simply a result of, legal racial equality.[22] As a counter to the "threat" of racial equality that abolitionism supposedly proposed, terming the mob's actions a "rescue" both mocked abolitionist efforts to help self-emancipated people (especially following the 1850 Fugitive Slave Act, which required them to assist in their re-enslavement) and defined the agency of the white womanhood in which Mary King was inscribed in these accounts. The assumption that King requires white men to rescue her from Allen, a Black man, would align her with both racism and anti-abolitionism. Her own contrasting account of imprisonment aligns her with anti-racism, abolitionism, and—importantly—the enslaved and the enslavable.

What the anti-amalgamationist genre fails to imagine is the possibility of the white woman as anti-racist—most explicitly figured here as the possibility of her interracial sexual desire and kinship relations. Even where they foreclose the possibility of such desire, abolitionist texts such as *Uncle Tom's Cabin* demand that their (assumedly white) readers extend sympathy to characters who are not (legally, even if visually) white.[23] Further, in abolitionist literature we find the mixed-race heroine more prominently figured, even, than the (here abolitionist) ideal of white womanhood.[24] Mixed-race characters' relation to race and their embodiment of racial dualism are at the center of these popular stories. The mixed-race heroine in abolitionist literature often appears in the role of the "tragic mulatta," whose tragedy lies not only with her inability to articulate or reconcile visual/legal/social racial identity, but with her position of precariousness or vulnerability. The "tragic mulatta" narrative differs most evidently from the captivity narrative because the heroines, though figured in many ways "like" the white women of captivity narratives, cannot be "rescued" by white men. If these women can be "rescued" at all in such narratives, this "rescue" is dependent on their own efforts, rather than on those of white men, who are generally depicted either as adversaries or as generally ineffectual in their efforts to assist the efforts of mixed-race women characters.[25] Whatever biological or rhetorical whiteness such characters may possess seldom translates to the structures of kinship with white men that would allow for their protection. White men in this genre usually do not acknowledge their kinship with mixed-race people; and even if they do, this kinship is legally illegitimate, rendering even well-intentioned white men powerless to protect mixed-race women from enslavement and all the dangers to which enslavement subjects them. Further, because the mixed-race heroine's self-identification is often aligned with Blackness rather than whiteness, the precariousness they experience also extends to their (actual or potential) children.

I want to suggest that Mary King, as she is articulated in Allen's account and in his reproduction of her correspondence, exhibits characteristics more like those found in the mixed-race heroine of abolitionist literary discourse than those available in the captivity narrative and anti-abolition and anti-amalgamation literatures. At the heart of this shared resemblance is the similarity of these characters' fugitive positions. Just as mixed-race heroines' visual whiteness is insufficient to protect them from antiblack racism, Mary King's genealogical whiteness is insufficient to protect her once she is understood to be in relations of interracial kinship. Like the mixed-race heroine, Mary King is positioned as precarious with relation to the white men who are better understood as her captors and adversaries than her rescuers. Her sexual desire for Allen and their future of shared domesticity in marriage places her in relations of interracial kinship (both to him and to their future children) rather than within the bounds of normalized white American domesticity. Both King's adversarial relation to white men and her kinship with Black people work to figure her fugitivity—a fugitivity that aligns her with Black and enslaved people via her relation to her white family and to the American nation.

The transferal of the captivity narrative from white supremacist arguments about Native people to those about Black people reflects a kind of lumping together of nonwhite people in anti-amalgamationist discourses invested in preserving an imagined white sexual and reproductive "purity." As Pascoe shows (and as I will discuss further in chapter 5), the stakes of interracial marriage are framed differently for white-Native pairings than they were for white-Black pairings in the nineteenth century. While prioritizing the transfer of property to white men is one explanation for this difference, the other is differences in white views regarding the potential of Native or Black people for assimilation into the nation. Notwithstanding these differences in white supremacist attitudes toward Native and Black people, the issue of captivity evidences a conflation of supposed Black and Native relations to white sexuality and white women in particular.[26] As white racists adapt the captivity narrative to describe Mary King's relationship to William Allen, the relationship between antiblack and anti-Native attitudes becomes more apparent. In both kinds of captivity narratives, assumptions about white supremacist sexual desire, preference, or "taste," as Lemire would have it, stipulate white women's attitudes toward nonwhite men. This stipulation masks white supremacist violence by placing the straw man of white victimhood in its stead. It also demarcates the bounds of white kinship and domesticity.

In this we can more fully see the relationship between captivity and fugitivity as two sides of the same coin—the former describing concerns about incorporating white people into nonwhite structures of kinship and domestic spaces, and the latter as excluding nonwhite people from the boundaries of family and nation. The lie of Mary King's captivity, then, is not simply a refusal to acknowledge her incorporation into a Black family via her marriage to Allen, but also to mark her, by virtue of this relationship, as unfit for inclusion in the white nation. This relationship between captivity and fugitivity is circular in nature, representing a kind of queer temporality that cannot be explained in terms of linear cause and effect. This argument is paradoxical. King must be a captive because a white woman cannot have willingly married a Black man. But she must be Black because a white woman cannot be a fugitive to white kinship and nationhood. This circular, queerly paradoxical temporality is represented in Mary King's re-racialization as mixed race. By describing her as not "fully" white—at least not in the sense of adhering to white supremacist versions of whiteness—King is always already re-racialized as Black in her fugitivity, even as the competing narrative of her whiteness frames her relationship as captivity. This circularity exhibits the racist logic of racialization.

By blaming Mary King's abolitionist upbringing or education by "her Amalgamation-preaching parents" for her "inappropriate" marriage choice, as the newspaper account of "Another Rescue" described events, the common conflation of abolitionism (the Kings were, in fact, abolitionists) and amalgamation becomes apparent. [27] Abolitionism, such arguments held, is a slippery slope, and the emancipation of enslaved Black people will inevitably lead to other, even more radical, forms of equality. As Karen Woods Weierman notes: "the proslavery press dubbed abolitionists 'amalgamationists,' equating support for emancipation with the endorsement of intermarriage. Actual intermarriages also tested the commitment of abolitionists to racial equality."[28] Similar to Elise Lemire's idea of race as dependent upon sexual racial "preference," this association posits race as an alignment with a particular political ideology. The underlying implication of the conflation of racial ideology and embodiment is that a political position could rhetorically re-racialize a person. In part, the conflation of physical and ideological racialization aligns whiteness with white supremacy and Blackness with a spectrum of political positions that include racial egalitarianism. Still, these two concepts of race—as sexual racial preference and as political affiliation—are connected.

For example, charges that the Republican Party, in its leanings toward abolitionism, also supported more radical views on "amalgamation" sparked a heated debate during the season leading to the 1864 presidential election. These public discussions, and literary frauds, led to the coining of the word "miscegenation" in the anonymously published pamphlet by David Goodman Croly and George Wakeman, *Miscegenation: The Theory of the Blending of the Races, Applied to the American White Man and Negro* and texts such as L. Seaman's *What Miscegenation Is! And What We Are to Expect, Now that Mr. Lincoln Is Re-Elected*.[29] They also caused Lincoln himself to denounce claims that he supported interracial marriage, just as he also denounced any support for the right of Black people to vote or serve on juries. Lincoln most famously declared his belief in a "natural" aversion to interracial marriage among white people in an 1857 speech, remarking on "that counterfeit logic which concludes that, because I do not want a black woman for a *slave* that I must necessarily want her for a *wife*." Lincoln continues, "I need not have her for either. I can just leave her alone. In some respects she is certainly not my equal."[30] Democrats' insinuation that Lincoln was a "black Republican" conflated the political position in support of abolition with the charge of supporting amalgamation by suggesting Lincoln's abolitionism also implied a sexual preference for African American women.[31]

More interesting for Allen's narrative are the connections between abolitionism and amalgamation evident in the abolitionist rhetoric that he employs, and in the characteristically abolitionist sympathy that Allen and King evoke from their few supporters. In Allen's presentation, the relation between amalgamation and abolition appears in terms of a shared potential for persecution or "fugitivity"—the precarious position, or "impermanence," of the enslaved, which points to the perpetual possibility of they (or their loved ones) being uprooted, and relays the fugitive position of the self-emancipated following the Fugitive Slave Act. For King and Allen, this fugitivity appears in the threat that the larger white community poses for the couple, even when not formally threatened by law. I mean to suggest here a sense of the word "fugitive" similar to that of Stephen Knadler, who uses it to "designate the counter hegemonic cultural work of influential people of color who, like Frederick Douglass in his own fugitive slave narrative, sought to intervene in whiteness's multiple racial formations by reevaluating its heterogeneous meaning."[32] In this sense, we might regard the fugitivity of white characters such as Mary King as inflecting another meaning of whiteness—one that is not definite or stable, but which is positioned in precarious proximity to Blackness and therefore sympathetic to the racially fugitive position of the enslavable.

This proximity is why both John Porter and his wife, Sarah, use the language of abolitionism to describe the King family's endeavors to prevent the couple's marriage, calling to mind the enslavement of African Americans as Mary King's escape from her family is coupled with the rhetoric of fugitivity. Sarah Porter, having knowledge of their intended elopement and emigration, writes to Mary King, "Now, dear Sister, farewell, and as you depart from this boasted 'land of liberty and equal rights,' and go among strangers, that you may, indeed, enjoy liberty, be not despondent, but cheerful, ever remembering the message of your angel mother."[33] We might surmise that this message of King's deceased mother was one of abolitionism—even, perhaps, a radical brand of abolitionism that preached racial equality, that rare anti-racism which would endorse King and Allen's marriage.[34] In this context, King's imprisonment becomes a perpetual fugitive state as she and Allen make plans to elope. No longer believing that their marriage is supportable in the United States, the couple—like some of the nation's most prominent self-emancipated people following the 1850 Fugitive Slave Act—emigrated to England.

There is a difference between the legal racial marking by which "women who crossed the color line became black in terms of their legal status," and the re-racialization of Mary King within the genre of the mixed-race heroine.[35] Still, both constructions of white womanhood are governed by structures of kinship which orient white women who would marry nonwhite men and bear mixed-race children. As Porter reads Mary King in the tradition of the mixed-race heroine, he not only reveals King's purported "protectors" as impinging upon her personal freedom, but also as threatening her future, racially "mixed," family. When King's potential family is taken into account, this reading reveals her changed relationship to the nation and an understanding of familial bonds akin to those who are enslaved or enslavable: because of this marriage choice, King considers herself, like the fugitive, unwelcome—and even in danger—in the United States. Like Eliza, who is removed to Liberia at the end of Stowe's novel, Mary King makes her ultimate home outside the United States. As she writes of her and Allen's homelessness as they are about to emigrate, King casts herself in abolitionist language, as her marriage choice has made her an outsider to the nation and race of her birth: "I feel that I have no home but in the heart of the one I love, and no country until I reach one where the cruel and crushing hand of Republican America can no longer tear me from you."[36] Not only can she no longer align herself with "Republican America," but she also regards the nation, like the white mob, as a threat to her chosen kinship ties.

If we did not know these words to be Mary King's, they could just as easily be those of Eliza Harris, writing to her husband, George. The coupling of "home" and "country" in King's letter sounds not unlike the image of domestic happiness Eliza dreams of while at the Quaker settlement, where "She dreamed of a beautiful country,—a land, it seemed, to her of rest . . . and there, in a house which kind voices told her was a home, she saw her boy playing, a free and happy child."[37] Eliza awakes to find herself (temporarily) safe in the Quaker home, "her child . . . calmly sleeping by her side," and "her husband sobbing by her pillow."[38] Her dream suggests that this "beautiful country" where she and her family can find "a home" is not the United States, as her later flight to Canada confirms. Though Stowe's narration of Eliza and

George Harris's emigration becomes a rather patriarchal account once they are reunited ("what a blessing it is for a man to feel that his wife and child belong to *him!*"), with Stowe attributing the larger voice to George's political ruminations rather than Eliza's thoughts for the remainder of the novel, the image of Eliza as both a fugitive and a mother remain in the foreground of *Uncle Tom's Cabin.*[39]

A significant fact of Stowe's plot is that it is not Eliza herself but her son, Harry, who has been sold. The image not only of an enslaved woman, but of a mother to an enslaved child therefore becomes the definitive conveyer of literary abolitionist sentiment. Burnham argues that Eliza is rendered white in her fugitivity, in popular illustrations of her crossing the ice of the Ohio River with her child.[40] Although Stowe undoubtedly draws upon whiteness's ability to evoke sympathy for her mixed-race Black characters, Eliza's and her child's fugitivity is dependent upon their legal Blackness—their ability to be enslaved and sold. If, as Burnham argues, whiteness is what allows Stowe's mixed-race characters to escape slavery (as was the case for some people who, like Ellen Craft, emancipated themselves by passing for white), Blackness is what imperils them. In the case of Mary King, however, it is not her own Blackness (in any visual or legal sense) but her relation to Blackness that puts her in danger. The refiguring of King as a mixed-race person uses the metaphor of a biological relation to Black people in order to illustrate King's condition of being related to Black people through marriage and (future) motherhood, suggesting that the difference between biological and nonbiological relations vis-à-vis Blackness is negligible. This is not the case as it pertains to King herself, but it becomes so when we consider King not simply as an individual but as part of a family that includes Allen and their future children. I will return to Mary King's figuring as the mixed-race mother more specifically in my final section.

"The Story of the *Quadroon* Girl"

When William Allen reads the mixed-race heroine, it is not the popular image of Eliza that sparks his interest. Rather, his reading of *Uncle Tom's Cabin* focuses on Cassy, the "quadroon" woman whose more radical place in the text is often overshadowed by the popular focus on Eliza. While Porter reads Mary King as somehow more like Eliza than the normative model of white womanhood, Allen shows how we might also read King in the tradition of Cassy. As Allen relates his impression of the recently published *Uncle Tom's Cabin* in a May 1852 letter to the *Frederick Douglass' Paper*, he writes,

"The story of the *Quadroon* girl, second book, thirty-fourth chapter, exceeds anything that I have ever read, in all that is soul-searching and thrilling." It is with Cassy that Allen seems to best identify, as he holds Tom as having "too much piety" and offers a familiar critique of the colonization chapter describing the ultimate fate of Eliza and George Harris. Allen writes, "I believe, as you do, that it is not light the slaveholder wants, but *fire*, and he ought to have it. I do not advocate revenge, but simply, resistance to tyrants, if it need be, to the death."[41] Nobody responds to the tyranny of slavery with so much "fire" as Cassy, whose ghostly revenge on Simon Legree is unequaled in the novel. It makes sense that, though seemingly forgotten by moderate abolitionist white people, Cassy would be a memorable character for more radical abolitionists. Although Cassy is described as being as visibly white as Eliza, her vehement—often violent—opposition to her and her children's enslavement presents her as a more dangerous figure than Eliza. Though Eliza's resistance is characterized by a bravery that is inspired by motherly affection and which continually places herself in danger, Cassy is not averse to harming her white enslavers (be it physically or psychologically) if necessary.

Although Cassy's story offers a familiar, generic narrative of the "tragic" mixed-race heroine, she nonetheless defies this literary trope (as Eliza also does), in part because she does not die at the end of her narrative, but instead escapes her final enslaver and is later reunited with her living children. In this, Cassy seems ahead of her time. She simultaneously evokes more radical abolitionist texts than Stowe's, such as Richard Hildreth's *The Slave: or Memoirs of Archy Moore* (1836), and anticipates postwar narratives of race and reunion, such as Lydia Maria Child's *Romance of the Republic* (1867), and Frances Ellen Watkins Harper's *Minnie's Sacrifice* (1869) and *Iola Leroy; or, Shadows Uplifted* (1892), to which I will return in chapters 3, 4, and 6.[42] Despite Cassy's radical presence in the text, Leslie Fiedler argues that her story "fades from the mind even after we have just read *Uncle Tom*," and Carolyn Vellenga Berman adds that Cassy often goes unmentioned in both early reviews of the novel and in recent Stowe scholarship.[43] Writing on *Uncle Tom's Cabin* has closely attended to the debates that surrounded the text's reception in 1852 and 1853—a debate that, though inflected by various positions of gender, nation, region, class, and race, has often prioritized the white, middle-class abolitionist readership with which Stowe's writing is usually associated. Although contemporary and critical African Americanist perspectives on Stowe have garnered more attention in recent scholarship, discussions of these perspectives often center around critiques of Stowe's views on colonization or her stereotypical depictions of Black characters.

A more radical employment of Stowe's mixed-race characters and construction of sentiment emerges, however, when we more closely examine the complexities of Black readers' responses to Stowe's novel. As Martin Delaney argued of Stowe, "she knows nothing about us, the free colored people of the United States."[44] However, these "free colored" people were among Stowe's earliest readers. The significance of Cassy in Allen's reading of Stowe, then, may lie in his readerly position as a free, northern, racially mixed man; a radical abolitionist; an anti-colonizationist; an integrationist; and an "amalgamationist." When this position of readership is taken into account, it is just as unsurprising that Allen finds Cassy's story particularly striking as it is that the increasingly popular discussion of Stowe's novel finds its way into Allen's narrative. While a more moderate abolitionist readership may readily allow Eliza's story to subsume Cassy's, it makes sense that Stowe's African American readers—especially those who readily critiqued the colonizationist ending of her novel—might also recall the single character who enacts a ghostly revenge on Simon Legree, the embodiment of the larger system in which "Uncle Tom" shows ultimately invest the entirety of that system and all its evils. My attention to Allen's emphasis on Cassy suggests that it matters whether any single reader of Stowe more closely identifies with George Harris, Cassy, or even Topsy, rather than with the Shelbys, the Birds, or Aunt Ophelia. Critics of abolitionist literature, in particular, ought to take the possibility of such readerly positions into account.

The structure in which Mary King resembles the generic trope of Stowe's Eliza can be explained by the same structure by which Cassy would become a memorable figure in white readings of *Uncle Tom's Cabin*. Both matters have to do with the relation of race to reading practices. By this I do not only mean that these practices are dependent upon the race of the reader, but refer to the practices by which race itself is read. William Allen's interest in Cassy seems exceptional when read next to the predominantly white readerly responses to the novel—that is, it can be contrasted against the failure of white readers to identify with Cassy, or with assumptions that mixed-race characters would be better able to garner white sympathy than Black ones, particularly if they support colonization. John Porter's suggestion of identifying Mary King with Eliza Harris points to a different readerly response, and the possibility for cross-racial identification with Stowe's enslaved characters.

By reading Allen and King's story in relation to those of both of Stowe's mixed-race heroines, Eliza and Cassy, we escape the underpinnings of the moderate, persistently racial separatist brand of abolitionism with which Stowe's novel concludes for the more radical readings that characters such as Eliza and Cassy might have to offer Stowe's readers. As Porter's letter and Allen's emphasis suggest, the possibilities for interracial identification go beyond the simple equation that white identification or sympathy depends upon Black proximity to whiteness (either in visual description, education, or ability to be assimilated in some version of American nationalism). Both King's rejection of white male patriarchy and her articulation of interracial kinship here foster that kind of identification, and better inform any reading of Allen's narrative.

Despite the fact that she is never in danger of actual legal enslavement, Mary King is forcibly confined in the attempt to separate her from Allen. King declares her devotion to her fiancé and distress over the prevention of their marriage, twice calling herself a "prisoner" held captive and under surveillance by family members who would prevent her marriage.[45] King's narrative of imprisonment also informs us that she has been deemed a transgressor against the white racist society that holds her, and is therefore in need of either punishment or pardon. The "committee" that first approaches Allen and King upon the mob's arrival escorts King to her father's house, and addresses her in these terms. Allen recounts that one member of the group "advised her also to go around among the ladies of the village, and consult with them, and assured her that he would be glad to see her at his house." Allen tells us that the "tone" of this speech is what evokes King's indignation: "The speaker evidently thought the young lady would receive it all as a mark of gracious favor, and as assuring her that though she had been 'hand and glove' with a coloured man, he would nevertheless condescend to overlook it."[46]

The mob's suggestion that King would either welcome or require the "gracious" pardon of white racists for her racial/sexual transgression is countered with King's indignation, her continued profession of love for Allen, and her ultimate state of fugitivity. She and Allen eventually leave the United States to avoid racial persecution—at a time when other African Americans figure as fugitives, either avoiding captivity in the North or, when possible, escaping to Canada or Europe, where they do not face the very real risk of re-enslavement. King's response refuses the mob's placement of her as either a captive damsel or a repentant transgressor of white racist codes, but insists that these white captors or pardoners are her personal adversaries.

The matter of rejecting the white racism that these accounts would foist upon her is truly personal for King, and to ascribe these views to her is to significantly change her story. While the "prejudice against color" that is primarily directed at Allen is willing to "pardon" King, it does so only at the expense of recasting her in racist terms: as a racial-purist damsel, rather than a race traitor. "The Fulton Rescue Case" article evokes a letter of response to the *Syracuse Journal* from Mary King's brother, William S. King, in which he "describes Miss King as repulsing [Allen] with her abhorrence of the idea of amalgamation."[47] In this account, King (very cordially) thrice rejects Allen's repeated proposals of marriage, as her brother attests that "she had always expressed her abhorrence of the idea of amalgamation."[48] In a weak attempt to support this claim, Allen also receives—and rejects the validity of—a letter (written not in Mary King's hand, but in her sister's, as she is allegedly too ill to write) breaking off the engagement.

We see here that assumptions of King's capacity for loving Allen become a question of the capacity for interracial sexual desire that her would-be "rescuers" attribute to her. That is, white racist assumptions about King and Allen's relationship predicate the impossibility of her sexual desire for him while admitting his desire for her and reframing it negatively against her supposed inability to reciprocate that desire. A surprising letter to King's father from Thomas Knowland, a Mississippi enslaver whom Allen calls a "specimen of Southern chivalry," asks permission to correspond with Mary King. Like the "rescue" mob, Knowland regards King as having "escaped" from an "ignominious connection" with Allen. Further, he tells Mr. King, "Your daughter [is]—innocent, as I must in charity presume—because deluded and deranged by the false teachings of the abolition Institute at McGrawville."[49] Echoing Shakespeare's Brabantio, who claims that Othello must have used some kind of "magic" to sway Desdemona's emotions,[50] Knowland is unwilling to assume that King could reasonably desire marriage to a Black man, but insists that she must have been "deluded and deranged"—brainwashed by abolitionists (who "must" also be amalgamationists).

This version of events does not square with the rest of Allen's narrative, of course. Allen makes it clear that his feelings toward King had always been "fully reciprocated,"[51] and reproduces letters in which King assures him of her continued love and devotion during their separation.[52] Reading the first letter he receives from King following their separation, Allen attests to his fiancée's devotion, writing that "Miss King,—though she could be persecuted—could not be crushed."[53] He further recalls the emotional difficulty King must have endured, his ever deeper feelings for her "after she had passed through that fiery furnace of affliction," and calls her continuance of their engagement "a moral heroism."[54] King's continued devotion to Allen is framed by placing her in this precarious, fugitive position—that of both estrangement from the white community and susceptibility to physical danger from it—a position which Porter's comparison likens to the state of people who are in danger of legal enslavement.

Like the Harrises and Cassy's family, Allen and King eventually decide to emigrate from the United States in order to secure their own safety—and the safety of their future family. King's position becomes more precarious still when read in light of the possibility of her motherhood. The fact that interracial sexual desire can lead to the literal embodiment of racial mixture places the white woman involved in interracial sexual relations in a precarious position: her sexual encounter may result in the literal (re)production of nonwhite people, as the children she bears from such encounters will not be designated "white" like herself. The potential for bearing racially mixed—that is, legally Black—children adds another dimension to King's fugitivity.[55]

Extending her fugitivity to the Black children that she would later bear, Cassy's motherhood—and especially, the infanticide of her last child because she is unwilling to see them suffer in slavery—is particularly poignant. Keeping in mind Stowe's appeals to white mothers to compare enslaved children with their own, King is in the particular position of a white woman whose children are not necessarily safe from potential enslavement, as the Fugitive Slave Act poses a threat even to free-born African Americans, and as the ideology of hypodescent would have it, partial whiteness is negligible. Harriet Jacobs, in *Incidents in the Life of a Slave Girl*, challenges the ability of white mothers to fully sympathize with the plight of the enslaved mother and her experience of reunion with her children when she asks, "O reader, can you imagine my joy? No, you cannot, unless you have been a slave mother."[56] This text reminds us of the difference—a difference that cannot be overemphasized—between Mary King's position and that of women who are, themselves, enslaved. What King exhibits in her "flight for freedom" as a white woman whose marriage and emigration are not hindered by law is the very kind of privilege Jacobs lacks and the resources for which she attempts to compensate in her narrative of motherhood. My next chapter will deal more explicitly with the condition of enslaved mothers in its discussion of racialized maternity and interracial kinship.

Apart from the extreme threat of the enslavement of free African Americans, King and Allen's mixed-race family is unwanted in their white community, as a western New York paper announcing their marriage makes explicit when it comments, sarcastically, "It is well they should emigrate, to show admiring foreigners the beauties of abolitionism."[57] King comes to articulate her own fugitivity in relation to the white community in her letters. Though initially offered "protection" and possible "pardon" from the white mob, in a letter written just before her elopement, King speaks not only to estrangement from the white community but to the danger of physical violence to herself: "should the public or my friends ever see fit to lay their commands upon me again, they will find that although they have but a weak, defenseless woman to contend with, still, that woman is one who will never passively yield her rights. *They may mob me; yea, they may kill me; but they shall never crush me.*"[58] In defiance of the threat of white male violence, King displays something resembling the "fire" that Allen attributes to Cassy. However, we would do well to note that King has not yet experienced the feelings of being "crushed" that Cassy has when we first encounter her in Stowe's novel as a woman who has been enslaved, sexually coerced if not raped, separated from her living children, and who has committed infanticide to save another child from the horrors of enslavement that she has determined unbearable. Mary King is not simply like an enslaved mixed-race woman, but rather practices of reading race liken her to enslaved mixed-race women in popular fiction. This process reveals how her "interracial" kinship ties to William Allen (and their potential children) bring racialized and genre-based reading practices to bear on Mary King's whiteness.

From Desire to Kinship

The seemingly slight differences between William Allen's narrative and Louisa May Alcott's loosely related story "M. L." illustrate this point in their different locations of and allowances for "interracial" desire. While Sarah Elbert presents the connections between these two stories and argues that Alcott's is based on her knowledge of Allen and King's case, a fundamental difference exists between the two narratives. This lies in the fact that Alcott stops short of fully acknowledging the possibility of a white woman's fully-informed interracial desire. This difference is central to understanding Alcott's story and its limitations.[59]

In "M. L.," the rich and beautiful, but kinless, Claudia falls in love with the musical, noble Paul Frere. The couple is happily engaged when the jealous Jessie Snowden discovers part of a letter Paul had written but could not bring himself to send to Claudia, revealing his history as the son of a wealthy Spanish planter and an enslaved "quadroon" woman. After his father's death, Paul was separated from his half-sister Nathalie and sold with the estate, to suffer in slavery until he escaped and appealed to his now-wealthy, married sister, who purchased him and gave him the financial assistance necessary to start a new life as a free man. Although she is surprised at Paul's revelation, Claudia remains determined in her devotion to him, and the couple is married—against the advice of Claudia's many friends. The story closes with a narrative of a happy couple, with Paul gaining both kin and country through his marriage to Claudia, and Claudia's former life of frivolity now replaced with new Christian meaning and substance in anti-racism. The "interracial" couple is triumphant at the story's close, and Claudia's commitment to Paul recasts her familiar model of white Christian feminine virtue in beliefs that support interracial marriage. Alcott's revision of the virtuous white woman is not dependent on her preservation of racial "purity," but in her ability to incorporate the nonwhite Paul into her own family structure, which serves as a microcosm of the racially integrated national and Christian community.

Although the ultimate anti-racist message of Alcott's story is quite clear, Claudia's early love for Paul is predicated on her initial ignorance of his racial difference, which distinguishes her ultimate desire to continue her relationship with him from Mary King's initial entry into an interracial relationship with Allen, having full knowledge of the probable opposition they would face. Sarah Elbert argues that "Claudia's romantic love for Paul becomes 'true love,' in nineteenth-century feminist parlance, precisely as her racial identity (whiteness) is challenged," that is, her own whiteness—socially constructed—is deconstructed through this allowing for "interracial" sexual desire.[60] However, as Elbert also recognizes, "her wealth, beauty, and 'whiteness,' ... ensure that she is a voluntary outcast, and therefore her privilege remains intact."[61]

Claudia differs from Mary King in her position as a "voluntary outcast" by virtue of the choice that Alcott forgoes for her heroine—that which allows the "white" woman's desire to be directed toward a man who is already known to be Black. Interracial sexual desire is diverted in Alcott's story, as the desire that preexists knowledge of racial difference fails to refigure white womanhood at its origins. Because her connection to Paul is already established, it need only be continued—a somewhat easier matter for the narrative in that it does not need to account for Claudia's desire for a Black man. Claudia's desire is both explained and mitigated by the fact of Paul's visual whiteness. Instead of initiating a kinship relation that is known to be interracial, Alcott's story only asks that Claudia perpetuate a preexisting promise of love and marriage. She does not offer Paul her love in the text, but simply refuses to take back that declaration on the basis of her new knowledge of his race. In some respects, the story begins from a narrative position that is unable to prohibit interracial desire. It has already occurred; no "natural" forces repel Claudia from Paul, and the desire that has already been expressed cannot be undone.

If we take this initial desire as a potential relation of kinship—a relation of potentiality that cannot be broken once desire has been articulated—Claudia and Paul's story resembles even more closely the narrative of interracial sibling kinship between Paul and Nathalie. Paul and Claudia's relationship is, at its outset, structured similarly to his relationship to his half-sister, Nathalie. Unable or unwilling to deny her connection to Paul, Nathalie goes so far as to take responsibility for her brother when he arrives on her balcony asking for her help. She asks him, "'Who should help you if not I?'"[62] In this, Nathalie serves as a model of true womanhood, which precedes Claudia's and structures Paul's relationships with all (white) women. His "reverence for womanhood" stems from this fraternal encounter, which causes him to look on all (white) women as a brother would.[63] He tells Claudia, "Since then, in every little maid, I see the child who loved me when a boy, in every blooming girl, the Nathalie who saved me when a man, in every woman, high or low, the semblance of my truest friend, and do them honor in my sister's name."[64] One might ask whether Nathalie's relationship to Paul renders her less white or, at least, more proximate to Blackness via this relation. Although Nathalie and Paul's kinship is mediated by a white relative (their father), Paul's reverence for Nathalie lies in the fact that she could have denied her own kinship with him (a point of white privilege), but that she has instead chosen to acknowledge that kinship.

However, recognizing a mixed-race brother may be less scandalous than accepting a mixed-race lover. It is significant that this sibling relationship mediates the romantic one between Paul and Claudia, as Paul requires from Claudia not a lover's passion, but a sister's pity as he pleads "give your abhorrence to the man who dared to love you, but bestow a little pity on the desolate boy you never knew."[65] Claudia's elevation depends upon the story's comparison of the two women: as Nathalie was Paul's "angel of deliverance," Claudia becomes his "strong sweet angel."[66] The recognition of Paul as kin seems accessible to these women, in part, because figuring them as "angels" dismisses any sense of racial contamination resulting from this kinship. In this configuration of "angelic" compassion, their kinship is rendered abstract; it is a kinship more humanistic than biological, more along the lines of figuring a national, rather than a nuclear, family.

Paul's position as a universal brother (read also in his name, Paul Frere), permeates the text as the couple's "interracial" marriage stands in for other forms of interracial national family. Through his marriage, we find that "Paul was no longer friendless and without a home, for here he found a country, and a welcome to that brotherhood which makes the whole world kin."[67] Here we not only read Paul as Claudia's individual lover, but as a universal brother to the white American nation—a nation that must acknowledge its own history of interracial kinship.[68] Paul's relation to his white sister (and assumedly his white wife) as "her proud protector" and "her willing servitor" indicates that he does not pose the usual "threat" of overly sexualized Black masculinity.[69] In his marriage to the kinless Claudia, Paul is positioned to take the place of the father and brother she never knew. That Paul's own father crossed racial boundaries in his own sexual relations is not insignificant: Paul embodies this boundary crossing, and his own sexuality is not bounded by notions of racial containment. Still, the more potentially radical reading of Alcott's story lies not in the interracial romance plot, but in this reading and its suggestion of American (inter)racial (re)union. What is most salient here is what remains unsaid, and what the characterization of Claudia-as-angel might allow readers to forget: the fact that interracial marriage (like other marriage in the nineteenth century) is likely to produce mixed-race people. Presented as a narrative of interracial brotherhood, the amalgamation narrative is replaced by a somewhat "safer" one of integration.[70]

Rethinking Mary King's generic function in Allen's narrative allows us to understand John Porter's reframing of the white woman as he compares King with Stowe's Eliza. Although the familiar characterizations of white femininity evidenced in literary genres such as the captivity narrative, anti-abolitionist writing, and anti-amgalgamation writing are central to understanding how nineteenth-century literary texts challenge Western notions of race and racialization, King is not best understood through these literary tropes. I am thinking especially of abolitionist literature's ubiquitous depictions of mixed-race characters ("tragic" and otherwise), which challenge the claims of racial essentialism central to political systems (systems that govern enslavement, marriage, citizenship, and so on) that are dependent upon the differentiation of white people from people who are not white. Allen's narrative pastiche allows us to read King through different literary genres comparatively. If unraveling the imagined sexual threat of the Black man and registering the real threat of white male patriarchy aligns King with Stowe's mixed-race heroines rather than with the popular model of the white damsel, these generic characterizations indicate how racialization is itself a literary practice.

In her discussion of the captivity narrative, Burnham shows how "the moving bodies of captive women . . . are inscribed by tensions between, on the one hand, their service to national or cultural reproduction and, on the other, the threats they pose to such reproduction."[71] The next two chapters turn to reproduction as I discuss the genealogies of kinship that travel between parents and children. We see glimpses of these possible directions in the character of Young Otello's visualization of Desdemona's embodiment of Blackness in pregnancy and in the specter of Mary King and William Allen's future children. The discussion that follows will take up these and other sites of reproduction's trajectories of racialization. The "fiction" of race as literary genre is not unrelated to ideas of fiction in the notion of "fictive" kinship. As writers such as Harriet Jacobs and Charles Chesnutt, and scholars such as Frances Smith Foster and Annette Gordon-Reed, have shown, enslaved people's emancipation efforts often depended not only upon individual ambition, treatment, circumstance, or desires, but was often predicated on relationships to family members and others in the enslaved community. As in the case of Mary King, we need therefore to consider the larger web of relations in order to understand reactions to racism, and also, I argue, to practices of racialization.

II

Reproduction

GENEALOGIES OF
(RE)RACIALIZATION

Mothers and Mammies

Racial Maternity and Matriliny

> Rear'd not beneath a parent's eye,
> A stranger to each kindred tie,
> On who but thee can I rely,
>
> My Mammy.
>
> —M. Belson [Mary Elliot?], "My Mammy"

LOUISA MAY ALCOTT'S best-known story of interracial family and post–
Civil War reunion is the 1863 tale originally published as "The Brothers."[1] The
title reveals the story's conceit, defining the mixed-race, formerly enslaved
Robert's relation to "Marster Ned," his white, enslaver half-brother. The narrative of interracial sibling kinship frames the Civil War and racial conflict
as familial matters, preparing readers for a new narrative of national reunion
that is even more necessary because it also constitutes familial reconciliation. Even more emphatically than Alcott's "M. L.," it suggests the national
implications of interracial kinship, and much like that story, it positions
white women at the center of these implications. By depicting relations of
interracial kinship between Civil War soldiers, Alcott places the white mili-
tary nurse, Faith Dane, in the position of mother to white, Black, and racially
mixed "boys." Here the white woman is the facilitator of interracial kinship.
The white and Black brothers need not be in competition for Faith's love. She
mothers her boys equally, standing in as a surrogate mother to the nation.

This positioning of Faith Dane as a figure of interracial motherhood oddly forecloses her participation in interracial sex—the thing that would generally create such relations of interracial kinship in the first place. While Alcott's alternative title, "My Contraband," frames the story around the relation between Nurse Dane and Robert (the "contraband" soldier), "The Brothers," in its foregrounding of the relation between two men, directs attention away from the subject of Faith's sexual desire. Alcott's story ultimately refuses to pursue an interracial romance plot, though it suggests its possibility, as Sarah Elbert and other readers of Alcott and race have suggested.[2] Faith's position at the center of the story, suggested by the possessive pronoun in "My Contraband," draws attention to the possibility for interracial sexual desire in the story. Faith's desire is not restrained because of any general inclination against amalgamation, but is thwarted more specifically by her preoccupation with Robert's status as a previously enslaved person. At the moment in which Faith touches Robert and "in an instant the man vanished and the slave appeared," the construction of difference in legal personhood rather than racialized appearance takes precedence. It demands that Faith's further affections for him are maternal in nature.[3] As Elbert notes, "Alcott thus insists that it is the man, tragically conscious of social boundaries and the consequences of crossing them, who forces Faith Dane to see her whiteness. Faith's sexual attraction to the 'man' is immediately disarmed by his performance as the 'slave,' and she resumes her own mask of comforting mother and, not incidentally, her dominance."[4] By resisting the teleology that logically links interracial motherhood to interracial sex—a kind of queering of interracial genealogies—Alcott's story preserves Faith Dane's whiteness. Unlike Kate Chopin's Désirée, Faith is not re-racialized by interracial motherhood. This seems to be because Faith's position as mother appears in this story (unusually) not as a result of sex at all, interracial or otherwise, but in lieu of it. Still, Alcott's hinting at this possibility of Faith's sexual kinship shows yet another trajectory for interracial genealogy.

Differing from Désirée's baby's re-racialization of his mother, the preservation of Faith Dane's whiteness seems to depend upon understanding her interracial motherhood as pretense. Redirecting Faith's motherly relation to both white and Black "boys" around the terrain of interracial sexual desire reinscribes motherhood as a form of stewardship, reflecting some of the racial hierarchy of enslavement. Viewing Faith as a suitable mother (but not a suitable lover) retains the hierarchy of race relations between Black men and white women. As mother, Faith retains a position of power and is regarded as a caregiver, rather than an equal. This relation of white motherhood to Black

"One hand stirred gruel for sick America, and the other hugged baby Africa." — PAGE 76.

3.1 NURSE TRIBULATION PERIWINKLE HOLDING BABY AFRICA. "ONE HAND STIRRED GRUEL FOR SICK AMERICA, AND THE OTHER HUGGED BABY AFRICA." LOUISA MAY ALCOTT, *HOSPITAL SKETCHES AND CAMP FIRESIDE STORIES* (BOSTON: ROBERTS BROTHERS, 1869). COURTESY OF THE AMERICAN ANTIQUARIAN SOCIETY.

children is rendered visible in an illustration of Tribulation Periwinkle nursing Baby Africa, in Alcott's 1869 collection, *Hospital Sketches, and Camp and Fireside Stories* (see figure 3.1). Positioning a white mother as steward to the Black nation re-genders the paternalism inherent in proslavery arguments, which often claimed white people as proper caregivers to Black people, who could not be expected to care for themselves outside the system of plantation slavery. Like Nurse Periwinkle, Faith Dane is similarly positioned as a white mother to the Black nation, and Black people are understood as perpetual children in Alcott's story. The presence of the Black woman in the background of the illustration also signifies her displacement. If Nurse Periwinkle must tend to "Baby Africa," the implication is that Black mothers are maternal failures, either through their own fault (as Daniel P. Moynihan would later blame Black mothers for the economic and social conditions of Black families) or by the burden of structural inequalities that denied most Black women access to the same educational and economic privileges that facilitated traditional models of white motherhood.[5]

Another potential reading of the figure of the white woman exists, however, if we take seriously the possibility of Nurse Periwinkle's kinship to Baby Africa or Faith Dane's mothering of Black "boys." I want here to suggest a more radical version of white mothering of Black children than is usually understood by the Black mother's displacement or absence. Reading Faith Dane as a potential mother to a Black child is provocative when one considers the model of Mary King as a white mother to Black children, one who may even have prioritized these children over her biological white family and the nation of her birth. Faith Dane's imagined motherhood changes, particularly, when we imagine the possibility of interracial sexuality that the title "My Contraband" suggests—a possibility that might result in bearing her own Black children. If Faith Dane and Nurse Periwinkle are understood also as capable of being biological mothers to Black children, rather than being surrogate or figurative mothers only, the prospect of interracial kinship might lead us to different potentialities for white motherhood.

Imagining this suggestion of biological motherhood, the image of Nurse Periwinkle can also be read as returning to the possibility of sexual desire between Faith Dane and Robert. Here we might reread Robert's assumption of Faith's surname, not just as a child who has inherited it, but perhaps as a lover in a reversal of gendered marital name exchange. Putting aside the more obvious problem of figuring power relations between the white woman and the Black man in this story, we are left with the possibility of interracial kinship: in this case, both in interracial sexual kinship and in interracial motherhood. As seen in the dangers of a "begrimed" Desdemona, the fact that sexual desire can lead to the literal embodiment of racial mixture (i.e., the production of racially mixed bodies) places the white woman involved in interracial sexual relations in a racially precarious position. While white women have often been read as key protectors and preservers of whiteness, their interracial sexual encounters may result in the (re)production of the racial Other: the children white women bear from such encounters will not be designated "white" like themselves. Barbara J. Fields mentions interracial motherhood and hypodescent in her discussion of the absurdity of biologically construed race, referring to "the well-known anomaly of American racial convention that considers a white woman capable of giving birth to a Black child but denies that a Black woman can give birth to a white child."[6] When read in this light, the suggestion of interracial sexual relations in "My Contraband" also hints at the possibility of white women—like Mary King—bearing racially mixed children like Robert. Taking these additional possibilities for interracial kinship seriously, we arrive at another reading of Nurse Periwinkle and Baby Africa: a reading of familial relations, rather than of national/racial stewardship or paternalism. If we think beyond these usual understandings of kinship as a metaphor for understanding either the nation or assumptions of racial dependency and stewardship, we can better understand depictions of white women who are at the center of interracial kinship relations— particularly in potentially procreative sexual relations and in relations of motherhood.

In this chapter I turn from parsing the particular distinctions of white women's interracial motherhood in order to examine slippages between differently racialized relations of biological and surrogate maternity. I here read the corresponding literary/cultural figures of the mother and the mammy, particularly in narratives that rearticulate motherhood or "mammyhood" when the racial definition or identification of these characters becomes unclear. Reading this relation in the dual mother-mammy figures of Charles Chesnutt's "Her Virginia Mammy" and Mark Twain's *Pudd'nhead Wilson*, I will discuss how these slippages between mother and mammy relations are, themselves, informed by racial figurings that, when changed or changeable, make the racialized mother/mammy distinction itself unclear. I introduce the mother-mammy or the mammy-mother as a figure in its own right here, as parallel biological and surrogate maternity are intertwined in complexly racializing genealogical relations. Motherhood and mammyhood are both racialized and racializing kinship relations in these texts. That is, they are relationships in which either the kinship of (usually biological) motherhood or the ersatz kinship of mammyhood are defined by racial identification and difference in the narratives discussed.

I refer to the relation of mammyhood as one of "ersatz kinship" here, following Sterling Brown, because I want to acknowledge that characterizations of the mammy as a member of the white family mimicked plantation slavery's pretense of Black contentment and naturalized white supremacist models of patriarchal stewardship.[7] What I mean by "ersatz kinship" is different from what is often referred to as "fictive kinship"—practices of cultural kinship in which Black enslaved families often engaged in lieu of or in addition to the biological kinship ties that practices of enslavement made difficult to maintain. I dislike the term "fictive kinship" for its seeming prioritization of biological genealogies, as though biological kinship relations are not also created or imagined in some way. Fictive kinship relations might be regarded as "real" in a way that ersatz kinship relationships like the mammy-child relation cannot. Unlike the latter, fictive kinship might be regarded as a form of deliberate resistance to enslavement in which people created kin when kin had been stolen from them. The ersatz kinship of mammyhood, however, is a coerced product of slavery meant to mask slavery's violence by perpetuating the lie of enslaved people as contented members of their enslavers' families while also obscuring the fact of enslaved Black women's kinship to their own biological children.

The texts discussed in this chapter each take up the combined or ambiguous figure of the mammy-mother as central for structuring both kinship relations and racial identification. However, I treat these intersecting figures (and the extent and nature of their intersection) for different ends. In their retrospective presentations of antebellum narratives, Twain's and Chesnutt's mammy figures are positioned against the sentimental celebrations of plantation life, as represented in the novels of Thomas Nelson Page and Thomas Dixon, and in the poetry of Sarah Piatt—writers who tend to depict what has now become a stereotypically derogatory version of the "Black mammy," one rather similar to the image so adored in Chesnutt's story. Chesnutt does not simply reproduce this image, however, but revises it in his narrative, and Twain similarly calls into question the notions of racialization and biological maternity that figure his central character. Even as Page claims that "no one can describe what the mammy was, and only those can apprehend her who were rocked on her generous bosom, slept on her bed, fed at her table, were directed by her unsleeping eye, and led by her precept in the way of truth, justice, and humanity,"[8] these authors already complicate the figure of the mammy in texts that expose Page's and Piatt's mammy figures as mere caricatures. Just as the trope of the mammy masks Black motherhood, the acknowledgment of Black maternity in the mammy-mothers of the texts I discuss reveals multiplied, queer maternal genealogies. By positioning mammy-mother characters whose dual relationship reflects a parallel genealogy of relation to the same child, these texts skirt around the fact of maternal surrogacy in the mammy and its inherent problems of white supremacist power. Instead, we are left with parallel genealogical relations—relations that ought not, by definition, to coexist—in a queering of normative genealogies of biological and surrogate maternal relations.

First I will discuss the racializing implications of Black motherhood and mammyhood. These relations of kinship and ersatz kinship both work to construct race, and, as I will show, their non-exclusionary relationship to one another presents another genealogy of kinship that might be understood as queerly resisting both biological and patrilineal teleologies. Next, I read Charles Chesnutt's short story, "Her Virginia Mammy," in order to introduce the categories of mother and mammy as not only interrelated but overlapping in texts invested in a national history of both race-based enslavement and racial mixture. Chesnutt's revision of the plantation nostalgia image of the mammy illustrates how the distinctions between the racialized categories of mother and mammy are blurred. This blurring reveals how queer genealogies of kinship are enacted in these sites of racialized maternity. Roxy, the mammy-mother of Mark Twain's *Pudd'nhead Wilson*, challenges the barriers of kinship and racial relations as she shifts between performing both roles to the same child. As a mother-mammy figure, Roxy's mixed race reflects upon the ambiguity of her maternal relationships, challenging assumptions about biological motherhood. In both Chesnutt's and Twain's texts, children's racialization is enacted not only through biological kinship with Black mothers but in the queer simultaneity of genealogical motherhood as it exists alongside an alternative ersatz kinship relation to motherhood in mammyhood.

Black Mammies, Black Mothers

In her 1872 poem, "The Black Princess," Sarah Piatt describes a Southern woman's nostalgic reminiscence of her mammy.[9] Piatt's poem is the epitome of plantation nostalgia, the perpetuation of the enslavers' pretense of happy plantation families. Insisting upon loving relationships between enslaved people and their enslavers, the supposed innocence of childhood becomes the poem's mechanism for masking racial oppression.[10] Fixing the figure of the mammy in such an idealized childhood, Piatt's poem reads, initially, as glorifying the mammy's apparent grace and beauty:

> Court lace nor jewels had she seen:
> She wore a precious smile, so rare
>   That at her side the whitest queen
>   Were dark—her darkness was so fair.
>
> Nothing of loveliest loveliness
> This strange, sad Princess seemed to lack;
>   Majestic with her calm distress
>   She was, and beautiful, though black.

The poem's evaluation of the "Princess's" "lovely" appearance accompanies what is revealed as rather backhanded praise, dependent upon negatively racialized descriptions of Blackness. As we read that "her darkness was so fair" and that she was "beautiful, though black," it becomes apparent that Blackness functions here only in derogatory terms, with these compliments given not in praise of Black beauty but only in spite of the woman's dark skin. Resembling the black/white imagery of William Blake's poem "The Little Black Boy," "The Black Princess" gives its readers a familiar impression of a Black person's honorary and obligatory "whitening" in heaven.

More interestingly, in the poem's last lines, we read not only the adult speaker's qualified reverence for this figure, but also her belief in the genuine nature of her mammy's love for the white child she has raised. So great does this speaker suppose her mammy's love was for the white child that it extends even from death, as the "black princess" still longs for that child from the place of her eternal reward in heaven:

> And in her Father's house beyond,
>> They gave her beauty, robe, and crown:
> On me, I think, far, faint and fond,
>> Her eyes to-day look, yearning, down.

What we read in these last lines is an astoundingly ignorant imagining of Black womanhood, which is unlikely to resemble the lived experiences of real women's servitude. It may well be the case that Piatt's speaker really did love her mammy, and that her mammy loved her. Nevertheless, however deep we might understand the affections between a Black mammy continually "yearning" for the white child even "in her Father's house beyond," her condition of earthly enslavement, the inherent violence of slavery, and the power relations implicit in Black feminine domestic servitude mark the mammy-child relationship as always suspect in its inability to ever be truly reciprocal.

Although the word "mammy" originally seemed to function rather innocently as a diminutive of "mother," by the nineteenth century it had come to designate a relationship explicitly *other* than biological motherhood, applied to wet-nurses or foster-mothers. The *Oxford English Dictionary* acknowledges that the figure of the mammy is explicitly racialized in the United States, referring to its common usage from the nineteenth century forward as "a black nursemaid or nanny in charge of white children."[11] While this definition acknowledges Black women's history as servants in white homes, the history of slavery and Black women's forced reproduction compounds the problem.

In their glorification of white children's relations with Black women, popular depictions of the mammy, like Piatt's, refuse to acknowledge existing racial power structures by which these women were either enslaved or employed by white families, or to acknowledge Black women's relationship to their own biological children. Referring to the phenomenon of mammy love as ersatz kinship, Sterling Brown calls Thomas Nelson Page's idealization of the mammy as a regional and national figure "honest if child-like," adding that "I am sure that he loved his mammy to death."[12] In this, Brown recognizes that depictions of the mammy often mask the racialized violence to which Black women were often subjected. In this masking, the figure of the mammy has been perpetuated well beyond the antebellum period, functioning to promote national, regional, and racial reconciliation, as well as postbellum white supremacy.[13] Because of her unique position as the caretaker of children, the mammy is embedded in a set of complex power relations, in which the power structure between adult and child or enslaved and (current or future) enslaver becomes complex.

Ultimately, examining problems of race and representation central to constructing the figure of the mammy indicates how this figure is more fluid than in usual renderings of the derogatory stereotype, both positioned against and able to perform notions of what is posited as an exclusively "white" motherhood. As Page writes, "She [Mammy] was far more than a servant. She was a member of the family in high-standing and of unquestioned influence. She was her mistress's coadjutress and her wise adviser, and where the children were concerned, she was next to her in authority."[14] Here Page suggests an idealized comparison (though not an equation) of the mother's and the mammy's maternal roles. Drawing attention to the ties of race and kinship that drive stories about mothers and mothering and mammies and "mammying" also illuminates both the complexities of race and racial mixture at work in these texts, and the ways that race remains dependent upon the particular articulation of kinship relations.

Patricia Hill Collins calls the mammy a "surrogate mother in blackface."[15] Like Blackface Desdemona, the mammy is a figure who is racially marked, not by Blackness itself but by the minstrel tropes that inform this popular image. This marking also maps relations of racialization inherent in the dual mother-mammy. What Collins calls the "matriarch," the Black mother "represented a failed mammy, a negative stigma to be applied to African-American women who dared reject the image of the submissive, hard-working servant."[16] It is a mistake, however, to regard these racialized roles of Black maternity as simply oppositional. In practice, they overlapped, as a single woman could occupy both the mother and mammy role simultaneously. This dual role of white supremacist racialization worked not in opposition but in tandem, even as one role was prioritized over the other. To separate the mammy from the Black mother is to misunderstand the labor these women did. The desexualization of the mammy denies both her maternity and her labor. The mammy is a necessarily sexual being because she is a necessary mother under slavery. To work as a wet-nurse is to have breasts that provide milk intended for one's own biological child.

The surrogacy of the mammy's motherhood is dependent upon her own relationship as mother to Black children, even as this relation is denied. Mary Niall Mitchell describes the contradictory ways in which Black women were "considered maternal when they care for white children, but not when they cared for their own children."[17] This contradiction can be seen in the necessity of differentiating the mammy from the mother, but also in the ways the role of "mammy" has been racialized as Black, denoting a particular relation to Black children, as well as to white ones. In David Macrae's *The Americans at Home*, the contradiction of separating mammy from mother comes into view in a section on the "influence of slavery on the blacks": "'I was once whipped,' said a negro servant at New Orleans, 'because I said to missis, 'My mother sent me.' We were not allowed to call our mammies 'mother.' It made it come too near the way of the white folks.'"[18] In this scene, we see the denial of Black motherhood in the reservation of the term "mother"—what MacCrae calls "the ordinary names indicative of family relationships"—for "white folks."[19] This denial works even as the word "mammy" brings to mind different relations of racialized maternal care and structures of white supremacist power.

The dual workings of the figures of the mother and the mammy are manifest in the emphases on biological and nonbiological kinship in relations of mothering. As the familiar law of the Virginia colony tells us, "*Partus sequitur ventrem*. The child follows the condition of the mother."[20] This law speaks to how both enslavement and legal racial identification were formally dependent upon a child's racial identification with her mother, regardless of the father's race. Moreover, it shows us how maternity becomes a force for racialization in nineteenth-century American literatures. As an iconic figure of American literature and culture, the visual image of the Black mammy is most commonly associated with cultural figures from Aunt Chloe in Harriet Beecher Stowe's *Uncle Tom's Cabin* to Hattie McDaniel in the 1940 film *Gone With the Wind*. In this iconic visual image of portly, big-breasted, dark-skinned, smiling, desexualized women, we see one of if not the single most hypervisible image of African American womanhood. The mammy becomes a stereotypically derogatory image by denigrating particular bodily characteristics and in the figure's hypervisibility, as its persistent presence tends to mask other versions and experiences of African American womanhood, including the realities of both the sexual exploitation of enslaved African American women and the history of their resistance to white supremacy.[21] While the mammy might be regarded as an antithesis to models of white republican motherhood in these iconic imaginings, this figure does have some role in preserving whiteness through its reproduction. The figure of the mammy as a happy and loyal caregiver to white children reproduces whiteness to the extent that she raises—and helps to racialize—white citizens who may later grow up to realize and act upon the racialized power structures that govern their relation to this maternal figure.

In addition, the figure of the mammy masks the lived experience of African American women *as mothers*—that is, as women who, their respective relationships to their white charges aside, are not coerced or paid for the love and care they give to their own children. Under this mask, the mother's biological children are most often figured as absent or neglected out of necessity for the mammy's care of the white children who demand prioritization. This image of the Black mammy-mother can be seen in Joyce J. Scott's sculpture *No Mommy Me*, which depicts a Black child displaced from her mother's care as she tends to a white child (see figure 3.2).[22] Here we find the Black mother physically positioned in competing, racialized relations of caregiving to white and Black children. The Black child clings closely to his mother's skirt as she holds the white child with arms outstretched, as though symbolically distancing him from her. The dual mother/mammy role reflects the irony that Black women were valorized in the role of mammy but denigrated as mothers by white supremacist culture. The worry of the Black child in Scott's sculpture—that this mother might care more for the white children in her care than for her own Black children—is Piatt's ideal. This implication is, of course, steeped in antiblack racism, which imagines both the white child as inherently worthy and loveable and the Black child as inherently unworthy and unlovable (or, at the very least, as unharmed by maternal neglect).

Exploring this figure's dual role, Kimberly Wallace-Sanders regards "the mammy's characterization as biological *and* surrogate mother" in American cultural representations within the context of a national, white patriarchy.[23] My discussion here focuses on figures of intertwined motherhood and mammyhood and the ways these figures construct the image of the mixed-race mother in relation to both notions of idealized white motherhood (as

3.2 JOYCE J. SCOTT, *NO MOMMY ME I,* 1991, LEATHER AND BEADS, 18×7×5½.
PHOTOGRAPH COURTESY OF THE MARYLAND INSTITUTE COLLEGE OF ART.

suggested by Faith Dane and Tribulation Periwinkle) and the stereotype of the Black mammy. Scott's sculptures represent the mammy as alternating between the roles of mother and mammy via her relationship to a Black child and a white one. My texts for reading the intertwining of mother and mammy queer the ties of maternal kinship and mammies' ersatz kinship by working beyond this alternating model. Rather, these texts show the mother-mammy as able to perform both roles to the same child, in a queer genealogy that merges these relationships. Rather than alternating between these two roles, as we might imagine the figure in Scott's sculpture doing, we see mother and mammy converge. The Black child who clings to his mother's skirt cannot be displaced but is ever-present in this convergence. In Chesnutt's story and Twain's novel, we see narratives of a Black woman character who is figured as both mother and mammy to the same child. This intertwining of kinship and ersatz kinship roles works as a kind of queer genealogical relation in its parallel operation. Genealogies of both the mother and the mammy are at work in these narratives of racialization.

Her Virginia Mother

In "Her Virginia Mammy," Chesnutt's protagonist, Clara Hohlfelder, is disturbed by the fact of not knowing her biological genealogy. Orphaned at a young age and having been adopted by loving people to whom she has for unknown reasons never felt a sufficiently close bond, Clara resists accepting her lover's proposal in part because she does not know what familial roots she would bring to the marriage. Chesnutt's response to the popular genre of plantation nostalgia fiction shows that Clara finds especial comfort not only in the revelation of her biological connections to the "first families of Virginia," but also in the emotional encounter with her own "Virginia mammy" of the story's title.[24] During a chance meeting that reveals the familial ties Clara had been hoping to discover, Clara is reunited with Mrs. Harper, who ultimately reveals herself to be Clara's long-lost mammy.

Mrs. Harper provides the missing details of Clara's parents' lives, the shipwreck by which they were separated, the supposed death of the lost child, and her own re-enslavement, which kept her from immediately restoring Clara to her "people." She tells Clara, "Yes, child, I was—your mammy. Upon my bosom you have rested; my breasts once gave you nourishment; my hands once ministered to you; my arms sheltered you, and my heart loved you and mourned you like a mother loves and mourns a firstborn."[25] These lines serve as the revelation of kinship for which Clara has been longing. While "their name and their blood" are all that Clara's parents seem to have left her, the encounter with her "dear Virginia mammy" is sufficient to fill Clara's yearning for the "kith or kin" she had previously thought herself without.[26] Despite the fact that Clara is left with no chance of ever being reunited with any of her biological kin, the meeting of mammy and child is framed clearly in terms of kinship rather than as a meeting between Clara and a mere former servant of her family. Importantly, this kinship seems sufficient for Clara. As the two women kiss, "One put into her embrace all of her new-found joy, the other all the suppressed feeling of the last half hour, which in turn embodied the unsatisfied yearning of many years."[27] The image Chesnutt provides is that of a mother and child reunited.

From these details, it is possible to gather something about the complexities of kinship in Clara's nostalgic view of race relations in the Old South—a South that never was, except in antebellum proslavery arguments of white patriarchal benevolence and the late-nineteenth and early-twentieth century plantation narratives that these arguments continued to inform. In Clara's nostalgic imagination—an imagination that has evidently been informed by positive images of slavery in the antebellum South—the plantation system extends an umbrella of kinship to the enslaved people who interact closely with the families they serve. The fact that Clara recognizes her "Virginia mammy" as a sufficient kinship relation to fill the void unable to be occupied by her adopted mother (who, she admits, "could not have loved me better or cared for me more faithfully had I been her own child," but to whom she has always felt "a subtle difference"), reveals the significance of the idealized mammy relation[28] Clara does not seem to regard this relation as a form of ersatz kinship, but as a bond of significant and real belonging that seems to surpass even her relationship with the adoptive mother who raised her.

Although the term "mammy" had come to designate a relationship explicitly *other* than biological motherhood by the mid-nineteenth century, connotations of familiarity (often associated with childhood) are here retained. This familiarity, confounded with childhood memories of love and care, remind us of the term's historical use by children as an appellation of genuine affection. As enslaved or employed women performed the duties of early childcare (and for children whose affections to their primary caregivers might not yet have been imbued with the racism inherent to Southern plantation slavery), the antebellum era presents the mammy-child relationship as one of close proximity to (or, at times, even closer than) the mother-child relation. What Clara seems to crave is contact with someone whose relation to her reaches back to the earliest years of her childhood. Clara hopes to gain some sense of herself from this early relation.

Chesnutt disrupts the plantation nostalgia genre with the implication that Clara's nostalgia is as suspect as that of Piatt's speaker in "The Black Princess." The violence of slavery and the power relations implicit in Black feminine domestic servitude, however, mark the mammy-child relationship as suspect, always imbued with the stain of racial hierarchy. However deep we might understand the affections between "Black mammy" and "white child," American racial formation is founded on assumptions of racial essentialism that prevent any conflation of the duties of white biological kinship with relations between "white" enslavers and "Black" enslaved people or free Black servants (regardless of any biological relations between them.) That is, even as the term "mammy" suggested the false family of plantation slavery, it also denied any conflation of that relation with the clearly recognized familial obligations between white kinfolk.

Clara does not doubt Mrs. Harper's likening of the mammy to the biological mother, however, as she describes her care and love as maternal. She regards her mammy's performance of these mothering acts as sincere enough to justify her own strong feelings of kinship, and she assumes these are reciprocated. In effect, the mammy's performance of motherhood produces a shared affect of kinship in a way that adoptive motherhood cannot in Clara's view. In this respect, it is important that Clara's Virginia mammy is not simply a servant of her family, but was, during Clara's youth, enslaved by them. A familial model of plantation slavery is therefore essential to Clara's understanding of the mammy. Mrs. Harper's affection, in this light, is explained through popular assumptions about the patriarchal system by which enslaved people are interpolated under the guise of kinship relations that rendered enslaved people as "uncle," "aunt," or "mammy."

Wallace-Sanders describes the mammy figure of nineteenth-century American culture as "a mother who frequently displaces white mothers and has ambiguous relationships with her own children."[29] In the particular familiarity of the mammy relation, this figure is sometimes usurped by the more distant white mother, rendering white women's relationships with their own children equally "ambiguous." Clara embraces this displacement as she romanticizes the mammy-child relationship, interpreting the labor of the breasts that nourish, the hands that minister, and the arms that shelter as labors of love, rather than those of a hired or enslaved body. Clara accepts the affection of the woman she believes to have been her family's "colored nurse" at face value. Never does it occur to her that the violence and white supremacy of

Southern slavery might influence a Black woman's feelings toward her white charges, nor does she think about her mammy's relationship with or obligations to her own biological children.

The familial appellations of plantation slavery imply a false structure of kinship between enslaved people and the people who hold them enslaved, but they also subtly acknowledge a system in which many enslaved people were biologically related to their enslavers. The presumably inherent division between mammy and mother is therefore ironic in light of the biological ties that are known to have existed between enslavers and enslaved people under the system of plantation slavery. In this respect, kinship appellations such as "aunt" and "mammy" subtly acknowledge a system that is distinctly unable to maintain the racial barriers on which its legality is based.[30] In the case of "Her Virginia Mammy," though, the intimate relationship between mammy and child approximates that of mother and child. Clara does not need an acknowledgment of blood relation to explain her connection to the older woman who she so closely resembles, but ironically—or perhaps, fittingly—the emotional encounter between Clara and Mrs. Harper is heightened by the fact she is revealed to be not Clara's mammy, but the biological mother for whom Clara has been yearning.

Everyone except Clara—the reader, Chesnutt's narrator, Mrs. Harper, and Clara's fiancé, Dr. Winthrop—recognize the family resemblance between the two women. Ultimately, however, Mrs. Harper chooses not to reveal the secret that would refigure Clara's understanding of her own whiteness. Dr. Winthrop understands the situation but, taking a visual cue from Mrs. Harper, he too remains silent rather than upset his fiancée's fantasy. We understand Dr. Winthrop as fully understanding Clara's beliefs about the importance of inherited "name" and "blood," while not caring much about these himself—even as he will knowingly marry a mixed-race (though effectively passing) woman. These metaphors of race are symbols of Clara's investment in white womanhood insofar as they serve for her as a sort of dowry—the only "property" that she brings to her marriage. These matter little, however, when Clara's surname will be lost as she assumes her husband's in marriage and as her racial genealogy is more likely to remain hidden because she is not even aware of her own racial passing.

Clara's naive assumption that Mrs. Harper was "the colored nurse" and not the wife and mother described in her story, speaks to Clara's inability to escape essentialist notions of racial determination, despite her experience teaching "colored" dance pupils of various shades, some of whom "were undistinguishable from pure white."[31] Mrs. Harper tells Clara that her mother "also belonged to one of the first families of Virginia and in her veins flowed some of the best blood of the Old Dominion," and Clara therefore assumes that her mother was white in the conventional, essentialist, and legal sense. Although Clara does not understand, Mrs. Harper alludes in her claim to racial intermixture within these Southern white families, complicating not only Clara's but her own race beyond Black/white dualism.[32]

In light of the complications interracial kinship brings to a story about mammies and mothers, Chesnutt's piece does more than just "ironize" blood, as Eric Sundquist suggests.[33] It challenges the prioritization of biology for determining either race or kinship, complicating the ways in which both race and kinship are simultaneously enacted. Mrs. Harper's performance of the role of mammy to her own biological daughter necessitates a racial performance as well—one that perpetuates Clara's nostalgic imagining of this figure. One irony of this scene is that while this biological mother's love is real, her participation in the racial stereotype of mammyhood simultaneously reinscribes her own race in essentialist terms. As Mrs. Harper allows her daughter to pass for white (while not even acknowledging that she is doing so), she also allows her own maternal love for her biological child to be filtered through the lens of the apparent racial servitude of the mammy's devotion.

What Chesnutt's story so deftly shows us is how easy the slippage between mother and mammy might be when notions of race itself remain malleable. In Mrs. Harper's performance of racialized maternity, her role of ersatz kinship serves to racialize her biological daughter—but not in the usual genealogical ways. By denying biological kinship, she preserves Clara's assumed whiteness. We see here that the mammy is a racialized figure of motherhood whose genealogies of both kinship and ersatz kinship contributes to racial construction. While Black mothers are known for passing on their enslaved and racial status to their biological children, Black mammies also construct the whiteness of the children they raise—usually via uneven structures of power and unwilling participation in the ersatz kinship of plantation slavery. As Mrs. Harper willingly articulates herself as mammy to her own daughter, she flips the script of hypodescent, using cultural understandings of the mammy-child relationship to racialize her own daughter as white. Still, in Chesnutt's plot, everyone but Clara knows the "truth" of both her biological relationship to Mrs. Harper and thereby her "true" race. Putting aside this point of racial essentialism, however, we are left with a protagonist whose whiteness is—unlike Désirée's—no less altered than it was at the story's opening, when she knew nothing of her biological genealogy. By presenting Clara's mother as both having the potential to re-racialize her as Black and to preserve—even to reinforce—her assumed whiteness, Chesnutt endows the Black mother with a kind of queer genealogical racializing potential. In the conceit of this open secret, Mrs. Harper is herself written as a figure who occupies parallel relations of kinship and racialization, as a mammy-mother. The dual role of mammy and mother works similarly in Mark Twain's *Pudd'nhead Wilson*, where we see a protagonist who enacts the racializing potential of her own relations not only to her own child but to that of her enslaver as well.

Roxy's Racial Genealogies

Like "Her Virginia Mammy," *Pudd'nhead Wilson* emphasizes the racialization inherent in (white) mother and (Black) mammy tropes.[34] Roxy, the enslaved mother of Valet de Chambre and mammy to Thomas à Becket Driscoll, illustrates how genealogies of racialization are complicated by racialized relationships. Roxy (Roxana) is a mixed-race Black woman who is able to simultaneously embody both the mother and mammy roles, and her shifting performance of motherhood or mammyhood extends racial genealogies to the children in her care. Wallace-Sanders correctly observes that "neither Roxy nor Mrs. Harper is a stereotypical mammy figure," and argues further that "both mammy characters fall into a uniquely hybrid stereotype, the mulatto mammy . . . a fascinating mixture of the two well-known stereotypes: the mammy and the tragic mulatto."[35] The hybrid category of the "mulatto mammy" is insufficient for discussing the particularities of kinship in Twain's text, however, where both mammy and mother relations are intertwined with racialization. Roxy (like other late-century mixed-race figures such as Iola Leroy and her sentimental abolitionist foremothers, Stowe's Eliza Harris and William Wells Brown's Clotel) embodies the contradiction of a race-based system of slavery that does not reflect the realities of racial mixture and ambiguity that are, themselves, a direct result of the patriarchal plantation system.

Twain's narrator ruminates on the contradiction of Roxy's race throughout *Pudd'nhead Wilson*, and this commentary, as with alternative readings of Mary King, reveals the difficulties of reading racialized kinship relations. Roxy's mixed-race maternity is dependent upon the narration of her kinship relations to her own son and to the child of her enslaver. Although the essentialist beliefs of Twain's characters are evident and unsurprising, Twain's narrator seems unconvinced by conventional notions of how any amount of "black blood" serves to racialize Roxy or her child as Black. We read that Roxy's child, "thirty-one parts white . . . too, was a slave, and by a fiction of law and custom a negro."[36] While Twain's narrator does not seem entirely convinced that either Roxy or her child is *really* "a negro," Twain's plot depends upon the notion that there *are* both "negroes" and "whites," though it may be argued that he paints racial difference not as essential but as created through socially constructed inequality. The "fiction of law and custom" that Twain cites here is the process of race-making that Omi and Winant call racial formation.[37] This "fiction" of hypodescent is no less emphatic in its racializing capacity because it departs from a blood quantum model of racialization. However, as Twain makes his readers aware of the social means by which Roxy's race is constructed, we can also see how, via this racialization and her kinship position as mother and mammy, Roxy occupies social relations by which her racialization also projects race onto the two children. She reproduces race through her relations to them.

Like other mammy figures, Roxy is mammy to one child and mother to another, nursing and rearing the child of her enslaver alongside (or even instead of) her own. However, the two children Roxy tends to are virtually identical, undistinguishable from one another by anyone other than Roxy, their primary caregiver. Roxy's relation to and unique knowledge of the children is what allows her to switch the infants' places in the act that sparks the novel's identity-driven plot. This switch changes the boys' identities, and their racialization, by sole virtue of Roxy's relation to them. Her position as mother to one child and mammy to the other enacts this racialization—in relative terms. Initially, at least, it is through their respective relations to Roxy that each child assumes their identity as either white and free or Black and enslaved.

The fact of these changes in identity challenge the notions of kinship through which racial identity and belonging are usually constructed and enacted. Twain's emphasis on Roxy's racial mixture causes Wallace-Sanders to read Roxy as belonging to the hybrid literary type of the "mulatto mammy."[38] If characters such as Roxy and Mrs. Harper are hybrid figures though, the most compelling evidence of this hybridity is not their own racial identification, but their ability to move fluidly between the roles of mammy and mother. Both Twain and Chesnutt "draw innovative parallels between passing over the color line and passing from mammy to mother," but unlike Mrs. Harper's, Roxy's movement between kinship and racial relations is not unidirectional.[39] Roxy's shifting between the roles of mother and mammy illustrates how she simultaneously performs and interpolates not her own but others' racialization through these roles and their attending racial genealogies.

As a white-looking woman who might be able to "pass" were it not for the racially marked dialect of her speech, Roxy's very existence calls into question antebellum beliefs about racial dualism and essentialism. Our first glimpse of Roxy easily dispatches with notions of "Blackness" as visible. We read that:

> From Roxy's manner of speech, a stranger would have expected her to be black, but she was not. Only one-sixteenth of her was black, and that sixteenth did not show. She was of majestic form and stature, her attitudes were imposing and statuesque, and her gestures and movements distinguished by a noble and stately grace. Her complexion was very fair, with the rosy glow of vigorous health in the cheeks, her face was full of character and expression, her eyes were brown and liquid, and she had a heavy suit of fine soft hair which was also brown, but the fact was not apparent because her head was bound about with a checkered handkerchief and the hair was concealed under it. Her face was shapely, intelligent, and comely—even beautiful.[40]

Even if Roxy's Blackness is not visible, it is audible—or rather, legible—in Twain's text. The dialect that marks Roxy's speech sets her apart from other potentially tragic mixed-race heroines, most of whom display the privilege of white ancestry not only in their physical appearance, but in their adherence to normative representations of speech. Unlike Roxy, her most prominent predecessors (including Eliza, Clotel, and Iola) speak in standard English, a sign that, in the tradition of moderate abolitionism, they may be more immediately suited for racial uplift than their uneducated or illiterate (and also visibly darker) counterparts. Roxy's speech is a continual reminder to the reader of her enslavement, and later, when she is freed, her social immobility. This speech, like all dialect, does not become legible on its own, however, but—like that of Blackface Desdemona—is visible only in relation to others' speech, which appears as unmarked by dialect (read: white). Roxy's "one-sixteenth" of Blackness, then, is visible not in her person but only in her performance of race. Her "very fair" complexion, the "rosy glow of vigorous health" in her cheeks, and "fine soft hair" do not reveal assumed biological traits of Blackness, nor do her "majestic form and stature," "imposing and statuesque" attitudes, or "noble and stately grace" fit with racist tropes. On the contrary, her "shapely, intelligent, and comely—even beautiful" face are marks of whiteness that immediately set her apart from the by now well-established mammy stereotype of a homely, unsexed matron.[41]

In addition to her appearance, Roxy's performance of race is specifically coded *as a relation*, to both legally white people and to her fellow enslaved companions, as "She had an easy, independent carriage—when she was among her own caste—and a high and 'sassy' way, withal; but of course she was meek and humble enough where white people were."[42] Roxy's racial performance is not simply one of Black subordination, however. Her visible whiteness makes Roxy subject to the colorist prejudices, by which she views herself in closer proximity to white gentility than the darker-skinned enslaved people on the plantation. The first conversation of hers that we read reveals both her race and her ideas about colorist hierarchies. While her and Jaspers's dialect are similarly marked, Roxy's rejection of Jaspers reveals that she ascribes to colorism, articulating racial hierarchies even among the mutually enslaved. The fact that Roxy's "got sump'n better to do den 'sociat'n wid n[—] as black as [Jaspers] is" is later revealed in her supposed preference for a white mate, and one of high birth at that.[43] Barbara Chellis argues that in this, Roxy "accepts the class structure as completely as any other white member of the Dawson's Landing community."[44] This assertion merits more closely examining the extent to which Roxy, by virtue of her dual role as both mammy and mother, is alternately empowered and disempowered in her struggle against racial hierarchies.

A large part of Roxy's personal history is omitted as Twain fails to explain the conditions of the relationship between Roxy and Colonel Cecil Burleigh Essex, Chambers's biological father. Leslie Fiedler argues that "there seems no doubt that [Twain] thought of the union between Roxy and Essex as a kind of fall," likening this union to that of James Fenimore Cooper's Cora and Uncas.[45] Fiedler disregards the significance of both racial mixture and gender in this equation, however, as Cora's whiteness is compromised in a way that Essex's is not by an interracial union. Here, the relation between a white woman and nonwhite man such as those of the previous chapters does not work under the same set of social assumptions as that between a white man and a Black, enslaved woman. The genealogy of racialization flows in gendered directions. Michael Rogin argues that "the white woman is missing from *Pudd'nhead Wilson*" in his discussion of miscegenation and violence.[46] That bearing a mixed-race child has no effect on Roxy's racialization illustrates the uneven workings of hypodescent and its gendered limitations for nonnormative genealogies of race. As a man, Essex does not have the racial vulnerability of someone like Mary King. Already a mixed-race heroine, these workings of racialization cannot refigure Roxy as a white woman in the text.

The status of Roxy and Essex's child—a familiar trope in narratives of enslaved women's reproduction—illustrates the limitations of white male racial genealogies. Leslie Fiedler writes that "if the fathers of the South are Virginia gentlemen, the mothers are the Negro girls, casually or callously taken in the parody of love, which is all that is possible when one partner to a sexual union is not even given the status of a person."[47] However we regard Roxy's feelings toward Essex, this "parody of love" is suggested by the fact that Roxy's apparent pride in her child's paternity by a first-family Virginian "of formidable calibre" is far from a legal claim.[48] The ultimate revelation of her son's paternity does him no material good. Although she is visibly white, Roxy's status as enslaved also renders her child enslaved—a person who is both socially and legally "fatherless."[49] As Hortense Spillers's evacuation of kinship suggests, the child's status as property has negated the paternal kinship relation. With this negation, the construction of race via hypodescent also negates the efficacy of genealogical whiteness.

Moreover, while Chellis gives Roxy every amount of agency in her union with Essex, stating that "she had mingled her blood with the F.F.V.,"[50] she also fails to acknowledge that Roxy's "blood" has already been "mingled" with white enslavers, most likely under circumstances which imply the exploitation of enslaved, Black women. Although the evidence of racial mixture is invisible in Roxy's person, we see the workings of hypodescent in her own racialization. Her actions throughout the story play with the relations of kinship that are so closely connected to ideas of race and identity. By switching the assumedly "white" Thomas á Becket Driscoll and the "Black" (though as visibly as "white" as both Tom and herself) Valet de Chambre, Roxy usurps family hierarchy and the racial essentialism by which one child is heir to his father's estate and the other (though his father was also a "First Family Virginian") can, at the whim of the other child's father, be "sold down the river."

In the act of switching her enslaver's child for her own, Chellis argues that Roxy is "a reversal of a type, the kindly Negro mammy who loves and protects the white child . . . Instead, she enslaves the white child, putting him in a position to be sold down the river, depriving him of his freedom just as surely as the white man has deprived her of hers."[51] Alternately, Myra Jehlen absolves Roxy in a way, regarding the "maternal economy" of the text as dealing with the distribution (but not the production) of whiteness-as-property.[52] Both of these readings misconstrue, to some extent, Roxy's agency within the system of enslavement. Roxy can move around the players within this system, but she does not have the power to make any quantitative change to the game. Moreover, her efforts are ultimately reversed—in true tragic form, concluding with just what our heroine attempted to prevent: it is Roxy's own biological son who is, in fact, "sold down the river" at the story's conclusion. One possible assumption here is that essentialist notions of race are restored at the story's close. But Twain also calls this fiction of race into question, exposing the process of racialization, in general, as arbitrary. Effecting the children's re-racialization, we might view Roxy's actions in light of their potential resistance to the hierarchy that makes the one child her enslaver. In this respect, she certainly does work against the iconic trope of the mammy. Rather than give an ethical evaluation of how Roxy works with the system of plantation slavery, though, I would like to examine how Roxy's unique place within that system—as both a mammy and a mother—allows her to work within it.

Ironically, it is in her capacity as a victim of slavery—racialized by the rules of matriliny and hypodescent—that Roxy has the power to re-racialize the children in her care. Doing so, Roxy contributes to the construction of both Blackness and whiteness. In her capacity as mother-mammy, she is the only caregiver who recognizes the children enough to make this switch. And it is through her own performance of the racial relations between them that effects their re-racialization. As Roxy switches the almost identical babies and we are spiraled into the racial fiction Roxy has created, Twain presents notions of socially constructed race against assumptions of essentialism. Once she has exchanged the children's places (simply by changing the clothes of one with the other's), we see her practice performing her corresponding mother and mammy roles in relation to them:

> She got up light-hearted and happy, and went to the cradles and spent what was left of that night "practicing." She would give her own child a light pat and say, humbly, "Lay still, Marse Tom," then give the real Tom a pat and say with severity, "Lay *still*, Chambers!—does you want me to take sump'n *to* you?"
>
> As she progressed with her practice, she was surprised to see how steadily and surely the awe which had kept her tongue reverent and her manner humble toward her young master was transferring itself to her speech and manner toward the usurper, and how similarly handy she was becoming in transferring her motherly curtness of speech and peremptoriness of manner to the unlucky heir of the ancient house of Driscoll.[53]

As we can see in the *Century Illustrated Magazine* illustration of this scene (figure 3.3), the performance Roxy enacts in relation to each child in the

ROXY AND THE CHILDREN.

3.3 ROXY AND THE CHILDREN. DRAWN BY LOUIS LOEB. ENGRAVED BY M. HAIDER. *CENTURY ILLUSTRATED MAGAZINE*, VOLUME XLVII, ISSUE 3 (JANUARY 1894): 328. COURTESY OF THE UNIVERSITY OF WISCONSIN–MADISON LIBRARIES.

baby-switching scene determines not only their racialization but also her respectively racialized relationships with them. One child becomes "white" and the other "Black," in effect, because Roxy is able to place them—and herself—into these racialized relations. Regarding the children's physical likeness to one another, and thinking of race as, at least to a certain extent, a social construction, Roxy correctly surmises that racialization requires that each child learn the intricacies of racial identity both with relation to one another and to their respective mother-mammy.[54] Because the boys are still only infants, Roxy easily teaches them to assume their newly assigned roles.

This act, which sparks the main plot of *Pudd'nhead Wilson*, distinguishes Roxy from more typical representations of the mammy figure by simultaneously representing Roxy's own motherhood. Unlike typical depictions of dark-skinned mammies throughout the nineteenth and twentieth centuries, the magazine illustration shows the difficulty of relating Roxy to either child based on visual cues alone. Her ability to switch the boys is oddly dependent upon not only her son's ability to "pass" as white but also on her own skin privilege. Regarding Roxy as Twain's reversal or satire of the mammy is appropriate not only for this upsetting of stereotype but in the importance of Roxy's prioritization of her own child over that of her enslaver. In this respect, Roxy rejects the role of mammy for that of mother, though in an admittedly complicated façade, by which she must also perform the mammy relation to her own biological son.[55] As a visually white woman who performs this role, Roxy not only whitewashes the image of Black motherhood, but that of Black mammyhood as well. Importantly, the agency that Roxy is given here is a result not of her biological motherhood alone, or any privilege of her relative whiteness, but of her dual station as both mammy and mother. She alone is in a position to switch the babies precisely because she is the only one who can tell the children apart. The exchange of racial identities is therefore enacted only through the children's respective kinship relations to herself, and as she enacts those relations she becomes the pivot of Tom's and Chambers's racialization and re-racialization.

Importantly, Roxy's feelings of love and kinship toward her own son are what prompt her to enact the switch in the first place. We see Roxy's motherly pride in an early scene in which Pudd'nhead Wilson compliments both children in Roxy's charge. "They're handsome little chaps. One's just as handsome as the other, too," Wilson tells her. She responds, "Bless yo' soul, Misto Wilson, it's pow'ful nice o'you to say dat, caze one of 'em ain't on'y a n[—]. Mighty prime little n[—], I allays says, but dat's caze it's mine, o'course."[56] Though Roxy feels motherly love for her biological son, she acknowledges the social hierarchy that would prevent others from such a comparison with the son of a respected white family and attributes her own preference as a result of her biological maternity alone. Moreover, Roxy's love of her son is not in spite of his race, but because of it—because he is her own. The precarious condition he has inherited marks his race, but also his need for motherly love and protection—that which Twain's white characters, even Chambers's own white relations—are unlikely to give. And, although Roxy is undoubtedly already familiar with the precariousness of slavery at the story's opening, she is particularly alarmed when she comes to fully realize that her child is in as precarious a position as herself: "Her child could grow up and be sold down the river! The thought crazed her with horror."[57]

Roxy's baby-switching recalls both this horror and her earlier, abandoned, plan for saving her son: suicide and infanticide. She initially tells Chambers, "Come along, honey, come along wid Mammy; we gwyne to jump in de river, den de troubles o' dis worl' is all over—dey don't sell po' n[—]s down de river over *yonder*."[58] Only the case of Margaret Garner (to which I will return in the next chapter) is necessary to illustrate that the option of infanticide is no mere plot device on Twain's part, but reveals the actual consideration (particularly when the Christian promise of Heaven is taken seriously) that enslaved people sometimes viewed death as better than enslavement. To kill herself in order to send (and accompany) her child to Heaven is an act of motherly sacrifice for Roxy. As James Grove calls Roxy "a life force countering the sterility and irony surrounding her," he may well have the maternal devotion of this scene in mind.[59] While Chellis chastises Roxy's actions as akin to that of her enslavers, Porter acknowledges that "the aggression unleashed . . . by Roxana's plot is driven out of control by the horror that provokes it."[60] Put simply: Roxy's available choices are limited. Enslaved mothers were often denied the ability to perform the protective duties of motherhood because of the system that denied enslaved people both freedom of action and access to kin from whom they were likely to be separated by either sale or death.[61] The power that Roxy grasps, however, is interesting in its ability to racialize—a power most often discussed as imposed upon Black mothers who pass on their race along with their enslaved status, rather than a power they might use in their own, active construction of relative racializations.

The figure of the enslaved mother functions in opposition to the privileged and protected place afforded to white motherhood. Switching her own child with that of her enslaver, Roxy collapses the mammy/mother dualism as she not only moves between but melds the two roles in her relation to both Tom and Chambers. She cannot change roles completely as the reader is always aware of the "truth" of her maternal relations, but her actions in these roles still have enough effect to propel the plot of Twain's novel. The agency Roxy is afforded by this collapse is short-lived, as she performs the role of mammy in relation to her own son. While feelings of biological kinship drive Roxy to switch the babies, her performance of both kinship and racial relations keeps the respective children in their places. The boys grow up, and Roxy raises them in accordance with these new relations of race and kinship relative to herself, and with predictable results. Her son becomes the haughty young man who believes he will be the future enslaver of the plantation, and the enslaver's child becomes a man who anticipates his own lifelong enslavement.

The relationship between Roxy and her biological son is, until the revelation of his true identity, no longer a mother-child relation, but one of mammy-and-child and enslaver. This is perhaps the clearest marker of Roxy's construction not only of Blackness but also of whiteness. Twain collapses the relation between mother and mammy in the text though, as we read further about Roxy's adoption of the role of mammy to her own child: "He was her darling, her master, and her deity, all in one, and in her worship of him she forgot who she was and what he had been."[62] The narrative almost forgets this too, as the problem of referring to the two boys presents a problem for the omniscient narrator, for while the reader is in on the secret, so to speak, the characters remain ignorant of Roxy's switch. At the outset, Roxy's performance as both mother and mammy in forming the children's newly raced roles is also enacted by Twain's narrator, who acknowledges the problem in naming the children. This problem of naming is initially solved when the narrator declares, "This history must henceforth accommodate itself to the change which Roxana has consummated, and call the real heir 'Chambers' and the usurping little slave 'Thomas à Becket'—shortening this latter name to 'Tom,' for daily use, as the people about him did."[63] As "this history" correspondingly switches the boys' names to reflect their assumed roles rather than their original identities, Twain's narrator is willing to maintain the performance of identity—as Roxy does—and as the men (who do not initially know that they have been re-racialized) do. The switch of re-racialization that Roxy enacts is so convincing, then, that even the omniscient narration also begins to perform it. This acknowledgment is further evidence of the efficacy of Roxy's racial construction.

What Roxy sacrifices in this reassignment of identities is any affective attachment she might elicit from her own son. While Roxy's relationship with the young man now known as "Chambers" is seldom shown in Twain's novel, her relationship with "Tom" is degraded from one of child and mother to that of enslaver and enslaved. In some of the story's most disturbing scenes, we see Tom beat Roxy—the woman who is really his biological mother. Ultimately, he sells her "down the river" just as she is enacting yet another motherly sacrifice by offering herself up to be sold (though she has legally gained her freedom by this point in the story) in order to preserve his white inheritance. What might be most disturbing about these scenes is that they may not elicit the same horror from some readers were it not for our knowledge of Roxy's biological relation to the grown man now known as Tom. Myra Jehlen presents this as a shift in the text, "where the injustice if racial inequality was first measured by the violation of Roxy's natural motherhood, now inequality will be justified by the spectacle of the emancipated and empowered Tom's unnatural sonhood."[64] This "unnatural sonhood" is reversed, however, as Roxy uses her knowledge of "Tom's" true birth to extract the support that he initially denies her. If Roxy cannot get Tom's support by appealing to his affection for his "mammy," she will get it by blackmailing him with the truth that she is his biological mother.[65]

Roxy's position as mother might be viewed not simply as another imitation of the enslaver, then, but as an enactment of maternity, and as an enactment of the racializing relations inherent in the mother-mammy. As the white matrons are rather quickly dispensed with or pushed to the fringes of Twain's story (we almost forget that Tom Driscoll's Aunt Pratt is still alive, until she sends the telegram informing him of his uncle's death), Roxy is doubly correct in stating that this Tom "hadn't no mother but me in de whole worl."[66] With no living biological mother, Tom's only maternal figure is his enslaved "mammy." Even when in conversation with Chambers, Roxy prioritizes her relationship with the other boy, invoking her position as Tom's mammy, but without revealing to the man who believes himself to be her son the truth of his birth. It is in this role as mammy, and not with the truth of her biological motherhood, that Roxy presents herself as someone who has a right to know the details of Tom's business, asking "Was I his mother tell he was fifteen years old, or wusn't I?"[67] However, when Roxy initially attempts to gain Tom's sympathy by virtue of her position as mammy, she fails. It is only after he recognizes her position as his own biological mother (simultaneously realizing the power she holds over him and the danger he faces were she to reveal that relation) that Tom submits to the role of a dutiful child.

The confusing identities of the two boys—and their confusing racialized relation to Roxy—continues to present a problem for the narration's representation of the text's kinship relations, even after the convenient name changes the narration enacts early on in the novel. While still calling the original Chambers "Tom" even after he knows the fact of his birth, the text now refers to Roxy as "his mother."[68] These two moves (the naming and the kinship relation in "Tom" and "his mother") should, logically, be mutually exclusive in the text. The fact that they are not suggests the story's acknowledgment of the conflation of the mother and mammy roles that Roxy simultaneously performs. This excess of names and relations in the text is too much for the narration itself to support. In this way, Twain's narration in *Pudd'nhead Wilson* represents the difficulty of dealing with the overabundance of names and identities, as well as Roxy's role as mother and mammy. As Tom continues to call Roxy by the more ambiguous appellation "mammy," rather than "ma," we see how Roxy's biological motherhood, even when recognized, is never completely free from her role as mammy. It seems that, as in the case of Macrae's *The Americans at Home*, the relation of "mother" is reserved for "white folks." Thus, even in having his mother revealed to him, Tom remains "motherless" under the system of slavery that would interfere with the mother-child relation.

Still, the synchronous existence of "Tom" and "his mother" in the text is an assertion of Roxy's underlying motherhood. Mark Patterson explains Roxy's role as mammy, a "surrogate" or "adoptive" mother to Tom in a system that does not allow for "the equality of maternity."[69] The text, however, does not seem so sure of this division between Roxy's maternal roles. The narration's switch in naming is itself confusing, emphasizing the precarious and simultaneous nature of these identifications, and calling to the reader's attention Roxy's role in enacting these shifts through her own acknowledgment of kinship with the two children. As she is about to voluntarily allow herself be sold again into slavery for Tom's benefit, she asserts that her motherhood is just as valid as a white woman's. She asks him, "Ain't you my chile? En does you know anything dat a mother won't do for her chile? Dey ain't nothin' a white mother won't do for her chile. Who made 'em so? De Lord done it. En who made de n[—]s? De Lord made 'em. In de inside, mothers is all de same. De good Lord He made 'em so."[70] Complicating this act of universal motherhood ("In de inside, mothers is all de same") is the fact that, as Patterson recognizes, "A 'white' mother . . . could not sell herself into slavery."[71]

Roxy's particular sacrifice, then, is one reserved for the figure of the Black mother. More than justifying the inclusion of Black mothers in a realm of universal motherhood, her particular expression of maternity does not transcend Roxy's legal Blackness but depends upon it.

From the complex relationship between Tom and Roxy, a reader might expect an equally complex parallel in Roxy's relation to Chambers, the child who is the biological child of her enslaver but was raised in the position of her own son. The rather conspicuous disappearance and reappearance of Chambers is one of the text's many oddities. By switching the babies, Roxy attempts to privilege her own son while condemning her enslaver's heir to slavery, but whatever mother-child relationship that the new Chambers might have gained as a result of this switch seems to have been lost. As Roxy disinherits the original Tom Driscoll, she does so twice—by disinheriting the child of her enslaver from his position of inheritance and by later disinheriting this same child who believes her to be his mother from that kinship relation as well. An extension of this discussion might take into account the presence (and absence) of Chambers in the story, in his partially articulated kinship relations to both Roxy and Tom, as well as his final position as a white man who was raised as a Black enslaved man, which becomes Twain's revision of the familiar "tragic mulatto" trope, rendered more complex because Roxy herself does not fit neatly into this role. Additionally, Chambers himself seems confused by his racialized genealogies. We read in the conclusion that Chambers, restored to his inheritance and whiteness, "continued the false heir's pension of thirty-five dollars a month" to Roxy. This financial support of his mammy-mother is an indication that Chambers does not abandon his affection for the woman he thought was his mother, and perhaps even that he is unable to assume the white supremacist role that would make her his mammy.

The story's close does not prioritize these affective kinship relations, however, but turns to the science of individualism rather than that of race or kinship to restore the identities of Valet de Chambres and Thomas Driscoll. In the evidence Pudd'nhead Wilson presents to the court regarding the children's fingerprints, the question of identity becomes one of name and of individual bodily consistency, but importantly *not* one of race or kinship. Neither man is proven to be "white" or "Black" by this evidence, nor is Roxy's maternity clearly identified. Rather, the altered fingerprint records alone indicate that a change has been made, and Roxy is identified not maternally but circumstantially—as the only person in a position to have made the switch. The science of fingerprinting stands in as a science of individual identity against popular theories of scientific racism by which Black and other nonwhite people were supposedly "proven" inferior to white people throughout the mid- to late-nineteenth century.[72] The scientific courtroom drama at the end of *Pudd'nhead Wilson* is essential; the detective story plot is no more separable from the racial melodrama of the story than are Twain's (conjoined?) twins.[73] And David "Pudd'nhead" Wilson is, after all, the titular character.[74] Perhaps what makes the tale so tragic is how close Pudd'nhead (who must understand the implications of the justice he enacts) brings it to remaining a farce.[75] Twain's ambiguous ending has Tom, Roxy's biological child, "sold down the river" as punishment for his crimes, and restores Chambers to his original position as white enslaver.[76] Tom's story proves as tragic as Chambers's inability to fit into either white or Black society, as it falls short of condemning the system of Southern plantation slavery.

By centralizing Pudd'nhead Wilson as the person Twain's tale is ostensibly "about," Roxy and her role are shifted to the background of some (if not most) discussions of the novel.[77] James Cox notes the dual role of Roxy and Pudd'nhead Wilson in creating and recognizing Tom's identity, as he emerges "almost as if they were his parents," and also notes a somewhat fraternal relationship between Pudd'nhead and Tom through their filial relation to Judge Driscoll.[78] This reading assumes the necessity of a father—which Roxy's child, of course, does not have. As Roxy is the person the text most clearly identifies as either child's parent, we might rather imagine a fraternal relationship between Tom and Chambers, triangulated through their relationship to her, or as nineteenth-century topsy-turvy dolls.[79] Not simply two sides of the same coin, however, the two boys' racialized relationship to one another—like the relationship between Alcott's white and Black brothers is figured through Faith Dane—is extended through Roxy. This can be seen in a cover illustration for a late-twentieth-century Bantam edition of Twain's novel (see figure 3.4). While Tom stands confidently with his back to Roxy's skirt (in stark contrast to the clinging child of Scott's image), Chambers peeks around from behind, seemingly as unsure of his place in this racial narrative as Twain's readers must be. In addition to Tom and Chambers' pairing, the pairing of Pudd'nhead and Roxy presents "parents" with different relations to Tom's and Chambers' genealogy. Through the science of fingerprinting, the identification of these men's original identities provides them with a genealogy of sorts, but the science of fingerprinting is divorced from taxonomies of race.[80] The white titular character therefore lacks the power of racialization even as he can determine these men's original identities by matching their fingerprints. Their racialization is not a matter of science but remains

11598-7 ★ $1.25 ★ A BANTAM BOOK

Pudd'nhead Wilson
by Mark Twain

WITH AN INTRODUCTION BY LANGSTON HUGHES
COMPLETE AND UNABRIDGED

3.4 ROXY AND CHILDREN. *PUDD'NHEAD WILSON.* COVER ILLUSTRATION, FIRST
BANTAM EDITION, 1977.

a "fiction" of social agreement—an agreement that the mammy-mother has the power to rework.

Literary discussions of the twins Angelo and Luigi in *Pudd'nhead Wilson* generally have taken for granted the author's explanation of the "literary Cæsarean operation" by which he has extracted the one tale from the other.[81] But what this backdrop of twins and twinning leaves in the text is a clear counter-relationship for Roxy's nearly twin boys. If we take seriously the claim that *Those Extraordinary Twins* is a metanarrative for *Pudd'nhead Wilson*, another version of national romance, the tale of racialized twinning does not result in anything resembling fraternity.[82] Although Wallace-Sanders notes that "*they share a birthday and a mother, which, in effect, makes them twins,*" this narrative of the interracial national family (as in Alcott's "The Brothers") is constructed triangularly—as their relations are reinforced or reimagined through their shared mother-mammy.[83] Roxy's switching of the boys is itself an additional kind of "twinning," a multiplication, rather than a mere exchange of genealogies. Once the switch is enacted, it—and all of its attendant identifying, relating, and racializing—cannot fully be undone. The racializing genealogies that Roxy has reassigned remain residually present at the end of the novel, even as the boys' original genealogies and relations to Roxy are again overlaid on top of them. This residual genealogy is a kind of queering as the racialized relations that ought to be mutually exclusive—as in the scenes in which we see "Tom" and "his mother" (whom he calls "mammy") remain present. These queer, contradictory but still overlapping genealogies appear as excess in the text. The confusion we read in Twain's narration signals an unease with Roxy's multiplied genealogies.

Unlike positive literary renditions of Black motherhood by Twain's contemporaries Charles Chesnutt and Frances Ellen Watkins Harper, Roxy does not have the means to create a truly loving kinship relation with her biological son, who seems to have been irrevocably tainted by the system of plantation slavery that is painted as equally harmful to the characters of both enslavers and the enslaved. The story's odd "restoration" of "Tom" to his supposedly "rightful" position of enslavement and the relegation of "Chambers" to the unhappy liminality reserved for racial ambiguity leaves no family for Roxy to preside over. In *Pudd'nhead Wilson*'s tragic conclusion, essential (and legal) categories of race and kinship override not only Roxy's visible whiteness or her enslaved Blackness but also her enactment of racialized maternity, as Twain leaves her biological son—and hence her own motherhood—without a clear place in the conclusion of the novel. In the twinning of Tom and Chambers, and the dual role of Roxy as mother-mammy, we are left with a kind of queer genealogy of excess kin.

The twinning of Tom and Chambers in much of the discussion of *Pudd'nhead Wilson* stems, in part, from this inability to place Roxy's biological son in a clearly defined relation of kinship to her. While Tom comes to perform the role of Roxy's enslaver, the text's refusal to provide a clear picture of Roxy and Chambers' relationship is a result of what we might call his genealogical queerness. His re-racialization as white also involves a bizarre process of losing his mother—an ironic reversal of kinlessness as his mother becomes his mammy. Even Chambers's presence at the story's close seems like a queer genealogy of the novel, as he returns to the plot that had almost completely discarded him when Roxy made the exchange that relegated her future enslaver to slavery. Roxy's relation to this surrogate son also seems excessive, in the sense that is overdetermined. Although we are to understand that the dutiful son, acknowledging his adoptive relation to Roxy despite the revelation of his biologically construed whiteness, provided for her financially in her old age, we are left unsure about the nature of their relationship. In part, Roxy is an inconvenient relation, the tie that relegated him to an upbringing of enslavement, but which cannot be cut nevertheless. Most emphatically, we never view Roxy as a mammy to this grown man, though this relation most accurately describes the legality of their relation. Nor can we fully understand Roxy as this man's mother in a text that insists upon the prioritization of biological relations at its conclusion, and which has chosen not to depict the details of their relationship. Were it not for Roxy's enslavement (on which the plot of the novel is, of course, dependent), we might be better able to parse these relationships. In the case of Roxy as mammy-mother, we see how the enslavement of African American people becomes an excessive factor in determining their kinship relations. My next chapter will focus on this excess content of enslaved kinship.

Kinfullness

Mama's Baby,

Racial Futures

My skin-folks but not my kinfolks.
—Zora Neale Hurston, *Dust Tracks on a Road*

IN JOHN ANDERSON COLLINS'S 1855 poem "The Slave-Mother," a self-emancipated woman, upon being recaptured, refuses to acknowledge her infant in order to secure his freedom. If recognized as being hers, according to the distinctly American law of genealogical—matriarchal—racialization, *Partus sequitur ventrem*; the child would follow the enslaved condition of the mother.[1] This mother's knowledge of the law and denial of kinship is presented as an act of profound maternal affection, since denying the mother-child relation renders the child free. In the poem, we read that:

They bound her fast, but no reply
The torturing whip or hand-cuff wring;
With one long, sad, despairing cry,
Her babe upon the ground she flung,
And, as her heart were turned to stone,
With madness flashing from her eye,
Refused the helpless one to own,
Or listen to its moaning cry.

Fast driven on with curse and blow,
No mercy hoping in her wo,
One thought alone can give her rest,
And soothe a mother's aching breast;
Better, her nature to deny,
Than that loved child in slavery die.

Recognizing the fact that her (seemingly light-skinned) child is racialized through her relationship to him, the move Collins's "slave-mother" makes here is not unlike Roxy's in *Pudd'nhead Wilson*. Both mothers assume their children are best served by freeing them from slavery, even if this necessitates denying themselves this kinship relation. Like Roxy, the despairing mother of the poem believes she can best mother her child by denying her own maternal "nature." The situation reveals the peculiar condition of the enslaved mother, whose relation to her children does not determine parental rights but their legal status as enslaved.

As the legal inheritance of enslavement subsumes or prevents other relationships, kinship itself is imagined to be evacuated by slavery. This is what Hortense Spillers refers to as "kinlessness" and Saidiya Hartman describes as the process by which "the slave loses mother" and becomes "no longer anyone's child."[2] We can see the condition of a mother who has no legal right to her child more clearly, perhaps, in Frances Harper's 1854 poem, also titled "The Slave Mother," in which the narrator describes the relationship between an enslaved woman and her child:

He is not hers, although she bore
For him a mother's pains;
He is not hers, although her blood
Is coursing through his veins!

He is not hers, for cruel hands
May rudely tear apart
The only wreath of household love
That binds her breaking heart.[3]

Harper's poem illustrates the condition of enslaved motherhood as burdened by the contradictory cross-purposes of mother love and enslavement's matrilineal inheritance. In this poem, we see an image of the enslaved mother that is quite common to antislavery literature. Drawing on the sentimental, readers might find sympathy with enslaved people through this point of entry. Collins's poem draws upon this popular image of the sympathetic mother and produces a related image: the resistant enslaved mother. The mother's deft logic in this moment of emergency lies in her understanding that her own kinship relation is the lynchpin that connects enslaved Black bodies with the biological reproduction of slavery. Recognizing this does not merely render her kinship a burden—the enslaved woman is not merely disempowered here—but resistant as she frees her child by refusing to recognize the maternal (i.e., legal) relation.

As in Collins's "The Slave-Mother," the most iconic figure of enslaved Black womanhood is represented as another type of "childless mother"—the mammy, a woman forced to mother the white, free children of her enslaver, but with no legal parental claim to her own. While popular images of the mammy displace Black children and Black matriliny in favor of relations of enslavement, and while the violence of slavery disrupted patterns of Black kinship, the fullness of Black matriliny is another persistent trope. As enslaved women were wrenched from their children, they also clung to them, sometimes managing to wrench their kin from the hands of their oppressors. We recall the powerful image of Sojourner Truth as she walks away from her enslaver's house in pursuit of her son. He had been illegally sold out of the state although New York's gradual emancipation would have granted his freedom. Her 1850 narrative tells us that "When Isabel [Sojourner Truth's given name] heard that her son had been sold South, she immediately started on foot and alone, to find the man who had thus dared, in the face of all law, human and divine, to sell her child out of the State; and if possible, to bring him to account for the deed."[4] Even though the law was on her side, it is remarkable that Truth was successful in getting her son returned to her. Here we see an enactment of the iconic power of Black matriliny and the persistence of racial trajectories that would extend into new generations. A counter to Truth's role as a caregiver and wet-nurse to the children of her enslavers, her account of Black motherhood extends beyond the legal battle she won to retrieve her son and to her larger racial legacy. Truth's matrilineal kinship is multigenerational. In a photograph taken in 1863, she holds a picture not of her son but her grandson, James Caldwell, who served as a member of the Fifty-fourth Massachusetts Infantry Regiment in the Civil War (see figure 4.1). The generational skipping over of Truth's own children in this portrait suggests another queer genealogy of the "childless mother" trope, as even the effectually childless enslaved mother might produce Black lineages beyond her scope. This shows how, despite kinlessness or the "loss" of one's mother (though a real and affectively valid experience of antiblack violence), extending toward larger generational scales reveals a kind of racial prescience. In this way, we

Sojourner Truth,

4.1 SOJOURNER TRUTH SEATED WITH PHOTOGRAPH OF HER GRANDSON, JAMES CALDWELL, OF CO. H, 54TH MASSACHUSETTS INFANTRY REGIMENT, ON HER LAP [BATTLE CREEK, MICHIGAN]: [1863] PHOTOGRAPH: ALBUMEN PRINT ON CARD MOUNT; MOUNT 7 × 11 CM (CARTE DE VISITE FORMAT). COURTESY OF THE LIBRARY OF CONGRESS, LILJENQUIST FAMILY COLLECTION.

might understand that kinlessness looks backward toward loss, but also iron-ically suggests its own future-leaning counter of racial kinfullness.

The phenomenon of "kinfullness" that I introduce in this chapter describes not an absence but the fullness of kinship and its racializing powers. This phe-nomenon works simultaneously alongside but counter to the violence of kin-lessness, extending our understanding of the relationship between kinship, race, and reproduction. I here build on the discourses of sexuality and racial (re)production I have explored earlier to begin expanding outward toward racialization's broader scope. The experience of the enslaved mother cannot be fully explained by the state of kinlessness that Spillers uses to describe the state of enslaved African American families. When notions of belonging manifest in the triumph of property over kinship, the enslaved mother and the child might also be characterized by excesses of kinship—kin*full*ness, rather than kin*less*ness.

While Spillers uses kinlessness to articulate the prevention of enslaved people from full participation in kinship relations, I introduce the alterna-tive concept, kinfullness, in order to attend to the additional content of ra-cialized kinship. Nancy Bentley notes this excessive, nonfamilial, content of the condition, writing that "Kinlessness is a sign of social death but also a source of interminable life, an unbounded 'future increase' detached from any enforceable claims or obligations that belong to heirs."[5] I speak here to the "unbounded future increase" of not only enslaved motherhood but also racialized motherhood more generally. "Future increase" does not necessar-ily produce kin but it does necessarily produce race. The figure of the en-slaved mother thereby creates slippages between reproductive and racially productive futurity.

Speaking to not only individual racialization but also racial production, by "kinfullness" I also mean to refer to the racialized content of kinship, to kinship as racially pregnant in excess of mere interpersonal relations but bearing the weight of larger racializing scales. Kinfullness's excess is twofold: First, it describes the baggage attached to kinship through the matrilineal inheritance of slavery. Not simply an inheritance of racialization, this genea-logical baggage is extra, possibly unnecessary or even unwanted, as we see in the case of slavery's matrilineal inheritance. It shows how racialization spills into kinship, interfering with other genealogical relationships. In the case of Collins's poem, kinfullness does not indicate that the mother's kinship itself is excessive (just as kinlessness does not indicate an actual lack of even bio-logical kinfolk), but that her kinship has been filled instead with the excess content of inherited enslavement. I describe slavery's inheritance as excessive in order to momentarily disaggregate kinship from this legal status, to highlight this inheritance as imposition, even as it was naturalized by white racist ideology, to denaturalize slavery as it was produced by virtue of this relation. Both mother and child are freed at the close of Collins's poem and are therefore able to experience the "natural" relation between mother and child, unencumbered by the excess juridical content of inherited enslavement. That is, they experience their relation as one of kinship that has been extracted from the burdens of reproducing slavery.

Second, kinfullness refers to the simple numerical excess of relations available for racialization. Racial hypodescent is itself a manifestation of kinfullness, as the usual mode of racial construction for mixed-race people necessarily ignores some kinship relations while prioritizing others. Kinfullness also speaks to the concerns (or anxieties) that come to bear upon kinship choices: what kinship relations might be produced by sexual couplings, or created in domestic spaces of the family, and which kinship relations are recognized or denied in genealogies that also racialize? Kinfullness produces an odd reversal of Zora Neale Hurston's sentiment, expressed in this chapter's epigraph, "My skin-folks but not my kinfolk" (more popularly rendered "All my skinfolk ain't kinfolk"), which disaggregates affiliations of race and kinship. According to the rules of hypodescent, not all kinfolk are necessarily skinfolk.[6] Nonnormative kinship sometimes follows lineages of choice rather than biology, and interracial kinship sometimes separates lineages of descent and racialization. At stake in the stories of racially mixed characters discussed in this chapter is the production of race itself, which results from the processes of acknowledging and rejecting certain kinship relations.

This chapter therefore focuses on literary texts in which characters' racial identifications affect how they construe kinship relations, and vice versa, extending previous chapters' conversations about interracial sexual kinship to retheorize other relationships between race and family. In the texts I discuss here, I show how the directionality of race flows toward the production of Blackness. Here we see how race is reproduced in two ways: first, through the queer, unilinear (matrilineal) genealogy of hypodescent; and second, through Blackness's multigenerational persistence, even when threatened with racial destruction by the rendering of enslaved families or individuals' "passing" as white. I turn first to a more general discussion of African American and interracial kinship and its non-heteronormative constructions. Recognizing nonwhite kinship relations as already queer according to white supremacist, patriarchal, and heteronormative understandings of kinship allows us to better understand how nonnormative kinship requires innovations of language and the revisions of literary tropes. I then turn to Frances Ellen Watkins Harper's *Iola Leroy, or Shadows Uplifted* to discuss both its revisions of the language of racialized relations and its presentation of the mother as the central kinship relation by which racial identity is determined and embraced.

Following from my discussion of the mother-mammy in the mixed-race mothers of "Her Virginia Mammy" and *Pudd'nhead Wilson*, I then read the mixed-race figures of anti-passing plots as illustrative of the process of race-making and the workings of what I call kinfullness therein. Representing racially mixed characters who choose to identify with Black, enslaved, mothers rather than white, free, fathers, *Iola Leroy* shows how race is constructed via a matrilineal mode of inheritance, race, and political affiliation that ultimately will come to defy the inheritances of slavery and racial oppression with which they are associated. I then discuss the emergent "new maternal negro" of Chesnutt's *The Marrow of Tradition* as revising not only the mammy figure, but also the materteral (the feminine of "avuncular") and similarly racialized figure of the aunt. This figure hereby appeals to universal motherhood while still struggling with the familial and national drama of interracial kinship. Last, I turn to the history of Margaret Garner—as reimagined in the nineteenth- and twenty-first centuries—in order to revisit the relationship between kinlessness, kinfullness, and futurity.

Fictive Kin, Othermothers, and the Language of Queer Kinship

What interests me most about Collins's version of the iconic enslaved mother is the mother's articulation of the relationship between kinship and enslavement. The poem's play on the language of possession and belonging exposes the contradictory language of kinship and racial relations. Collins's enslaved mother, when asked if the child is her own, states, "I have no child! this stranger one/Belongs to freedom—not to me," reworking legalized notions of inherited slavery and familial belonging.[7] That the "stranger" child would "belong" not to a parent but to freedom itself exposes the system that prioritizes legal status over parental rights. But also, we are to understand familial relations as lost in the necessity of giving up one's child in order to avoid their captivity. Because the enslaved mother's impossible position as a "childless mother" does not erase but reinscribes that kinship relation, her refusal to acknowledge the relation that would enslave her child is ultimately corrected. The mother's exceptional devotion to her child is ultimately rewarded later in the poem, when a judge declares both the child and the woman free, because the would-be enslaver cannot prove ownership. The mother's sacrificial refusal of kinship is not lost on the judge, however, as he proclaims, "This childless mother?—Let her go!"[8] The paradox of the phrase "childless mother" articulates the familial denial that would free this child from the matrilineal inheritance of enslavement. That this child does not "belong" to her—the ironic state of "childlessness" that this woman assumes in order to free her child—is illustrative of slavery's destruction of kinship.

Christina Sharpe finds something similar to the "childless mother" in her discussion of Allan Sekula and Noël Burch's *The Forgotten Space*. In this 2010 film, Aeriele Jackson is described as a "former mother" because the state has taken away her children.[9] Sharpe notes the oddness of characterizing Jackson's motherhood as "former." She is placed outside time, framed as a "childless mother" of sorts in a post-slavery version of kinlessness that upsets the supposed permanency of kinship and confuses the language of relationships. Kinfullness stands as an alternative to kinlessness, addressing the contradictory relations of enslaved motherhood in American literature—a representation of racialized maternity that is abundant with various, sometimes conflicting, notions of kinship. The excess content of kinfullness reveals the contradictory nature of the judge's characterization, as the enslaved woman cannot be a "childless mother" other than under the peculiar legal auspices of slavery. These paradoxical kinship examples illustrate the limitations of the normative language used for describing complex relations of racialized kinship. As with the mother-mammy relations of the previous chapter, the words we have used to describe normative kinship relations are often insufficient for working out the complexities of kinship, particularly as this relates to race. Further examination of the racialized language of kinship is therefore necessary in order to show how alternative language might allow for the recognition and explanation of complex racialized relations and their queer genealogies.

We read, early on in *Pudd'nhead Wilson*, that the other people enslaved on Percy Driscoll's plantation "were not related."[10] The narrator's denial of kinship here calls to mind the denial of kinship ties in the system of plantation slavery, in which biological kinship relations between enslaved people were interrupted by the geographical relocation of commerce or the threat of death, and which nevertheless produced other kinds of kinship ties.[11] Carol Stack's notion of "fictive kin" describes one way enslaved people countered the force of kinlessness under enslavement: by forming relations that extended beyond biological genealogies.[12] Berlin and Rowland describe this as enslaved people's extension of kinship into other forms of communal belonging and responsibility:

> The line between household and community was permeable and open, encompassing not only relationships by birth and marriage but also various fictive kin who became honorary "aunts" and "uncles," "brothers" and "sisters." Slaves considered all such kin, whether honorary or blood members of the family, to be "their people," and the slaves' ethos gave them special responsibility for their people. That responsibility, born of the frequent separation of parents and children, husbands and wives during slave times, continued to inform African-American family life during the Civil War and after.[13]

My hesitance about using the phrase "fictive kin" to describe adoptive kinship relations between enslaved people lies in the suggestion that this nonbiological kinship is "fiction" when compared with biological and legal kinship relations. By dint of contrast, cordoning biological and legal kinship from "fiction" reifies them, frames them as "real" and "legitimate." The term "fictive kin" risks sentimentalizing biological and legal kinship relations, even as the system of plantation slavery created biological relations between enslaved people and enslavers through the rape of enslaved women. Biological kinship is itself sometimes a fiction of pretended family, as such relations do not necessarily function as kin, and legal kinship is sometimes a function not of biology but of recognition. Legal prioritizations of normative forms of kinship create hierarchies that have sometimes excluded even biological kin from familial belonging and legitimacy. The biological and legal are not always relations to be celebrated, nor do these categories necessarily overlap.

Laws denying enslaved Black people the right to marry and laws preventing interracial marriage contributed to different formations of kinship that did not prioritize legal relations. Proponents of marriage freedom would argue in various contexts for the importance of marriage, as a civil right that ought not to be denied, such as the claim made in William Wells Brown's *Clotel; or, the President's Daughter*, that "Marriage is, indeed, the first and most important institution of human existence . . . the most intimate covenant of heart formed among mankind."[14] Critiquing more recent discussions of the movement to legalize same-sex marriage, Judith Butler recognizes that when marriage is the norm for structuring kinship, other forms of family-making are excluded. Butler writes, "The enduring social ties that constitute viable kinship in communities of sexual minorities are threatened with becoming unrecognizable and unviable as long as the marriage bond is the exclusive way in which both sexuality and kinship are organized."[15] While the stakes of recognizing kinship are different in this twenty-first-century context than they were in the nineteenth century, the normalization of the heterosexual, patriarchal, nuclear family that persists into the present is based on the same set of oppressive epistemological claims.[16]

US marriage laws have, historically, extended their reach well beyond the couples who either enter or do not enter into legal marriage contracts. In her study of anti-miscegenation law, Peggy Pascoe notes how marriage law becomes a marker for policing kinship more generally. "Marriage proved to be such a fruitful ground for the growth of white supremacy because it reached well beyond the realm of romance . . . When societies decide who can and who can't legally marry, they determine who is and isn't really part of the family."[17] Scholars rightly trace these exclusions from gendered normalcy to exclusions of kinship, of life, of humanity. Katherine Frank shows how "the institution of marriage was viewed as one of the primary instruments by which citizenship was both developed and managed in African Americans."[18] Accordingly, Black resistance to normative imperatives like that of respectability has often challenged the heteronormative models of kinship that marriage legitimates. Roderick Ferguson notes this regarding some African American freed-people's rejection of heteronormative marriage and monogamy in their domestic and family structures.[19]

Discourses on marriage have accordingly extended beyond normative romantic gender roles to normative familial roles. As Cathy Cohen explains this phenomenon, "many of the roots of heteronormativity are in white supremacist ideologies," in which "regulated nonnormative heterosexuality" comes to bear not only on the policing of sexuality but also of marriage and family relations.[20] The mother (and particularly the single mother) has borne the brunt of criticism when she diverges from the normative. A litany of Black feminist scholars have recognized the various ways nonnormative Black kinship relations have been denigrated by white supremacists, and how such denigration has overwhelmingly organized around the disparagement of Black mothers. This denigration can be traced from proslavery arguments that enslaved mothers cared less for their children than white mothers do, to Daniel Patrick Moynihan's disparagement of Black matriarchy, to President Ronald Reagan's use of the phrase "welfare queen" as a disparaging dog-whistle code for Black mothers, to twenty-first-century media dismissals of grieving Black women whose children have been murdered by police or white supremacist vigilantes.[21] In all of these we see something that is also familiar in the nineteenth-century US context: a pattern of refusing

Black mothers the same status and affective sentimentality with which white motherhood has been associated, marking motherhood itself as a racialized relation of heteronormative kinship.

Patricia Hill Collins notes Black women's significance in framing the very limits of belonging, most clearly articulated through kinship relations. As perpetual outsiders, she writes, "African-American women, by not belonging, emphasize the significance of belonging."[22] Black women are not just markers of belonging, however, but often structure belonging through women-centered kinship relations. The prioritization of biological motherhood for childrearing is an additional problem of patriarchal heteronormativity against which Black kinship structures have worked. One counter to such normative kinship structures is language that acknowledges the multiplicity of kinship relationships. We see this, for instance, in discussions of the people Rosalie Riegle Troester calls "othermothers," women whose caregiving for children did not follow biological genealogies of childbearing.[23] The fact that othermothers are not necessarily surrogate figures that displace biological motherhood illustrates a queer genealogy of its own in its departure from the prioritization of the heteronormative, nuclear family. Othermothers can exist alongside biological mothers, showing, as Collins states, "that vesting one person with full responsibility for mothering a child may not be wise or possible."[24] "Othermothers" and "bloodmothers" can coexist within a kinship structure, offering clear alternatives to the model of matriliny that prioritizes singular, biological motherhood above all else. This queer genealogy names alternative (though not necessarily competing) genres of maternal kinship. The importance of such alternatives for gender and sexuality studies becomes apparent when such nonnormative arrangements have most often been ascribed to the absence of Black fathers. Black feminist writers have focused instead on the centrality of women to Black structures of the family and the multiplication of maternal figures that such structures sometimes produce. As Ruha Benjamin writes, "to be subordinated . . . also entails inhabiting subterranean spaces where it is possible to forge new forms of kinship."[25]

I return to these discussions of mother-like relations in order to show how kinship relations are tied up in—and complicated by—the language we use to describe them. The term "othermother" implies the mother relation as unique. Structures of kinship that do not mirror the nuclear, biological family require feats of language that must deviate from heteronorms. The multiplication of mothers in this example offers a queer form of kinship, as parallel genealogies of kinship and race diverge from normative chronologies. Such a proliferation of kin also creates confusion in a language system that prioritizes single genealogical lineages. This excess of kin—this kinfullness—becomes visible in the problems of language that terms like "othermother," "bloodmother," and "fictive kin" seek to address. Similar to Twain's problem of narrating "Tom's" relationship to "his mother," the naming of nonbiological kin is often disorienting. Like strictly biological understandings of kinship and racial inheritance, heteronormative language struggles to contain and represent the excesses of more complicated relations.

While I will discuss the narrative of *Iola Leroy*'s titular character at length in the next section, the novel's subplots attend specifically to the language of race and relation as they revise popular themes of plantation nostalgia to show enslaved people's perspectives on slavery. Harper unravels the myth of the happy plantation family in her depictions of enslaved people's relationships with former enslavers and their search for their own family members during Reconstruction. Throughout the novel, the biological kinship ties established and rearticulated throughout the narrative also function as racial ties. Such ties were often broken through the system by which people were sold regardless of biological family relations, preventing the performance or maintenance of kinship roles. To acknowledge slavery's damage to families, Harper revisits the language of slavery as she relates this to the language of biological kinship. What she reveals is that such language is often confusing and even contradictory, exposing the conflict between slavery and kinship that produces linguistic slippages and requires deliberate shifts of language.

Significantly, *Iola Leroy* evidences the dual, racialized meaning of the term "mammy." An ambiguous designation of racialized maternity, Harper uses this to refer not only to Black nurses tending the white children of their enslavers, but also as a title of affection used by Black people for their own biological mothers. Iola Leroy refers to the enslaved Black woman who cared for her as a child as Mammy Liza, and this woman remains distinct from Iola's biological mother. However, other characters, such as Ben Tunnel and Salters also refer to their own mothers as "Mammy." The affectionate interchanging of "mother" and "mammy" in scenes of Black kinship illustrates the slippery nature of this term, while also pushing against uses that would erase Black kinship from the figure of the mammy, who is not simply kinless but necessarily has children of her own, even though she may be separated from them.

As in this chapter's first example, Collins's "The Slave-Mother," the enslaved mother's legal relation to her own child's enslavement does not negate maternal affection. In Collins's poem, Black motherhood is perfected in the sacrifice of a relation to one's own child because that relation bears the legal burden of reproducing slavery—an admittedly problematic relation in which maternity is best enacted when it is denied. Despite these problems, this antislavery text (like other depictions of enslaved mothers) works against the idealized image of the mammy who is characterized by her relation to white children, a relation that also necessitates her (legal, physical, psychological) absence from her own children. But in Harper's Reconstruction-era novel, this absence is not necessarily permanent. Her juxtaposition of these two uses of "mammy" reveals the persistence of familial relationships even under slavery. *Iola Leroy* depicts this persistence in formerly enslaved Black families' struggles for reunion following emancipation. The figure of the mother is, of course, central to Harper's Black families.

Beyond varying her uses of this term of racialized maternity, Harper plays upon naming and titles of respect as her characters navigate relationships between ersatz kinship relations with enslavers and truly affective kinship relations within Black families. Harper positions the "uncle" figure (common to antebellum and plantation nostalgia fiction in popular texts like Harriet Beecher Stowe's Uncle Tom and Joel Chandler Harris's Uncle Remus) alongside a plotline involving Iola's and Henry's biological uncle. Uncle Robert is, then, not a designation of imagined kinship under plantation patriarchy, but one indicating a biological kinship relation: Robert is the brother of Iola and Henry's mother, Marie. As Robert is revealed as a maternal uncle, the "uncles" who surround him at the story's opening (i.e., Uncle Daniel and Uncle Ben Tunnel) are refigured in light of this common trope of plantation slavery and its various nonbiological kinship relations, ersatz and otherwise.

Uncle Daniel, for example, alludes to familiar stock figures of plantation nostalgia in his devotion to his young white enslaver. He claims "I used to nuss Marse Robert jes' de same as ef I were his own fadder," and argues that he "beliebs [Marse Robert] lob'd me better dan any ob his kin."[26] Although other enslaved people are understandably suspicious of what love he believes "Marse Robert" to show, Daniel's love is presented as genuine here, and for this honest devotion he is rewarded. Affective relationships between enslaved people and their enslavers (not unlike kinship relations) may have been complex.[27] Daniel here expresses a complicity with imagined kinship roles, despite the inherent violence of the power relations that seem to deny the possibility of genuine love between enslaver and enslaved. The modern reader cannot help but find themselves at least a bit disconcerted by Daniel's early articulations of enslaved devotion. His paternal love mimics the usually gendered role of the mammy as enslaved caregiver. However, he serves as an important point of comparison for the novel's biological kinship relations, which have the potential to bind formerly enslaved families together in shared racial identification and familial belonging, even as these relationships are first discovered.

Daniel is not, of course, representative in his devotion to his enslaver. The novel's strategic renaming of Mrs. Johnson, a white former enslaver, is a logistical move not unlike *Pudd'nhead Wilson*'s dealing with two versions of "Tom" in the text. Over the course of the novel, "Mrs. Johnson" comes to refer to two different people: a white enslaver woman and a Black formerly enslaved one. But, unlike the uncertainty that Twain's confusion implies, Harper articulates this name shift as a deliberate act of familial respect. We read that Iola's Uncle Robert "had been separated from his mother in his childhood and reared by his mistress as a favorite slave."[28] This mistress, Mrs. Nancy Johnson, "had fondled him as a pet animal, and even taught him to read."[29] Even though Harper's narrator assures her reader that "notwithstanding their relations as mistress and slave, they had strong personal likings for each other," neither a slave mistress's alleged kindness nor a "strong personal liking"[30] compares with kinship. Robert's one stated grudge against his enslaver is the fact that she has sold his mother away from him. He tells Daniel, "I ain't got nothing 'gainst my ole Miss, except she sold my mother from me. And a boy ain't nothin' without his mother. I forgive her, but I never forget her, and never expect to. But if she were the best woman on earth I would rather have my freedom than belong to her."[31] Robert's "except" here is indeed a great one. It is in this "except" that we see biological kinship ties usurping the fiction of the plantation family that places white masters and mistresses in the position of patriarchs and matriarchs to supposedly devoted Black slaves, who figure in proslavery discourse and white plantation nostalgia fiction as perpetual children. Articulating the truth of Robert's familial allegiance, the narration eventually comes to call Robert's mother "Mrs. Johnson," changing references to his enslaver, who shares this legal name, to "Miss Nancy."

In a system in which the patriarchy (and matriarchy) of white enslavers prevents enslaved fathers and mothers from maintaining kinship ties and duties, the Black mother is often framed as a rival to the white plantation mistress—particularly when the two women's children are fathered by the same man. In the vein of plantation fiction which Harper might be most vehemently opposing (by authors such as Thomas Dixon and Thomas Nelson Page), enslaved Black (and especially, mixed-race) women appear as heartless seducers of white men and dangerous usurpers of white womanhood. Authors writing against such depictions work to reveal the sexually vulnerable position of enslaved women, whose legal position makes them or their female ancestors more likely to have been victims of rape than seducers, and to emphasize a notion of shared feminine virtue akin to that more prominently associated with white womanhood. This assertion of Black women's respectability is visible in Harper's transfer of Robert's mistress's name to his mother.

While Robert's shifting of "Mrs. Johnson" from his enslaver to his mother indicates his ability, after emancipation, to assign his filial duty where his true affections lie, the story of Robert's relationship with his enslaver pairs his preference for biological kinship relations with the imagined kinship of plantation slavery. We see this in his encounter with Miss Nancy after the war and his reunion with his mother:

> She hardly knew how to address him. To her colored people were either boys and girls or "aunties and uncles." She had never in her life addressed a colored person as "Mr. or Mrs." To do so now was to violate the social customs of the place. It would be like learning a new language in her old age. Robert immediately set her at ease by addressing her under the old familiar name of "Miss Nancy." This immediately relieved her of all embarrassment. She invited him into the sitting room and gave him a warm welcome.[32]

Nancy's refusal to address Robert with the formal title of "Mr." here is juxtaposed against her designation as "Mrs. Johnson" prior to this scene. The narration not only represents this shift of title, but articulates its enactment: "'What,' said Mrs. Johnson, as we shall call Robert's mother, 'hab become ob Miss Nancy's husband? Is he still a libin'?'"[33] The formerly enslaved characters then continue to call their former enslaver "Miss Nancy," but now the "Mrs. Johnson" by which the narrative had previously referred to the white woman is transferred to her Black counterpart. The reassignment of names, like Robert's ultimate abandonment of his enslaver to go in search of his mother, couples the articulation of kinship ties between formerly enslaved people and the assertion of Black womanhood as both respectable and respected, on a par with (if not superior to) white womanhood in the novel. As the narrative makes clear which Mrs. Johnson is Robert's mother, as if to avoid confusion (and perhaps to add insult to injury) it strikes the other Mrs. Johnson from the text: To leave two Mrs. Johnsons in the novel would be excessive. It would be equally excessive to conflate a plantation mistress's affections for maternal love and care. Emancipated from these pretenses of plantation family, Robert is able to perform the proper duties of a son. The narrative's newly assigned "Mrs." also asserts the respectability of Robert's mother, showing that the text itself is willing to articulate what Miss Nancy cannot bring herself to speak.

A similar move occurs in Jourdan Anderson's delightfully witty "Letter from a Freedman to his Old Master," addressed to his former enslaver, Colonel P. H. Anderson. Jourdan Anderson calls his own wife "Mrs. Anderson," noting that this appellation doubles that of Colonel Anderson's wife. He emphasizes the import of giving his wife this title: "The folks call *her* Mrs. Anderson."[34] In Anderson's letter and Harper's novel, the politicized naming of Black women asserts a kinship relation that works against notions of plantation stewardship. In both of these cases, we understand that the previous address of white women as "Mrs." while depriving Black women of this title indicates a difference in legal kinship relations, as enslaved Black women did not have access to the legal form of marriage designated by the title "Mrs." It is also an act of antiblack microaggression, by which we understand these titles or lack thereof to either give or deny respect, but also to articulate respectability and respectfulness as racialized relations. Respect and "respectability," of course, describes relations that have been racialized historically. As these texts demand this version of white women's respectability for Black women, they also articulate a prioritization of respect's directionality.[35] Both Anderson and Harper's Robert use "Mrs." not only to mark these women as deserving of respect, but also in order to describe their own familial relation to them as respectful.

Before the war, another enslaved man, Ben Tunnel, claims a similar devotion to his mother, which causes him to remain with her rather than escape with his fellow enslaved friends. Although he tells Robert that he "love[s] freedom more than a child loves its mother's milk," his comrades' desertion to the Union army leaves him "hushing his heart's deep aspirations for freedom in a passionate devotion to his timid and affectionate mother."[36] We see here that sometimes the condition of slavery, rather than biological relatedness, determines these characters' recognition of kinship, as Ben reveals that he believes his enslaver to be his biological father. Recognizing no kinship ties with the man who does not acknowledge him as his son (and who has no legal obligation to do so), Ben's mother becomes the determining kinship relation in his life, as much as she is the determining racializing relation. Enslaved, he follows the condition of his mother, and accordingly inherits his Black self-identification from her, rather than from his white father.[37] This enslaving father, like the white Mrs. Johnson, is an excessive kinship relation, to be discarded in favor of the shared racial identification of the maternal relation here. In this paradox of the simultaneous kinlessness and kinfullness by which Ben chooses certain kinship relationships while rejecting (or being denied) others, we see how excesses of familial ties might also produce difficulties for navigating racial identity and inheritance for mixed-race people. As the novel's mixed-race protagonists trace these queer genealogies of their own racialization, certain lineages must be prioritized and some must be excised from racial inheritance.

Iola Leroy's "Condition of the Mother"

In the early chronology of *Iola Leroy*'s titular character, we read a familiar story in the well-established tradition of mixed-race heroine fiction: Young Iola, raised as the white, privileged daughter of a Southern planter and his wife, and educated in the North, has no knowledge of her Black ancestry, and she holds no real means for identifying herself with the Black people whom she knows only as servants. She can hardly anticipate the chain of events that are, however, unsurprising to Harper's readers: her father will die unexpectedly, her mother's manumission will be found faulty and their marriage determined illegitimate, their children will be listed among the property of the estate, and the sad fate of Iola and her brother Harry is to be sold by their father's unsympathetic relatives. The revelation that Iola and Harry's mother was mixed-race and enslaved results in their choice to identify with their mother's race—as Black people. Upon obtaining their freedom, they begin to search for their mother. Ultimately, this narrative of racially ambiguous bodies frames racial malleability as determined by kinship relations, as these characters construct their newly racialized selves over the course of a story in which their previously lost Black kin are restored to them.

W. E. B. Du Bois's 1899 photograph of an African American woman that Koritha Mitchell chose for the cover of the 2018 edition of Harper's novel reminds us that Iola's own embodiment is of a white-presenting African American woman.[38] Iola Leroy is a woman embodied in such a way that she is able to "pass" as white in the novel's early chapters (despite her ignorance of her racial genealogy). "Passing" by definition assumes a fixed starting point of racial identification. By this logic, people who are "really" Black (due to various imagined quantities of "Black blood") may struggle with the possibility of being taken for—but never *being*—white. Harper frames *Iola Leroy* in terms of racial recognition, which emerges as a function of her characters' recognition of their African American kinship ties. What Harper illustrates here is a different form of kinfullness than Collins's "The Slave-Mother": It presents not as the legal excess of racialized kinship, but as a literal excess of kinfolk. Iola's condition of kinfullness manifests itself in an overabundance of kinship relations, as the conflicting white and Black family members suggest potentially conflicting racial affiliations. The result of this conflict is that mixed-race Black people, even if they might "pass" for white, often chose to identify with their enslaved mothers rather than their enslaver fathers.

Like Harper's 1869 serialized novel, *Minnie's Sacrifice*, *Iola Leroy* is what P. Gabrielle Foreman calls an "anti-passing narrative," depicting characters who discover and ultimately identify with their Black genealogies.[39] Recognizing *Iola Leroy* as an anti-passing narrative is important for understanding how Harper positions these texts in conversation with abolitionist literatures of the antebellum period and the plantation nostalgia fiction of the late nineteenth and early twentieth centuries. The anti-passing genre is also important for understanding what may look like an irony of racialization in the ways in which Harper's protagonists reconstruct race. If the phenomenon of "passing" is itself a kind of re-racialization, anti-passing seems to risk adhering to essentialist notions of race. The crux of anti-passing literature is the assumption that passing is possible, and that for ambiguously raced bodies, racial identification becomes a choice. The anti-passing narrative is a narrative of racial hypodescent, as Harper's characters' Blackness emerges as a function of recovering their African American relations. In *Iola Leroy*, racial identification here becomes not simply a choice of identification but one of kinship, as its main characters' Blackness depends ultimately upon who they embrace (and who they reject) as family. The origin story that Harper here revises (in which a child who has been raised as white discovers their Black ancestry only in adulthood, and at the moment that she herself becomes a victim, rather than a beneficiary, of racial oppression) here upsets bedrock notions of racial essentialism and genealogical inheritance. What Harper illustrates here is a different form of kinfullness than Collins's "Slave-Mother." Kinship relations that are initially conceived along the lines of what Nancy Bentley calls "bare genealogy" are reconfigured along lines that couple biological relatedness and shared racial identification via a racialized—and here necessarily maternal—kinship.[40]

Harper's emphasis on motherhood highlights the mother-child relationship as primary to the novel's aspirations for racial determinacy and uplift. Foreman notes the prominence of mothers in early African American women's writing, explaining that Harper and others wrote protagonists who attended to Black women's agency, in part, "by recuperating an economically, legally viable and racially inflected motherhood."[41] Black mothers are not kinless in Harper's novel, but are the reproducers of shared kinship ties and shared racialization. The author's motherhood, even, is foregrounded in Harper's dedication of the novel to her daughter, Mary:

TO MY DAUGHTER,

MARY E. HARPER,

THIS BOOK IS LOVINGLY DEDICATED

This centering of the child-mother relation in *Iola Leroy* is emphatic through-out the novel, in both Iola's search for her mother following the Civil War and in her maternal Uncle Robert's similar search for his mother, Iola's grandmother.

Iola Leroy does not merely foreground maternal relationships but priori-tizes them among the narrative's excessive kinship relations. This prioritiza-tion illustrates the queer workings of hypodescent, as racial inheritance does not follow dual, heteronormative genealogies, but single, maternal ones. Despite Harper's focus on biological relationships, biology is not the crux of the novel's framing of kinship so much as racial identification is. Mixed-race Black characters align themselves racially—and politically—with cer-tain biological family members while simultaneously rejecting kinship with others. Like Iola, enslaved or formerly enslaved characters in the novel come to ignore certain biological kinship ties—like those between enslavers and enslaved people—and to articulate kinship instead along lines of shared ra-cial identification rather than biological genealogy alone.

Throughout the novel, race is thereby produced and reproduced not simply through biological genealogies but according to which kinship rela-tions are acknowledged and which are rejected or forgotten. That her hope of reconciliation with her mother has "colored all my life," as Iola says, is a telling metaphor for the rest of the story, in which this relationship binds maternal kinship and racial reproduction.[42] In this way, the novel exhibits matrilineal Black kinship, rather than plantation patriarchy, as having the "so-cial efficacy" that Hortense Spillers and others have shown is denied under enslavement.[43] Harper's centering of Black motherhood further reveals the ersatz kinship relations between enslaver and enslaved, distinguishing emphatically between the figure of the Black mother and that of the Black mammy. In what must have appeared to Harper's post-Reconstruction readers as a familiar defense of slavery, the visibly white and still unknow-ing Iola Leroy's initial anti-abolitionism is based on the picture of her own father as a "kind" enslaver. Now removed to the North for her education, in true plantation nostalgia form, Iola recalls her youth and the close relations between the families of white enslavers and enslaved people on the plantation where she was raised.[44] Iola claims, "I love my mammy as much as I do my own mother, and I believe she loves us just as if we were her own children."[45] Once Iola Leroy has learned the truth of her biological mother's (and hence her own) Blackness, though, this claim is exposed as dubious; much of the rest of Iola's story focuses on her persistent search for and reunion with her biological mother. This is accompanied by her corresponding forgetting of Mam Liza, whom Iola never seeks out, and the fond memory of whom almost disappears from the story.[46] The only other time readers are reminded of Mam Liza is when Aunt Linda's "motherly" manner "seemed to recall the bright, sunshiny days when [Iola] used to nestle in Mam Liza's arms, in her own happy home."[47] While this may seem like a lapse in racial solidarity, it is also a refusal to sentimentalize the mammy-child relation or to elevate it to the status of kinship.

The mammy is therefore revealed as ersatz kin, as Iola's initial pretense about her commitment to Mam Liza proves false. Given Iola's previous declaration of affection for her mammy, choosing to seek out one woman and not the other seems at least somewhat arbitrary. Importantly, the dialect-speaking, illiterate Aunt Linda does not remind Iola of her biological mother. This makes Iola's later reminiscence of her mammy rather curious amidst the novel's prioritization of biological kinship ties (grandmother, mother, uncle, and brother) rather than the larger support system of nonbiologically related but similarly raced and enslaved people. Only immediate biological kin constitute Iola's familial obligations. We here remember that the relationship Iola has had with her mammy was that of a white child of enslavers, not as an enslaved Black person. Unlike many of her white contemporaries, Harper does not idealize the figure of the mammy or sentimentalize even this mammy-child relationship. The ersatz kinship relations of plantation slavery are a red herring of sorts in the novel, as kinship between an enslaving family and the enslaved people it holds captive are continually revealed as false. While the violence of this enslaving family is not as apparent as that of Tom's in *Pudd'nhead Wilson*, Iola's re-racialization similarly fails to retroactively change her racialized relationship to her mammy. Not all Black people are kin to one another in this novel, even as race is determined in relative terms. Mam Liza is, perhaps, true to the idea of "My skin-folks but not my kinfolk" from Iola's perspective of racial solidarity. Even as the novel directs us toward racial uplift, kinship is both exceptional and foundational.[48] While shared racial identification and kinship are not simply to be conflated, kinship—and mothers, especially—are the rock upon which racial identification is built.

Although shared racial identification does not necessarily produce relatives, Black mothers reproduce race. This racial reproduction allows racial uplift to become possible, despite the violence that chattel slavery has done to enslaved families. *Iola Leroy* maps the persistence of the enslaved family by placing the mother at its center, and by tracing the genealogies of racialization to new generations of relatives. After the Civil War, we find members of the novel's rendered families in a religious camp meeting. "In that meeting were remnants of broken families—mothers who had been separated from their children before the war, husbands who had not met their wives for years."[49] *Iola Leroy*'s most poignant depiction of these separations is that between an enslaved mother and child. Alongside the various tales of grown children longing for their lost mothers, the scene of initial parting is presented by an older, dark-skinned emancipated woman named Harriet, who we learn is Robert's mother and Iola and Harry's maternal grandmother. Harriet gives witness to this event in what is both one of the most familiar and one of the most heart-wrenching scenes of Harper's novel, in which a formerly enslaved woman recounts her separation from her children and her wish for her reunion with them:

> Bredren an' sisters, it war a drefful time when I war tored away from my pore little chillen . . . When my little girl . . . took hole ob my dress an' begged me to let her go wid me, an' I couldn't do it, it mos' broke my heart. I had a little boy, an' wen my mistus sole me she kep' him . . . Many's the time I hab stole out at night an' seen dat chile an' sleep'd wid him in my arms tell mos' day. Bimeby de people I libed wid got hard up fer money, an' dey sole me one way an' my pore little gal de oder; an' I neber layed eyes on my pore chillen sence den. . . . But I'se prayin' fer one thing, an I beliebs I'll git it; an' dat is dat I may see my chillen 'fore I die.[50]

What is heart-wrenching about this scene is not its exceptionality, but its familiarity. But what is familiar here is not only Harriet's painful memory of family separation but also her prayer to be reunited with her children. Just as scenes of separated and sold families were prominent in antebellum antislavery writing, Black newspapers reflected their readers' hopes for post-slavery familial restoration. One such example published in the *Christian Recorder* in 1886 reads:

> Information wanted of my mother, Jane Ross. She belonged to a man named Captain David Taylor, who lived on Eastern Shore, Maryland. She was sold away down South. Any information of her will be greatly

received by her daughter, Minnie Blake, formerly Minnie Ross, 206 Dean Street, Philadelphia, Pa.[51]

People searching for lost kin published "Information Wanted" advertisements like this one in postbellum Black newspapers.[52] Readers of newspapers like the *Christian Recorder* (in which Harper published both poetry and fiction), would have likely connected this scene of Harriet's history and hope to the larger post-war landscape in which Black people like Minnie Ross sought out lost kin, illustrating the violence slavery enacted upon Black family and also kinship's importance to Black people and communities. Harper's image of Black motherhood revises that of the slave-mother, to show not simply the denial of kinship but the aftermath of slavery, in which the hope (even if unfulfilled) of finding lost kin is restored.

Information wanted advertisements and Harper's camp meeting scene show how, even in the physical absence of kin, articulations of kinship persist. In light of this persistence, it is no surprise, perhaps, that Harper's novel focuses on matriliny as multigenerational. There is no separating the intertwining of motherhood and racial reproduction in the text. But the racial reproduction necessary for uplift necessarily extends toward generational futurity. In addition to theories of racial hypodescent, the impetus for reproducing race has long been associated with the policing of women's reproductive bodies. As the novel shifts Iola's initial narrative of privileged, white, middle-class womanhood to the "race-woman" of Black educational uplift, Harper's anti-passing politics positions racialized matriliny as foundational for the deliberate, radical racial reproduction of Blackness. Iola's and Henry's Black identification extends their anti-passing politics to their deliberate reproduction of Blackness. Both siblings marry Black people and recognize the generational implications of this decision. Harry chooses Miss Delaney, a dark-skinned Black woman, and Iola ultimately marries a mixed-race Black man, Dr. Latimir, refusing the white (though upstanding and initially sincere) Dr. Gresham's proposals of marriage.

Although Iola, her brother, and their mother were all white-presenting people, her refusal to marry a white man implies that she will be less likely to have children who are able or willing to pass as white. Moreover, the decision shows us that Iola understands her own maternity to be racialized as Black. She knows that, even if she were to marry a white man and agree to "pass" as white herself, that it may be impossible for her future children to do so. Iola therefore cites not simply the color line but the possibility of her own reproduction of Blackness as the "insurmountable barrier" that divides her and Dr. Gresham, even while he argues, "Your complexion is as fair as mine. What is to hinder you from sharing my Northern home, from having my mother be your mother?"[53] Even though Iola has experience living in the North as a white woman, she refuses the necessary passing this would entail, simultaneously refusing to replace her own mother with a white mother-in-law. But what ultimately convinces Dr. Gresham is Iola's explanation of racial reproduction. She asks, "'Doctor,' . . . and a faint flush rose to her cheek, 'suppose we should marry, and little children in after years should nestle in our arms, and one of them show unmistakable signs of color, would you be satisfied?'"[54] Iola does not only identify with Black people, but she understands herself as likely to reproduce Blackness.

Here we see that *Iola Leroy*'s matrilineal genealogies of racialization are multigenerational; they are also multidirectional. Just as the recognition of visibly Black children would bind Iola to Blackness, so does the recognition of her elder kin, as Iola loses a position of employment because of her association with her Black family. One of Iola's coworkers observes that "there was an old woman whom Iola called 'Grandma,' and she was unmistakably colored. The story was sufficient. If that were true, Iola must be colored, and she should be treated accordingly."[55] While Iola's would-be husband, Dr. Latimir, "was a man of too much sterling worth to be willing to forsake his [Black] mother's race for the richest advantages his [white] grandmother could bestow," Iola sees that her own grandmother's Blackness implies her own, regardless of her other kinship ties.[56] Even while race is figured as matrilineally inherited, it does not necessarily follow an unbroken linear trajectory. Blackness might resurface after skipping a generation (as Iola imagines it might), even while visual Blackness is not a determiner of racialization. Not heteronormatively genealogical and not linearly predictive, racial reproduction is queer indeed.

These multigenerational and nonlinear kinship bonds that drive *Iola Leroy*'s racial identification position the figure of the mother as essential to racial uplift, extending her role well beyond normative kinship. While slavery often stifled the ability of enslaved mothers to perform this kinship role to their own children, emancipation presented a challenge for mothers and would-be mothers to meet the demands of an American motherhood that, in the national imagination, is figured as both white and middle class. Miss Delaney, Harry's fiancée, notes the importance of Black mothers to the perception of the race as a whole. We read that "One day she saw in the newspapers that colored women were becoming unfit to be servants for white people. She then thought that if they are not fit to be servants for white people, they are unfit to be mothers to their own children, and she conceived of the idea of opening a school to train future wives and mothers."[57] Vashti Lewis interprets Harper's confrontation of such derogatory images of Black women that were popular in the 1890s as marked by what she characterizes as "schizophrenic overtones," observing that "Although this critique on black women may have delighted white readers, certainly women of African descent only a generation removed from slavery must have found insulting the implication that diminished capacity of black women to nurture white children was a necessary impetus for someone to teach them (or for them to learn) parental skills."[58] It is curious that Harper leaves unclear what skills, exactly, formerly enslaved mothers need to learn. But taken within the larger context of racial uplift, we see the role of the Black mother poised not simply as a matriarchal kinship relation, but as a community leader.

Reading the Black mother within the context of racial uplift necessitates extending this figure's role from the scale of the familial to the national. Upon hearing Iola's paper on the "education of mothers" at a parlor meeting, the Reverend Eustace remarks that "the great need of the race is enlightened mothers" who (with the help of "enlightened fathers") can help to raise a generation of children who will function as citizens of the American nation.[59] If we read in Harper's complex women characters writing that sometimes embraces and sometimes works against models of gendered, racialized respectability, we can perceive a layer beyond the most simplistic reading of this narrative of uplift, in which formerly enslaved Black mothers must become fit for national participation. This additional layer of Harper's uplift narrative extends familial relations and responsibilities beyond the scale of the nuclear family to a larger community of racialized kinship (a scalar shift I will explore further in the conclusion to this book).

Devoted Mothers and Devalued Kin in Charles Chesnutt's *The Marrow of Tradition*

Even more emphatic than *Iola Leroy*, perhaps, in its extension of kinship's scale is Charles Chesnutt's representation of the "new maternal negro," a figure of racialized maternity that refuses both the stereotypical mammy and the imitation of white motherhood. Janet Miller in *The Marrow of Tradition* is a character who is placed in diametrical opposition to the Black mammy. Woven together with Chesnutt's retelling of the Wilmington riot and his depiction of Tom Delamere's blackface performance, the novel depicts what William Andrews refers to as "a kind of spectrum of southern racial opinion and class identity."[60] In this spectrum, one finds Chesnutt's more progressive African American characters alongside "familiar stereotypes of the southern romance," one of which is Mammy Jane Letlow.[61]

Chesnutt's version of the familiar trope plays on popular representations of this figure. At its heart is the Black woman's genuine love for the white children she has nursed. In our very first glimpses of her, she proclaims to her white employer, Olivia Carteret, "Will I come an' nuss you' baby? Why, honey, I nussed you, an' nussed yo' mammy thoo her las' sickness, an' laid her out w'en she died. I would n' *let* nobody els nuss yo' baby; an' mo'over, I'm gwine ter come an' nuss you too."[62] Chesnutt couples this image of the devoted Black nurse with her admiration for Olivia's child, who has "sech fine hair fer his age" and "sech blue eyes," along with his physical strength and well-fed appearance.[63] This mammy-child relationship rivals that in Sarah Piatt's imaginings.

Mammy Jane is not only a mother figure to the white child; she emerges from a long history of enslaved Black mammyhood and, now in the Reconstruction era, attempts to train younger Black domestic servants to be content with their positions. As Mammy Jane tells Major and Mrs. Carteret, "I's fetch' my gran'son' Jerry up ter be 'umble, an' keep in 'is place. An' I tells dese other n[—]s dat ef dey'd do de same, an' not crowd de w'ite folks, dey'd git ernuff ter eat, an' live out deir days in peace an' comfo't."[64] Mammy Jane's nostalgia for the "Old South" of plantation slavery is explicit in the text, as she tells Mrs. Carteret, "None er dese yer young folks ain' got de trainin' my ole mist'ess give me. Dese yer newfangle' schools don' l'rn 'em nothin' ter compare wid it. I'm jes' gwine ter give dat gal a piece er my min', befo' I go, so she'll ten' ter dis chile right."[65] Though no longer enslaved, the love and devotion to the three generations of children she has nursed in Olivia Carteret's family are seemingly enough to keep her in this role of contented servitude.

Chesnutt posits figures of plantation nostalgia like Mammy Jane and her grandson Jerry in sharp contrast to his (mostly mixed-race) characters, who are presented as clear models of Black social uplift.[66] The younger nurse assigned to the Carteret family (who never was enslaved herself and appears to be too young to remember slavery) has no emotional ties to white plantation families and does not understand the near-kinship affections Mammy Jane holds for the Carterets. "These old-time negroes, she said to herself, made her sick with their slavering over the white folks, who, she supposed, favored them and made much of them because they had once belonged to them,— much the same reason why they fondled their cats and dogs."[67] Recognizing the contradictions of white former enslavers bearing any real love for the people they enslave, the young nurse's work is clearly not a labor of love, as Chesnutt explains: "For her own part, they gave her nothing but her wages, and small wages at that, and showed them nothing more than equivalent service. It was purely a matter of business; she sold her time for their money. There was no question of love between them."[68]

It is Janet Miller, however, who provides the clearest contrast with Mammy Jane. Early on, we learn about Janet's white relations from Mammy Jane (who, of course, "knows all 'bout de fam'ly").[69] She tells Doctor Price, "Dis yer Janet, w'at 's Mis' 'Livy's half-sister, is ez much lik her ez ef dey wuz twins. Folks sometimes takes 'em fer ne er-nudder,—I s'pose it tickles Janet mos' ter death, but it do make Mis' 'Livy rippin'."[70] Unlike Roxy's "twin" boys, however, these sisters have no living parent through which to triangulate their relationship. Their father, now dead, never publicly acknowledged Janet as his daughter while he lived. Mammy Jane is wrong in her assumption that Janet can derive joy from her family resemblance to the half-sister who refuses to acknowledge their relation. We read that "Janet had a tender heart, and could have loved this white sister, her sole living relative of whom she knew. All her life long she had yearned for a kind word, a nod, a smile, the least thing that imagination might have twisted into recognition of the tie between them. But it had never come."[71] Rendered kinless by her white family's racism, Janet instead reproduces Blackness, forming a family of her own. She marries a Black man (Doctor Miller) and they have a son.

As the story unfolds, it is confirmed that both Janet and Olivia's father was Samuel Merkel. Subsequent to the death of Olivia's mother, Janet was born to Merkel and Julia Brown, his maid, who had formerly been enslaved by his wife's family. Olivia, after her mother's death, had been raised by her aunt Polly, with whom her father had had a long-heated dispute about his insistence on keeping Julia in the house. Much of the Carteret family's plotline surrounds the mystery of this affair's details. Olivia, who believes herself to have been her father's only legitimate child and has inherited his entire estate, discovers that her father had left a will (which had previously been hidden by Olivia's aunt, Polly Ochiltree), leaving some land and money to Julia Brown and her daughter Janet, but the majority of his estate to "my dear daughter Olivia Merkell, the child of my beloved first wife."[72] In this, Olivia discovers that her father had married Julia Brown (though their marriage would have been rendered illegal due to the anti-miscegenation laws of the state at the time) and acknowledges his paternity of the child in an undelivered letter to his first daughter before his death.

The complexities of this particular family drama are as significant as they are familiar. Chesnutt's interracial plantation family exhibits popular anxieties about racial reproduction, interracial kinship, and the possibility of the cross-racial inheritance of property. As Peggy Pascoe argues, at the heart of anti-miscegenation law is not simply the belief that racial sexual mixing was unnatural, but the fact that white supremacist ideologies were highly invested in preserving white property and inheritance.[73] Characterizing the racial melodrama of Olivia Carteret and Janet Miller as "Chesnutt's use of the family as a metaphor for the crisis in American racial politics," Eric Sundquist connects the drama of "Negro domination" with that of "Negro" kinship.[74] Racial integration and the "threat" of racial equality are "family crises" for Chesnutt's characters: We learn that Polly Ochiltree has stolen Merkell's papers in order to disinherit Julia's child, so that Olivia can inherit her father's entire estate. Further, when Aunt Polly dies, she plans to leave her house and land to Olivia's child rather than her other nephew, Tom Delamere, specifically because she believes that the Carteret child "would never sell them to a negro."[75] If white supremacy is dependent upon keeping wealth in white families, the erasure of the color line in interracial marriages and the production of mixed-race children thoroughly disrupts this system. Accordingly, the system by which white men are not legally obligated to acknowledge their children born to Black mothers ensures that their property will not pass to their nonwhite kin.

Chesnutt presents a family drama that de-emphasizes the imagined threat of Black men's sexual violence toward white women in favor of one highlighting the racial and sexual competition between Julia Brown and Polly Ochiltree. The source of both kinds of racial anxiety is the same: the threat of upsetting white racial reproduction.[76] While Polly contrives to paint Julia as a Jezebel figure (twice she calls her a "hussy"), she reveals her own heartlessness as she relates the episode in which she casts Julia and the child Janet out of Merkell's house.[77] Horrifyingly, Polly admits, "I could have killed her, Olivia! She had been my father's slave; if it had been before the war, I would have had her whipped to death."[78] The image Chesnutt gives us of their confrontation shows the cruelty of the white matron, contrasted with the quiet, passive grief of the Black mother. Later, when the town is in an uproar over Polly Ochiltree's apparent murder by a Black man (though the reader knows that she has been killed by her own nephew, Tom Delamere, in blackface), Chesnutt persists in highlighting the real danger of white violence toward African Americans. This culminates in the death of Janet and Doctor Miller's son, killed by a stray bullet during the race riot in which white men attempt to enact "revenge" on the town's Black citizens for Polly Ochiltree's death.

While Janet has, until the novel's end, been painted as a parallel mother figure to her sister, Olivia, here their paths diverge. Just after Janet's son's death (and while the riot has dispersed all the town's white doctors), Olivia's child is in need of medical aid, and the Carteret family seeks the help of Doctor Miller. Because he initially declines to leave his grieving wife's side, Olivia arrives to entreat him to do otherwise. Though Doctor Miller is mired with grief and anger at the white violence that has killed his son, when Olivia throws herself at his feet, he is moved by her resemblance to his own wife. "He had been deeply moved,—but he had been more deeply injured. This was his wife's sister,—ah, yes! but a sister who had scorned and slighted and ignored the existence of his wife for all her life . . . This woman could have no claim upon him because of this unacknowledged relationship. Yet she *was* his wife's sister, his child's kinswoman. She was a fellow creature, too, and in distress."[79] Doctor Miller leaves the decision up to his wife, and Olivia plays on both her motherly and sisterly sympathies to persuade her. "'You will not let my baby die!'" she tells her, "'You are my sister;—the child is your own near kin!'"[80] This appeal is not entirely unfounded, for Janet shows sympathy for her sister: "She was greatly interested; she herself was a mother, with an only child. Moreover, there was a stronger impulse than mere humanity to draw her to the stricken mother."[81]

It seems, then, to be the biological tie to her sister and the child—and not simply the bonds of universal motherhood—that drives Janet's sympathy. Later, though, she admits to a hierarchy in these kinship relations, telling Olivia, "'My child was nearer . . . He was my son, and I have seen him die. I have been your sister for twenty-five years, and you have only now, for the first time, called me so!'"[82] Although she rejects her sister's all-too-convenient acknowledgment, Janet ultimately instructs her also grief-ridden husband to go to the Carteret's aid by an act of what seems like motherly sympathy. Stephen Knadler regards this act as "threaten[ing] to shatter no mere sacred image of whiteness (or blackness for that matter) but to disrupt its *form*," by which he describes the novel's "deconstruction of whiteness as rhetorical performance."[83] In Janet's case, she disrupts any exclusively white claim on motherhood and also threatens the very boundaries of whiteness, as acknowledging her relation disrupts constructions of white family. Janet also reveals herself, the mixed-race Black mother, as the figure able to embrace interracial kinship.

Janet's embodiment of universal motherhood in this scene is what Samina Najmi calls Chesnutt's "cautious hope for racial awareness on the part of white women, especially the white woman as mother," and provides the novel with a marginally happy ending.[84] Although Janet rejects her sister's convenient recognition of kinship, she is unwilling to allow her nephew to die as a result. The partial reconciliation in the interracial family presents some hope for the national racial reconciliation that Chesnutt presents as a possibility through the Carteret-Miller family drama. Knadler argues that it is in Janet's role as mother, and the recognition of universal motherhood that allow for this hope for reconciliation. He writes "to assure her son's life, Olivia Carteret must recognize that the ideal type of womanhood . . . is embodied in her "dark" Other."[85] This white recognition of the Black potential for universality—along with an acknowledgment of the existing ties of interracial kinship in the United States—are presented as necessary steps toward racial equality in Chesnutt's novel.

It was not such a universal claim to which Olivia appealed, however. We read that "This was the recognition for which, all her life, she had longed in secret . . . but it had come, not with frank kindliness and sisterly love, but in a storm of blood and tears; not freely given, from an open heart, but exhorted from a reluctant conscience by the agony of a mother's fears."[86] The novel may leave readers who are intent upon a narrative of race and reunion unsatisfied in the absence of a reciprocal articulation of sisterhood between white and Black mothers. While Elizabeth Ammons argues that *Iola Leroy* appeals to "a sisterhood of mothers," the failure of biological sisterhood to produce satisfying emotional kinship ties frustrates this figurative sisterhood in *The Marrow of Tradition*.[87] This sisterhood proves excessive in the text, as Olivia's initial reluctance to acknowledge interracial kinship is coupled with Janet's unwillingness to allow that kinship tie to be articulated solely for the benefit of a white future. Just as Mammy Jane's mammy-love is marked as insufficient to produce interracial kinship ties that will reflect upon the national family, Janet does not perform the role as loving sister to a white woman. Instead, she promotes racial uplift only in her role as a sort of surrogate-mother to a white child. As the "new maternal negro," Knadler describes Janet as an "untragic mulatto" in her refusal "to renounce her white parentage or to be ashamed of her blackness."[88] Through her distance from the submission of the Black "mammy," but with the potential for interracial kinship, Janet becomes a newly raced figure, in line with Chesnutt's own dreams for racial uplift being achieved by characters like Janet and Doctor Miller.

Janet's racialized relations do not only frame her as a mother, however, but also as a sister, as Chesnutt's ending becomes a kind of metaphor for women's interracial solidarity in the United States: white women will ask

Black women for help when needed, all the while denying solidarities of sisterhood and excluding women of color from mainstream white feminism. In her discussion of Caribbean literature, Elizabeth Maddock Dillon describes "sororal" as "a set of relations between sisters or siblings that is distinctly horizontal in opposition to the vertical structure of genealogical reproduction."[89] Olivia's racial anxieties include the fear that her recognition of Janet will result in the same kind of horizontal racial transfer, similar to sexual kinship. The question of what it means to have a Black sister, then, presents the worry that Janet's race will somehow reflect onto Olivia's, that recognizing their family's interracial relations will cause Blackness to overflow into the lives and relational racializations of its white members. *The Marrow of Tradition* ultimately illustrates the limitations of sororal relationships for interracial kinship, as white women's recognition of Black women as kin are framed as contingent. Here, these sisterly relations are yet another casualty of kinfullness—they present as excessive, too much for white womanhood to bear, except in cases of rare necessity. Dillon describes "lateral relations that generate no offspring" in a relation she characterizes as "that of siblings, not that of reproductive parentage."[90] But even as these relationships are not reproductive of bodies, these anxieties of interracial family show how they are potentially productive of race, in this queer genealogy of futurity that extends beyond the reproduction of children.

In addition to being a mother in her own right and an (unacknowledged) sister, Janet is an aunt to the white child she helps to save. In this biological family relation we see a subtle nod to the conflation and confusion of the kinship relations that mark Black women. Mammy figures are sometimes also referred to in these terms, as "Aunt" So-and-So, by white and Black children alike. In Harriet Jacobs's *Incidents in the Life of a Slave Girl*, for example, the uncareful reader might be confused by the fact that Linda's biological grandmother is widely referred to as Aunt Martha while Linda's biological aunt and Martha's daughter is called Aunt Nancy. The sometimes interchangeable naming of mammy and aunt confuses the maternal for the materteral, and both appellations articulate a similar pretense that these enslaved Black women were part of a big, happy interracial "family" of enslaving and enslaved people. As the new maternal negro, however, Janet appears in this story not as an "Aunt" but as an aunt, offering assistance to a dying child with whom she shares a blood relation and who she does not choose to punish for his older family members' wrongs.

Although the novel's potential for racial reconciliation is rendered more possible because of an acknowledged kinship relation between Black and white people, this possibility is deferred. Janet's care for her white sister's child in this moment can never compete with Mammy Jane's genuine love, and the sisterly affection that might accompany this act is tenuous. While the novel construes these kinship relations as literal, Chesnutt suggests a more general relation that rejects imagined barriers of racial dualism in the formation of an integrated national family—a family that is clearly not yet reconciled at the end of Chesnutt's novel. Chesnutt's refusal of the fully reconciled interracial family is a move that distinguishes *The Marrow of Tradition* from plantation nostalgia fiction. By showing a fraught interracial national family (though a family, in the biological sense), Chesnutt resists any impulse to place Janet in a role resembling the mammy figure. By prioritizing the importance of her own child's death, her begrudging refusal to let her sister's child die rejects the kinship her half-sister would now acknowledge (though only for the sake of her child, it seems) for a model of motherhood that does not necessitate this biological kinship relation. Rather, it is her relation to her own child that drives her to help the Carteret baby and not her own biological ties to him. In this way, the white child is de-prioritized, even though he is the child who lives.

The extent of the problematic interracial kinship that Janet Miller resists might be read in contrast to the imagined "yearning" of Sarah Piatt's iconic mammy, which more closely resembles Mammy Jane's nostalgia. Janet Miller poses a poignant counter-narrative to the "mammy" trope as a mixed-race Black woman who does not yearn for the white child of her mother's former-enslavers, but for her own child. The stakes of mammy-lore are clear here, as kinship and servitude are conflated in the mammy figure and the accompanying Black child is de-prioritized for the white one. The Millers' dead child, like Twain's "Tom Driscoll," shows the results of the white child's usurping powers. Chesnutt's novel paints a picture of interracial kinship ties as reluctantly acknowledged though biologically present in the history of the American nation. Moreover, he presents these ties as needing to be rejected—or at least checked—by the new maternal negro's refusal to prioritize the white child—and, by extension, her refusal of an exclusively white national futurity.

The most extreme version of a Black mother's radical refusal of racialized kinship might be seen in the case of Margaret Garner. After emancipating themselves in 1856, while she and her family were being pursued by enslavers, Garner infamously killed her two-year-old daughter (and attempted to kill her other children) in order to prevent them from being returned to slavery. In an 1857 poem based on Garner's infanticide, "The Slave Mother, A Tale of the Ohio," Harper describes Garner's reasoning:

I will save my precious children
   From their darkly threatened doom.
I will hew their path to freedom
   Through the portals of the tomb.[91]

Following familiar antislavery arguments that death is better than slavery, and Christian theological beliefs in a utopian afterlife, Garner's logic was not unique. Garner's extreme act resonates as a refusal of the racial reproduction of kinlessness, projecting the mother-child relationship instead into a future beyond the world in which their kinship is bound up with the excesses of inherited enslavement. I next turn to a twenty-first-century interpretation of Garner's life in order to examine the ways that interracial kinship relations come to bear upon the connections between childhood and futurity, which are complicated by the mortality of enslaved children.

Margaret Garner's Futurity

In Toni Morrison's libretto for Richard Danielpour's 2005 *Margaret Garner: A New American Opera in Two Acts*, the workings of time and futurity re-direct the focus away from the usual sentimentalization of Garner's killed children. The opera focuses around the lives and relationships of enslaved people—notated by arias that muse on nostalgia, loving duets, and direct appeals to God. In the opera's first act, the song "A Little More Time" illustrates the relationship between enslaved kinship and the future. The "slave chorus" and main characters sing: "A little more time / more time with the children we love . . . / time with our brothers. / We feel the mercy of our Lord God / with the grace of a little more time."[92] The lines continue to include more familial relationships, as the characters wish for "More nights to curl like a vine / in our husband's arms," "More days to bask in the light / of our lover's eyes," "Our fathers' graves, / we can still attend / with sweet William and Columbine" and for "Time with our mothers."[93] As in Morrison's depiction of Sethe in *Beloved*, Margaret's relationship to her children is one of desperate love, couched in the ever-present anxiety about her condition of enslavement. Margaret is depicted as a mother who deeply loves—and needs—her child. Cilla (Robert's mother and thereby Margaret's mother-in-law) warns her, "emphatically" the libretto tells us, "It's dangerous, daughter, / to love too much. / The Lord giveth / and the Lord taketh away."[94] Enslaved motherhood is a state of desperation, made precarious by the looming possibility of kinlessness.

The family escapes to Ohio, but not without some trouble. Cilla will stay behind, saying she is "too old to tread new waters."[95] Margaret and Robert's initial conversation is about their future in freedom, calling the "free" state "a beautiful place for a future." Margaret demands, "Tell me. Tell me what the future will be like," and the couple plans the beautifully and excruciatingly mundane: planting a garden, mending clothes, being paid for one's labor.[96] It is an idyllic future of happiness, with their children "tumbling in clover and / rosemary" and swimming in "clear water / until their skin glitters like brass."[97] It is also a future of security, as they sing, together, not only of the future's arrival, but of its permanence: "That is how it will always be."[98] It is at this moment of futuring that Margaret and Robert are discovered by their former enslaver (and Margaret's rapist) Edward and the other enslavers. Now captured, Margaret finds herself "out of time." Robert is killed and Margaret begins killing their children. She slits the throat of the first and stabs the younger child, singing of a recursive future, "Never to be born again into slavery!"[99] The next scene opens thus:

Act II

INTERMEZZO

Total darkness envelops the stage. Gradually, the image of Margaret, alone, becomes visible. Her state of mind is changing; the intense isolation she feels in this moment "out of time" is mirrored by the dislocating blackness that surrounds her.[100]

Margaret's out-of-timeness defeats the earlier scene's future-gazing. As the notes tell us "With defiant grandeur, Margaret embraces her life's circumstances."[101] She has abandoned her own and Robert's thoughts for the future and seems heartbreakingly resigned.

In a case resting on whether Margaret is guilty of murder or simply of the destruction of property and a violation of the Fugitive Slave Law, Margaret is tried and sentenced to death. However, as Margaret stands at the gallows, the judges grant clemency and a stay of execution. Cilla steps forward to tell Margaret "You will live, my daughter."[102] But Margaret refers to her own future in a different scale of time, a different futurity. She sings:

Oh yes. I will live.
I will live.
I will live among the cherished.
It will be just so.
Side by side in our garden.

It will be just so.
Ringed by a harvest of love.
No more brutal days or nights.

(making eye contact with Cilla in the crowd)

Goodbye, sorrow . . .
Death is dead forever.
I live. Oh yes, I live![103]

At this moment, the stage directions tell us that *"While the crowd's attention is focused elsewhere, Margaret deliberately trips the trap door's lever and hangs herself."*[104] The nature of Margaret's resignation to a future happiness only in death recalls an old problem of antislavery literature, namely, that satisfaction in this heavenly future rests upon the diminishment of a search for justice in this world. In antislavery literature, justice is often problematically displaced to the afterlife, removed from human responsibility or possibility on earth.

The opera does not end with Margaret's death, however, but with the other mother figure, Cilla, echoing Margaret's reference to the afterlife, "Soon, soon my bold-hearted girl / I'll be there. I'll be there."[105] Here, instead of hope for Garner's reunion with her own children, another mother figure repositions Garner as child, to be reunited with a loving parent in the otherworldly future. There is danger, of course, in idealizing Garner's killing of her children, just as there is in idealizing children and childhood itself. Either sentimentalized according to nostalgic past imaginings of childhood or weighted with the burdens of enacting some ideal of futurity, children often figure not as individual people in themselves, but as representations of reproduction's infinite potential. Garner's act is one of desperation, in her view the best choice among a scope of limited and terrible options. Retelling Garner's story does not, as abolitionists understood, celebrate child murder, but denounces the situation in which murder becomes the most appealing choice for a mother. Danielpour and Morrison's opera brings this mother-child relationship to the foreground, so as to illustrate not only this tragic act of adult deliberation and decision, but also refiguring Garner so as to make more visible her vulnerability as a victim of this system in which she has so few choices available. I read this version of Garner's story for its intertwining of time and family, as kinship relations become a function of time itself. Enslaved children wishing for "Time with our mothers" gives way to Margaret and Robert's musings about their family's happiness in a future that "will always be." In these relations of time we can reimagine kinlessness as a theft not only of relations as slavery absents the very bodies of loved ones, but also a theft of time—not only of laboring time, but also of relating time. Here we recall Frederick Douglass remembering that "My mother and I were separated when I was but an infant—before I knew her as my mother"—and understand that a son and mother have not only been physically stolen from one another, but their time together has been stolen as well.[106]

Not just stolen kinship but interracial kinship creeps into Margaret Garner's story, revealing something more about how race figures in these genealogies of time. In her court address during Garner's trial, white abolitionist Lucy Stone Blackwell framed the problem of Margaret Garner as one of interracial kinship, specifically citing Garner's mixed race—and that of her children—as evidence of white supremacist sexual violence. Stone observes: "The faces of the negro children tell too plainly to what degradation female slaves submit. Rather than give her little daughter to that life, she killed it."[107] African American women antislavery writers such as Harriet Jacobs and Frances Harper emphasized the threat of sexual violence against enslaved girls in their writing. Harper includes this in her poem inspired by Garner, as her protagonist muses that:

> My baby girl, with childish glance,
>   Looks curious in my anxious eye,
> She little knows that for her sake
>   Deep shadows round my spirit lie.[108]

African American abolitionist Sarah Remond cites Garner similarly in an 1859 lecture, using her story to call out the sexual abuse of Black women by white enslavers.[109] Garner's own mixed-race body further becomes evidence of racism's circular production of race, as white supremacist violence itself creates even more Black bodies upon which that violence can be enacted.

In Thomas Satterwhite Noble's 1867 painting, *The Modern Medea*, neither the enslaved mother nor her children bear obvious visual markers of mixed-race genealogies (see figure 4.2).[110] Garner is imagined only as phenotypically Black, a trope of enslaved motherhood not entirely unlike the mammy, whose loyalty to the white family prevents her own "natural" motherhood. Representing this individual (mixed-race) Black mother in a manner so closely resembling the trope of Black motherhood most often associated with white children, Noble's painting recalls the irony by which Black women, imagined to be bad mothers themselves, were perfectly well trusted to raise their oppressors' white children. By depicting neither Garner nor

THE MODERN MEDEA—THE STORY OF MARGARET GARNER.—Photographed by Elliott, from a Painting by Thomas Noble.—[See Page 318.]

4.2 ENGRAVING AFTER THOMAS SATTERWHITE IN *HARPER'S WEEKLY* 11 (MAY 18, 1867): 318. COURTESY OF THE AMERICAN ANTIQUARIAN SOCIETY.

her children as visibly mixed race, Noble also erases any visual markers of sexual assault in Garner's genealogical history. Removing this evidence of the violence of white masculinity, Garner is represented as a "bad" mother who is left to face trial by white men who are not depicted as perpetrators of violence in their own right, but only as witnesses to hers. Leslie Furth argues that this painting's positioning shows "an ambiguity as to who is to blame" in Garner's and the white men's gestures toward the children, registering both the mother's "defiance and desperation."[111] But limiting the tragedy of Garner and her family's enslavement to this event alone is to miss the point of slavery's generational violence. Garner is not simply tragic because of her act of killing, but because of the act of her children's conception in slavery and in the continued enslavement she imagines for those still living. The children clinging to Garner's skirts bear a slight resemblance in their positioning to the Black child of Scott's *No Mommy Me*, and in the image of Twain's Roxy discussed in the previous chapter. The close contact with and tugging of the mother's clothes blends parental familiarity with the desperation of this violent scene. It speaks to why Garner's killing of her own children produces more horror than more mundane killings of enslaved children might. This familiarity resists violence, even violence done out of love.

The resemblance between these images of enslaved mothers and children, though slight, suggests the fraught relationship between interracial kinship and slavery's generational inheritance. Elizabeth Livermore's "The Fugitives," serialized in the *Independent Highway* in 1856, imagines Garner's mammyhood as Lucretia (Livermore's Garneresque character) takes an odd moment to recall, "my little playful Missus! Shall I ever see her again?"[112] The connections between racialization and relation are what call up Livermore's imagining of Garner as both mother and mammy, supplying the narrative of tragic Black motherhood with another, seemingly excessive, relation to the white child. Similar to Piatt's mammy, who "looks yearning down" from Heaven upon her white child, Livermore puts this concern over white children in the mouth of Lucretia in an unlikely moment that inexplicably seems to displace her desperate care for her own children. Livermore here prioritizes Lucretia's concern for white children over her radical resistance to the racial reproduction of slavery that her act of infanticide accomplishes.

In the broader sense, Garner's infanticide enacts what Dillon refers to in the eighteenth-century Atlantic enslaving colonies as "the end of the line," "a trope in which white genealogical lineage is ruptured, and the European patrilineal family meets its reproductive demise."[113] Garner refuses interracial futurity, refuses the reproduction of Blackness enacted by white supremacist violence, refuses the excessive burden of racially productive genealogy. The stakes of this refusal extend even beyond the pathos of the killed child and have been imagined well beyond the nineteenth century. To refuse racial futurity is not only to become kinless—to "lose your mother" as Saidiya Hartman describes it—but also to be haunted, as in Morrison's *Beloved*, or to be caught in a recursive paradox of time travel, as in Octavia Butler's *Kindred*.[114] To deny a racial future is not only to end the racial line, but to be forever mired in the excesses of race and racism.

In actuality, Garner did not kill herself on the scaffold as she does in the opera but was returned to slavery along with her still-living husband and remaining children. Another of her children was drowned in a March 1856 boating accident, in which Garner is also believed to have attempted to drown herself.[115] This infant (Garner's youngest) is the child with whom she was pregnant in January when she fled with her family and killed her daughter. As the *Liberator* reports, Garner herself claimed to be happy that her child had died rather than endure a longer life enslaved. Just as the violence of Garner's story reaches back from this event of killing her children to the origins of inherited slavery itself, it also reaches forward to future children and

4.3 THOMAS SATTERWHITE NOBLE, *JOHN BROWN'S BLESSING*, C. 1867. OIL ON CANVAS, 84¼ × 60¼ IN (214 × 153 CM), OBJECT NUMBER: 1939.250. COURTESY NEW-YORK HISTORICAL SOCIETY.

future enslaved generations. The proliferation of children in Noble's image of Garner raises questions about how and why Noble both ages and multiplies Garner's single slain infant. Does this account for the later, drowned child? Does it imagine other children of Garner's who will die in slavery? Does Noble simply find that two children add to this gruesome spectacle of infanticide?[116] This excess of children speaks too to kinfullness's excess baggage, as Garner's genealogy of racial inheritance proliferates bodies and enslavement and suffering, even as she attempts to remove one of her children from this trajectory.

Noble's painting *John Brown's Blessing* (of the same year as *The Modern Medea*; figure 4.3) revisits the image of a Black woman and her child, as a woman holds her baby up for Brown to touch, as he is on his way to the gallows. *John Brown's Blessing* connects this child, an image of Black futurity, with the white man to be hung for treason after inciting an uprising of enslaved people. The future that Brown could not enact in his own rebellion but to which his violence and his violent execution contributed saw a changing landscape of racial inheritance. Noble creates both of these paintings in a post-slavery and postwar moment that frames them as historical events viewed from an uncertain future. Brown can be safely viewed from a moment in which he might be understood to have contributed to the future of Black freedom that his death could not foresee. Without the inheritance of slavery, interracial kinship might not hold quite so much excess baggage, but racialization would still occur not only in bodies and in families, but in the domestic space of a white supremacist nation.

My next chapter, on the narrative of Mary Jemison, will take up the possibilities of interracial kinship beyond the excesses of a society based on slavery by turning to the ways these queer genealogies are framed by native kinship and domesticity. While Mary King and William Allen sought to remove themselves from the United States as they established their interracial family, Mary Jemison described herself as similarly unwilling to raise her own mixed-race children within that domestic, national space. Jemison's differently figured belonging within the Seneca nation provides a model of domestic possibility against which we might then regard the limitations of interracial kinship for national reunion in the United States.

III

Residency

DOMESTIC RACIAL RELATIONS

Mary Jemison's Cabin

Domestic Spaces

of Racialization

> To him she was a white woman, and he knew stories of white women
> being taken by Indians.
> —Rayna M. Gangi, *Mary Jemison: White Woman of the Seneca*

A HISTORICAL MARKER on the Chambersburg trail in Buchanan Val-
ley, Pennsylvania, memorializes the location of Mary Jemison's capture by
the Shawnee. The plaque reads: "The monument marking the home of the
'White S[—] of the Genesee' prior to her capture by the French and Indians
is 3 miles north. The remainder of Mary Jemison's life was spent as an Indian."[1] More commonly known as the "White Woman of the Genesee" than
by this racist epithet, Jemison's racialization was essential to the telling and
retelling of her life story. The daughter of Scotch-Irish parents who emigrated
to North America, Mary was a child when she was captured in 1758. Her parents, two of her brothers, and her sister were killed by the Shawnee, and she
was adopted into a Seneca family. She ultimately married Indian men, raised
her children among the Seneca, and lived as a member of this community
for the rest of her long life. It was not until 1823 that James Seaver sought her
out and heard her life story, writing and publishing his "as told to" narrative
the following year.[2] By that time, Jemison's biography was situated within
an established genre of white women's captivity narratives. This genre has
contributed to what Native studies scholars such as Lisa Brooks, Margaret

Newell, and Pauline Strong have critiqued as the prioritization of a relatively small number of white captives relative to Native Americans enslaved during the colonial period.[3] The genre also relied on an assumption of clear racial distinctions between white and Native people and overwhelmingly failed to imagine the possibility of kinship between them.[4]

But Jemison's narrative offers more complicated scenes of kin-making and domestic proximity than the strict generic conventions of captivity narratives afford. This is because Jemison's kinship with her subsequent husbands, her children, and even the African American people she lives with for a short time, refigures her white womanhood into something else—even as she continued to be known as "the white woman" throughout her life and was memorialized as such after her death. Monuments to Jemison bear both her likeness and specific references to her whiteness. These monuments reveal how the racialization of Native people cannot be reduced to biological relatedness. Ironically, the persistence of Jemison's whiteness reveals how Indigenous identity and belonging are not reducible to race. Any claims to Jemison's whiteness cannot preclude the Seneca kinship relations that refigure her as Indian. Even in the racist language of the plaque, we see how white memorializers (including Jemison's amanuensis) clung to Jemison's whiteness even as they attempted to reckon with how interracial kinship ties reframed her racialized identity.[5]

A statue at Jemison's gravesite in what is now Letchworth State Park in western New York State, near where Jemison once lived (see figure 5.1), does not focus only on this dual racialization, but frames Jemison's kinship relations. Here Jemison is not memorialized in her old age, but as she may have appeared when she traveled across this space as a young woman, fleeing the US government's attempts to eradicate her community. The statue also depicts Jemison as a mother, carrying her child—a Seneca child who is also under threat from settler colonialist violence—on her back (see figure 5.2). By depicting Jemison thus, as a figure in relation, rather than as simply and individually racially embodied, this statue presents a glimpse of the kinship relations by which Jemison's racialization might be best understood. Put another way, Jemison's kinship with Native people extends racialization beyond the scale of her own body to relationships within her family and community, and to a larger political stage. Even as Native people are problematically racialized against a backdrop of whiteness, Jemison's racialization does not align with essentialist notions of race, but instead with notions of identification through kinship and community relations that actually prioritize Indigenous theories of identification and belonging over white supremacist ones.

5.1 STATUE OF MARY JEMISON AT HER GRAVESITE, LETCHWORTH STATE PARK, NEW YORK. PHOTOGRAPH BY STEPHAN FIELDER AND SUE ANN FIELDER.

5.2 STATUE OF MARY JEMISON AT HER GRAVESITE (BACK), LETCHWORTH STATE PARK, NEW YORK. PHOTOGRAPH BY STEPHAN FIELDER AND SUE ANN FIELDER.

Taken together, these monuments to Jemison speak not only to her re-racialization as Indian (a simplification of Jemison's identification as Seneca, a category which extends beyond racialization and to matters of tribal belonging and sovereignty), but also evidence racialization across various scales of domesticity via Jemison's relationships within and to the domestic spaces she occupies. Just as the statue of Jemison speaks to a particular moment of her embodiment within a threatened Native space, the historical monument with which I began speaks to Jemison's racialization by way of placing her within a particular space. As it marks the location of her capture, it slips deftly to note also how Jemison's movements in this space accompany her racial identification, explaining that "The remainder of Mary Jemison's life was spent as an Indian." The plaque commemorates neither some revelation of ancestry nor a bodily transformation. The statue of Jemison carrying her child proves a more apt marker of Jemison's relationship to white and Seneca identification. Not simply a matter of individual embodiment, racialization happens in relation and simultaneously at multiple scales. Expanding our notion of racial relation from body to family to community to nation, we must therefore take into account the spaces in which these various scales of racialized relations occur.

In this chapter I read the cultural construction of a woman born white who becomes Indian by a process of racialization and re-racialization that is relational rather than generational, and which is also informed by the domestic spaces she inhabits at various scales. Much as Iola Leroy frames her own re-racialization by virtue of which kinship relations she recognizes and which she ultimately rejects, Mary Jemison's re-racialization is similarly framed through relations of kinship. Moreover, Jemison's kinship relations and race are both worked out not only in her interpersonal relations, but in shared relations in and to domestic spaces. Jemison's racialization is dependent upon the spaces of racialization she and the other people in relation to whom she is racialized inhabit.

Expanding the scale of my first two sections to treat race as not simply bodily or reproductive, this chapter and the next deal with larger, spatialized conceptualizations of race in domestic spaces that are not necessarily fixed but which are contested and shift via processes of settler colonialism and nationalist expansion, and which are precarious in times of revolutionary and civil war. These contested, shifting, precarious spaces of the nation are also the contested, shifting, precarious spaces for racialization. In the texts that are the focus of this chapter and the next, racialization extends beyond the body and even the family in its relationality toward a trajectory of spatial expansion, to larger relational (though not necessarily generational) gene-alogies of race. Focusing on this larger scale, we can understand Jemison's re-racialization simultaneously in her relationship to kin and her relationship to domestic spaces. In keeping with Amy Kaplan's theorization of "manifest do-mesticity," I note two complementary registers of the "domestic" here, both on the scale of the dwelling spaces of the home and in the domestic spaces of nations. The second register is fraught with the contestations of Indian removal, sovereignty, and forced "domestic dependency" by which settler colonialist nations seek to impose both registers of the domestic upon Na-tive peoples. This chapter therefore reads Jemison's narrative in light of the nonbiological kinship and queer domestic relations that dominate her narra-tive, and that ultimately articulate her kinship, domestic, and racial relations.

Reading kinship not as biological relatedness but as cultural, domestic relations of behavior, we see a different version of what in other contexts is sometimes termed "fictive kinship," illustrating how biological ideologies of relation (and, by extension, racialization) are not the only ones available. The Native kinship relations I discuss here dovetail with notions of African American kinship discussed in the previous chapter, illustrating how kinship genealogies might be (re)framed alongside and against white supremacist and settler colonialist notions of kinship and domesticity. This reframing reveals the link between biological kinship and racialization to be more ten-uous than we might otherwise imagine. Taken in the larger context of her narrative, Jemison's domestic relationships with her Seneca family, to white settler-colonialists, and to fugitive African American people become telling indicators of the rejection and adoption of kinship ties and the relations of domesticity and fugitivity that enact Jemison's queer re-racialization as the Seneca Indian "White Woman of the Genesee."

Jemison's narrative reveals her supposed whiteness as culturally con-structed despite its pretense about race's biological fixedness. In this con-struction, Jemison's narrative is nevertheless in conversation with the na-tional trope of the white woman as represented and revised in the genres of the captivity narrative and the anti-miscegenation narrative. I begin with Jemison's relation to space as one of fugitivity. Framed by white settler co-lonialist violence, removal, and misreadings of her need or desire to be "re-deemed" by white society, Jemison finds herself in relations of domestic kin-ship with not only Seneca but with Black men, as she navigates Indigenous and settler colonialist spaces. I take up the tension between the Western bio-logic of racial identification and the Native cultural logic of kinship at work in Jemison's tale of adoption in order to show how Jemison's racialization as white is modeled on normative, white supremacist models of kinship and belonging. I then move to a discussion of her subsequent marriages, connecting the history of legal racial determination in federal Indian law and "anti-miscegenation" law to the particular position of a woman whose landed property is determined both by white patriarchal and Native matrilineal systems. I here connect domestic spaces at the scale of familial home and the "domesticated dependent nations" of federal Indian law with the model of white womanhood in the frontier romance's anxieties regarding interracial romance and republican motherhood. I resist the too-easy slippage between domesticity and cultural belonging to focus instead on how domestic spaces themselves contribute to racialization at multiple scales as the locus of cultural and racializing relations.

Lastly, I draw upon models of white womanhood in theories of republican motherhood and manifest domesticity to show how the role of women in the early national period was dependent upon assumedly biological kinship relations and corresponding domestic spaces, and what is at stake in early republican literatures that call this prioritization of biology into question. Jemison's residency and fugitivity here mirrors Native residency and removal at various scales. What is regarded as a frontier space for white settlers remains, for Jemison, a domestic rather than a foreign space. By foregrounding Jemison's relationship to Native domestic spaces, I show how Jemison's cabin operates as both a fugitive space and an Indigenous one, in which Jemison resists white settler encroachment and removal on multiple domestic scales. Reading Jemison's relationships to and within this space allows readers to see how Native relations of kinship, identification, and belonging work against white supremacist, colonialist frameworks for producing both family and race.

Mary Jemison, Fugitive

In the autumn of 1779, Mary Jemison found herself separated by war from her husband Sheninjee, homeless, and with five children to feed. As General Sullivan's campaign across western New York State threatened the Seneca people with its program of attack and starvation, Jemison recounts that:

> they destroyed every article of the food kind that they could lay their hands on. A part of our corn they burnt, and threw the remainder into the river. They burnt our houses, killed what few cattle and horses they could find, destroyed our fruit trees, and left nothing but the bare soil and timber.[6]

Having waited out the danger, her community then returned to their lands, she says, "but what were our feelings when we found that there was not a mouthful of any kind of sustenance left, not even enough to keep a child one day from perishing with hunger."[7] Displaced and without food, as the weather grew increasingly cold and stormy, Jemison took her children to the Gardow Flats, land along the left bank of the Genesee River. This land, not yet populated by Seneca who would later resist removal to Buffalo Creek Reservation or by the white settlers whose encroachment would prompt their displacement, is not without residents. Jemison tells us: "At that time, two negroes, who had run away from their masters sometime before, were the only inhabitants of those flats. They lived in a small cabin and had planted and raised a large field of corn, which they had not yet harvested."[8] For these men and for Jemison and her family, this is a fugitive space, one of temporary safety and racialized domesticity.

Before what Jemison recalls as the harshest winter in her memory, she hires herself out to help harvest the men's corn, and thereby provides for her family. The irony of her situation is complex. She remembers: "I have laughed a thousand times to myself when I have thought of the good old negro, who hired me, who fearing that I should get taken or injured by the Indians, stood by me constantly when I was husking, with a loaded gun in his hand, in order to keep off the enemy, and thereby lost as much labor of his own as he received from me, by paying good wages."[9] On orders from George Washington himself, Sullivan's army had succeeded in severely threatening Jemison's and her family's access to food and shelter. It is clear to Jemison that "the enemy" is the white Continental Army rather than the local Indians who both she and her children recognize as kin.[10] The irony of this scene reminds us of both the perceived vulnerability of white women on the frontier and the actual vulnerability of Seneca such as Jemison and her children during the Revolution. But Jemison's laughter here is eclipsed by the further irony of her would-be-defenders: two formerly enslaved Black men— unlikely protectors of white womanhood in American literature of the 1820s.

The homesteader's failure to comprehend Jemison's own Indianness resembles another story of cross-racial protection, in *An Authentic Narrative of the Seminole War; and of the Miraculous Escape of Mrs. Mary Godfrey, and her Four Female Children.* The "miracle" that saves this white family from native violence is the help of an enslaved Black man. Godfrey's husband has left his family to fight the Seminole and she ultimately flees their home after she "heard the frightful yells of the approaching savages, and saw the dwellings of her nearest neighbors in flames."[11] They flee into the swamp and are compelled to hide there for four days, on such little subsistence that Godfrey worries she will not be able to produce enough milk for her six-month-old baby. The youngest child's "pitiful moans" give their location away to "a straggling black, who had enlisted in the cause of the enemy."[12] He is carrying an axe and Godfrey, assuming that he means to harm them, begs him to spare her children. The man then drops his tool and assures Godfrey and her children of their safety. He returns later to bring them food, water, and blankets. He warns them when he thinks it is unsafe for them to remain there, and helps them back to their white community, the narrative tells us, "although at the risk of his own life."[13]

The reasoning this man gives for sympathizing with Godfrey and her children is, perhaps, predictable. The narrative explains:

> that he had two children who were held in bondage by the whites, that to enjoy his own liberty he had left them to their fate, and something now seemed to whisper him, that if he should destroy the lives of her innocent children, God would be angry, and might doom his little ones to a similar fate by the hands of the white men in whose power they were![14]

Michelle Burnham describes how this scene produces "sympathetic identification across, rather than within, racial boundaries," as the man compares Godfrey's children to his own.[15] There is reason for this sympathy, of course, but that does not negate these people's different relations to power and violence in this space. The narrative depends upon framing white settlers as innocent, nonparticipants in, or beneficiaries of the settler colonialist violence done to Native people. Thomas Godfrey has gone to fight against the Seminole, likely threatening Indian families with starvation and violence, much as his own family is threatened. And white settlers like the Godfreys are holding this Black man's children enslaved.

In the cases of both Jemison and the Godfreys, we see the literary employment of white womanhood's domestic relations confounded. The *Authentic Narrative*'s visual and narrative framing of white innocence distorts relations of racial power in this settler space. The scene in which a fugitive Black man meets Godfrey and her children (see figure 5.3) is reminiscent of other images of white women's apparent vulnerability, recalling images like the title page to Rowlandson's narrative and Clay's "Female Intrepidity," discussed in chapter 2. Unlike the women in these images, however, Godfrey and her children are framed as completely vulnerable, without any apparent means to protect themselves and without male protection. This protection arrives in the form of the very man who initially seems to be a threat. The axe-bearing Black man

AN

AUTHENTIC NARRATIVE

OF THE

SEMINOLE WAR;

ITS CAUSE, RISE AND PROGRESS,

AND A MINUTE DETAIL OF THE

HORRID MASSACRES

Of the *Whites*, by the *Indians* and *Negroes*, in Florida, in the months of December, January and February.

Communicated for the press by a gentleman who has spent eleven weeks in Florida, near the scene of the Indian depredations, and in a situation to collect every important fact relating thereto.

PROVIDENCE :

Printed for D. F. Blanchard, and others, Publishers.

1836.

5.3 FRONTISPIECE, *AN AUTHENTIC NARRATIVE OF THE SEMINOLE WAR; ITS CAUSE, RISE AND PROGRESS, AND A MINUTE DETAIL OF THE HORRID MASSACRES OF THE WHTIES, BY THE INDIANS AND NEGROES, IN FLORIDA, IN THE MONTHS OF DECEMBER, JANUARY AND FEBRUARY.* NEW YORK: D. F. BLANCHARD, AND OTHERS, PUBLISHERS, 1836. COURTESY OF THE AMERICAN ANTIQUARIAN SOCIETY.

is the seemingly unlikely protector of the white family. In Jemison's case, we read a different kind of irony that a woman born white is at risk at the hands of the US government's campaign against Native communities and sheltered by self-emancipated African Americans. Both moments of danger illustrate the complexities of settler colonialist violence and also the relevance of fugitive domestic spaces for forming racialized relations of kinship and power.

The swamp in which Godfrey and her children hide and in which the above scene occurs is one kind of fugitive space, shared by enslaved Black people, Native people—and white people. As Tiffany Lethabo King notes, "Often when Black and Indigenous people encountered one another their meetings were mediated by the violence of an evolving humanism organized through their captivity and death."[16] Here, interracial alignments resist such racist forms of humanism. The man who Godfrey calls, in her own narration of the events, "the humane African (our deliverer)" is also a fugitive in this space, in danger of capture and re-enslavement.[17] The cross-racial sympathy of this scene might also be described as a shared relation not to power but to place. As Mark Rifkin writes: "Quotidian interactions offer kinds of routine contact that accrete, generating forms of collective being-in-the-world that do not necessarily coincide with state-sanctioned modes of determining belonging but that produce experiences of enmeshment with others. In addition to one's relation to other bodies, histories of contact might include an engagement with the land."[18] The kind of "enmeshment with others" in physical spaces of "engagement with the land" are not entirely dependent upon state-sanctioned modes of belonging, even though they are often informed by them. In Jemison's narrative, too, engagement with the land is key, as the nation-state organizes domestic national spaces in part by encouraging certain kinds of domestic familial spaces, while threatening others.

Taken in the entirety of its irony, the above episode of Jemison's fugitivity is more than just one example of the several ways that she fails to function within the bounds of white womanhood, but reveals something more fundamental about the way whiteness itself is working throughout her narrative. While most scholarly discussions of Jemison have either ignored or given minimal attention to the autumn and winter she and her children spent with the two African American men who helped save them from starvation, attending to the significance of these events—and the space in which they occur—gives insight into the ways Jemison's tale reveals an identity generated by associations of kinship and domesticity that are dependent upon cultural or behavioral relationships rather than biological ones, and in which

Jemison's racialization can be seen as a function of her relationships to and within domestic spaces.

This relationship between Jemison and the two African American men for whom she harvests corn becomes a domestic relation as well as a relation of exchanged labor. Homeless with her family before the arrival of what was indeed a historically harsh winter, Jemison remains with these men in their cabin until she can build a home for herself and her children. She relates that "deprived of a house, and without the means of building one in season, after I had finished my husking, and having found from the short acquaintance which I had had with the negroes, that they were kind and friendly, I concluded, at their request, to take up my residence with them for a while in their cabin, till I should be able to provide a hut for myself."[19] Not only do we see the irony that Jemison does not need protection from the Indians, but the fact that she and her children live for a time in the same cabin as two Black men—the safest available domestic space—explodes the normative trope of the vulnerable white woman in her narrative and reinscribes the bounds of domesticity around a decidedly interracial space.

The initial arrangement of hired, seasonal labor thereby becomes a different kind of domestic relation—one of necessity, and that which is difficult to define. We get little information about the time Jemison and her children spend in this domestic space. However, she calls these men "kind and friendly," saying that she stays with them after they invite her to do so, and asserting that with them, "I lived more comfortably than I expected to through the winter."[20] However brief, this period of Jemison's life and this space of domesticity seem essentially important for understanding her narrative. Once a "stranger" among the Seneca, and given a home, made a "homeless fugitive," and a "weary wanderer" by the Continental Army, Jemison is taken into an African American domestic space in which she and her children could be supported. Jemison's vulnerability in the space of this cabin and in relation to the spaces of the burgeoning US nation-state aligns her with both her Seneca family and with this fugitive household.

This space of interracial domestic relations defies Anglo-Protestant assumptions of domestic space and kinship, showing yet another way Jemison finds herself (both culturally and geographically) outside the bounds of white womanhood. I find it difficult to describe this domestic space in part because it defies normative expectations and language for describing relationships of cohabitation. The space might therefore be termed a "queer" one in that it functions outside the bounds of heteronormative domesticity. More than an anecdotal event in Jemison's tale, the winter Jemison and her children spend in the cabin of these self-emancipated men is representative of how her narrative resists conventional underpinnings of white womanhood, speaking to the ways Jemison does not conform to the models of white, heteronormative femininity and domesticity usually associated with literatures of the early republic, such as the captivity narrative. The significance of these events is duly noted by G. Peter Jemison (a descendant of Mary's) in his epilogue to Rayna M. Gangi's novelization of Mary Jemison's narrative. I quote G. Peter Jemison at length as his comments most appropriately address the significance of this part of Mary Jemison's story. He writes:

> Mary survived the terrible winter of 1779–80 because of two escaped slaves and their generosity. She and her five children were given refuge in the home of these two African-Americans, within Seneca territory, beyond the reach of the American Army and its path of total destruction. The irony of African slaves believing they are protecting a white woman from the Senecas, when it is the American Army that she is fleeing, could not have been imagined by a Hollywood writer.[21]

Mary Jemison's racialization occurs and reoccurs within interracial domestic spaces. Her inability—or perhaps, rather, her refusal—to keep "foreign" (i.e., nonwhite) elements outside the domestic space of the home illustrates her own failure/refusal to adhere to models of white republican womanhood. That is, Jemison's racialization occurs at multiple scales—the bodily, the familial, and the national—that call attention to racialized relations within various kinds of domestic spaces.

In this chapter and the next, I use the word "domestic" in the two senses that Kaplan develops in her dual understanding of the relationship between the heterosexual, nuclear family home and the imperially expanding American nation. These meanings of "domestic" work in tandem to create cultures of belonging within such spaces. As Laura Romero writes, "the politics of culture reside in local formulations—and in the social and historical locations of those formulations."[22] Although they focus on individual figures' or characters' racialization through interracial kinship relations, the texts I discuss in this and the next chapter are involved in race-making on multiple scales. By expanding the scale of racialization's implications beyond the body, interpersonal relations, and the family, these texts frame racialization as having larger implications for the nation, and even for the stakes of race itself. This is to say, despite their focus on (real or fictional) individuals, these texts are nationally oriented. As they narrate stories of race's bodily construction and (re)construction, each of these texts is not simply about the figures at their center, but about the racialization of the nation and race-making at a larger scale.

The national implications of domestic spaces become clear when we consider the stakes of Jemison's racialization for her relationship to the United States, a domestic space that is racialized as white. As Jemison is re-racialized outside the iconic white womanhood that is also associated with national (re)production, the intertwining of whiteness and heteronormativity becomes clear. Heteronormative domesticity is itself one product of settler colonialism. As Rifkin explains, "a heteronormative understanding of proper sexuality (monogamous, marital, procreative, structured around the nuclear family) has been crucial in inserting Native peoples into structures of settlement."[23] Mary Jemison's queer racialization is a product of nonnormative relations of kinship and domesticity. Rifkin holds that the "generational inheritance of sensations" is, among other things, a "means for (re)imagining and (re)connecting to place."[24] My discussion of domestic spaces (including the "queer" space of Mary Jemison's cabin) similarly speaks to this connection to places and spaces that frame and help to constitute kinship and other racialized relations. Attending to these relations to space gives insight into Jemison's removal from and resistance to white kinship. By foregrounding Jemison's relationship to this Native space, we see that Jemison's cabin operates as both a fugitive space and an Indigenous one, in which Jemison resists white settler encroachment and removal on multiple domestic scales.

The time that she spends with these Black men in their cabin at Gardow is not the only period of Jemison's fugitivity. As June Namias, Chris Castiglia, and others note, Jemison ultimately resists "white 'protection' or 'rescue'" from the family of her adoption and marriage.[25] Much like Mary King, she remains a lifelong fugitive from the forms of white womanhood to which white men wish to return her. Though shortly after her adoption, Jemison initially expresses a wish to be "liberated from the Indians and to be restored to my white friends and my country,"[26] she later refuses to return to the white settler community when given the opportunity. Following the Seven Years' War, when the British government actively attempted to recover white captives from the Indians to return them to white society, Jemison decided not to leave the Seneca, feeling that her familial ties to them were stronger than any biological ties she might have to white people elsewhere. Because bounties were offered as a reward for redeeming captive white people, Jemison recounts the danger of her being forcibly "redeemed" despite both her decision to stay with the Seneca and the decision of the council chiefs that "as it was my choice to stay, I might live amongst them quietly and undisturbed."[27] As a young widow following the death of her first husband, Jemison recounts the particular danger she encounters from a Dutchman who wishes to redeem her against her will.

Jemison positions herself as a fugitive of sorts in this account, writing that "as I was fully determined not to be redeemed at that time, especially with his assistance, I carefully watched his movements in order to avoid falling into his hands . . . He gave up the chase, and returned: but I, fearing that he might be lying in wait for me, stayed three days and three nights in an old cabin at Gardow, and then went back trembling at every step for fear of being apprehended."[28] This position of fugitivity—hiding in a cabin at Gardow—is a familiar relation to place in Jemison's narrative. The episode repositions Jemison from being a white captive of the Shawnee in the earlier captivity plot to a position not unlike that of the two self-emancipated men she meets in 1779. Without Jemison's consent, her proposed "redemption" by a white man seems little better than the sale of another human for profit. The logic of Jemison's physical movement away from (even theoretically well-meaning) white people with whom she no longer identifies is similar to the condition of Mary King prior to her and William Allen's emigration in 1853, or perhaps even akin to that of her fugitive African American housemates. Essentially, Jemison hides in this cabin from a white man who threatens to capture and sell her away from her family. This episode of fugitivity in the cabin at Gardow echoes the shelter Jemison and her children received in the interracial space of the fugitives' cabin. The irony of her position here—as one who is redeemable (or, we might say, saleable) *because* she is white—grates against the danger of her previous position, as one subject to starvation and exposure to the elements due to a white government's campaign against Indian tribes, and as a woman who aligns her and her children's position with that of formerly enslaved Black men. This attempt to redeem Jemison is also an attempt to reorient her to the space she inhabits—an attempt at "domestication" that demands not only her allegiance with the white family, but her removal from the Native space of kinship and sovereignty.

As Jemison's Seneca brother, Kau-jises-ta-ge-au, weighs in on the matter of her redemption, however, the narrative reinvests her with traces of white womanhood that hearken to the captivity narrative and the frontier romance. Quarreling with an elder of the tribe as to whether or not Jemison should be redeemed, she recounts that "my brother frankly told him that sooner than I should be taken by force, he would kill me with his own hands!"[29] Had this scene occurred earlier, during the captivity narrative portion of the text, one might too easily read Kau-jises-ta-ge-au more as one of the figures in

John Vanderlyn's 1804 painting *The Death of Jane McCrea* than as a figure of brotherly protection. Jemison's account of her affection for, and the affection she received from, her brother makes this a more complex scene, though. Remembering his special "kindness . . . natural mildness of temper, and warmth and tenderness of affection," she states, "If he had taken my life at the time when the avarice of the old King inclined him to procure my emancipation, it would have been done with a pure heart and from good motives."[30] Read in the tradition of the genre of the frontier romance rather than the captivity narrative, this brotherly sentiment becomes strikingly familiar, as the death of a female relation is presented as preferable to the degradation she might suffer when forcibly taken by an enemy. Had a brother of James Fenimore Cooper's Cora Munro uttered these words, they would surely have been read by most readers as a chivalric last attempt to protect white feminine honor (i.e., virginity and hence, racial reproduction). Admittedly, such a death, even at her brother's hand, does not appeal to Jemison, but as she is reunited with her brother, her kinship ties with her Seneca family are reinforced.

Amid Jemison's various articulations of kinship and belonging, these moments of Jemison's racialized fugitivity illustrate how racializing relations occur not only within the bounds of domestic spaces (like the African American men's cabin or the Seneca lands at Gardow) but also in racialized relations to that space. Like the historical marker of her initial capture, Jemison's narrative will similarly conflate the bounds of kinship and space, as she says of her Seneca family, "with them was my home; my family was there."[31] A space might contain and create kinship relations, or kinship relations might characterize one's relations to and relations within a particular place. The narrative of Mary Jemison's adoption shows how her physical residence within the Seneca community accompanies the establishment of her kinship, as "home" and "family" signify the domestic space that will ultimately shift her political and racial allegiances.

Adoption, Domesticity, and Scales of Racialization

The designator "white" that so frequently accompanies depictions of Mary Jemison reminds readers of the supposed permanence of biological identifiers and the potential transience of cultural ones—meaning, although Jemison can and does become Indian in Seaver's narrative, she never ceases to be white in these imaginings.[32] The characterization of Jemison as a "white Indian" seems itself to be another paradoxical phrasing of racialization, but it reveals something about the relationship between these categories. From one perspective, it evidences the very problem of regarding "Indian" as a racial category rather than one of tribal citizenship or sovereignty. In this understanding, this pairing seems to contrast "white" and "Indian" as designating different modes of identification and belonging—one biological, the other cultural. But from another perspective, it reveals something more about the nature of white racialization. This characterization of Jemison as a "white Indian" reveals the discord between settler colonialist and Indigenous framings of racial, national, and familial belonging, and ultimately the refusal of the latter to be subsumed by the former. In doing this, it also reveals how Jemison's racialization works not only individually but at larger domestic scales, in spaces of domestic habitation, Native residency, and the "frontier" encroachments of white settler colonialism.

As G. Peter Jemison reminds readers regarding Mary's familial status among the Seneca, "Adoption in the 18th century meant something more than an Indian name; it included rights and responsibilities which Seneca women inherited at birth, for we are a matrilineal society."[33] Throughout her narrative, Jemison continually describes this relation to her adopted family as comparable to a blood relation, emphasizing the fact that her adoption creates a kinship relation that is not inferior to biological kinship. She recounts, "I was ever considered and treated by them as a real sister, the same as though I had been born of their mother."[34] Jemison's new sisters diligently teach her their language and make her accustomed to their way of life, and thereby bring her into a cultural kinship that bears no hint of being a substandard form of family. For the intended Anglo-American audience of Jemison's narrative, however, these familial relations can only be explained by their comparison to blood kinship. Even in interpreting her adoption, the referent of blood relations and their recognition is continually in the background of Jemison's tale. It is not enough that we learn that she has become these women's adopted sister; she must explain this cultural kinship relation to her predominantly white readership "as if" it were a relation of blood. In her adoption ceremony, the Seneca women who will become Jemison's sisters couple welcoming their new sister with mourning a brother who has been killed. Their lamentation at his loss is immediately followed by the introduction of their new family member as they say, "'His spirit has seen our distress, and sent us a helper whom with pleasure we greet. Dickewamis has come: then let us receive her with joy! She is handsome and pleasant! Oh! she is our sister, and gladly we welcome her here. In the place of our brother she stands in our tribe. With care we will guard her from trouble; and may she be happy till her spirit shall leave us.'"[35] Jemison explains that she has been brought into their family to replace a brother who had been killed, noting that this is a common practice among Indian communities who lose members in war. This welcoming hearkens to Jemison's physicality in shared familial spaces, as "In the place of our brother she stands in our tribe." The substitution of an adopted sister for a supposed blood relation implies that the weight of kinship rests in cultural or behavioral incorporation rather than biological determination. This holds even truer when we recognize that assuming their lost brother was biological kin would be a matter of conjecture. In truth, we do not know whether this brother was biologically related to them. Consanguinity here does not necessarily determine kinship. Jemison's status as sister is equal to that of her new family's dead brother in this equation ("she is our sister," not merely "like" a sister), as the adoption articulated in this welcoming reception fully incorporates her into the family structure.

In his discussion of Jemison's adoption, Tuscarora historian Elias Johnson frames adoptive kinship explicitly in terms of corresponding notions of racial belonging. He writes, "When Mary Jemmison [*sic*] had been formally named De-he-wa-mis, they called her daughter and sister, and treated her in all respects as if she had been born among them and the same blood flowed in her veins . . . There was no difference in the cares bestowed, no allusion was ever made to the child as if it belonged to a hated race, and it never felt the want of affection."[36] As kinship is established, racial difference is seemingly negated. Jemison expresses similar feelings of kinship, regardless of biological relatedness, as she remembers her Seneca sisters. She recounts "the warmth of their feelings, the kind reception which I met with, and the continued favors that I received at their hands, rivetted [*sic*] my affection for them so strongly that I am constrained to believe that I loved them as I should have loved my own sister had she lived, and I had been brought up with her."[37] These articulations of kinship, along with Jemison's domestic location among her Seneca family and the replacement of familial affections, slip easily into her re-racialization, just as the historical marker explains that "The remainder of Mary Jemison's life was spent as an Indian."

While Desdemona's whiteness inhered in her (racially marked) body, Jemison's is imagined as a function of how, where, and with whom we might "place" her. In one sense, this "placing" is metaphorical, a function of genre, as in readings of Mary King's story. Removing Jemison from the realm of the captivity narrative and placing her, instead, alongside the frontier romance or even as Native autobiography, the whiteness of this figure changes. In another sense, this "placing" is quite literal, as Jemison is racialized by and within the domestic spaces she inhabits, which become spaces for racialized relationships. As such domestic spaces operate at various scales, I will first attend to the smallest, in the realm of the family. Here we see a narrative of Jemison's physical removal from her white family and placement into a Native family, a removal and placement that effectively re-racialize her. And, like the re-racialization of Desdemona, Jemison's racialization is decidedly gendered; this capacity for re-racialization is applicable specifically to white women. In Jemison's case, however, race is imagined not to adhere to her gendered body, but her gender determines her transferability to differently racialized domestic spaces of belonging. This belief about white women's racialization reveals the underlying imagined "threat" governing the captivity narrative: the idea that white women's physical removal from white society and white family (and hence white male domination)—not only their participation in interracial sex—threatens their whiteness. In Jemison's case, it is not simply captivity but adoption—signaling a permanent rather than a temporary removal from white society—that displaces her whiteness.

The idea that white women, through adoption, might be physically removed from whiteness and placed into another space of racialization is not unique to Jemison's narrative. We see this theory of gendered racialization play out in the determination of Indian identity in federal Indian law, particularly in the infamous court of Chief Justice Roger Taney. Ironically, this belies ideas of race as permanent and as biological. Narratives of white women's racial precariousness suggest the construction of race beyond the bodily scale. The 1846 Supreme Court case of *United States v. Rogers* begins with a question of jurisdiction for a murder trial.[38] Whether William S. Rogers (a white man who claimed to have been adopted into a Cherokee tribe) was to be tried by federal or Cherokee courts depended upon the legal determination of his racial identity. As the case approached the Supreme Court, Rogers's alleged murder of Jacob Nicholson took a back seat to the question of identification it raised: can a white man, adopted into the Cherokee tribe, become an Indian? Eric Cheyfitz points to a tension between bio-logic and cultural logic in determining Native American identity in the discourse of federal Indian law, illuminating the problem of determining Indian identity solely on the basis of blood quantum while diminishing the importance of tribal recognition and community. Two potentially conflicting definitions of "Indian" emerge from this tension. Discussing *United States v. Rogers*, Cheyfitz writes, "it should be emphasized, adoption by the community did *not* make an 'Indian,' a Western racial-political category, but a community member, a person belonging to a Native cultural category."[39] Ultimately, the case is specifically concerned with a biologically and racially conceived legal definition of "Indian," and concludes that Rogers, though adopted by the Cherokee tribe, is "a white man, of the white race, and therefore not within the exception [of the law in relation to Indians]."[40] The peculiar wording of the *Rogers* decision, which explicitly refers only to white men, Cheyfitz notes, "suggests white youths and white females *can* become Indians through the cultural logic of adoption."[41] This distinction aligns with theorizations of white women as racially precarious in their potential to reproduce nonwhiteness.

Apart from their gender difference, William S. Rogers's adoptive situation is not dissimilar to Jemison's: he was a white man who claimed to have been adopted into the Cherokee community, and he had married a Cherokee woman with whom he had several children. Upon his adoption into the Cherokee tribe, Rogers claimed that he "became and continued to be one of them, and made the same his home, without any intention of returning to the said United States."[42] As with Jemison, Rogers's relation to Indians is framed as the confluence of kinship and space: with them was his home; his family was there. This case illustrates how personal racial identification is insufficient for determining racialization. However, the court is not concerned with whether Rogers or Nicholson are accepted members of a Native community, the situation of their homes among—and comprised of—people who identify as Cherokee, or their relationships with Indian people or culture, as the *Rogers* decision refuses this logic of racialization. The court's final verdict tells us that Rogers "is not an 'Indian,' within the meaning of the law" because "no white man can rightfully become a citizen of the Cherokee tribe of Indians, either by marriage, residence, adoption, or any other means, unless the proper authority of the United States shall authorize such incorporation."[43] The emphasis on Rogers's apparently biological whiteness suggests that there is no way to become Indian in this determination, either via relations of kinship or the occupation of racialized domestic spaces.

Ultimately, the Rogers case is more concerned with who has the authority to determine Indian identity than with questions of what constitutes that identity. The case of *Rogers* also raises questions of blood quantum in its legal rendering of Indian identity, as it asks whether an 1834 trade act (interestingly called the Nonintercourse Act) can be applied to

> crimes committed by natives of the Indian tribes of full blood, against native Indians of full blood only; or do the said section and proviso have reference also to Indians (natives), or others adopted by, and permanently resident within, the Indian tribes; or have they relation to the progeny of Indians by whites or by negroes, or of whites or negroes by Indians, born

or permanently resident within the Indian tribes and limits, or to whites or free negroes born and permanently resident in the tribes, or to negroes owned as slaves, and resident within the Indian tribes, whether procured by purchase, or there born the property of Indians.[44]

I quote here at length to convey the complicated nature of this passage, which links notions of biological relatedness with relations of adoption, residency, and reproduction. Examining these things together, we see the problem of the metaphor of "blood" for determining identity in a society in which racial mixture, in its many possible forms, is undeniable.[45] The logic of blood quantum posits racialized identification as individual, independent of interpersonal relations of kinship and the occupation of racialized spaces. Moreover, this individualization of Indian identity means that one can be Indian even without access to Indian land, language, customs, or kin. By rendering "Indian" a purely biological, bodily category for racialization, the cultural basis for identity formation is replaced with something that the United States government can regulate. This framing of identity therefore threatens to devalue cultural practices and relationships as essential to Native identity by reducing them to the individual, bodily scale.

If the ideology of the different claims for men and women's racializing potential in the case of *Rogers* holds, the logic of whiteness and Indianness is a gendered logic with implications for expanding scales of racial reproduction. The logic that positions white women as particularly racially vulnerable suggests queer, "horizontal," and unidirectional genealogical trajectories of race. Karen Oakes points to this difference in her discussion of the unidirectionality of re-racialization, as "a European American woman could become a Seneca, but a Seneca woman, even a physically white Seneca woman, could never 'become' European American. Nor, for that matter, could her 'Indian' children."[46] The case of *Rogers* also suggests that either racialized Indianness might be transferred to women's bodies more easily than to men's (i.e., through the familiar heterosexual encounter by which men "give" and women "receive" race) or the cultural construal of "Indian" can be adopted more readily by women (who, perhaps in alignment with narratives of captivity, are perceived as more susceptible to cultural mobility than men). In either case, the result is that white women are positioned at the center of discourses of interracial marriage and racial reproduction. This positioning frames Indigenous kinship and belonging along the lines of what Rifkin calls "queer... forms of family formation" that resist settler colonialist norms of sexuality and nationhood.[47] This includes Jemison's own racial reproduction.

Kimberly TallBear notes how, throughout US history, "Growing the white population through biological reproductive heterosexual marriage . . . was crucial to settler-colonial nation-building."[48] The kinds of family formation in which Jemison participates refuse to reproduce whiteness, circularly connecting her own individual racialization to its genealogical (and geographical) reproduction. The domestic spaces in which Jemison and her family reside reveal intricate connections between racialized sexuality and racialized/racializing domestic spaces.

Sex, Land, and the Scales of Frontier Romance

A Narrative of the Life of Mrs. Mary Jemison is in direct conversation with literary texts that (like federal Indian law) come to impress upon relations of interracial kinship and domestic arrangements between white people and Native Americans in contested geographical spaces for racialization. Jemison's story has elicited numerous attempts to place her within the framework of the white woman's captivity narrative, attesting to an ongoing desire to render her story appropriate to the conventions of the genre, while wrestling with the problem of how to place a figure who is nevertheless often described in "transcultural" terms.[49] Scholars have had much difficulty placing Jemison's narrative within the genre of the captivity narrative because Jemison herself defies the role of the captive, ultimately choosing to stay with the Seneca—whom she regards as kin—throughout the rest of her long life. The text is therefore better understood in relation to other popular American literatures of the 1820s, as the discussions of writers such as Harry Brown, Annette Kolodny, and Ezra Tawil suggest, or—in keeping with readings by Susan Walsh and Laura Mielke—as Native autobiography.[50] In truth, the model of white womanhood with which Jemison is most closely related is not the captivity narrative but the frontier romance. This genre illustrates the intertwining of anxieties regarding the racialization of white women and the implications of racial reproduction for racialized settler and national spaces. In novels such as Lydia Maria Child's *Hobomok* (1824), James Fenimore Cooper's *Last of the Mohicans* (1826), and Catharine Maria Sedgwick's *Hope Leslie* (1827), the figure of the "white woman" in (potential or actual) interracial kinship relations with and occupation of domestic spaces alongside Native people is central to the storyline. These texts show the perceived dangers of the failure of white republican motherhood, as white women who refuse to reproduce structures of white domesticity refuse to reproduce the nation.

The moniker "White Woman of the Genesee" does not simply racialize Jemison but also locates her within Seneca territory. This relationship between racialization and residency illustrates the interlocking scales of domesticity that connect the racialized and sexualized body to spaces of home and nation. Jemison's continued residency within this space of Native identification, which she continually negotiates via her kinship relations, including those of refusing to reproduce whiteness, resists the kinds of white-settler colonial nation-building to which TallBear refers. She explains how "white bodies and white families in spaces of safety have been propagated in intimate co-construction with the culling of black, red, and brown bodies and the wastelanding of their spaces."[51] Jemison's racial reproduction refuses to be coopted for this kind of settler-colonialist propagation. Even while claims of Mary Jemison's whiteness persist, her narrative refuses a major trajectory of cultural whiteness in Jemison's relationships and residency within the domestic spaces that—quite literally—set her apart from the white womanhood of settler colonialism.

Jemison's relationship to Native domesticity is simultaneously formed through her relationships to kinship and land. This fits with popular discourses of republican motherhood, in which concerns about sex, family, domesticity, and property are not easily separated when questions of legitimacy and inheritance are taken into consideration. As with the popularity of *Othello* in the United States, it is clear why the emphasis on Jemison's marriages to two subsequent Indian husbands would be of particular interest to Seaver's readers (either as titillating or horrifying details) despite the difference of her narrative from prevalent tales of white women and Indian men in the frontier romance. As with Mary King and Desdemona, however, we would be mistaken in regarding objections to interracial marriages as solely concerned with maintaining either the racial or cultural "purity" of white women. Peggy Pascoe and others have argued that white anxieties about interracial marriage in the United States were deeply invested not only in interracial sex but also in the retention of white privilege regarding the inheritance of property and, especially, land. While laws prohibiting interracial marriage were inextricable from issues of gender and sexuality (with many laws dealing specifically with demarking the racial groups with whom white women could not legally marry), Pascoe notes that "marriage between white men and Indian women was ... intimately linked to American land settlement," and therefore often recognized by legislators.[52] Here we see the connections between familial domesticity and the domestic realm of the nation, as Native, non-heteronormative domesticity upsets settler colonialist projects of allotment, inheritance, and nation-building, as well as those of racial reproduction. As the case of *Rogers* suggests, the perceived difference between the potential for white women and white men to become Indians might also be characterized as a greater governmental interest in the identification of potential citizens (white men) than in noncitizens (women and Indians), and in those individuals' relationships to land that could be claimed for US nation-building.

If, as Pascoe holds, marriage was used "to confirm the land and property rights of White husbands," marriages between Indian men and white women—two already legally disenfranchised groups when it came to property rights—do not figure heavily in the literature on anti-miscegenation law in the United States.[53] June Namias similarly identifies concerns regarding Indians and land that were prevalent during the early part of the century as coming to bear upon depictions of relations between white women and Indian men, explaining the racist justifications for Indian removal—"Certainly beastly men did not deserve to keep American land"—as paralleling anxieties about sexual relations between white people and Indians.[54] This parallel risks metaphorically figuring white women as potential "property" as well—the sexual property which supposedly "beastly" men do not deserve to "possess."

Namias acknowledges that "along with the will to take over Indian lands there appears to have been a covert anxiety that Indian men could indeed serve as attractive and companionate sexual partners."[55] One of its most significant divergences from the majority of women's captivity narratives (and the rhetoric of racially and sexually "pure" white womanhood one would expect to find there) is Jemison's relation to Indian men. Once adopted into a Seneca community, Jemison expresses no need for protection from Indian men, though she does describe white men as threats to her and her family. Jemison's is not a story of violation or degradation at the hands of Indians, as even the circumstances of her arranged marriage end in what she only describes as a loving relationship. Still, even as she recounts the virtues of her first husband, a Delaware man named Sheninjee, Jemison must account for their interracial relationship as a potential problem for her Anglo-American readers. She nevertheless describes their relationship in terms of companionate marriage and happy domesticity, writing that:

> Yet, Sheninjee was an Indian. The idea of spending my days with him at first seemed perfectly irreconcilable to my feelings: but his good nature, generosity, tenderness, and friendship towards me, soon gained my affection;

and, strange as it may seem, I loved him!—To me he was ever kind in sickness, and always treated me with gentleness; in fact, he was an agreeable husband, and a comfortable companion. We lived happily together till the time of our final separation, which happened two or three years after our marriage.[56]

Jemison makes no further reference to the union of a white woman and an Indian man as a problem in her narrative, but this marriage seems to solidify Jemison's sense of belonging with the Seneca. Significantly, Jemison describes her feelings for Sheninjee explicitly as love. Resisting the racial proscriptions that would deny an Indian man ever to be "an agreeable husband, and a comfortable companion" to a white woman, Jemison's narrative provides an unusual—though not completely unheard of—account of a successful interracial marriage.

The implications of interracial sex for interracial domesticity thereby paints a clear trajectory from bodily racialization to racialization's larger scales. The frontier romance genre would dramatically illustrate these connections between sex, racial reproduction, and the racialized spaces of the nation, showing how expanding scales of domesticity translate spaces of sexual kinship into spaces of national belonging. The phenomenon by which white women who marry and reproduce with nonwhite men were said to forsake their racial identity is now familiar in this study, indicative of associations of white women's sexuality with racial allegiance to those we see in earlier readings of Desdemona and of Mary King.[57] And, as with Mary King, racial allegiance might translate easily to political alignment when one becomes kin to people who are oppressed by the state. In her discussion of the controversial marriage between Harriett Gold and Elias Boudinot, for example, Theresa Strouth Gaul similarly recounts the couple's "increasing embroilment in Cherokee politics" following their marriage, confirming fears that such political alignments might accompany kinship.[58] In the context of settler colonialism and nation-building, these political alignments are very explicitly to do with cultural and racialized relationships to the land itself.

The frontier romance genre places relations of sex and domesticity within the setting of the racially contested space of the frontier. Doing so, it presents a parallel between its racialized characters (and white women characters, in particular) and the US nation as similarly contested spaces of/for racialization. In these stories, white women and the land on which they reside are similarly racially precarious. Moreover, the circular relationship between racialized bodies and racialized spaces is what makes republican motherhood an essential concept for understanding the expanding scales and stakes of interracial domesticity. Cooper's and Sedgwick's frontier romances, for example, are both nationally and decidedly spatially oriented novels in which we can see how individual characters' (re)racialization have larger implications for national racial construction. By extending racialization from the bodily and familial to the national scale, these novels gesture toward the alternate theory of racialization I have been describing here, though not explicitly.

One of the most prominent early republican literary discourses on Indian-white interracial marriage is, curiously, about two marriages that never literally occur: Cora Munro's would-be forced marriage to Magua, and her marriage-in-death to Uncas in James Fenimore Cooper's *Last of the Mohicans*. Cooper writes that interracial marriage would be but a "horrid alternative" to Cora's death.[59] Here, interracial sexuality threatens Cora's claim to white womanhood and its couched assumption of sexual/racial purity. This threat is mitigated, of course, by Colonel Munro's revelation that his daughter Cora, born of a different mother than her fairer sister Alice, is "descended from that unfortunate class who are so basely enslaved to administer to the wants of a luxurious people."[60] That is, Cora does not have the claim to white womanhood that her sister does, according to societal rules of hypodescent. As Colonel Munro explains his daughter's racial genealogy to Duncan Heyward, "these unfortunate beings are considered of a race inferior to your own."[61] Cassandra Jackson notes the complicating of racial genealogy and sexuality as "Cooper injects slavery into the center of the national conversation about the expulsion of Native Americans," also evidencing the "mutually beneficial relationship between the practice of slavery and Indian removal."[62] The nation is built, then, through violent racial relations in domestic spaces.

Like Hawkeye's supposed cultural (though importantly not "cross-blooded") Indianness, Cora's cultural whiteness appears subordinate to her hypodescended racial genealogy. Still, she seems to have enough purchase in white womanhood for Hawkeye to reject the Delaware funeral song about the "future prospects" of Cora and Uncas at their dual interment. We read that he "shook his head, like one who knew the error of their simple creed," and that "[h]appily for the self-command of both Heyward and Munro, they knew not the meaning of the wild sounds they heard."[63] Though not suitably white enough to marry Duncan Heyward, Cora is apparently still white enough that these white men reject any semblance of her marriage to an Indian, even in death. Still, this imagined iconicity of Cora's whiteness—like Desdemona's—seems subject to racial marking. Though established, it is precarious, potentially changeable. Cora's failure of white womanhood is clearest in the text's refusal of her racial reproduction. Because her racial genealogy renders her unable to reproduce whiteness, Cora must be the "end of the line"; she cannot contribute to and must therefore be removed from the future white nation.

While *The Last of the Mohicans* is careful to foreclose any possibility of white-Indian marriage, Catharine Maria Sedgwick's more controversial *Hope Leslie* does not exclude white-Indian marriage from the captivity plot. In this story line, Hope's sister Faith is captured by the Pequot chief Mononotto, who has come to reclaim his children, Magawesca and Oneco, who have been servants to the white settler-colonist family who have adopted Hope and Faith. Several years later, Magawesca informs Hope of her sister's condition, telling her that she has married Oneco (who had saved her life on the occasion of her captivity) and helps to arrange a meeting between Hope and Faith, only for Faith and Magawesca to be captured by English soldiers. Although Magawesca is imprisoned, Faith is restored to the care of her sister's guardians. But Faith is not happy with her return to white domesticity; she remembers little of her sister or her childhood and can no longer speak or understand English. Ultimately, Faith is rescued by her husband Oneco, and returns to the family of her marriage. Like Mary Jemison, Faith resists the narrative of captivity in her refusal to reenter white society. Faith is never permanently reclaimed in *Hope Leslie*; her choice to remain with her Indian husband and family still stands at the conclusion of Sedgwick's novel.

Faith's Indianness is described in both cultural terms and in terms of kinship with her Pequot family, which has replaced what she no longer feels for her white sister. At their last meeting, we read that "there had been nothing in the intercourse of the sisters to excite Hope's affections," and thus she recognizes that Faith can no longer be her sister in feeling, despite their biological relation.[64] Further, Sedgwick describes Faith's sexual kinship in terms of its equivalency to biological relations, as Magawesca tells Hope that "she is dear to Mononotto as if his own blood ran in her veins."[65] This "as if" equates Faith's marriage with a blood relation, just as Mary Jemison's adoptive kinship is represented in terms of its equivalence to biological kinship. With Faith, as with Mary Jemison, kinship that is marked by relations of behavior rather than genealogy has not simply supplanted biological kinship but must be regarded on equal terms. Ultimately, the (re)racialization of both Cora and Faith, like Mary Jemison, illustrate race's relational, rather than genealogical, movement, and also the expanding spatial scales for race's simultaneous instantiation in relations to bodies and to nations.

As white republican mothers are tasked with keeping the proverbial racial Other out of the domestic spaces of the home, and therefore the nation, the frontier romance presents such women in terms of white supremacist anxieties that are not simply about sex but about nation-building in settler-colonial spaces. Jemison's narrative, too, contains fodder for such anxieties, which extend outward from Jemison's racialization to larger scales of domesticity. Perhaps the most compelling reason Jemison gives for remaining with the Seneca is her fear of how her children might be treated in white society, even by her biological relatives. Following the Revolutionary War, when her brother again offers her the opportunity to return to white society (though the chiefs wish her now-grown son, Thomas, to remain) she explains:

> Another, more powerful, if possible [reason for remaining, apart from not wanting to leave Thomas] was, that I had got a large family of Indian children, that I must take with me; and that if I should be so fortunate as to find my relatives, they would despise them, if not myself; and treat us as enemies; or, at least with a degree of cold indifference, which I thought I could not endure. Accordingly, after I had duly considered the matter, I told my brother that it was my choice to stay and spend the remainder of my days with my Indian friends, and live with my family as I had heretofore done.[66]

Significantly, Jemison expresses no similar fears about raising her half-white children among the Seneca. There is a conspicuous absence of dualism in Mary Jemison's narrative when she discusses her white and her Indian families: she explains her feelings of adoptive kinship in terms of blood relations and she names her "Indian children" after her blood relatives who have been murdered by the Shawnees, obscuring the supposed racial lines of separation between those she identifies as kin. But the domestic spaces she occupies for the remainder of her life reveal her prioritization of Seneca kinship and belonging, as her relationships to these spaces of domesticity racialize her and her family.

Much like Mary King, Jemison understands how white racism threatens her family and she (quite literally) positions herself accordingly. The frontier romance often frames this positioning in terms of where—and with whom—characters like Cora and Faith might belong. Interracial kinship is a fugitive kinship in this sense, as women like King and Jemison must seek spaces of safety for their nonwhite families. This fugitive kinship is also incompatible with white, republican motherhood. If, as Kerber holds, "the model republican woman was a mother"—and particularly, a mother of sons—she was a mother of *white* sons (i.e., future republican citizens) and not the Seneca children that Mary Jemison raises, children who might be figured as potential enemies (or, at the very least, "foreigners") by Jemison's biological relatives.[67] In Child's *Hobomok*, the question of reproducing republican citizens plays out in terms of assimilation and removal from white domestic spaces. Mary Conant decides to marry Hobomok after her true love, Charles Brown (a white suitor rejected by Mary's father because of his religious beliefs), is believed to have been killed at sea. Mary eventually comes to describe Hobomok as "almost like an Englishman" in his suitability as a companion, and the couple have a son together.[68] Still, their happiness is foreclosed when Mary's initial betrothed returns, alive(!). Hobomok graciously steps aside, divorcing Mary and literally disappearing into the west so that she and Charles can be together.

Perhaps more surprisingly, Child's novel compensates for the problem of interracial motherhood through the complete assimilation of Mary Conant and Hobomok's son into Anglo-American culture. Raised by his mother and Charles Brown after his biological father's departure, we read in the novel's conclusion that Charles Hobomok Conant is fully incorporated into the white society of this nuclear family and educated at Cambridge in England. Moreover, "his father was seldom spoken of; and by degrees his Indian appellation was silently omitted."[69] Retaining only the names, religion, and culture of his white parents, the Indian child becomes, in effect, white, despite any biological claims to "mixed" race. Though many white Americans regarded African Americans as "beyond the reach of mixture" (as Thomas Jefferson famously claimed), the belief that Indians both could and ought to be assimilated into white society was rather common in the early republic.[70] This form of genocidal erasure through assimilation would, of course, become most prominent in attempts to assimilate Native children into white settler-colonialist societies by removing them from their communities and placing them in residential boarding schools or adopting them into non-Native families. Charles (Hobomok) Conant's ability to "become" white also allows for the retention of his mother's whiteness. An ultimately redeemable heroine in no small part due to the re-racialization of her son, Mary Conant is a potential prototype for the white republican mother as (despite interracial sexual kinship) she manages to (re)produce the white family.

Unlike Jemison, Mary Conant is therefore able and willing to contribute to the reproduction of the white nation, both by reproducing an apparently visually white male child and by producing the domestic space of the culturally white home. While this focus on companionate marriage may seem to obscure other factors of spatial and legal domesticity, in effect, *Hobomok* is a precursor to what Lydia Fisher calls antebellum "domestication narratives," as its ending sufficiently contributes to the project of nation-building that Fisher describes by expelling the "savage" elements of both the child and the woman from the home.[71] The child that Mary Conant raises will produce descendants who Child's readers can easily imagine constituting the early republic. Jemison's narrative, on the other hand, appears at least on the surface to foreclose a corresponding image of Seneca domesticity. The narrative places special emphasis on the violent deaths of her sons (Thomas and Jesse are murdered by their brother John, who is later murdered as well) while telling surprisingly little of the kin who survive her—Jemison's three surviving daughters and thirty-nine grandchildren. Seaver's narrative of Jemison's sons is therefore not only sensationalist but revisionist, as they trace these supposed failures of kinship in lieu of pursuing others. While Jemison's sons definitely matter in her narrative, they do not matter in all of the ways Seaver—and perhaps white readers—might expect them to. Their deaths do not represent the definitive "end of the line" for Jemison's family, which will extend her legacy of inheritance according to Seneca ideologies. That is to say, this legacy is both matrilineal (traced via daughters rather than sons) and Seneca (counting tribal belonging as inherited from Jemison herself, rather than adhering to racializations that would mark her as white). As we liken Jemison's narrative to the frontier romance, a nationally oriented literary genre, we might also recognize its alternative representation of scales of Seneca domesticity. This domesticity returns us to the contested spaces of tribal sovereignty that Jemison inhabits throughout her narrative.

Mary Jemison's Cabin

Mary Jemison's home perhaps has as its clearest geographic referent the domestic space of Gardow Flats (see figure 5.4). Even as she leaves the cabin of the African American men, she takes up residence in this space for most of the rest of her life. She tells us, "As that land became my own in a few years, by virtue of a deed from the Chiefs of the Six Nations, I have lived there from that to the present time."[72] On this land, Jemison hid in another cabin from the Dutchman who wanted to separate her from her family, and it is part of this land that she would later have stolen from her by a white settler with a nefarious claim of kinship. The land at Gardow is where Jemison and her daughters farmed to feed their family, where she became known to her neighbors as "the White Woman of the Genesee," and the home she ultimately had to

GARDEAU,—THE HOME OF THE " WHITE WOMAN,"—1872.

5.4 GARDEAU, THE FORMER HOME OF MARY JEMISON, AS IT APPEARED IN 1872, JAMES E. SEAVER, *A NARRATIVE OF THE LIFE OF MARY JEMISON, DEH-HE-WÄ-MIS*, SIXTH EDITION. BUFFALO, NEW YORK: PRINT HOUSE OF MATTHEWS BROS. & BRYANT, 1880 [C. 1877], PAGE 4. COURTESY OF THE AMERICAN ANTIQUARIAN SOCIETY.

leave to live out her remaining days at Buffalo Creek Reservation as the frontier of Jemison's narrative became more heavily populated by white settlers.

After living as a fugitive in this domestic space of self-emancipation and Native resistance to colonial imperialism, Jemison's relationship to Gardow would follow a familiar pattern, with infringements upon and thefts of Native lands, both at the hands of the federal government and those of individual white opportunists. The circumstances of Jemison's relationship to the land on which she lives and works are particular to her position as a "white woman among the Seneca"; that is, a woman whose land ownership is dependent upon both her position as a woman in a matrilineal society, as well as her position as a "white woman" whose marriages were with Indian men—men who do not have the same claims upon a wife (or her property) that white men would have under US laws of coverture. It is through her Seneca community that Mary Jemison acquires the land on which she lives with her family following the Revolutionary War, that she and her daughters farm, and where she resides into her old age. Through the 1797 Treaty of Big Tree (by which the Seneca sold all land east of the Genesee River), Jemison was formally granted land on Gardow Flats. Although this claim was opposed by

Red Jacket, a prominent member of the Seneca community, this land claim helped to further establish Jemison's identity as an Indian woman. However, as June Namias tells us, Jemison, her second husband Hiokatoo (a Seneca man who she married after her first husband's death), and their children are by this time positioned both geographically and metaphorically "between the encroaching white world and the beleaguered Indian one."[73] In 1816, white neighbors convinced Jemison to petition for US citizenship in order to gain legal title to this land. This she did, and gained official title to the land when she became a US citizen in 1817.

Jemison's relationship to Gardow foreshadows later attempts to force Native people into relations to land as individual property owners, rather than as members of sovereign tribes. The Dawes Act (also known as the General Allotment Act) of 1887 took land rights away from tribes and granted land ownership to individuals. It also promoted white settlement on "excess" land, continuing earlier white supremacist arguments that the Native "misuse" of land justified US programs of genocide and removal. The stakes of holding title to an Indian land claim becomes clear with the 1823 Supreme Court case, *Johnson v. M'Intosh*, involving a single plot of land in Illinois, sold to different people by both by the Piankeshaw and under a grant from the United States. The case was concerned with distinguishing "possession" from "ownership," questioning "the power of Indians to give, and of private individuals to receive, a title which can be sustained in the courts of this country."[74] After Jemison was granted citizenship she continued to live at Gardow Flats with some of her children and, with the title to her land, was able to give or sell portions of it to some of her white neighbors.[75] By gaining title to this land, Jemison's dealings became more secure than were she to have remained a non-titled possessor, but she did not have complete control over these legal dealings, which from this point forward were facilitated (not necessarily in Jemison's own best interests) by white male agents. According to her narrative, when Mary Jemison meets George Jemison, a man claiming to be a cousin biologically related to her through her white father, she allows him to use some of her land and to move his family there. With the help of one of Jemison's white neighbors and due to Jemison's own inability to read English, this supposed "cousin" then succeeds in swindling Jemison out of over four hundred acres in an agreement by which she had meant to give him only forty. Namias notes the significance of a white man scheming Jemison out of her land as representing another way in which she is marked as an Indian woman, as attempts to strip Jemison of her relationally and culturally defined Native identity are also accompanied by the eventual loss of most of her land.[76]

Despite these perpetual assaults on her land, Jemison's residency at Gardow serves to form spaces not of contestation but shared domesticity. The winter of 1779/80 also presents an extraordinary example of the domestic virtue by which Jemison is so closely characterized in Seaver's introduction, and one which he incorrectly associates with her whiteness: hospitality. Seaver writes, "Although her bosom companion was an ancient Indian warrior, and notwithstanding her children and associates were all Indians, yet it was found that she possessed an uncommon share of hospitality, and that her friendship was well worth courting and preserving."[77] Seemingly, Jemison's whiteness is that which allows her the capacity for this exceptional virtue of domesticity—a capacity that Seaver implies might have otherwise been inhibited by her familiar and familial associations with Indians. While Seaver tells us that "Many still live to commemorate her benevolence towards them when prisoners during the war, and to ascribe their deliverance to the mediation of 'The White Woman,'" the narrative that follows does not mark such hospitality as an expressly white—or "woman's"—quality.[78] It does, however, resemble the hospitality she receives in the cabin of the two self-emancipated Black men who help shelter and sustain her and her children. We read further in Seaver's introduction that "Her house was the stranger's home; from her table the hungry were refreshed . . . She was the protectress of the homeless fugitive, and made welcome the weary wanderer."[79] Once a "stranger" among the Indians and given a home, and made a "homeless fugitive" and a "weary wanderer" by the Continental Army before being taken into an African American domestic space in which she and her children could be supported, this brand of hospitality is not merely a "white woman's" virtue but the empathetic result of Jemison's experience with people who are willing to grant hospitality across racial lines.

Jemison's Seneca mother provides another example of hospitality, as she directs her children in the interpersonal relations that meant Mary was welcomed into their family. When one of Jemison's sisters wants to bring her to watch the public execution of prisoners, their mother chides her daughter, warning against taking Jemison to see a scene that might deepen her sadness at losing her biological family. The sympathy Jemison's mother exhibits here resembles the sympathy for the "stranger" that Seaver holds as exceptional in Jemison, and would err in attributing to her capacity as a white woman. If Jemison learns something of hospitality and sympathy from the two African American men with whom she and her children share a home, or from her Seneca mother who is so mindful of her sensitivity, these lessons in virtue cannot simply be attributed to her whiteness. Rather, the Anglo-American household that Jemison fails/refuses to produce is paralleled by the models of hospitable, interracial domesticity that she perpetuates.

I turn to Mary Jemison's cabin at Gardow—the one she shares with the two African American men, or where she hides from the Dutchman set on redeeming her, or that in which she and her Seneca family reside during their years there—as a marker that ties interracial models of domesticity to the domestic spaces in which such domestic behaviors of kinship take place. A domestic structure in the contested domestic space of the frontier, the cabin is precarious in many of the ways Jemison herself had been. Over almost half a century of her life residing in this domestic space, Jemison's land would dwindle as she and other Seneca were compelled to sell land at Gardow and other portions of their territories. In 1831, apparently because she had become "uncomfortable among the growing numbers of white settlers in the region," Jemison moved with her daughters to the Seneca's Buffalo Creek Reservation, near the city of Buffalo, New York. Jemison would sell her remaining two square miles of land at Gardow Flats two years before she passed away at the reservation in 1833.[80] This does not conclude Jemison's residency, however. Her remains were reinterred in the grounds of a Seneca Council House at what is now Letchworth State Park in western New York. Near her grave stands the "Jemison family cabin," which belonged to her daughter, Nancy, and which used to stand near her own at Gardow Flats (see figure 5.5). The cabin holds artifacts that belonged to Mary Jemison herself, including the original door to her cabin at Gardow.[81] Jemison is memorialized not only as a racialized individual, then, or only in relations of racial reproduction as in the statue depicting her and her child, but also in this marker of her residence. The cabin memorial speaks to Jemison's legacy of racialization, as a domestic structure that is framed belonging not only to her but to later generations of the Seneca kin whom she would produce.

The cabin of Jemison and her kin marks Native residence on this land, but the absence of additional markers of Native residence is misleading. Other domestic structures would be also be (re)moved, mirroring the patterns of violent displacement endured by other Seneca who once lived at Gardow. Practices of Indian removal contributed to the "vanishing" Indian trope, which sought to naturalize Native removal as "disappearance" from the land, downplaying the violence of settler-colonialist removal and genocide. As *An Authentic Narrative of the Seminole War* describes white settlers as "unfortunate families who were compelled thus to leave their late peaceful homes" as they fled violence from the people Native to that land, this framing of "home" and white victimhood is predicated on denying the original

5.5 JEMISON FAMILY CABIN, LETCHWORTH STATE PARK, NEW YORK. PHOTOGRAPH BY STEPHAN FIELDER AND SUE ANN FIELDER.

displacement of Indigenous people.[82] This historical revision appears in the contemporary context of US multiculturalism under the guise of universalizing relations to the land itself, in the pretense that "we are all immigrants" to the North American continent. Philip Deloria describes the popularity of this sentiment in white depictions of Native people during the Jacksonian era of removal, as popular images of Native people sought to erase a history of violent settler colonialism in order to imagine "one aboriginal, nature-loving family" that is "bound by a universal web of blood connections and their relations to the earth."[83] The next chapter takes up this kind of national imagining and appropriation of interracial kinship to extend the scales of racialization even further, from the genealogical scales of the racialized nation to evolutionary scales as well. Kinship expands racialization from space into time, implying a racialized nation that is defined not only geographically but also by its perpetuation into racialized futures that nevertheless cannot be predicted through linear genealogies or white supremacist ontologies.

Racial (Re)Construction

Interracial Kinship and the Interracial Nation

Race is a cultural, sometimes an historical fact.
—W. E. B. Du Bois, *Dusk of Dawn*

IN HIS NOTORIOUS *Notes on the State of Virginia*, Thomas Jefferson wonders "Whether the black of the negro resides in the reticular membrane between the skin and scarf-skin, or in the scarf-skin itself; whether it proceeds from the color of the blood, the color of the bile, or from that of some other secretion." He ultimately determines that race is "fixed in nature, and is real," no matter what "its seat and cause."[1] Despite the white supremacy and racial essentialism on which these ponderings are premised, Jefferson's metaphors are useful. Taking up the question of where race "resides" allows us to contemplate the specific limitations of Jefferson's search for race's bodily location and return instead to race's movement. I began this book with the metaphor of race's material transfer from the skin of one body to another in Desdemona's begriming, and I end with the expansion of race's spatial and temporal scale beyond individual racialized bodies. Here I mean to discuss the implications of interracial kinship that extend from the domestic spaces of family to queer genealogies that produce and reproduce the racialized and re-racialized nation.

One problem with Jefferson's racist analysis is that he attempts to locate race within the bodies of (only) Black people rather than, say, within the state of Virginia itself. Another problem, of course, is Jefferson's elision of racial mixture. When he argues that Black bodies cannot be politically incorporated into the (necessarily white supremacist) nation and may therefore necessitate removal "beyond the reach of mixture," he makes a temporal error.[2] By 1781, when Jefferson completed the first version of his text, he should have known that the proverbial ship of removing Black people "beyond" mixture with white people had sailed. Even at this early moment of nation-making, racial mixture was not a future threat but, as Du Bois might have it, (always) already a "historical fact." Early Americanists well know both this fact and Jefferson's error, which is exacerbated by the larger hypocrisy of his own racial reproduction. By attending to Jefferson's racism as a slippage of bodily, national, and temporal scales of racialization, we get at the crux of racial construction and its circularity.

Even in a landscape dominated by white supremacist theorizations of race's nature and significance, uncertainties about race as a category and radical opposition to racial oppression expanded understandings of race's complexity. The discourse of racial mixture was one particularly fruitful arena in which that complexity reveals itself. As Ralina Joseph explains, "the very ability to 'mix' races rests upon the premise that race is a stable and singular entity."[3] The texts I discuss here struggle with race's inability to be contained as their authors imagine the unwieldy nature of race's genealogies. In this chapter, I trace interracial kinship from past to present to future, also showing how genealogies of race are imagined to operate in increasing spatial scales from body to home to nation. Just as Mary Jemison's cabin reframes domestic space outside heteronormative, white patriarchal, and settler-colonialist frames of home, conceptions of the domestic nation are reframed by interracial kinship.

The novels I discuss in this chapter depict interracial families in their specific context within and in relation to the interracial nation. An evolutionary scale of interracial kinship emerges in Jerome Holgate's dystopian amalgamated city; Lydia Maria Child's language of interracial family reunites and reconstitutes a nation divided; and William Wells Brown's revisions of the mixed-race heroine frame a nation already and irrecoverably amalgamated at its founding. In these texts we observe interracial kinship as emerging reality, futurist possibility, or past and perpetually recurrent history. The relationships between these temporal scales are not teleological but queerly circular, as race is continually formed and re-formed at these various scales. For this reason, I do not organize this chapter's texts as dealing with chronological processes of race-making but understand that each of these texts understands racialization as oriented simultaneously toward more than one temporal moment. While I treat the language of mixed-race racialization and re-racialization in Holgate's and Child's texts, this is coupled with the recurrent namings and renamings that (as with *Pudd'nhead Wilson*) confuse discussions of Child's and Brown's novels, as individual names recur in their characters' queer inheritances and are changed or revised in subsequent novelistic retellings. These shifts in naming, too, are queerly circular, reminding us of the gothic apparatus by which familial/national/racial genealogies are never left in the past or with their individual bearers, but persist with the sustained possibility of their ghostly reappearance.

I begin by discussing the significance of queerly circular racialization as "racial reconstruction," acknowledging racial formation as never static or finished but always in the process of its own remaking. I then work through three literary imaginings of mixed-race people and their implications for theorizing race itself and the stakes of racialization in light of race's queer circularity. Holgate's *Sojourn in the City of Amalgamation* conflates racial scales of body, city, and nation, showing how these scales for racialization are not teleologically descended from one another, but mutually and simultaneously produced. The relationship between racialized bodies and racialized populations is not genealogical, then, but an ontological paradox in which each produces the other. I turn to Child's *A Romance of the Republic* to explore the linguistic as a metaphor for racialization that offers an alternative to essentializing notions of mixed "blood" and the biological more generally. Holgate's *Sojourn* and Child's *Romance* might be understood as opposite sides of the same coin. The former depicts a dystopian future of forced interracial kinship that inevitably produces national conflict, and the latter a utopian postwar future of racial reconciliation. These novels paint interracial kinship as unnatural and natural, respectively, and in the process make arguments not only about the morality or social acceptability of racial mixture, but also about the nature and conceptualization of race itself. Discourses of race as biological and as visual have dominated the language used to talk about it. Discussions of race (including, I will admit, my own) have therefore been inundated with metaphor as race is imagined as blood or, more often, as color.[4] Child's *Romance* shifts the dominant discourses of race as bodily and as visual toward a metaphor of the lingual, allowing readers to imagine race's malleability and unpredictable genealogical movement. Last, I take up Brown's *Clotel* in order to read his critique of racial essentialism as a temporal shifting of racial reproduction toward its inescapable circularity. Brown presents the project of racial reconstruction from a starting point of racial mixture rather than racial essentialism, exposing racialization and re-racialization as already queer in their resistance to any single teleology, as even siblings might be racialized differently from one another.

I deliberately place this discussion late in the book, even while discussions of these kinds of interracial kinship might have made logical sense earlier—even initially. I do this in part to emphasize the circularity of these theories of racialization. At the end we are, it seems, at a possible starting point of this conversation. Processes of racialization are not teleological but logically circular (more commonly called tautological), having no clear beginning or endpoint in their reasoning. By here introducing what might otherwise have been a starting point, I gesture toward the temporal queerness of racial genealogies, which we have seen sometimes follow nonlinear trajectories through time. I also delay this particular discussion of mixed-race bodies and their implications in order to avoid foregrounding the most seemingly racially essentialist arguments of this project, even as racial essentialism looms large as an unavoidable backdrop for anything termed "interracial." By placing this discussion of racial essentialism late, rather than early, I also hope to avoid anything like a narrative of racial progress from past to present as I unfold these theories of racialization. Instead, I mean to show how even the most essentialist discourses of race are themselves recursive, unfolding theorizations of race (and racism) that remain persistently relevant for the present moment, at which I will arrive in my conclusion.

Racial Reconstruction

Returning to the discussion of futurity, time, and circularity with which I ended part II, we might recall Morrison's gesture in *Margaret Garner* to the theft not only of kin but also of time. Garner removes kinship relations from worldly time, projecting these relationships into an interminable future. Garner's disruption of racial reproduction cannot be confused for what Nancy Bentley refers to as "interminable life," however, but as the disruption of structures of time and genealogy enacted by racial oppression. If normative genealogies are bounded by both heteronormative and worldly time, antiracist resistance defies familial and even ancestral loss by locating kinship relations outside time itself. This intertwining of time and family also speaks to a longer genealogical time, and the ties of kinship that are created—or not created—through genealogies of racialized inheritance. When we talk of genealogy we are really discussing time on a particular, generational, scale. In this scale of time we can see not only how relations are and are not made, but how racialization does and does not adhere to normative temporal inheritance. On this larger scale, one yet unarticulated truth within my study that has nevertheless informed the workings of racialization and relations throughout is a fact known perhaps better in the long nineteenth century than in our own historical moment: that mixed-race people are not a cure for racism. We need only look to Frederick Douglass, for example, a man who was likely biologically related to white people, to understand how this genealogical fact seems to have done little good in shielding him from various forms of white supremacist violence.

This chapter turns to narratives of mixed-race people that illustrate the queer circularity of racial reconstruction. Rather than simply rehashing nineteenth-century discourses of racial mixture, I seek to draw out the spatiotemporal connections these discourses make between body, family, and nation. These scalar dimensions of race prompt us to figure race's queer genealogy as recursive, not linear. Tracing race from body to family to nation (both as myths of racialization have done and as I have, perhaps ironically, organized the trajectory of this book) ultimately brings us full circle. If the white body reproduces the white family, which thereby reproduces the white nation, then that nation is supposed, in turn, to reproduce white bodies. Both the reasoning and the trajectory of this equation is circular: If the body is white, then the family is white; if the family is white, then the nation is white. Correspondingly, the nation is white because it is comprised of white families, which are white because they are comprised of white bodies. While this pattern would repeat into infinity, the confusion in this genealogy lies in its circular logic. Viewed in light of the simultaneous formation of race in individual bodies and in the larger racialization of populations, this racial genealogy reveals not simply the directionality of race's trajectories but their never-ending cycle.

Racial construction is never a complete process but is always part of a cycle of racial reconstruction. As we examine the processes of race-making with which my study is concerned, we can see that race is never simply "made" or even named, but in a perpetual state of making and remaking, articulation and rearticulation. I refer to the circular logic of race's collapsed scale and recursive teleology as racial reconstruction—the continual formation and reformation of race that has implications from the bodily to the national scale, and which is never completed but which necessarily continues *ad infinitum*. In this understanding of racialization, we might therefore recognize its social construction as impermanent, since bodies are not simply racialized but find themselves implicated in a constant state of race-making.

The argument that racialized bodies ultimately produce/are produced by racialized nations proves little about racial (re)production, revealing only the constant flux of racialization—not simply its construction but the necessity of its continual reconstruction. This logical fallacy becomes most evident, perhaps, in nineteenth-century discourses of racial mixture. White supremacist conceptions of the nation understand nation-building as inherently linked to white reproduction, and therefore the interracial family becomes a threat to the state. The imagined threat of nonwhite people to the state manifests itself often not in terms of power but in terms of place—that is, where race resides. Interracial bodies do not maintain imagined racial "purity," and integrated spaces do not maintain racial segregation. These facts simultaneously reveal race's location (at multiple scales) and its temporality, as race does not simply move through physical and temporal genealogies but around and within them.

In *Dusk of Dawn*, W. E. B. Du Bois declares that "Race is a cultural, sometimes an historical fact" in the midst of a dialog in which he acknowledges both genealogies of racial mixture and the circumstances by which Black people would be relegated to a particular, racialized location in a specific geographic space.[5] Here Du Bois shows that he understands notions of racial hypodescent, but his theorization of race is not simply essentialist. In this passage, Du Bois also connects scales of bodily and national spaces of racialization, admitting that he is related to white people "by Blood" and explaining that "the black man is a person who must ride 'Jim Crow' in Georgia."[6] What he comprehends here is the relationship between race's operation at different scales, as race does not simply "reside" in the body (as Jefferson would have it) but in the nation's larger racializing spaces, such as the Jim Crow car. Du Bois's scalar conceptualization of race is also evident in the process by which his autobiographical writing leads seamlessly into a sociological theory of race. In his "autobiography of a race concept," he refuses to extract individual racialized experience from this larger theoretical discourse of race, just as he refuses to figure race in purely individualized terms. Moreover, Du Bois's text figures racial construction as something that is not fixed or predetermined but unfolds over time—like autobiography. Importantly, Du Bois locates his experiences of race's larger "Problem" by gesturing to a temporal scale. It is, he writes, "the central problem of the greatest of the world's democracies and so the Problem of the future world."[7] Du Bois' bodily "Problem" reveals an autobiography of racial conception that is already complicated by racial mixture. That his race would be located not simply in the "mixture" of racialized "blood" but in the Jim Crow car reveals the recursive nature of race-making.

At the heart of racialization in a white-supremacist system is the anxiety that race, whiteness in particular, is precarious. This fear is in keeping with racial reconstruction's recursive structure, its queer circularity. The construction of race is often an attempt to pin it down, to define and delimit and control racialization through not only theoretical but political and legal means. Racialization is often just this—an attempt. To construct race is, culturally and historically, to attempt the impossible task of compartmentalizing racialized bodies that are already unable to compartmentalize race. Tracking the (imagined) locations of race at various scales has therefore been a wide-scale project of white supremacy. State-level anti-miscegenation laws, for example, reveal spaces of interracial kinship-as-threat, imagined as necessary for preserving white supremacy. Peggy Pascoe writes that "After the American Revolution . . . some Americans began to welcome the prospect of marriage between the self-consciously 'white' citizens of the new United States and the Indians whose land (quite literally) grounded the emerging nation." "Amalgamation" between white and Native people was even endorsed by such prominent figures as Thomas Jefferson, Patrick Henry, and William H. Crawford.[8] This was not the case for white-Black marriages, however, which were differently concerned with the inheritance of white property, even as these forms of white supremacy worked in tandem with one another. Anti-miscegenation laws were specific about which populations of nonwhite people white people were prohibited from marrying. The capacity of different races to be absorbed into the white nation apparently varied. While the complexity of anti-miscegenation laws paints an incomplete picture, their presence does illustrate an imagined movement of race that might also be used to metaphorize scales of racialization.

A series of maps show the presence of state anti-miscegenation laws in 1835, 1853, and 1867 (see figures 6.1, 6.2, and 6.3).[9] These are the respective years in which the main texts discussed in the final three sections of this chapter were published, and this span shows the physical movement of such laws as they spread across the still-expanding nation. Predictably, antiblack racism was often a specific component of this legislation, and—like all laws—it did not necessarily prevent interracial couplings (even while it may have prevented the issuing of legal marriage licenses) but made such couplings legally punishable until the Supreme Court overturned the marriage laws. The *Loving v. Virginia* case deemed anti-miscegenation laws

1835

■ Laws prohibiting interracial couples

■ No laws prohibiting interracial couples

☐ Official statehood precedes laws prohibiting interracial couples

▨ Not yet a state

6.1 LEGAL MAP: WHERE WERE INTERRACIAL COUPLES ILLEGAL? 1835. COURTESY OF
UNIVERSITY OF WISCONSIN–MADISON CARTOGRAPHY LAB.

unconstitutional in 1967—one hundred years after the last map I show here.[10] These maps therefore do not track interracial kinship but instead track the particular form of legislation against it; they track attempts at race-making. We see here a national scale of white supremacist efforts to contain race, attempts not only at racially constructing the nation but at reconstructing race in the national imaginary.

Like the transfer of blacking makeup from Othello to Desdemona, the spread of laws prohibiting interracial marriage across the nation suggests a metaphor for race's imagined transfer—or rather, the imagined prevention of race's transfer. In each map, race is constructed and reconstructed. The history of anti-miscegenation law creates one kind of narrative about racial construction. Grounded in notions of racial essentialism, such laws illustrate which kinds of interracial sexual kinship and domesticity are and are not legitimated by the state. Like the racial fact of who does/does not have to ride in the Jim Crow car in Georgia in 1940, laws that dictated who could/could not legally marry also sought to construct the bounds of racialization itself in their very assumption that racial categories could be easily defined. Ironi-

1853

■ Laws prohibiting interracial couples

■ No laws prohibiting interracial couples

□ Official statehood precedes laws prohibiting interracial couples

▨ Not yet a state

6.2 LEGAL MAP: WHERE WERE INTERRACIAL COUPLES ILLEGAL? 1853. COURTESY OF UNIVERSITY OF WISCONSIN–MADISON CARTOGRAPHY LAB.

cally, anxieties about race have often been at their heart anxieties about racial mixture and the difficulties of delimiting racial boundaries, even as racists would seek to legislate them. Just as these maps cannot show the extent of racial mixture throughout the nation, neither have individual bodies. Much like these maps of legislating interracial sexuality, then, mixed-race bodies become sites not only for racial construction, but for race's continued reconstruction.

Unlike Iola Leroy, the mixed-race characters studied in this chapter are not all anti-passing figures. Neither do they simply pass into whiteness. They are, however, racially reproductive in a way that defies hypodescent and compiles race as racial mixture. Scholarship in Critical Mixed Race Studies has begun to examine racial mixedness as a form of racial identification in itself. This form of racialization risks a seemingly inherent tendency toward antiblackness in its refusal of oppressed identities in favor of this newly created, third category, of "mixed" or "multiracial" identity. As Ralina Joseph puts it, "mixed-race African American representations . . . continue to be delimited by the racist notion that blackness is a

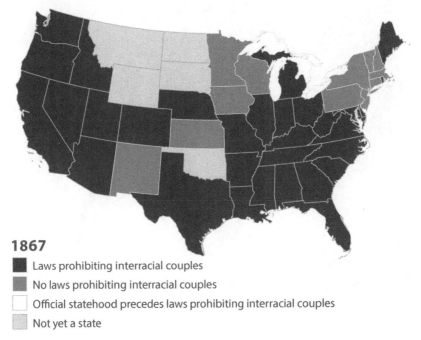

1867

■ Laws prohibiting interracial couples

■ No laws prohibiting interracial couples

☐ Official statehood precedes laws prohibiting interracial couples

▨ Not yet a state

6.3 LEGAL MAP: WHERE WERE INTERRACIAL COUPLES ILLEGAL? 1867. COURTESY OF UNIVERSITY OF WISCONSIN–MADISON CARTOGRAPHY LAB.

deficit that black and multiracial people must overcome."[11] Nineteenth-century narratives of amalgamation troublingly repeat this sentiment of antiblackness—or, as Du Bois would have it, the line of racial demarcation that defines where Blackness begins and whiteness ends—as a "problem." There is, of course, something anachronistic in imposing any twentieth- or twenty-first-century sense of "multiracial" identity upon nineteenth-century figures. While my primary texts in chapters 3, 4, and 6 grapple with antiblackness in their understandings of racial mixture, I am interested less in their potential for Blackness's erasure (a potential I want to acknowledge, nonetheless) than I am in their proliferation of racial (re) production, in ways in which Blackness is neither hypodescended nor entirely whitewashed.

The language used to discuss racial mixture reveals fundamental ideas about race. In this chapter, I read the language with which racial mixture was discussed in the nineteenth century as itself a subtle (even insidious) mode for racial theorization. The language of racial mixture is itself indicative of the queer circularity of racial (re)construction, articulated through race's imagined connections to body, family, and nation through both time and space. The scalar/temporal shift to which I turn at the end of this project shows again how queer racialization is not individualistic but spatially and temporally expansionist, collapsing the body/family/nation paradigm and revealing the circularity of this logical relation. Anxieties about what we may now more familiarly term "integration"—the mixing of races within US national spaces and among national populations—are, from the early republican period on, inextricable from anxieties about what later comes to be commonly called "miscegenation"—referring explicitly to interracial sex and reproduction. Both sets of anxieties are implied by and at times conflated within the term often used in early republican discourse on racial mixture: "amalgamation." The *Oxford English Dictionary* gives this popular definition of "amalgamation" as "The action of combining distinct elements, races, associations, into one uniform whole."[12] The term therefore comes to refer both to the creation of "amalgamated" national populations as well as "amalgamated" bodies. It is with this dual notion of "amalgamation"—and the simultaneous scales of racialization at the level of the body, family, and nation that this term implies—that I read Holgate's *A Sojourn in the City of Amalgamation*.

What Amalgamation Is!

Jerome Holgate's *A Sojourn in the City of Amalgamation* is a racist dystopian novel concerned with anxieties about the interracial family and genealogy.[13] Written under the pseudonym "Oliver Bolokitten," Holgate's novel offers a profoundly racist vision of an integrated society. In Holgate's futuristic imagined city, white inhabitants enter interracial marriages not because of interracial love or romance (which Holgate cannot conceive), but because of a shared societal duty to Black people and to uphold abstract philosophical principles of amalgamation. Much of the novel is devoted to the traveling narrator's exploration of the city, and his ruminations on its logical and logistical problems. In the spirit of biological racism, *Sojourn* argues that the source of the supposed repulsion between Black people and white people (a point that Holgate both assumes and describes in the most racist parts of the text) is a physiological matter, lying in the "effluvia," which "exhales from [the] blood" of Black people and is received unfavorably in the noses of the white people, who must undergo a process of "perfuming" in an invasive "bottling operation" to counter their "natural" reactions to Black people's supposed odor.[14] These sensationally described, painful, and traumatic medical procedures are performed to render interracial couples more compatible, but they do not work entirely. Amalgamationist white people must constantly fight the apparent physical repulsion they feel toward their spouses, and some are unsuccessful, as white men frequently vomit in the presence of their Black wives.[15]

Though extreme to the point of absurdity in its racism, *Sojourn* is of the same cloth as any of the racist arguments against interracial kinship with which this project has been concerned. While this text is not known to have had a wide circulation beyond Holgate's local circle, this extremist novel is not an exceptional production but representative of a larger cultural racist sentiment that would be evidenced by legal prohibitions and social sanctions against interracial marriage and broader conversations about interracial sexuality, particularly those that deemed interracial kinship "unnatural." The anti-amalgamationist sentiment behind Holgate's *Sojourn* is common to early republican discourses on racial mixture, especially scientific theories of racialization and racism that have long been at the heart of Anglo-American discussions of race and particularly those involving questions of racial equality and national belonging. The conflation of abolition and amalgamation had become a common trope by the time of several anti-abolitionist riots of the 1830s. During the July riots of 1834, accusations of promoting amalgamation were directed at (and refuted by) prominent abolitionists such as William Lloyd Garrison and Arthur Tappan in the popular press. Elise Lemire links *Sojourn* to the July riots of 1834 in New York City, noting that the anxieties it expresses are very close to those expressed in the anti-abolitionist conflation of abolition and amalgamation in popular commentary on the riots by writers such as James Watson Webb. Much of the violence around these riots was directed at people who had been rumored to promote amalgamation.[16] In this sense, Holgate is in alignment with racist political cartoonists like Edward Williams Clay, the producers of blackface minstrel productions of *Othello*, and the white supremacist mob that would separate William Allen and Mary King. Holgate's representation of amalgamation presents interracial sexuality and kinship as a national crisis, an imminent threat to the white-supremacist nation.

Importantly, Holgate's illustrations of white supremacist anxieties reveal worries not about interracial futures, but the interracial present, as mixed-race bodies themselves become a point of obsession in addition to that of interracial sex. Recognizing the racially precarious nature of racially ambiguous bodies, discussions of theories of racial hypodescent, and anxieties about the reproduction of whiteness, we can also trace Holgate's obsession to a national ideology of assimilation. This racial trajectory is productive of race, but not reproductive. That is, it is concerned not only with racial reproduction but also with non-reproduction: Racial futurity is not guaranteed. Race might always be reconstructed. The theory of hypodescent is not just one of reproducing oppressed races, then, but also a theory of how whiteness might be absorbed, erased, folded into racial nonwhiteness. Hence white racist anxieties about racial mixing are always predicated upon not only others' racial proliferation, but of whiteness's disappearance. This white supremacist anxiety thereby masks its own violence. Similar to the captivity narrative's centering of white victimhood and obscuring of settler colonialist violence against Native people, anti-amalgamation literature imagines whiteness itself as under threat. This imagined threat necessarily conflates the scales of amalgamation, registering racialization in the racial mixture of the body, family, and nation. In this chapter, I am interested in moving between early republican discourses on racially "mixed" populations in the United States and growing anxieties about populations of racially "mixed" people, a conflation that represents the scalar and temporal genealogical dimensions as well as the stakes of racialization.

The assumptions of preexistent racial "distinction" that the term "amalgamation" necessitates evokes speciesist arguments of racialism and racism, which Holgate employs in his representation of a twentieth-century "amalgamated" United States. The scientific racist employment of species was, as David Walker charged, an attempt to deny various nonwhite people acceptance as part of the human family.[17] I turn to the scientific racism of evoking race-as-species in order to highlight how this type of racist rhetoric (for which Holgate's novel is, again, not exceptional but exemplary) pushes arguments about the racialization of the body, family, and nation even further, toward the even deeper genealogical scale of racializing humanity. As genealogies of interracial racialization are taken from body to family to nation to species, race's queer teleology produces a circular argument about race: races ought to be separate because races *are* separate. This argument's stipulation is disproven, of course, by amalgamation. The fact that supposed racial "purity" is not perpetually (re)produced presents a crisis for explaining racialization. Holgate's familiar anti-amalgamationist racism presents the interracial body, family, nation, and/or species as a dystopian crisis of racialization.

Throughout the novel, Holgate continually dodges the reality that the presence of mixed-race people proves: that these "racial gradations" are not as "distinct" as white racists have habitually imagined them to have been. The designation of racial "mingling" as "unnatural" led not only to debates about the integration of different racially designated populations in the United States, but also to assumptions about the ever-growing population of racially mixed people in the early American republic, a population that Holgate refuses to acknowledge in the present by projecting this racial mixture into a dystopian future. However, the present state of racial amalgamation appears in the figure of Boge Bogun, a mixed-race person whose racially conflicted body is described as—literally—at war with itself. This metaphor of bodily war echoes Alexis de Tocqueville's famous study of the United States, in which he characterizes "whites and emancipated Negroes . . . placed upon the same land like two alien nations."[18] Tocqueville predicts that "only two possibilities exist for the future: either Negroes and whites must blend together completely or they must part."[19] Framing these two possibilities as bodily rather than national conflict, Holgate's novel metaphorizes the interaction between and effectively collapses these scales of racialization.

While Holgate presents his novel as a description of a dystopian future of amalgamation, his works on biblical and American genealogy look backward to explain the racial makeup of the American nation. In *American Genealogy*, Holgate admits that the United States is already "amalgamated and constituting one people of a different extraction from any that now exists," but argues that "a suffusion of Anglo Saxon blood" is the predominant characteristic of the American population.[20] This genealogical discussion of the forming of an apparently white American population, like Holgate's work on race and biblical genealogy (via a familiar racialist argument about the origins of racial divisions in the twelve tribes of Israel), is related to theories of scientific racism and racialism that would gain popularity in the early American republic and against which anti-racist arguments articulating Black humanity would necessarily push.[21] Theological tracings of races to biblical history and (hence) inheritance, and scientific understandings of race as species, extend the scales of racialization well beyond the nation to Christendom and even humanity. Floating above the body/family/nation paradigm of racialization, then, we perceive the thread that confirms Walker's observation of the overarching attempt to deny humanity to nonwhite people. This can be seen in places like Louis Agassiz's changing views on whether Black people constitute a different species from white people, and Samuel Morton's and others' attempts to claim Egyptian history and civilization for white history by claiming that the ancient Egyptians were of the Caucasian race.[22] Other writings on "amalgamated" populations, like Benjamin Rush's 1799 writing on Blackness as a sexually contagious disease and Josiah Nott's 1843 discussion of "hybrid" people as an "unnatural" or "contaminated" population (because of their potentially interspecies conception and beliefs in the supposed eventual sterility of racially mixed people), help to make sense of the racism of Holgate's *Sojourn* and explain the connections between theories of race, family, nation, and human kinship.[23]

The non-presence of Black people in Holgate's national histories (despite their acknowledged presence in the geographical space of the American nation) implies the naturalization of racial separatism. This common view mirrors Thomas Jefferson's discussion of race in *Notes on the State of Virginia*, where, making claims about the apparent fact and significance rather than the nature of racial difference, he asks, "Will not a lover of natural history . . . one who views the gradations in all the races of animals with the eye of philosophy, excuse an effort to keep those in the department of man as distinct as nature had formed them?"[24] This naturalization of race manifests in Holgate's novel as an essentialist (rather than merely a separatist) racist argument, as Holgate uses the metaphor of species to describe racial difference. I am less interested here in Holgate's racist likening of Black people to nonhuman animals (a well-worn racist trope) than in the attention to the problem of classifying racially mixed people in his *Sojourn*. I would therefore like to consider this particular vein of racism—the attempted removal of Black people from categories of humanity necessary for membership in the American nation— alongside accompanying problems of acknowledging and understanding racially mixed people's position with relation to national inclusion or exclusion. Prior to writing *Sojourn*, Holgate had argued in support of colonization during a debate in his hometown of Utica, New York. There is, of course, a false philanthropy in Holgate's support for colonization, which is revealed at the end of his novel, and the positioning of his dystopia as a probable result of not allowing colonizationists to carry out plans to remove Black bodies from the United States.[25] This turn to colonization is in accord with racial separatist arguments along a broad spectrum of antebellum political positions.

Holgate's investment in racial separatism turns to the bodily scale of racialization in the novel's divergent *mise en abyme*, "The Memoirs of Boge Bogun, with an Account of the War which Took Place in His Own Body between the Differently Colored Particles of Flesh, and the Consequent Result." We read this story in part through this phenomenal person's memoir, in which he explains the union of his parents, "a stout bodied negro" and a beautiful "English lady," brought about by a "rigid amalgamationist" grandfather despite the fact that his "poor mother . . . abhorred the disgusting idea."[26] During his sojourn, our narrator attends an exhibition of Bogun, described as "a man half black, half white; the lower half being black, the upper half white; the line dividing the two colours being clear and distinct."[27] Unlike Rice's Young Othello, however, Bogun's racial division is not relegated to the surface of his body, but rather within. Holgate goes on to represent racial mixture as an internal war between "white" and "black" "particles" of Bogun's genealogy that are vying for his various body parts. Most of Bogun's story reads as a narrative of these battles. The physical illnesses white people experience in the novel's interracial relations are revisited here in the body of a mixed-race child of such a coupling.

Oddly (and despite the physical location of Blackness in the lower half of his body), the bulk of Bogun's memoir removes the question of interracial sex from the body/family/nation equation, recognizing amalgamation as already having happened at other temporal and generational scales even while confining the "problem" of amalgamation to an individual, bodily one. Bogun's illness, figured as battle scene between two competing populations, might then be understood in its possible effect on entire populations of white people, as suggested in the extremist position that amalgamation will result in the end of human existence, as scientist Josiah Nott suggests in 1843.[28] While Holgate's text imagines a futurist dystopia of racial mixing, the section in which he turns to the fetishization of the mixed-race body brings his discussion of amalgamation into a different scalar perspective. This section reveals Holgate's anxieties not about racial mixture as an imminent threat but as already having occurred. The war in Bogun's body has been won. Racial purity is not a presentist reality. The body of the nation is an amalgamated body and can only be un-amalgamated through violent means that may put the bodily whole into jeopardy.

The body of Boge Bogun is, of course, a microcosm of the city of Amalgamation itself and of the "amalgamated" American nation, as the problem of an already racially mixed United States is translated to a bodily scale. In the midst of his story, the white and black "particles of flesh" become, alternately "Whites" and "Blacks," and occasionally, "English" and "Africans." The ultimate triumph of the "Whites" is no small metaphor for the racial separatist project of colonization as we read that "From that time to this all has been quiet in my body."[29] By imagining the possible separation of the races and by relegating amalgamation and mixed-race people to a dystopian future, Holgate denies the contemporary and historical racial reality of the nation that includes racially "mixed" people who cannot be un-amalgamated as the two segregated halves of a "mixed" body. Holgate cannot parse racialization at the bodily level, and can only achieve it by moving to the larger scale of racial relations between sexual partners and national populations. The racial danger that looms here is that the war in Bogun's body has not been won definitively, but may resurface as another racial conflict—or racial (re)construction—either within his own body, or in subsequent generations. The "War which Took Place in His Own Body" is an ancestral war, a war of differently raced genealogies. The internal problem of bodily classification articulated in the question of how this body is racialized impends upon how people might treat that body in a white-supremacist nation. Holgate's most prominent representation of the mixed-race body is one that is quite literally internally conflicted. Although Holgate locates this conflict within the body (rather than upon it), the real conflict lies outside it, as the nation attempts to determine (and is in the process of continually determining) how racially mixed bodies might figure in the United States.

I turn now to another consideration of the language of race-making and racialized relations. Departing from bodily metaphors of race as color, blood, or "particles of flesh," as well as from the discourse of racial mixture as "amalgamation," Lydia Maria Child's *A Romance of the Republic* not only describes racial mixing as utterly natural but also calls attention to the confluence of constructing and articulating race. Child's post–Civil War novel imagines interracial kinship as a template for national racial reconciliation. This future-looking historical fiction works against the whirlwind of attempts to name race and racial mixture by offering a different metaphor for thinking about race: language. While, as Debra Rosenthal has discussed, the novel's naturalization of racial mixture works against racist scientific arguments about amalgamation as unnatural, *A Romance of the Republic* also poses the question: What does it mean to frame race as language—not simply to conflate race and something like "culture," but to use language as a metaphor for race and race's genealogical movement? This metaphor suggests that race does not necessarily have definitive or unilateral origins or markers but is figured and refigured through unpredictable trajectories and complexly intertwined genealogies. Much more than notions of blood or color, the metaphor of racial mixture as "polyglot" language is in keeping with the concept of racial reconstruction that I have discussed here.

The "Polyglot" Family of the Republic

Child's *A Romance of the Republic* demonstrates the rhetoric of white womanhood in antebellum and Reconstruction-era narratives of racial mixture and national kinship, reimagining the mixed-race heroine via a narrative of race and national (re)union.[30] While much attention has been given to the preservation of national racial separatism with regard to laws about interracial marriage and the denial of citizenship to nonwhite people, some narratives of race and kinship not only acknowledged the fact of racial mixture in nineteenth-century America but celebrated it. Like other mixed-race heroines both before and after them, Child's protagonists, Flora and Rosa, only learn of their mixed-race heritage following their father's death. Their parents' marriage, because of their enslaved mother's status, was not legitimate, and his impending debt (of course) causes the daughters to be sold with the rest of their late father's "property." After an appropriately sensational series of events, Flora and Rosa (who do not die) marry white men who are fully aware of their wives' African ancestry. Both women's husbands and Flora's adult son fight in the Civil War, surviving to return to their happy family, which does not hide the fact of their African American ancestry, but embraces it alongside other, European origins, all of which are assimilated into a model of the American "polyglot" family.

Countering anti-amalgamation literature like Holgate's *Sojourn*, Child rejects tropes of white women's racial "purity" in favor of a radically pro-amalgamation agenda. As in Brown's revisions of *Clotel* and in later African American revisions of the mixed-race heroine by writers such as Frances Harper, Julia C. Collins, and Charles Chesnutt, Child here departs from her earlier "tragic" mixed-race protagonists to write characters more closely resembling the heroic mixed-race figures of postwar African American women's fiction. Differing from the majority of anti-passing narratives, however, Child's mixed-race figures work to reimagine racial mixture not as a hypodescended branch of African America, but as the emerging predominant genealogy of white America. In one way, we might view Child's novel as exhibiting an early version of the "melting-pot" multiculturalism that would become increasingly popular over the second half of the twentieth century: *Romance* re-racializes its seemingly white women characters as mixed-race heroines who are uniquely able to incorporate racial mixture into models of the interracial family and therefore the interracial nation.

Critiques of Child's final novel acknowledge her problematic assimilationist framing of mixed-race heroines while disallowing other Black characters (i.e., those without known white ancestry, whose Blackness is visible, and whose formal education has not matched that of her privileged protagonists) from similar incorporation into the novel's forms of familial and national domesticity. When read in comparison with texts like Harper's *Minnie's Sacrifice* and *Iola Leroy*, Child's novel is decidedly less radical because of its inability to imagine mixed-race women who identify as and with Black people. Nevertheless, I explore the useful implications for rethinking the novel's re-racializations via the figure who holds the potential for reproducing not only whiteness but as reproducing the racially mixed family and nation.

The idea of the United States as an already amalgamated nation was not new by the time Child wrote *Romance*. Proponents of scientific race theory had argued that the Anglo-Saxon race was itself also inherently amalgamated. Most surprisingly, they presented this particular kind of amalgamation as an advantage, despite their simultaneous—and contradictory—arguments that the amalgamation of the Black and white races would result in degeneration or even in sterility and the ultimate end of the human race. In some sense, *Romance* (though somewhat condescendingly) figures other kinds of supposedly non-assimilable people (e.g., African Americans, Jews) as incorporable into the white family and white nation, much as writers like Thomas Jefferson argued that Native American people would be. Jefferson's argument for Native assimilation is a project of obviously genocidal "disappearing" of Indians from the national landscape in which whiteness was supreme, uncomfortably similar to Child's earlier incorporation of Charles ~~Hobomok~~ Conant into whiteness only through the erasure of his Indian name and kin. Child's novel's assimilationist project more clearly refigures whiteness as unthreatened by racial amalgamation because whiteness is itself already amalgamated in its capacity to absorb (certain kinds of) racial assimilation.

We might characterize Child's project in *Romance* not only as assimilating Blackness but as retheorizing whiteness, using the metaphor of language to produce not simply assimilation of other races into whiteness, but whiteness's inherent permeability to supposed racial difference. The "polyglot" family Child describes is a metaphor for this type of racially absorptive white racialization. At the beginning of the novel, Alfred King proclaims, "What a polyglot family we are! Your grandfather's Spanish, your grandmother's French, and your father's English, all mixed up in an *olla podrida*."[31] Later, Flora repeats this assessment, commenting on her children's use of the German pet name *Mein Lieber bruder*, in tribute to their father's birthplace. By the end of the novel, African ancestry has also been added to this mix. Child's novel reads as a response to racial separatist arguments about the nation, painting a picture of national postwar reunion that is not about the reconciliation of the North and South, but about the recognition of African American ancestry and an incorporation of this recognition into ideas about an amalgamated American identity.

Refiguring the white woman with regard to her participation in interracial kinship relations ultimately refigures both her participation in the racialized nation and the nation itself. Ending her novel with a happy, interracial, poly-glot family, Child offers another microcosm of the postwar national family. While Brown orients his novel toward the past by constructing his heroine through her relation to the third president of the United States, Child frames her "romance" in futurist terms, staging her mixed-race-heroine narrative in the landscape of Civil War drama that produces a new era of racialization. In *Sojourn*, Holgate compares race to both species and contagion. His pairing of animals is forced and unnatural, and is coupled by images of illness and disease. Alternatively, in Child's novel, the blending of plants in pairings and cross-pollinations and language's blending and cross-communication are naturalized. Imagining race in terms of plants allows Child to rethink race's genealogical trajectories as slipping seamlessly into a future of racial repro-duction.[32] Departing from narratives of white women's perpetuation of ra-cial purity, Child theorizes race as mixed, complex, and—importantly—not static, but continually remaking itself.

The fluidity of language in Child's "polyglot" families is a fitting meta-phor for the fluidity of racial construction. Like "amalgamated" races, lingual relations defy completely neat separation; neither are essentially discreet or fixed. Languages change and absorb parts of other languages, blurring boundaries and confounding notions of linguistic purity. Neither does the mixture of languages mark degeneration. In the metaphor of the "poly-glot" family, Child's conception of racial mixture is transferred from what is embodied to what is articulated. This moves race from the metaphor of amalgamated material to that of blended languages. We might regard Child's framing here as an argument about race's construction. It is made as it is spo-ken; it is malleable, it is transferrable, it is changeable, it can be amalgam-ated quite naturally. Languages cannot be definitively contained, but flow into one another over time, as words and phrases are adopted and absorbed, claimed and incorporated. Along these lines, Greg Carter likens racialization itself to its articulation, writing that "the meanings of [racial] mixture, the language we use to describe it, and its cast of characters have always been in flux."[33] Child similarly theorizes that race cannot be contained, that it is not essential or material but constructed, and that its definition lies in its naming.

Imagining amalgamation as polylingualism we see a theory of racializa-tion that mirrors race's relations in kinship and domestic spaces. Nationally located languages are also about space and place, as phenomena such as colo-nialism, emigration, and the creation of diasporic communities all allow for languages' movement into new spaces. Not confined by national borders or nationalized linguistic bodies, language travels across geographical space and time. Although linguistic genealogies may be known, they are not necessarily defining, as words and phrases can be adopted and adapted, transported and owned, appropriated and reappropriated until their origins are obscured and perhaps even irrelevant. Although constructed, language is painted akin to nature in Child's framing, as languages merge and are hybridized much like the races of her flowery characters. In Child's version of racial (re)construction, white racial inclusion is both problematic and optimistically expansionist. Beyond reading race as a function of cultural behavior rather than of biological descent, this metaphor characterizes race in a way that naturalizes queer genealogies, articulating race as relative, a matter of familial relationships of race-making. This metaphor also allows for the phenomenon of racial (re)construction.

How language might stand in as a metaphor for race is not hard to imagine. Jefferson laments the loss of those "Indian tribes already to extinguish" in a euphemism that removes the white, settler colonial causes of genocide, and also reframes genocide as a loss to white, settler colonialist knowledge.[34] Jefferson's lamentation turns quickly from a supposed interest in Native people to an interest in Native languages, as he muses that "[w]ere vocabularies formed of all the languages spoken in North and South America . . . and these deposited in all the public libraries, it would furnish opportunities to those skilled in the languages of the old world to compare them with these, now, or at any future time, and hence to construct the best evidence of the derivation of this part of the human race."[35] The language comparison Jefferson desires also leads to a comparison of racial relatedness, as he believes this linguistic study will provide some account of the "affinity of nations."[36] The relationship between race, nation, and language is unclear to Jefferson and was equally so throughout the nineteenth century, as those pondering racial differences and their historically genealogical relations parsed even the number of races differently. Most often, the "Indians" of North America were lumped into a single racialized category, distinguishing them from both white and Black people while erasing differences between and histories of treaties with sovereign tribes. To think of the possibility of linguistic relations between various "nations" is to position Indians differently—shifting the focus from imagined biological differences to cultural ones. Moreover, these cultural differences illustrate not simply difference but relatedness.

Framing racial mixture in terms not only of nature but also of language, Child's metaphor of the interracial family as "polyglot" imagines racial (re)production as a process of cultural intermixture. Here new elements are incorporated with ease, but even as they remain distinct within a language, they become now inextricable from it. As a polyglot nation, races of people, like words, become part of the national fabric. We can still detect their origins, but they are effectually integrated into the hybridized national tongue. New words might even be invented, formed from parts of disparate linguistic backgrounds. This too is allowable in the polyglot nation. This amalgamationist construction of the polyglot nation has a danger of being assimilationist, understanding the absorption of all race into American whiteness as "foreign" words might be adopted into American English. Racial intermixture need not be deliberate—and definitely not forced as Holgate imagines—but occurs as a matter of course. This may be the national future that is too frightening even for Holgate to imagine. While for Holgate this mixture is so unnatural that it must be mandated, for Child framing racial amalgamation in terms of polyglot language does not simply naturalize racial mixture, it recognizes race itself as socially constructed, through these articulations of family, race, and racial reproduction.

In their polyglot theorization of racial mixture, *Romance*'s interracial families illustrate racial amalgamation that does not always amount to absorption and erasure, even as it raises racialization and kinship as points of confusion for the narrative. Extending her depictions of re-racialization beyond her mixed-race heroines, Child also includes a baby-switching plot in her racial romance. The confusion of names and family relations in this plot mirrors the confusion of racialization, both preceding and resembling the case of Twain's renamed and re-racialized "twins" in *Pudd'nhead Wilson*. Gerald Fitzgerald (Senior) has sons with two women, his white wife, Lily Bell, and one of Child's mixed-race heroines, Rosa. When Rosa learns that her legal relation to Gerald is one of enslavement rather than marriage, she tries but fails to convince Gerald to free her and her yet-unborn child. Once born, both sons (conveniently) resemble their father. The scene of Rosa contemplating the two children, "one born to be indulged and honored . . . the other . . . born a slave, liable to be sold by his unfeeling father or by his father's creditors," foreshadows Twain's Roxy.[37] Rosa recalls, "They were so exactly alike that I could distinguish them only by their dress. I exchanged their dresses . . . and while I did it, I laughed to think that, if Mr. Fitzgerald should capture me and the little one . . . he would sell the child of his Lily Bell."[38] Rosa's biological son is thereafter raised as Gerald Fitzgerald and Lily's child.

This tangling of genealogies of race and kinship leads to predictable confusion in the novel's plot and among its characters, producing a familiar overabundance of kin that must be dealt with on a number of fronts, the most prominent of which is a linguistic one. These relational overabundances manifest in ways not unlike those in *Pudd'nhead Wilson* but produce further problems of articulation for Child's characters. As the novel's relationships between racialization and kinship are inextricable from one another, the complexity of articulating the latter reflect the similar complexities of the former. Child's characters incorporate interracial kinship relations into their polyglot configurations of family. When the young Gerald Fitzgerald learns the truth about his birth mother, race, and legal enslavement, his relationship with the woman who raised him is called into question. However, Lily Bell Fitzgerald, a white woman whose racism is real, complex, and never fully extinguished in the novel, clings to her relationship with the son she has raised. When Rosa tells her what she has done, Lily replies, "But whatever you may say, he is *my* son. I never will give him up. He has slept in my arms. I have sung him to sleep. I taught him all little hymns and songs. He loves me; and I will never consent to take a second place in his affections."[39] Perhaps surprisingly, her racism does not alter her affection for her son, but ideas about racial essentialism and kinship are challenged in her interest in Gerald's continued "passing" as her biological, assumedly white child.

In this proliferation of kinship relations, the text allows Gerald to recognize and have relationships with both his biological and "adopted" mothers. He shows how he is able to multiply his filial affection, explaining (regarding Lily), "I love her and always shall love her. It cannot be otherwise . . . It has been the pleasant habit of so many years. But ought I not to consider myself a lucky fellow to have two such mothers?"[40] Gerald also addresses the language with which he might relate to the woman who gave birth to him and the one who raised him, telling Rosa, "I don't know how I am to distinguish you. I must call you 'Rose-mother' and 'Lily-mother,' I believe."[41] Rosa and Lily's shared motherhood of Gerald is one example of the linguistic problem of "othermothers" discussed in chapter 4. Knowledge of Gerald's nonbiological relation and his mixed-race does not impede Lily's motherhood to him. While Lily's sentiment clearly articulates antiblack racism, its evasion of racial essentialism also raises questions of race's trajectories and associations. Regardless of birth, it seems that she believes herself to have passed her own whiteness on to her adopted son.

Meanwhile, as Rosa's birth son was raised by Lily and Gerald Fitzgerald, readers are led to believe that their birth child, who Rosa replaces with her own, died of yellow fever as an infant (along with his Black nurse Tulee). We later learn that both Tulee and the baby lived, though they had been claimed by slave traders and sold. Before they were separated, Tulee tattooed "G.F." on the baby's arm (he is also, conveniently, named Gerald Fitzgerald) so that he might be identified later. Following these initials, Rosa's birth child calls himself George Falkner, and ultimately marries an enslaved mixed-race woman, Henriet. Refusing the proliferation of kinship relations that Gerald (Junior) has embraced, Lily does not desire a motherly relationship with the child to whom she gave birth. She decrees that he ought never learn the identity of his birth mother, a request with which Rosa and Alfred King comply. George's cultural racialization is shown to be more important to Lily than notions of biological race, as she says, "it would be very disagreeable to me to have a son who had been brought up among slaves."[42] Moreover, she later cites George's marriage, rather than his upbringing, as the reason she denies his kinship, saying, "I shall never recognize any person as a relative who has a colored wife."[43] Lily's father, Mr. Bell, has similar reservations, but cannot bear the revelation about his grandson even as far as his daughter has.

Even more so for Lily's father than for Lily herself, kinship and inheritance ought to follow lines of racialization; the fact that they may not produces confusion that he cannot resolve. Mr. Bell complains that his biological grandson has a mixed-race wife, citing this as sufficient to disown him. He complains, "My property, it seems, must either go to Gerald, who you say has negro blood in his veins, or to this other fellow [George], who is a slave with a negro wife."[44] Mr. Bell's confusion about whether to prioritize his own genealogical kinship or his grandson's sexual kinship in matters of inheritance indicates two different modes of racialization about which he is simultaneously anxious. Ultimately, rather than perpetuating the confusion around mixed-race characters as tragedy, Child instead rids her narrative especially of white men who cannot embrace interracial kinship, keeping only those (like Alfred King and Franz Blumenthal) who can. Mr. Bell does not live out Child's text; his racism renders him unable to be incorporated into the novel's complex structures of racialized family. The senior Gerald Fitzgerald also disappears (suspiciously coinciding with the disappearance of two people he held enslaved) and is presumed dead.

While Gerald Fitzgerald the younger benefits from the multiplication of his mothers, the two brothers become doubles in the text, though not rivals but rather dual inheritors within the national family. Gerald Fitzgerald Junior and George Falkner meet during the Civil War while both are fighting for the Union army. The two become fast friends before Gerald (Junior) dies in the Battle of Bull Run. Although he remains unacknowledged by his birth mother, George also escapes having to deal with her racism or her rejection, instead learning about his biological genealogy from Alfred King, who becomes a kind of father figure to him while also arranging for Henriet's education so as to assume George's future middle-class station. Alfred King offers George "my influence and my fatherly interest" even while asserting "neither of your parents was related to me in any degree, or connected with me in any way."[45] George learns that he is "unmixed white," that he has "a right" to his father's name, and that the Gerald Fitzgerald he knew was his brother by the same father. George decides to change his name (back) to Gerald Fitzgerald, thus supplanting his previous two namesakes. More importantly, perhaps, than this history, Alfred also offers George (who has been previously enslaved) the economic support that will provide him with a comfortable future, though not one of excess leisure, arguing that "he will not be deprived of any of his pecuniary rights; and he is in a fair way to become more of a man than he would have been if he had been brought up in luxury."[46] Thus the novel resolves the baby-switching narrative in the larger context of the Civil War's familial losses and debts. Child's plot makes the racialization of both white and mixed-race Black people so confusing (as it admittedly must be in any retelling of Child's plot) as to render these distinctions (though ahistorically and perhaps even irresponsibly so) almost arbitrary.

George's story, however, has at its heart the racial (re)production of Blackness, though not through overcomplicated racial genealogies (biological or cultural), but through kinship relations. The narrative's interracial baby-switching results in a decidedly more complex racial aftermath than Twain's. Unlike Twain's Chambers, George does not seem destined to a life of confused racial liminality or discomfort. Mired in the complexities of interracial family and racialization, it is peculiar that *Romance* offers no commentary on how George/(Gerald?) understands his own racialization. This man, though born to white parents, has been raised as Black and has been enslaved and emancipated; his education and other opportunities have been limited as a direct result of his supposed race. His personal history seems decidedly "Black" in this respect. Most importantly, however, he has a mixed-race Black wife. It is this woman's presence in the story—her kinship and racialized relation to him—that illustrates the scalar dimensions of George's racial trajectory. Even if we consider (for a moment) the most essentialist reading of him as "originally" white, then Black, then white again, George's wife cuts through this trajectory of re-racialization with her own undeniable Blackness.

With Henriet and George's relationship, Child hereby refuses the simple antiblackness of this character's re-racialization. Because of his marriage, Blackness is not something he can or even wishes to escape, but something he embraces irrespective of his own racial embodiment and genealogy. Marking inherited racialization as oddly irrelevant, whatever George learns about his genealogical past, the (re)production of Blackness is anticipated in his future. While the presence of George/Gerald's wife seems to secure his reproductive, cultural, and even perhaps identificatory Blackness, his alignment with a white father figure like Alfred King might render him the kind of white man who can become kin with a Black-identifying woman, opening up possibilities for interracial kinship that gestures toward the book's imagined polyglot futurity. As we expand the question of George's identification from the bodily to the familial scale, we read a queer genealogy of racialization in which his clearest racialization stems not from his birth parents, but from Rose's nonreproductive act of switching up the plot's racial genealogies and from his familial intertwining with Henriet, a mixed-race Black woman who serves as a kind of counter to Child's heroines, who do not seem to identify with other people with Black ancestry even while they refuse to deny their own.

If we think beyond the polyglot family of Child's republican romance, of course, we must also consider the polyglot American nation at the scale of the racially (re)constructed national family. Rather than working to keep out the threat of the racial Other, as in Kaplan's presentation of republican motherhood, Child's heroines—in their preexisting embodiment of racial difference, their reproduction, and their queer genealogical racializations— bring racial differences into communion in the body of the national family.[47] As Teresa Zackodnik recognizes, the mixed-race heroine cannot help being a "highly political figure" in US literature.[48] This is, in part, because this figure is concerned with the very "questions of racial epistemology" that frame the nature of racialization and race-making upon which white supremacy depends, and which illustrates the ongoing processes of racial (re)construction.[49] Thinking beyond the bodily and familial scales of Child's heroines toward the implications of a polyglot national future of infinite racial (re)construction, we can see the broader implications of this linguistic metaphor for race. My examples of mixed-race heroines in this chapter focus on these scalar extensions of racial genealogy. As a character already positioned in interracial kinship, the mixed-race heroine has a different relation to interracial desire than assumedly white models of racial purity. These characters ultimately reposition and re-racialize the figure of the white woman in already amalgamated American genealogies that work to define the nation.

Like Child's polyglot reproducers of interracial family, Althesa, the nontitular daughter of Thomas Jefferson in William Wells Brown's *Clotel*, successfully passes for white and works against national racial-purist ideologies of white womanhood that necessitate her rejection of racial difference or her reproduction of whiteness. Neither Brown's nor Child's characters simply embody racial mixture, but rather reproduce it, indicating a shift toward a model of womanhood able to incorporate Black people into structures of the national multiracial family and retheorizations of the possibilities for racial (re)production. *Clotel* takes up racial (re)construction via the fact of the already mixed-race nation. Differing from the anti-passing narratives of mixed-race heroines discussed in part II, Brown's heroines veer uncomfortably toward the "tragic mulatta" figures of antislavery literature. By framing its own mixed-race heroine as the progeny of a founding father of the nation, however, *Clotel* situates the amalgamated body as a product of a nation of "diverse bloods," addressing preexisting and irrecoverable genealogies of interracial racialization at the national scale and indicating the larger stakes of racial (re)construction, which we can continue to trace (in queerly recursive nonlinear genealogies) to the present.

The President's Other Daughter

As Brown rewrites and revises his figure of mixed-race womanhood, he imagines alternative spaces and circumstances for racial construction, exposing race's queer genealogies and recursivity by representing the interracial family and nation as always already racially mixed and as perpetually reconstructing themselves. *Clotel* employs the familiar rhetoric of nineteenth-century antislavery literature's use of mixed-race bodies and mixed-race families to discuss a mixed-race nation from an opposing position to Holgate's amalgamation dystopia. And, contrary to Child's narrative of familial/national racial reunion, Brown locates racial mixture at the nation's founding. At the center of Brown's novel is a recasting of Child's 1842 story "The Quadroons," set in the historical context of Thomas Jefferson's children born to Sally Hemings. Brown's novel gives a fictive account of the children produced by this union, writing the common trope of the "tragic mulatta" alongside Jefferson's Declaration of Independence, both the progeny of our nation's "founding fathers."

As Child gestured toward the national racial future, she and other authors of plantation nostalgia and anti-nostalgia fiction also inevitably looked to the past. The history of racial formation in the United States has been an ongoing series of racial (re)constructions. Clarence E. Walker similarly discusses the United States as racially mixed even at its conception and addresses the myths by which the nation has been imagined as white. Reading Jefferson and Hemings as more appropriate "founding parents of the North American Republic" than George and Martha Washington, Walker argues for reading the nation as "a mixed-race society, not a white one," a sentiment in keeping with Brown's historical fiction.[50] Using the rhetoric of white womanhood in his critique of slavery, Brown challenges racial categories as problematic for the racially mixed nation he illustrates in *Clotel*, as many of the mixed-race women who are visually "white" in his narrative are (legally) enslaved. To this effect, both Brown and Child have been criticized for falling into the familiar trap of antislavery literature's use of mixed-race heroines to garner sympathy for enslaved people, based on the assumption that their white, middle-class audience will more easily sympathize with characters who are visually white and whose speech is not represented in dialect.

Despite these problems, Brown's novel exhibits some important examples of nonnormative genealogies of racialization, enacted in Brown's continual revision of the mixed-race heroine trope. While Frances Harper would ultimately do more work to revise the mixed-race heroine in *Minnie's Sacrifice* and *Iola Leroy*, Brown's revision of the mixed-race heroine in this and his subsequent editions of *Clotel* illustrates alternative teleologies of this figure's racialization.[51] In Brown's first edition of *Clotel* it is not the titular sister, but President Jefferson's other daughter, Althesa, who most clearly illustrates the potential slippage between the "tragic mulatta" and "white woman" tropes, and thereby the queer discontinuities of racialization.[52] Though both sisters are described as "quadroons," Clotel and Althesa meet decidedly different fates.

Clotel's narrative is familiar: She is abandoned by her white lover, Horatio Green. Since their union has been defined as illegal, Horatio is free to marry a white woman, leaving Clotel alone with their illegitimate child. Unsurprisingly, Clotel's narrative ends in her suicide. Althesa, however, is bought out of slavery by her ever-faithful beloved, the white, Northern-born Henry Morton. They live comfortably together as a married couple (though not legally so) until their deaths from disease in the normal course of life. While Clotel's story is a clear retelling of the "tragic mulatta" trope, Althesa's draws upon the sympathy of Brown's white readers by allowing her to function as a white woman throughout much of her portion of the narrative. There is nothing particularly exotic about Brown's depiction of Althesa, nor does she read as a "tragic" heroine in relation to Brown's other mixed-race women. The rhetorical function of Althesa depends upon notions of white womanhood that are inscribed both in white feminine beauty and the domestic role of the middle-class white woman as Althesa successfully passes for white (though her husband knows about her Black genealogy) until reaching a death that is *not* hastened by the brutal machinations of slavery. Althesa functions as white following her marriage. She dies in her own bed, next to her white husband, much as though she had successfully "passed" as a white woman, whatever her intentions may have been.

Althesa's story shows that, constructed through historical and social contexts though it is, race is constructed in ways that are not entirely predictable, nor entirely permanent. Despite this character's relative racial privilege, individual racialization is always in danger of racial (re)construction and must therefore be regarded alongside familial and national racial scales. Even if we regard Althesa as a "passing" figure, her re-racialization as white is temporary, not extending past her death. Any apparent whiteness she may possess is not inheritable by her children. Her daughters' racial genealogy is traced through their mother's and does not seem to have anything to do with their own, personal identification or appearance. Neither can their apparent whiteness be preserved by unions with white lovers because of their legally enslaved status. Their mother was fortunate, but they are not. Althesa's re-racialization is not permanent, and it is not genealogically transferrable to future generations. That their white ancestors outnumber their Black ones is beside the point according to the social rules of racial hypodescent. Here, as in passing narratives' great fear of the recursive return of Blackness (the aftermath of which we observe in Kate Chopin's "Désirée's Baby"), we see a lineage of hypodescent in which Blackness follows so fine a line that it might pass over a generation but never disappear entirely. Like Chopin, Brown poses racial passing as possible but as generationally temporary, refocusing the scale of interracial kinship from the body, to the family, to the nation by illustrating the conflation of these scales and the circularity of racialization across them. Thinking simultaneously in terms of past and future racializations at various scales, we here understand bodies, families, and nations in a perpetual state of racial reconstruction.

It is not the liminality of these mixed-race figures that allows for their often shifting performances of white womanhood, but the nature of queer racialization itself. Nineteenth-century discourses about race's perceptibility turns on the assumption of some kind of essential racial content that is always detectible. In truth, race may or may not be visible, and racial genealogies might reemerge in subsequent, nonsequential generations. This possibility of racial genealogical discontinuity is queer indeed. As in my previous chapters, I do not aim to essentialize race in this discussion of racial "mixture." Rather, my aim is to highlight the ways these characters are able to employ an existing national rhetoric of white womanhood in their simultaneous embodiments of visual whiteness and their performances of versions of white womanhood that sometimes reinforce and sometimes challenge the dominant trope. Brown's Althesa illustrates the precarious rhetoric of white womanhood and the limitations of racial reproduction that do not follow a guaranteed teleology. Problems of identifying and classifying racially ambiguous people and of understanding how interpersonal relationships respond to and create racial hierarchies are part and parcel to the project of racial (re)construction.

The particular brands of racism surrounding mixed-race people and interracial relationships (of various kinds) have often been about the tricky work of racialization. As Brown's novel shows, this kind of assimilation into whiteness is precarious even when passing is successful. Désirée's baby (or perhaps even her grandbaby) might, at any moment, exhibit evidence of racial mixture and familial proximity to nonwhite kin, revealing racial genealogies beyond individual features or identification. The case of Althesa indicates what will be reiterated for many generations later: The existence of mixed-race people has not and will not be a sufficient counter to racism. Without any real counter to antiblack oppression, assimilation will always be both precarious and contingent upon adherence to white supremacist models. But if we take seriously the power of race's social construction, it is not solely in bodily racial mixture or in the amalgamated family that race is reimagined, but through the narratives that are framed around race at all scales. Like the language of racialization and the various genres of writing about race, racial (re)construction is enacted and reinforced by its articulation and rearticulation in narratives that tell and retell—and which thereby theorize and retheorize—the story of how race is made.

Brown would revise his 1853 novel numerous times, first in *Miralda; or, the Beautiful Quadroon* (serialized in 1860 in the *Weekly Anglo-African*), in 1864 as *Clotelle: A Tale of the Southern States* (part of James Redpath's "Books for the Camp Fires" series that was marketed to Union soldiers), and for the last time in 1867 as *Clotelle; or the Colored Heroine* (published the same year as Child's *A Romance of the Republic*). One significant change Brown makes in these three revisions—and one that renders their cross-textual comparison confusing for scholars who discuss them—is his shifting of the title character from the "tragic mulatta" figure of *Clotel*'s iconic suicide on the Long Bridge to mixed-race heroines who live to see the end of these later novels.[53] Julia C. Collins makes a similar shift in *The Curse of Caste; or the Slave Bride* over the course of her novel's serialization in the *Christian Recorder* in 1865, as her story's focus veers from Lina, the enslaved "bride" of its title, to her daughter, Claire.[54] Brown's shift in naming across these revisions produces confusion among those writing about Clotel, Miralda, Clotelle, and Clotelle similar to that created by Twain's baby-switching and renaming and Child's proliferation of Gerald Fitzgeralds.

While Twain's and Child's renamings mark these characters re-racialization, Brown's (like Collins's) shift instead refigures the stakes of mixed-race racialization itself. Through these revisions, Brown re-centers his novel on mixed-race women who live and who marry Black men. This change is indicative of a larger shift in mixed-race-heroine fiction of the later nineteenth century.[55] Frances Harper's revision of the mixed-race heroine in *Minnie's Sacrifice* and *Iola Leroy* represents such a shift in mixed-race-heroines' clear racial identification not as liminal or tragic but as deliberately Black, despite their white family members and upbringing as white women. Brown's revisions of *Clotel* likewise reorient readers toward a different understanding of the mixed-race heroine and also toward a different genealogy of her racialization. Brown's iterations of mixed-race Black women do not necessitate the wholesale rejection of white family members for Black identification but allow white and Black genealogies to exist simultaneously in women who nevertheless identify as Black. Further (much like Child's George/Gerald), Miralda and the two Clotelles gesture toward the reproductive futurity of Blackness, with visibly Black husbands.

Miralda and the 1864 and 1867 versions of *Clotelle* conclude with the heroine's reunion with her white father, Mr. Linwood. All three novels give the same account of Linwood's racism: "Being brought up in America, and having all the prejudice against color which characterizes his white fellow-countrymen, Mr. Linwood very much regretted that his daughter, although herself tinctured with African blood, should have married a black man, and he did not fail to express to her his dislike of her husband's complexion."[56] Problematically relying on the mixed-race child to cure her white parent's racism, Brown reunites his heroine with her father as a salve to the racist, enslaving nation. Miralda/Clotelle and her husband, Jerome, convince her father to free the people he still holds enslaved, converting him to an anti-slavery (and an apparently antiracist) position. This family reunion serves, of course, as a metaphor for national reunion, but so does Brown's familial racial reconstruction. In his earliest novel, Clotel's daughter Mary (who lives to see the end of the novel) marries the mixed-race, light-skinned George Green. In Brown's three later version, however, Jerome is described as having a "dark complexion" and a "black complexion."[57] This detail inserts visible Blackness into Brown's final images of racial reunion and enables him to reimagine his conclusion of familial racial (re)construction as a different kind of Black futurity—one that refuses the generational whitening of dark skin and, perhaps at the least, the assimilation of Black people into a predominantly white (though amalgamated) nation in such a way that would render them invisible.

While *Clotel* can be critiqued for suggesting a future of genealogical whitening, Brown's later revisions refuse this racial (re)construction of white and African American reunion, instead suggesting Black futurity rather than Blackness's erasure. These representations conflate genealogical, identificatory, legal, and visual Blackness. However, Jerome's dark skin ensures Blackness's legibility, even where Miralda's/Clotelle's racialization as Black might become illegible.[58] As with Harper's *Iola Leroy*, marriage to a visibly Black husband (and the attendant increased likelihood of bearing visibly Black children) racializes the mixed-race heroine through these familial relations. Moreover, by signaling Miralda/Clotelle as a mixed-race Black woman, Brown's racial (re)construction of the mixed-race family (even as Linwood is not in danger of re-racialization, as white men seldom are) lay bare the fact of the white man's interracial sexual kinship. Like Harper's, Brown's later versions of racial (re)construction represents a kind of recursive return of Blackness as freely claimed, potentially countering oppressive legacies of imposed hypodescent. Here the queer directional return of Black racialization has the potential to reveal Black histories that have been suppressed.

Returning to Jefferson's legacy of racial discourse, Brown's framing of these novels around the former president's legacy would have later, racially reconstructive, resonance. Jefferson's and Hemings's children did not, of course, inherit their father's white, free status. Only two of these children—Eston Hemings and Madison Hemings—were freed in Jefferson's will. The former apparently resembled his father in many respects, including being light skinned enough to pass as white.[59] Eston Hemings married a free mixed-race woman of color, Julia Ann Isaacs, moved to Madison, Wisconsin, in 1852, and changed the family's surname to Jefferson, thereafter living as white people. Their two sons, John Wayles Jefferson and Beverly Jefferson, bore the names of their white, free, familial connections and served in the segregated Union army, both in white regiments. Though it is unclear when, exactly, knowledge about Black ancestry was foreclosed, Eston Hemings Jefferson's family ultimately did not pass knowledge of their African American ancestry on to subsequent generations. In 1998, genetic testing established the link between Eston Hemings Jefferson's descendant Julia Jefferson Westerinen's family line and that of Thomas Jefferson. This also confirmed the fact of Thomas Jefferson's African American descendants (though well-known and a topic of US political and literary culture since Jefferson's own lifetime) for some remaining Jefferson apologists.

The discontinuity of racialization that Althesa's narrative of passing exhibits would be the same type of discontinuity revisited upon Hemings's and Jefferson's descendants in the twenty-first century. Althesa's genealogy of temporary passing illustrates the recursive nature of racialization. Even as Althesa is (successfully) re-racialized as white, race will be reconstructed for her children. Brown himself would revise these genealogies of racialization in the subsequent revisions of his novel. Eston Hemings Jefferson's Black ancestry would ultimately be used to reveal his genealogical relations to both the white enslaver president and the woman Jefferson held enslaved, laying bare these legacies of antiblack oppression. Putting aside the (however important) essentialist problems and ethical difficulties of the phenomenon of racial "passing" for a moment, the revelation of Eston Hemings Jefferson's genealogy illustrates passing's spatiotemporal limitations. Passing may or may not be available to a racially embodied individual, but any individual body's ability to pass does not necessarily allow the projection of that passing into future generations.

Like the novels I discuss here, Eston Hemings Jefferson's racial genealogy shows us how race is continually—and relationally—reconstructed. Désirée's husband, Armand, had a mother who was apparently able to pass the skin privilege of white identification onto her son, but Armand was unable to pass white-skin privilege onto his own child. Clotel's sister, Althesa, successfully passes, dying in her own bed alongside her white husband, but her children cannot inherit her whiteness or their father's free status. We do not need to racialize Eston H. Jefferson's remaining descendants as "really" African American via the "one drop rule" of racial hypodescent in order to see how their racial genealogy illustrates the recursive racialization of racial reconstruction. There is no way to locate the genealogical moment/racial quantification at which point Eston H. Jefferson's descendants "stop" being Black and, accordingly, "become" white. We might know, rather, at what point his family ceases to experience the legal oppression of Black people and that Eston (and whatever family members were aware of their racial genealogy) must have worried about their possible re-racialization and the accompanying threat of antiblack oppression.

Lest we wonder (pessimistically) whether the experience of antiblack racism constitutes Blackness itself, racial reconstruction provides examples—as with Brown's later mixed-race heroines and with Harper's—in which Blackness's recursive racialization is empowering. Eston Hemings Jefferson's brother Madison Hemings acknowledged his paternity but refused to or was unable to pass as white. Annette Gordon-Reed writes that Madison Hemings thereby serves as a "metaphor for the condition of blacks in American society."[60] Madison Hemings understood the queer genealogies of racial hypodescent and embodiment. Eston and Madison, though born of the same parents, constitute parallel racial genealogies that produce racially disparate legacies for their descendants. That the reconstruction of Eston Hemings Jefferson's genealogy might retroactively re-racialize him or any of his descendants illustrates the confluence of bodily, familial, and national race-making. That these genealogies are traced retrospectively, through a white woman descendant, illustrates race's capacity to travel via queer genealogies of racial (re)formation that nevertheless converge around figures of white women as bearers of racial reproduction. The shifting re-racializations of Jefferson's and Brown's genealogies of the nation show us the ironically simultaneous historicity and arbitrariness of race-making, but also its continued power and efficacy. My conclusion turns to the power and efficacy of race-making in the present, via white women's continued (scalar and teleological) role in racial (re)production.

Conclusion

"Minus Bloodlines"

White Womanhood and Failures of Interracial Kinship

> Minus bloodlines, he saw nothing yet on the horizon to unite them.
> —Toni Morrison, *A Mercy*

IN 1867, the American Equal Rights Association (AERA) split over debates regarding the proposed Fifteenth Amendment. The association had advocated for voting rights for both African American people and white women, but the non-intersectional competition between gender and race was overwhelming. As a result, AERA split, and its former members divided into two new organizations: the American Women's Suffrage Association, founded by Lucy Stone, Henry Blackwell, and Julia Ward Howe (supporting the amendment), and the National Women's Suffrage Association, founded by Susan B. Anthony and Elizabeth Cady Stanton (opposing the amendment). Many middle-class white women (and some of the US suffrage movement's most beloved leaders) could not bear the thought of Black men gaining the right to vote before they did. While much has been written on the divide between Black men and white women in this struggle, we lose much if we fail to acknowledge the place of Black women in this debate.

Even following the ratification of the Fifteenth Amendment in February 1870, prominent Black women activists such as Sojourner Truth, Charlotte Forten, Frances Ellen Watkins Harper, Lottie Rollin, and Mary Ann Shadd Cary continued to fight for women's suffrage. What AERA's split illustrates is not the split between Black men and white women (despite prominent attention to Frederick Douglass's place in this debate) but between white women and Black women. Someone like Frances Harper could well have predicted this split. Speaking at the eleventh National Woman's Rights Convention in 1866, and sharing the stage with Elizabeth Cady Stanton and Susan B. Anthony, Harper spoke truth to power. She said, "I tell you that if there is any class of people who need to be lifted out of their airy nothings and selfishness, it is the white women of America."[1] Harper knew that white women, as a whole, could not be trusted to support Black suffrage, despite the history of Black women's (and men's—we see you, Frederick Douglass) engagement with women's rights activism. The split of AERA is just one indication of failed interracial sisterhood. That such sisterhood is metaphorical makes it no less real than other kinship ideals. I end this book with this turn to a political notion of metaphorical kinship—sisterhood—in order to further extend the possible scale of racialized genealogies. If the queer genealogies of racialization's unpredictable possibilities offer a larger takeaway in our twenty-first-century moment, it is that a turn away from essentialist theories of racial construction might allow us to more fully realize radical possibilities for interracial relations writ large.

Charles Browning's painting *Blackface* is an image that illustrates how, exactly, interracial sisterhood fails in this moment (see figure C.1). The painting shows a white, middle-class pretense at Blackness: a subject sitting in a privileged place that mimics the position of oppression. Coming full circle here to the Blackface Desdemona of chapter 1, I present this image as the alternative and parallel icon of interracial un-kinship. Blackface Desdemona is an iconic figure illustrating the imagined dangers of interracial kinship, showing how race's queer directionalities might have re-racialized white women. Browning's *Blackface* returns us to blackface as an image of appropriation rather than becoming, or even mimesis. It is a reminder that the (re)racialization I have described throughout this project is hardly the usual trajectory of race's flow. I introduce this at the end of my project as an emphatic reminder that interracial kinship does not necessarily result in racial (re)production that takes us away from white supremacy. I distinguish between whiteness and white supremacy in order to signal how my discussion attends not only to whiteness as a racialized position of identification within bodies, families, and nations, but also to the larger—related—structural force beyond these, a force with historical leanings toward racial oppression.

C.1 CHARLES BROWNING, *BLACKFACE*, 2005. COURTESY OF THE ARTIST.

Racial (re)construction occurs in illogical and unpredictable ways. It cannot be simply willed. As we have shown, racialization is not simply a matter of individual identification but of relation. As blackface minstrelsy illustrates most starkly, racial relations, though they might produce kinship, can also be appropriative. This image, taken with the possibility of interracial sisterhood in mind, dredges up unsavory images of white women's comparison of their civil-rights struggle to slavery. This relation to Blackness is not one of exchange, engagement, and love, but of inappropriate "love and theft," as Eric Lott puts it.[2] In this context, Browning's "Blackface" might be taken as a reminder that white feminism, try as it might to don Blackness, does not succeed in this approach, which always comes in lieu of actual interracial, ethical, and reciprocal engagement. The failure of AERA is not simply one of universalist principles or of political pragmatism, but of white women's failed interracial engagement with the Black women who were bound to lose out in the oversimplified question of whether Black men or white women ought to get the vote first.

White feminism's failure to be in kinship with Black sisterhood marks an ongoing failure of interracial kinship, and one with which I must conclude in order to bring my discussion into the present moment. Here, I bring the scalar implications of interracial kinship to bear on the teleological projection of race even to our present moment. I turn from white womanhood to white feminism in order to drive home the political implications of the history of racialization that has relied upon white women's racial (re)production. White women's and white feminism's ties to white supremacy are the lynchpin of interracial kinship's racial trajectories. In this future-oriented projection of (re)racialization, we might imagine the (re)production not only of whiteness but also of white supremacy. But even as I here center white women and the cultural racial baggage with which this position has been weighed down, this centering must be skewed, redirected, queered, and perhaps wrested away for the sake of future racial relations.

White Genocide

On January 7, 2017, I received an email sent to my and other University of Wisconsin–Madison faculty of colors' university email accounts, the subject of which was "The Problem of White Genocide." The email was a fountain of racist hate speech. It decried "diversity" at multiple scales—in integrated institutions of higher education, families, and nations—and criticized "mommy professors" for teaching anti-racism, declaring both diversity and anti-racism as inherently "anti-White." The beginning of the email read, in part: "ALL White countries and ONLY White countries are being flooded with third world non-Whites, and Whites are forced by law to integrate with them so as to 'assimilate,' i.e. intermarry and be blended out of existence."[3] This was a racist message about university instruction and research on race and racism. It was also a racist message about interracial family and mixed-race people. When I reported the email to my institution, the reply I received primarily addressed the concept of academic freedom. This reply failed to understand my specific reaction to the original email as a mixed-race Black woman. I eventually forgot about this email, only to recall it three years later when editing this portion of this book. I found the original email (I never delete; I keep all my receipts) and read it again. I shook with rage as I cut-and-pasted the above quotation into my notes. I care very much about anti-racist pedagogy and my academic freedom to teach in ways that I believe to be both intellectually rigorous and ethically responsible. But this email was not only an attack upon my pedagogical practices or even my scholarship; it was an attack upon my very existence, the existence of my family, and of my child.

I recount this twenty-first century example in order to illustrate how central racial reproduction remains for white supremacist anxieties. Even though the racializing system of hypodescent worked historically to maximize Black, enslavable labor for the benefit of white enslavers, it also became a threat to the reproduction of whiteness. This ironic twist that renders mixed-race people a threat to white supremacy even when they have white ancestry becomes visible when racial hypodescent results in the political alignments we see in Harper's anti-passing fiction or when genealogically white women like Mary King or Mary Jemison align themselves with non-white family rather than with white supremacy or even with white relatives. My twenty-first century example also includes a sexist hint at the gendered responsibilities of racial (re)production: it is no mistake that my colleagues and I are characterized here as "mommy professors" for our refusals to reproduce white supremacy. Coupling refusals to (re)produce white people with refusals to (re)produce white supremacy, the email unintentionally and rather ironically illustrates the nonbiological and nonheteronormative work of antiracist "mommy professors'" racial reproduction. By creating interracial families, classrooms, institutions, or communities, we threaten the white supremacist nation. In truth, the anxieties about "white genocide" expressed in this email echo those of nineteenth-century racist writers like Jerome Holgate and are best understood in conversation with the kinds of anxieties about amalgamation's threat to white supremacy that I discuss in this book.

The "miscegenation" debates that accompanied the 1864 election cycle, like the above racist email and some mid-nineteenth-century popular literature, were less interested in interracial sex than they were in mixed-race people. While antislavery literature would focus on mixed-race figures as a problem for a race-based system of slavery, these debates were invested in the even broader implications of such people's existence in a white-supremacist nation. David Goodman Croly and George Wakeman's proclamation that "The blending of diverse bloods [is] essential to American progress," was a purported call for America to abandon its endeavors to be an Anglo-Saxon nation, and to instead create national homogeneity not through exclusion but through amalgamation in the literal sense:

> It is clear that no race can long endure without a commingling of its blood with that of other races. The condition of all human progress is miscegenation. The Anglo-Saxon should learn this in time for his own salvation. If we will not heed the demands of justice, let us, at least, respect the law of self-preservation. Providence has kindly placed on the American soil, for his own wise purposes, four millions of coloured people. They are our brothers, our sisters. By mingling with them we become powerful, prosperous, and progressive: by refusing to do so we become feeble, unhealthy, narrow-minded, unfit for the nobler offices of freedom, and certain of early decay.[4]

Croly and Wakeman's pamphlet also predicts a future in which the duality of "white" and "Black" races is eliminated, presenting complete racial mixture as imminent, as well as desirable. This was not just an argument about sex, but about sex's genealogies. While this view of racial mixture is a parody of discourses on racial equality, it is not a far cry from the look toward racial mixture as an answer to the "problem" of seemingly irreconcilable racial dualism that emerges post-Reconstruction. As Du Bois presents it, the color line is a problem, and some thinkers imagine its resolution not in its crossing but only in its erasure. This erasure would be termed "white genocide" by white supremacists. Invested in the simultaneous (re)production of whiteness and white supremacy, they sought to avoid the figurative creation of interracial "brotherhood" and "sisterhood" by foreclosing its biological creation.

But what the unpredictable genealogies of interracial kinship have shown us is that mixed-race people—while heavily weighted in national literary, cultural, and political discourse—are a red herring. White people in interracial kinship relations are not guaranteed to acknowledge these relations.

And even when they do, this does not then guarantee racial solidarity with their mixed-race sistren and brethren. Further, even while hypodescent is the dominant framework in which race's queer genealogies operate, this is not a guaranteed rule about racial reproduction. Some people pass not only through whiteness, but also into it. Colorism complicates racial relations as white supremacy might be absorbed by anyone who touches it. Neither is the nature of white relations vis-à-vis interracial kinship a simple matter of numerical shifts toward mixture. Mixed-race people, even in their proliferation to ever more expansive scales and national populations, have never been and likely never will be able to thwart racism. White enslavers (like Jefferson) were long related to the people they enslaved, and this did not change their "hearts and minds" any more than relationships with women has brought about gender equity. Appeals to family, while building on the sentiment of individual relationships, often fall short in their failure to expand to outward scales of political responsibility to someone who is not one's own sister or daughter.

David Walker, in his *Appeal*, explicitly decries prohibitions on interracial marriage as inherent to the dehumanization of Black people. Unlike the Egyptians, he holds, Americans justify the enslavement of Black people "by telling them that they were not of the *human family*."[5] Walker is no grand promoter of amalgamation in practice but puts forward his argument on general principle. Explaining the relevance of interracial kinship to even larger scales of racism, Walker takes the long genealogical view of race's temporal and spatial scale. As he explicitly calls out the American racial separatism that would legislate against interracial marriage, he characterizes it as constituting dehumanization, regardless of whether African American people are literally believed to be nonhuman.[6] To trace generations of racial exclusion from the category "family" is ultimately to trace the racist exclusion of nonwhite people from humanity itself.[7] Walker's longer genealogical tracing of racial exclusion from family to humanity interrogates a premise of the body/family/nation trajectory by introducing the category of humanity into the body/family/nation teleology of race. Rejecting what we might appropriately call the "seminal" in favor of the axiological, Walker calls into question the premise of racialization that cannot be explained by assigning the same truth value to the racialized body, family, and nation, but which must address larger ethical definitions and exclusions.

Similar to how white-supremacist notions of racial purity involved scalar concerns about the larger implications and futures of racial mixture, Walker's concerns reached beyond questions of immediate familial relations and extended to a racially integrated notion of humanity that would have broader political implications. Walker supported racial mixture as a matter of principle rather than pragmatism. And it is the principle rather than the practices of this interracial kinship that are likely more efficacious, as they respond to racism's structural stakes. Croly and Wakeman's directive aligns with Walker's humanist principles. In its utopian framing of the deepest white-supremacist fears, however, it mistakenly conflates biological relation, the "commingling of . . . blood with that of other races," with an ideological shift toward the "demands of justice."

When we prioritize justice—such as racial equity—rather than interracial kinship (a possible though definitely not guaranteed means to that end), the true value of white womanhood comes into view. Throughout this project, I have shown that white women's racialization as not simply (re)productive of whiteness (or white supremacy), but exhibits the vulnerable nature of their own racialization. The possibility of white women's (re)racialization reveals race as not essential or permanent but rather as malleable. As literary and cultural depictions of white womanhood involved in interracial kinship relations shift expectations about race and kinship while inflecting upon popular understandings of literary genre and reading practices, the centrality of the figure of the white woman for reproducing race cannot be overlooked. This fact is evidenced by the history of policing white women's interracial sexuality, and hence their racial reproduction. The failure or refusal of white women to (re)produce whiteness is, of course, what has been termed by white supremacists "white genocide." If we take seriously this study of racial (re)production's queer genealogies, however, we must refuse to regard this racial (re)production as merely sexual in nature but as political.

White women are not (re)producers of race only because of their sometime role in biological reproduction, but because they constitute a cultural and political force toward racialization. White women are not just biologically significant, then, but politically so: they are a central force because women are not a minority population in the United States. We exist in numbers enough that—if aligned—would produce significant political change. That women, as a political force, have never aligned significantly across barriers of race, class, sexuality, or gender identity, is a product of white supremacy, a phenomenon that not only includes but is dependent upon the participation of white women. I argue here that the real threat of "white genocide" does not lie simply in the policing of white women's sexuality, but in the policing of their sororal alliances.

Failed Sisterhood and the Production
of White Womanhood in *A Mercy*

White women's failed sisterhood with women of color—like racism more generally—is a structural rather than an individual problem, and one with deep historical roots. Toni Morrison's 2008 novel *A Mercy* met a moment of national optimism and misguided discourses about a supposedly "post-racial" cultural moment with an allegory, of sorts, about national racial failures. In the relationships between the novel's women—and particularly in the women of color's respective relationships with the text's main white woman character, Rebekka Vaark, we see the simultaneous foreclosure of interracial kinship set alongside the (re)construction of white womanhood.

After the death of Jacob Vaark, his household includes his white widow along with three nonwhite women. These women—Florens (a Black girl), Lina (a Native woman), and Sorrow (a mixed-race Black woman)—have been variously sold to Vaark at different times, and the respective conditions of their enslavement are complex. The death of the white patriarch leaves the women in a moment of possibility and uncertainty. Near the novel's end, Morrison turns to the question of what will become of this queer household of nonnormative and ill-defined relations. Scully, a white indentured servant, observes and summarizes their situation near the novel's close:

> They once thought they were a kind of family because together they had carved companionship out of isolation. But the family they imagined they had become was false. Whatever each one loved, sought or escaped, their futures were separate and anyone's guess. One thing was certain, courage alone would not be enough. Minus bloodlines, he saw nothing yet on the horizon to unite them.[8]

Even though we see these women and Rebekka work alongside one another in the same domestic space over the course of the novel, with Jacob's death, the power relations between them become apparent. While the widow Vaark's future seems only to lie in the possibility of her remarriage, she can still reorient herself around a new kinship relation to white masculine power. If sexual kinship is racializing, Rebekka might solidify her own racialization as white by marrying again. When Rebekka is sick with smallpox and thought to be dying, we understand that she, herself, offers a small degree of power and protection to the women with whom she shares domestic space. Morrison describes Florens, Lina, and Sorrow as "three unmastered women," noting their inability to inherit, their femaleness, and their tenuous relationship even to the right to their own bodily selves.[9] What Rebekka has and these women lack is a kinship relation (even if only a potential kinship relation) to white masculinity, and the attendant privilege of her own relative racialization as white. Neither do these nonwhite women have any right to the shared space they inhabit. Morrison tells us that, "Female and illegal, they would be interlopers, squatters, if they stayed on after Mistress died, subject to purchase, hire, assault, abduction, exile."[10] As property or potential property themselves, and despite their previous domestic relations, these women have been excluded from forms and spaces of the normative white family.

Morrison's enslaved women also exhibit the signs of kinlessness produced by slavery and settler colonialism. Lina and Florens both exhibit "mother hunger—to be one or to have one," having been wrenched from their own mothers and without any viable replacement for this relationship other than through each other.[11] As their kinlessness is a product of enslavement and genocide, it figures as a kind of orphaning in the novel, and their lack of consanguinity seems to prevent them from any form of reparative adoption. Sorrow's first child is killed, and in her second she shows a ravenous delight, the arrival of which prompts her to rename herself "Complete." But one cannot help but wonder if Sorrow's Completeness is precarious. Moreover, these nonwhite women seem not to have formed sustaining kinship relations with one another; this is not a family of fictive kin. Morrison reminds us explicitly that "they were not a family—not even a like-minded group. They were orphans, each and all."[12] Foreclosing interracial kinship in its barest biological sense, mothers are not simply dead or lost forever in Morrison's novel, but sacrificed under circumstances of pure desperation. Florens's mother sells her in order to avoid her child's inevitable rape in slavery. Only Sorrow's motherhood is complete, and this too is utterly precarious by virtue of its accompanying race-making. However these women might be productive, they cannot (re)produce whiteness and this fact puts them at risk.

Neither is interracial adoption possible in A Mercy. The relationships Rebekka has with Lina, Sorrow, and Florens are decidedly not maternal. Any hope for family that these women have, it will have to be formed without the white woman. These nonfamily relations ultimately structure both the family's foreclosure in this novel and the process of racialization itself. In Morrison's final pages, we read about Florens's sale to Jacob Vaark, orchestrated by her own mother as she perceives an increasingly immediate need to protect her from the inevitable sexual assault of their enslaver. Addressing Florens, the woman we only see described via her relationship to her daughter as "a minha mãe" ("my mother" in Portuguese) explains her own racialization as consubstantial with her kinlessness. On the auction block, she tells us, "I learned how I was not a person from my country, nor from my families. I was negrita."[13] Just as race is relative to familial genealogies of racialization, so is this kinless, saleable form of Blackness determined by the removal from this assumedly pre-racialized structure of belonging.

Race is (re)produced in scenes about Florens and her mother, and it is produced through relations of kinship. Florens' mother does not inherit race from her family, but from white enslavers, who produce Blackness-as-enslavement. This tethering of Blackness and antiblack racism seems initially to evidence a foundational tenet of Afropessimism: the teleology of Blackness's (re)production as ontological death. But whiteness is also (re)constructed in Morrison's novel. Not only are Florens and her mother (re)racialized here, but Rebekka becomes a white woman (and a more clearly white supremacist one) over the course of her story. Rebekka is (re)racialized both in relation to her husband and in her non-kinship relations with Florens, Lina, and Sorrow. With no surviving children of her own, Rebekka does not find solace in nonbiological kinship. She neither adopts nor loves Florens or Sorrow. Rebekka's home seems to have some potential for sororal affection in the necessarily shared labor she and Lina share, but their relationship is not sisterly. Jacob's death sparks Rebekka's concern about her own self-preservation, and her whiteness can only be preserved independently of such interracial kinship relations. Unable or unwilling to reproduce biological whiteness or to form interracial kinship with the women around her, the white mistress ironically becomes kinless herself. In the nexus of racialization and kinship, it is perhaps the case that the white woman is the most kinless of all.

I close my discussion with Morrison's narrative of race's early instantiation in what would become the United States in order to remind us again of race's relativity. Here we have a foundational narrative of racialization that is dependent upon kinship's foreclosures. A Mercy was published in the landscape of Obama-era national hope for a supposedly post-racial future and speaks truth to the problem of framing interracial kinship as potential: it could always have been otherwise. Barack Obama's election presented many with a moment of imagining interracial kinship's ability to breed anti-racist futures if not race's "end" itself. But as Morrison shows, racial genealogies work in a variety of relational ways. Rebekka's whiteness and Florens's and Sorrow's Blackness and Lina's Nativeness all function as relations of kinship, formed in directionalities that even while they may predictably follow racialization, do not necessarily do so. Christina Sharpe's discussion of race as both logic and political project speaks to the absence of this necessity and therefore the need for deliberation in remaking kinship and belonging according to anti-racist ideals. She writes, "Whiteness is a political project and it is also a logic, by which I mean it is a calculus, a way of sorting oneself and others into categories of those who must be protected and those who are, or soon will be, expendable."[14] *A Mercy* shows us that these denials and racializations of kinship, the logics and calculus of racially related sorting, are not logically necessary, even if they are contextually unavoidable.

White Feminism and Its Possible Racial Futures

Morrison's fictionalized failure of interracial kinship, though set in the United States' pre-national history, is not a definitive moment for race's relative trajectories, but a representative one. Likewise, the failure of AERA was not the single defining moment of foreclosure for interracial sororal kinship, but one of many such moments. The history of white womanhood's failure to embrace interracial kinship that I outline here does not have a linear trajectory, but is recursive. Such moments of failed interracial kinship are part of the continued racialization and (re)racialization of white women not only as white but as white supremacist. While the genealogical (re)production of whiteness (and white supremacy) is difficult to detect, we would do well to recognize race-making not as a static state or even a clean trajectory through history, but as a process of continual re-instantiation and reinforcement. Neither whiteness nor white supremacy are simply inevitable, but must be created in their various personal and historical contexts. White women's racialization is formed and re-formed in these moments, keeping the figure of the white woman at the center of national structures of racism.

Herein lies the failure of white feminism: Despite interracial kinship and the queer genealogies of racialization that have sometimes (re)racialized white women beyond whiteness, the tendency of white womanhood toward political, structural white supremacy persists. These failures of anti-racist white womanhood do not mean that anti-racist white womanhood is inherently impossible, but illustrate the various ways that the workings of US racialization has most often aligned white womanhood with a white-supremacist patriarchy (sometimes with white women's complicity and sometimes without it). This alignment forecloses other available structures of kinship, namely of the kinds I have discussed throughout this project—which have been available and which have shaped US literature and culture since the nineteenth century, but which remain at the margins of racialization even as they illustrate these alternative, queer genealogies by which race has traveled. This alignment does not always take the face of overt racism, however, but emerges most often in more subtle ways that are still, at heart, profoundly unsisterly.

After the 2018 Women's March, a photograph of Alison Saar's Harriet Tubman Memorial in Harlem circulated widely. The statue, *Swing Low*, is located in the "Harriet Tubman Triangle" at the intersection of Frederick Douglass Boulevard, West 122nd Street, and St. Nicholas Avenue (see figure c.2). At the march, someone had dressed the figure of Harriet Tubman with a bright pink pussyhat, a highly-critiqued marker of a white feminist movement that has continued a long tradition of exclusion and privilege. A predictable flurry of critique erupted from Black social media. This included an Instagram post from Nicole Moore, founder of theHotness, an activist-oriented online journal written explicitly for and prominently featuring women of color. In her post Moore discussed the deliberate nature of this act and its inherently false activism.[15] I quote her post here in full:

> Yesterday after attending the NYCLU rally for immigrant and reproductive rights and hearing a diverse roster of speakers breakdown abortion access and #DACA politics; and then after doing me and going to Pilates I was checking out my TL and saw that someone put a damn pink pussy hat on the statue of Harriet Tubman in Harlem. #Pinkpussyhats in no way represent the rage, power, and constant radical, resistive stance of a Black feminist like revolutionary Tubman! I was pissed! All day I watched white women many, if not mostly, in their pink pussy hats marching who I never see the rest of the year at DACA rallies, at forums on violence against Black transgender women, or in #Harlem at meetings regarding afford-able housing or tenants rights. I was on 14th St and couldn't get back up-town fast enough last night to snatch that joint off her head. When I got there the hat had already been removed. Someone knew like I knew, the statue was fine as is. #HarrietTubman, like most Black women activists, do not need to don a pink pussy hat, a safety pin, or any other (white) feminist accoutrements to show that we are down with the movement! If recent elections aren't proof enough, WE ARE THE MOVEMENT! The time and energy used to knit this hat and to climb the statue to place it on top could've been used to help and support the real lives of Black women in Harlem. I wish white women would stop playing activist. 45 is a racist misogynist. This is no time to be cute! If you want to f*ck with a statue, go and show your disdain for the statue of J. Marion Sims the "gynecolo-

gist" who bought Black women slaves to conduct surgical experiments without anesthesia. Leave this statue alone! #BlackRadicalWomen are already good. We are enough and matter just as we are! #handsoffharriet #BlackHarlemLives #timesup #blacklivesmatter UPDATE!! FOUND OUT THAT @emancipated_negress SCALED THE STATUE AND REMOVED THE HAT! THANK YOU SIS![16]

Moore here describes the fundamental problems with this white-feminist use of Tubman's image. It follows a long history of white women's participation in mainstream feminist struggles for their own interests, while both relying on nonwhite women's labor in those struggles but also ignoring these women's own most pressing interests. Moore critiques white feminism's historical and continued alignments with white supremacy, referring to the current political moment in which 53 percent of white women helped to elect the forty-fifth president of the United States (here called "45"). These failures of white women to politically align themselves with nonwhite women in the twenty-first-century moment we are witnessing is not unlike that of Morrison's fictionalized pre-national family drama or AERA's decline.

Foisting a pink pussyhat on the image of Tubman is not unlike the act of blackface we see in Browning's painting and in the blackface minstrelsy I discussed in chapter 1. Both are appropriative acts that pervert images of Blackness in order to misconstrue the nature and political orientation of Black women. Both use Blackness in attempts at humor that miss the mark by failing to imagine an audience beyond the position of white privilege. Both acts elide the interests, activism, and very presence of Black women themselves. As Moore and others have explained, Tubman's life and work was more radical than the white feminist brand attempting to claim her. This claiming of Black feminist history, done in lieu of actual engagement with and work alongside Black women in the present, is an act of willful ignorance performed under the guise of interracial sisterhood.

Saar's statue depicts Tubman in the act of helping to free enslaved people—an illegal action in which Tubman repeatedly put her own life at risk. The back of Tubman's gown is embedded with tendrils attempting to drag her back to slavery. On the gown's front are images representing the people Tubman helped to emancipate. These faces are molded in the style of West African passport masks, which were carried by travelers and identified their tribe or nation. These were markers of family, and Saar deftly connects Tubman to not only these other enslaved people, but to their genealogies, as her presence in Harlem reaches forward to the genealogies of free Black

C.2 ALISON
SAAR, "SWING
LOW," 2008.
PHOTOGRAPH
BY JONATHAN
SENCHYNE.

people who would come to see her as an icon of Black radical activism, an inspiration for anti-racist struggles even in our present moment. But to understand Tubman's genealogies as racially essentialist would be a mistake. Tubman's racial genealogies are not simply biological but relational. For this reason, they cannot be simply appropriated by whiteness, but they might be productively engaged by it, even to the point of kinship.

What would mainstream white feminist engagement with radical, interracial sisterhood look like? Such sisterly care would likely involve white women's active presence in all the places Moore notes their absence: "at DACA rallies, at forums on violence against Black transgender women, or in #Harlem at meetings regarding affordable housing or tenants rights." That sisterly care would necessitate white women taking the time, as Moore suggests, "to help and support the real lives of Black women in Harlem." It may even enact a genealogical turn away from the (re)production of white supremacy, in which mainstream white feminism has historically been complicit. When the queer possibilities of racial (re)construction come into view, we can see more radical possibilities for white womanhood in particular—possibilities that have the potential to decenter white supremacy by halting its reproduction. This does not necessitate halting the reproduction of white-presenting bodies, of course, but of offering these bodies different racial/genealogical possibilities. As I have shown here, white genealogies do not *necessarily* tend toward whiteness in their racial (re)production. Other racial teleologies are possible. Whiteness must therefore be urged toward a genealogical future that does not reproduce white supremacy, but toward a more radically inclusive future—a future that will necessitate kinship with those who are Black and Brown and Indigenous and Queer. More radical racial constructions of white womanhood are necessary if these women are to be included in our intersectional, feminist futures. As race itself is continually (re)constructed, our moment is not *post*-race, but race might take new directions.

NOTES

Introduction

1 Kate Chopin, "Désirée's Baby" [1893], in *Bayou Folk* (Cambridge, MA: Riverside Press, 1895), 154.

2 Interestingly, the assumption Armand makes is not that Désirée has been unfaithful. A short story of similarly reappearing racial genealogies is Pauline Hopkins's "Talma Gordon," which includes accusations of sexual unfaithfulness. As Captain Gordon says, "I hurried away to your mother and accused her of infidelity to her marriage vows," which he does without first considering the possibility that a woman he had believed to be white had racially mixed ancestry. See Pauline Hopkins, "Talma Gordon" [1900], in *The American 1890s*, edited by Susan Harris Smith and Melanie Dawson (Durham, NC: Duke University Press, 2000), 115.

3 Alys Eve Weinbaum, *Wayward Reproductions: Genealogies of Race and Nation in Transatlantic Modern Thought* (Durham, NC: Duke University Press, 2004), 16, original emphasis.

4 As Anna Shannon Elfenbein holds, "Désirée's Baby" is, in Chopin's oeuvre, "the story most clearly patterned on the tragic octoroon formula." See *Women on the Color Line: Evolving Stereotypes and the Writings of George Washington Cable, Grace King, Kate Chopin* (Charlottesville: University Press of Virginia, 1989), 118.

5 Alisha Gaines, *Black for a Day: White Fantasies of Race and Empathy* (Chapel Hill: University of North Carolina Press, 2017), 8.

6 See, for example, Kimberly TallBear, "Narratives of Race and Indigeneity in the Genographic Project," *Journal of Law, Medicine and Ethics* 35, no. 3 (2007): 412–24; J. Kēhaulani Kauanui, *Hawaiian Blood: Colonialism and the Politics of Sovereignty and Indigeneity* (Durham, NC: Duke University Press, 2008); and Jean M. O'Brien, *Firsting and Lasting: Writing Indians Out of Existence in New England* (Minneapolis: University of Minnesota Press, 2010).

7 Jodi A. Byrd, *Transit of Empire: Indigenous Critiques of Colonialism* (Minneapolis: University of Minnesota Press, 2011), xxiii.

8 Elizabeth Freeman, *Time Binds: Queer Temporalities, Queer Histories* (Durham, NC: Duke University Press, 2010), xxii.

9 Holly Jackson, *American Blood: The Ends of Family in American Literature, 1850–1900* (New York: Oxford University Press, 2014), 7.

10 See Hortense Spillers, "Mama's Baby, Papa's Maybe: An American Grammar Book," *Diacritics* 17, no. 2 (1987): 74, and Saidiya Hartman, *Lose Your Mother: A Journey Along the Atlantic Slave Route* (New York: Farrar, Straus and Giroux, 2008), 85.

11 Alexis Pauline Gumbs, "Nobody Mean More: Black Feminist Pedagogy and Solidarity," in *Imperial University: Academic Repression and Scholarly Dissent*, edited by Piya Chatterjee and Sunaina Maira (Minneapolis: University of Minnesota Press, 2014), 255, original emphasis.

12 Darieck Scott, *Extravagant Abjection: Blackness, Power, and Sexuality in the African American Literary Imagination* (New York: New York University Press, 2010), 8, original emphasis.

13 Colin Dayan, *The Law Is a White Dog: How Legal Rituals Make and Unmake Persons* (Princeton, NJ: Princeton University Press, 2013), 118.

14 John Ernest, *Chaotic Justice: Rethinking African American Literary History* (Chapel Hill: University of North Carolina Press, 2009), 36.

15 Richard Dyer, *White* (New York: Routledge, 1997), 60.

16 Ernest, *Chaotic Justice*, 41.

17 Later in this introduction and in my conclusion, I address the antiblackness that attends such understandings of mixed-race Black people as "mixed-race" rather than Black. This problem is separate from, though not unrelated to, questions of colorism.

18 Critical Mixed Race Studies has recently taken up an important critique of white-centered racial mixture. See, for example, Greg Carter's discussion of this problem in *The United States of the United Races: A Utopian History of Racial Mixing* (New York: New York University Press, 2013). Work on interracial relations external from white people have also been the topic of much important work in nineteenth-century studies, including Julia H. Lee, *Interracial Encounters: Reciprocal Representations in African and Asian American Literatures, 1896–1937* (New York: New York University Press, 2011) and Hsuan L. Hsu, *Sitting in Darkness: Mark Twain, Asia, and Comparative Racialization* (New York: New York University Press, 2015).

19 Thomas Jefferson, *Notes on the State of Virginia* [1785], edited by David Waldstreicher (Boston: Bedford/St. Martin's Press, 2002), 176. Samuel Morton, *Crania Americana; or, A Comparative View of the Skulls of Various Aboriginal Nations of North and South America, to Which Is Prefixed an Essay on the Varieties of the Human Species* (Philadelphia: J. Dobson, 1839) and *Crania Aegyptiaca; or, Observations on Egyptian Ethnography, Derived from Anatomy, History, and the Monuments* (Philadelphia: J. Penington, 1844).

20 *Oxford English Dictionary*, s.v. "biologism" (accessed January 23, 2020, https://www.lexico.com/definition/biologism).

21 Cheyfitz uses the term "bio-logic" in opposition to a cultural logic of identification and identity formation, which he shows is a more appropriate paradigm by which to understand American Indian identity. See Eric Cheyfitz, "The (Post) Colonial Construction of Indian Country," in *The Columbia Guide to American Indian Literatures of the United States since 1945*, edited by Eric Cheyfitz (New York: Columbia University Press, 2006), 16. William Stanton discusses the development of biological understandings of race throughout the nineteenth century more generally in *The Leopard's Spots* (Chicago: University of Chicago Press, 1960).

22 Judith Butler, *Undoing Gender* (New York: Routledge, 2004), 103.

23 Kimberly TallBear, *Native American DNA: Tribal Belonging and the False Promise of Genetic Science* (Minneapolis: University of Minnesota Press, 2013), 31.

24 Jefferson, *Notes on the State of Virginia*, 176.

25 Katy L. Chiles, *Transformable Race: Surprising Metamorphoses in the Literature of Early America* (New York: Oxford University Press, 2014), 2.

26 Mark Rifkin, *The Erotics of Sovereignty: Queer Native Writing in the Era of Self-Determination* (Minneapolis: University of Minnesota Press, 2012), 4.

27 Christina Sharpe, "Lose Your Kin," *New Inquiry*, November 16, 2016 (https://thenewinquiry.com/essays/lose-your-kin/).

28 Julius Augustus Lemcke describes this in *Reminiscences of an Indianian* (Indianapolis: Hollenbeck Press, 1905), 196. Several contemporary writers on Civil War–era politics also mention this demonstration as significant. See James A. Rawley, *Race and Politics: "Bleeding Kansas" and the Coming of the Civil War* (Philadelphia: Lippincott, 1969), 167; James M. McPherson. *Battle Cry of Freedom: The Civil War Era, 1848–1865* (New York: Ballantine Books, 1988), 159; Eric Foner, *Reconstruction: America's Unfinished Revolution, 1863–1877* (New York: Harper and Row, 1988), 32; and Stephen H. Hartnett, *Democratic Dissent and the Cultural Fictions of Antebellum America* (Urbana: University of Illinois Press, 2002), 69. Throughout this book I have chosen not to represent the word "nigger" in my textual citations, but will represent this word as "n[—]" as I have here. I recognize the historical violence attached to this term and the importance of not eliding that violence in discussions of racism. However, I am tired of reading this word and I no longer see the illustrative value in repeating it, even in quotation, in my own work. I believe the force of racist violence is conveyed sufficiently in the quotations in which this term appears even without the word's direct quotation. My choice to represent this term as "n[—]" is meant to convey both the word's presence in these texts and my deliberate refusal of direct quotation. My methodology here follows the pedagogical principals that Koritha Mitchell discusses in her practice of not reading this word aloud that in her classrooms. See "Teaching & the N-word: Questions to Consider," on Koritha Mitchell's official website, accessed April 16, 2020, http://www.korithamitchell.com/teaching-and-the-n-word/ and Koritha Mitchell, "The N-Word in the Classroom: Just Say NO," March 4, 2019, in *C19 Podcast,* produced by Xine Yao, Paul Kotheimer, and Koritha Mitchell, podcast,

MP3 audio, https://podcasts.apple.com/us/podcast/s2e6-the-n-word-in-the
-classroom-just-say-no/id1275235064?i=1000431046556.

29 Elise Lemire, *Miscegenation: Making Race in America* (Philadelphia: University
of Pennsylvania Press, 2002), 4. While Lemire uses the phrase "sexual race preference" here, I choose the word "desire" rather than "preference" to highlight
these sexual-racial orientations. The word "preference" suggests a prioritization,
indicating that sexual desire is directed preferentially at persons of one specific
race rather than another. While it may be true that some people or characters
do sexually "prefer" mates of a particular race (whether for political, fetishistic,
practical, racist, or other reasons), this is not always the case. My reference to
"sexual desire" is meant to leave open various possibilities for the sexual impulses of the figures I discuss. Whether these impulses constitute hierarchical,
sexual, racial "preferences" (as was assumed about figures such as Desdemona
and Mary King) is a matter tangential to my discussion. The possibility that
their sexual desire is directed at nonwhite men in these narratives is the possibility with which I am most concerned.

30 Dorothy Roberts, *Killing the Black Body: Race, Reproduction, and the Meaning of
Liberty* (New York: Pantheon Books, 1997), 246.

31 For a discussion of how African Americans deftly pushed against the various
kinds of racist scientific discourse that would both exclude them and brand
them as inferior, see Britt Rusert, *Fugitive Science: Empiricism and Freedom
in Early African American Culture* (New York: New York University Press,
2017).

32 Jennifer Morgan, *Laboring Women: Reproduction and Gender in New World Slavery* (Philadelphia: University of Pennsylvania Press, 2004), 9.

33 Roderick Ferguson, *Aberrations in Black: Toward a Queer of Color Critique* (Minneapolis: University of Minnesota Press, 2003), 13.

34 P. Gabrielle Foreman, "Who's Your Mama? 'White' Mulatta Genealogies, Early
Photography, and Anti-Passing Narratives of Slavery and Freedom," *American
Literary History* 14, no. 3 (2002): 506.

35 On the latter point, see Jennifer Morgan, *Laboring Women.*

36 Ferguson, *Aberrations in Black,* 20.

37 Tavia Nyong'o, *The Amalgamation Waltz: Race, Performance, and the Ruses of
Memory* (Minneapolis: University of Minnesota Press, 2009), 6.

38 Toni Morrison, *Playing in the Dark: Whiteness and the Literary Imagination* (New
York: Vintage, 1992), 5.

39 Barbara Christian, "The Race for Theory," *Feminist Studies* 14, no. 1 (Spring,
1988): 68. Derrick Spires notes, similarly, how literary forms "such as the
sketches, short fiction, and poetry published in black and antislavery periodicals
and newspapers, did . . . important theoretical work." See Derrick Spires, *The
Practices of Citizenship: Black Politics and Print Culture in the Early United States*
(Philadelphia: University of Pennsylvania Press, 2019), 10.

40 Michael Omi and Howard Winant, *Racial Formation in the United States from the
1960s to the 1990s* (New York: Routledge, 1994), 55.

41 Mark Rifkin. *When Did Indians Become Straight? Kinship, the History of Sexuality, and Native Sovereignty* (New York: Oxford University Press, 2011), 34.

42 Lydia Maria Child, *An Appeal in Favor of Americans Called Africans* [1833] (New York: Arno Press, 1968), 200.

43 These photographs are from the William and Ellen Smith Craft Photo Album, in the Craft and Crum Families, 1780–2007 Collection, held by the Avery Research Center at the College of Charleston. The entire album is digitized here: https://lcdl.library.cofc.edu/lcdl/catalog/lcdl:39896.

44 My discussion of "kinfullness" has been developed separately from, though it is not entirely unrelated to, what Ruha Benjamin calls "kinfulness." See Ruha Benjamin, "Black AfterLives Matter: Cultivating Kinfulness as Reproductive Justice," in *Making Kin, Not Population,* edited by Adele Clarke and Donna Haraway (Chicago: Prickly Paradigm Press, 2018). My spelling—with a double "l"—means to recall Hortense Spillers' notion of kinlessness and specifically to replace this with an alternative (though not incompatible) theorization of kinship's fullness. I discuss my concept of kinfullness more extensively in chapter 4.

45 Lee Edelman, *No Future: Queer Theory and the Death Drive* (Durham, NC: Duke University Press, 2004), 4.

46 See Julian, Gill-Peterson, Rebekah Sheldon, Kathryn Bond Stockton. "What Is the Now, Even of Then?" GLQ: *A Journal of Lesbian and Gay Studies* 22.4 (2016): 495.

47 On race and childhood innocence, see Robin Bernstein, *Racial Innocence: Performing American Childhood from Slavery to Civil Rights* (New York: New York University Press, 2011).

48 Nyong'o, *Amalgamation Waltz,* 4.

49 Katherine McKittrick, *Demonic Grounds: Black Women and the Cartographies of Struggle* (Minneapolis: University of Minnesota Press, 2006), xii.

50 McKittrick, *Demonic Grounds,* ix, xi.

Chapter One. Blackface Desdemona, or, the White Woman "Begrimed"

Portions of this material were previously published in "Blackface Desdemona: Theorizing Race on the Nineteenth-Century American Stage," *Theatre Annual* 70 (2017), 39–59.

1 Anna Cora Ogden Mowatt Ritchie, *Mimic Life; or, Before and behind the Curtain. A Series of Narratives* (Boston: Ticknor and Fields, 1856), 103.

2 Ritchie, *Mimic Life,* 103.

3 Ritchie, *Mimic Life,* 104. In his discussion of this scene, Jeffrey H. Richards describes the corporality of this exchange of color as a reminder of the body that shatters the illusion of the embodied figures onstage. See Jeffrey H. Richards, "Chastity and the Stage in Mowatt's 'Stella,'" *Studies in American Fiction* 24, no. 1 (1996): 87–100.

4 Ritchie, *Mimic Life,* 104.

5 Even as I acknowledge the use of blackface makeup's failures to represent Black people in this chapter, the use of this medium metaphorized the racialization

of Blackness. That is to say, these performances were a form of antiblack racism that had very real, harmful effects upon actual Black people, whose existence was invoked even as they were absented from such performances. My capitalization of Blackness in this chapter is meant to acknowledge the importance of considering actual Black people and their racialization in this discussion and also to differentiate Black people from the blackface makeup that failed to represent them even as it reflected popular ideas about their racialization.

6 There were productions of *Othello* by entirely African American casts in the nineteenth century, and productions involving Native American people. Othello was also played by Afro-British and African American actors (such as Ira Aldridge) in England. However, Othello was not played by a Black man with an accompanying white cast in the United States until Paul Robeson's groundbreaking, controversial performance in 1943.

7 William Winter, "Shakespeare on the Stage: Fourth Paper: Othello," *Century Magazine* 82 (1911): 512.

8 "Othello's Costume," *Once a Week*, September 8, 1866, 274, original emphasis.

9 Ellen Terry, *Ellen Terry's Memoirs*, edited by by Edith Craig and Christopher St. John (New York: G. P. Putnam, 1932), 160. Kenneth Gross notes the mobility of Blackness, as it "does not stay with Othello alone" but "touches other characters, shifting place and face in often dreamlike ways," and also notes the metaphorical blackening of Desdemona's face. Kenneth Gross, *Shakespeare's Noise* (Chicago: University of Chicago Press, 2001), 104.

10 Abigail Adams, Letter to William Stephens Smith, 18 September 1785, Adams Papers, Digital Edition, Adams Family Correspondence, Volume 6, Massachusetts Historical Society (www.masshist.org/publications/apde/portia.php?id =AFC06d119). See Lois Potter, *Othello* (Manchester: Manchester University Press, 2002), 31; and Dympna Callaghan, *Shakespeare without Women* (New York: Routledge, 2000), 80–88. Discussions of stage makeup, femininity, and sexuality appear in Sujata Iyengar, *Shades of Difference: Mythologies of Skin Color in Early Modern England* (Philadelphia: University of Pennsylvania Press, 2005), 123–39; and Kim F. Hall, *Things of Darkness: Economies of Race and Gender in Early Modern Europe* (Ithaca, NY: Cornell University Press, 1995), 87–92. As late as the twentieth century, director Trevor Nunn expressed anxiety about blackface makeup's transfer. Discussing the need for Black actors to play Othello, Nunn observed blackface as an inherent impediment to a "physical relationship between Othello and Desdemona" onstage, arguing that "with a white actor in black make-up that's the one thing you can't have. If they touch each other, Othello comes off on Desdemona." See Alan Renton, "Honest Conversation: After a Seven Year Absence, Trevor Nunn Is Returning to Shakespeare," *Independent*, August 17, 1989, 10.

11 For similar discussions of white womanhood under threat of improper marking, see Jonathan Senchyne, "Bottles of Ink and Reams of Paper: *Clotel*, Racialization, and the Material Culture of Print," in *Early African American Print Culture*, edited by Lara L. Cohen and Jordan A. Stein (Philadelphia: University of Pennsylvania Press, 2012), 140–58; and Melissa Gniadek, "Mary Howard's Mark:

Children's Literature and the Scales of Reading the Pacific," *Early American Literature* 50, no. 3 (2015): 797–826.

12 For a discussion of the various uses of Desdemona as an icon of (white) womanhood, see Edward Kahn, "Desdemona and the Role of Women in the Antebellum North," *Theatre Journal* 60, no. 2 (2008): 235–55.

13 On how race studies can benefit from thinking about Shakespeare, see Ayanna Thompson, *Passing Strange: Shakespeare, Race, and Contemporary America* (New York: Oxford University Press, 2011), 5.

14 Celia Daileader, *Racism, Misogyny, and the Othello Myth: Interracial Couples from Shakespeare to Spike Lee* (New York: Cambridge University Press, 2005), 6–7.

15 Joyce Green MacDonald also discusses *Othello*'s later resonances in the Americas. See Joyce Green MacDonald, "Border Crossings: Women, Race, and *Othello* in Gayl Jones's *Mosquito*," *Tulsa Studies in Women's Literature* 28, no. 2 (2009): 315–36.

16 On the history of relationships between Black men and white women, see Martha Hodes, *White Women, Black Men: Illicit Sex in the Nineteenth-Century South* (New Haven, CT: Yale University Press, 1997) and *Sex, Love, Race: Crossing Boundaries in North American History* (New York: New York University Press, 1995); Joshua D. Rothman, *Notorious in the Neighborhood: Sex and Families across the Color Line in Virginia, 1787–1861* (Chapel Hill: University of North Carolina Press, 2003); and Cassandra Jackson, *Barriers Between Us: Interracial Sex in Nineteenth-Century American Literature* (Bloomington: Indiana University Press, 2004).

17 Morrison, *Playing in the Dark*, 6.

18 See Eric Lott, *Love and Theft: Blackface Minstrelsy and the American Working Class* (New York: Oxford University Press, 1995).

19 Angela C. Pao, "Ocular Revisions: Re-Casting *Othello* in Text and Performance," in *Colorblind Shakespeare: New Perspectives on Race and Performance*, edited by Ayanna Thompson (New York: Routledge, 2006), 37–45; Robert Toll, *Blacking Up: The Minstrel Show in Nineteenth-Century America* (New York: Oxford University Press, 1974); and Francesca T. Royster, "Playing with (a) Difference: Early Black Shakespearean Actors, Blackface and Whiteface," in *Shakespeare in America*, edited by Alden T. Vaughan and Virginia Mason Vaughan (Washington, DC: Folger Shakespeare Library, 2007), 35–47.

20 William Shakespeare, *Othello: The Moor of Venice. Texts and Contexts*, edited by Kim F. Hall (Boston: Bedford/St. Martin's Press, 2007), 5.3.386–88. Shakespeare's Folio and Quarto texts differ here, the former reading "My name" and the latter "Her name." I quote the Quarto's "Her" because this is the text in all but two of over two-dozen nineteenth-century American editions I have examined. Thanks to Virginia Mason Vaughan for indicating how the apparent shift in whose name is begrimed in Shakespeare's Quarto and Folio presents another opportunity to discuss the transfer of "race" from Othello to Desdemona.

21 Potter, *Othello*, 56.

22 On the prevalence of this interpretation, see James H. Dormon, *Theater in the Antebellum South, 1815–1861* (Chapel Hill: University of North Carolina Press, 1967), 276–77; and Charles H. Shattuck, *Shakespeare on the American Stage:*

From Booth and Barrett to Sothern and Marlowe (Cranbury, NJ: Associated University Presses, 1987), 47.

23 John Quincy Adams, "Misconceptions of Shakespeare Upon the Stage" [1836], in *Notes and Comments upon Certain Plays and Actors of Shakespeare, with Criticism and Correspondence,* edited by James Henry Hackett, 3rd ed. (New York: Carelton, 1864), 224.

24 Kim C. Sturgess notes *Othello*'s popularity in nineteenth-century American performance in *Shakespeare and the American Nation* (New York: Cambridge University Press, 2004), 15–17. Confirming that popularity even in the antebellum South, see Woodrow L. Holbein, "Shakespeare in Charleston, 1800–1860," in *Shakespeare in the South: Essays on Performance,* edited by Philip C. Kolin (Jackson: University Press of Mississippi, 1983), 98; Charles B. Lower, "Othello as Black on Southern Stages, Then and Now," in *Shakespeare in the South: Essays on Performance,* edited by Philip C. Kolin (Jackson: University Press of Mississippi, 1993), 201; and James Shapiro (ed.), *Shakespeare in America: An Anthology from the Revolution to Now* (New York: Library of America, 2014), xx–xxi. Marvin McAllister writes that *Othello* was also "by far the most popular stage African play in the eighteenth- and nineteenth-century United States" in *White People Do Not Know How to Behave at Entertainments Designed for Ladies and Gentlemen of Color: William Brown's African and American Theater* (Chapel Hill: University of North Carolina Press, 2003), 109. On the importance of race to New England productions of *Othello,* see Paraic Finnerty, *Emily Dickinson's Shakespeare* (Amherst: University of Massachusetts Press, 2006), 161–80. The US Supreme Court case of *Loving v. Virginia,* 388 US 1 (1967), determined that state anti-miscegenation laws were unconstitutional in 1967.

25 Virginia Mason Vaughan, *Othello: A Contextual History* (New York: Cambridge University Press, 1994), 64.

26 Shakespeare, *Othello,* 1.1.88–89, 110–11, 115–17. On these omissions, see James Andreas, "Othello's African-American Progeny," *South Atlantic Review* 57, no. 4 (1992): 41. The implied bestiality is also significant. As Winthrop D. Jordan notes, this racialized imagery also suggests "the sexuality of beasts and the bestiality of sex." See Winthrop D. Jordan, *White over Black: American Attitudes toward the Negro, 1550–1812* (Chapel Hill: University of North Carolina Press, 1968): 38.

27 Virginia Mason Vaughan, "Making Shakespeare American: Shakespeare's Dissemination in Nineteenth-Century America," in *Shakespeare in American Life,* edited by Alden T. Vaughan and Virginia Mason Vaughan (Washington, DC: Folger Shakespeare Library, 2007), 23–34; and Shapiro, *Shakespeare in America.*

28 Shapiro, *Shakespeare in America,* xx.

29 See, for example, [David Croly and George Wakeman], *Miscegenation: The Theory of the Blending of the Races, Applied to the American White Man and Negro* (New York: H. Dexter Hamilton & Co., 1864); L. Seaman, *What Miscegenation Is! And What We Are to Expect, Now That Mr. Lincoln Is Re-Elected* (New York: Waller and Willetts, 1865); Samuel S. Cox, "The Fate of the Freedman: Misce-

genation or Amalgamation" speech delivered in the House of Representatives, February 17, 1864 (Washington, D.C.: Office of "The Constitutional Union," 1864); and John H. Van Evrie, *Subgenation: The Theory of the Normal Relation of the Races, An Answer to "Miscegenation"* (New York: John Bradburn, 1864).

30 Josiah C. Nott, "The Mulatto, a Hybrid—Probable Extermination of the Two Races if the Whites and Blacks Are Allowed to Intermarry," *American Journal of the Medical Sciences* 6 (1843): 252.

31 On the practical nonnecessity of blackface performance, see Callaghan, *Shakespeare without Women*, 92.

32 Freeman, *Time Binds*, xxii.

33 Peggy Pascoe, *What Comes Naturally: Miscegenation Law and the Making of Race in America* (Oxford: Oxford University Press, 2009), shows how such anxieties were also invested in the preservation of "white" property and inheritance.

34 Benjamin Rush, "Observations Intended to Favour a Supposition that the Black Color (as it is called) of the Negroes is Derived from Leprosy," *Transactions of the American Philosophical Society* 4 (1799): 294.

35 Rush, "Observations," 294.

36 Jefferson, *Notes on the State of Virginia*, 176.

37 Mary Preston, *Studies in Shakespeare: A Book of Essays* (Philadelphia: Claxton, Remsen, and Haffelfinger, 1869), 71, original emphasis.

38 Adams, "Misconceptions of Shakespeare," 217–28.

39 Dormon, *Theater in the Antebellum South*, 277. On debates about Othello's color, see Holbein, "Shakespeare in Charleston," 99–101; Ania Loomba, *Shakespeare, Race, and Colonialism* (New York: Oxford University Press, 2002), 92; Tilden G. Edelstein, "*Othello* in America: The Drama of Racial Intermarriage," in *Region, Race, and Reconstruction: Essays in Honor of C. Van Woodward*, edited by J. Morgan Kousser and James M. McPherson (New York: Oxford University Press, 1982), 183–93; and Lower, "Othello as Black," 201–5.

40 Edelstein makes this point. See "*Othello* in America," 182, 184.

41 The word "photonegative" used to describe this casting first appeared in Miranda Johnson-Haddad's program notes for the fall 1997 production of *Othello* at the Washington Shakespeare Theater. On this production, see Denise Albanese, "Black and White, and Dread All Over: The Shakespeare Theater's 'Photonegative' *Othello* and the Body of Desdemona," in *A Feminist Companion to Shakespeare*, edited by Dympna Callaghan (Oxford: Blackwell, 2000), 226–47.

42 Sujata Iyengar writes about this production's racial critique in a different vein, indicating the false assumption that any Desdemona—even one played by a woman of European descent—would have "alabaster" skin any more than a black Othello might simply be understood as a "black devil" with "thick lips." See Sujata Iyengar, "White Faces, Blackface: The Production of 'Race' in *Othello*," in *Othello: New Critical Essays*, edited by Philip C. Kolin (New York: Routledge, 2002), 122.

43 The relevance of Black women to *Othello* is also evident in Djanet Sears's play, *Harlem Duet* (1997), which imagines a possible "backstory" for Othello via the

triangular relationship between Black women, Black men, and white women, and in Morrison's *Desdemona*, which I discuss below.

44 See Daileader, *Racism, Misogyny, and the Othello Myth*, 10; Hall, *Things of Darkness*, 9; and Joyce Green MacDonald, "Black Ram, White Ewe: Shakespeare, Race, and Women," in *A Feminist Companion to Shakespeare*, edited by Dympna Callaghan (Malden, MA: Blackwell, 2000), 194.

45 Lemire, *Miscegenation*, 5.

46 Preston, *Studies in Shakespeare*, 71, original emphasis.

47 Preston, *Studies in Shakespeare*, 66–67.

48 Shakespeare, *Othello*, 1.2.63, 73.

49 See, for example, Thomas Jefferson's articulation of this belief in *Notes on the State of Virginia*, 176.

50 John Quincy Adams, "The Character of Desdemona" [1836], in *Notes and Comments upon Certain Plays and Actors of Shakespeare, with Criticism and Correspondence*, edited by James Henry Hackett, 3rd ed. (New York: Carleton, 1864), 245. For a positive nineteenth-century reflection on Desdemona, see Mrs. (Anna) Jameson, "Desdemona," [1832] in *Characteristics of Women, Moral, Poetical, and Historical* (New York: John Wiley, 1848).

51 Adams, "Misconceptions of Shakespeare," 244, 245.

52 Adams, "The Character of Desdemona," 246; and Adams, "Misconceptions of Shakespeare," 245.

53 Adams, "Character of Desdemona," 235.

54 Edelstein, "*Othello* in America," 185.

55 See W. T. Lhamon Jr., *Jump Jim Crow: Lost Plays, Lyrics, and Street Prose of the First Atlantic Popular Culture* (Cambridge: Harvard University Press, 2003), 20–25.

56 T. D. Rice, *Otello, A Burlesque Opera* [1853], in *Jim Crow, American: Selected Songs and Plays*, edited by W. T. Lhamon Jr. (Cambridge: Harvard University Press, 2009). On this adaptation's relation to Shakespeare's original and its nineteenth-century models, Gioachino Rossini's opera *Otello* (1816) and Maurice Dowling's burlesque, *Othello Travestie* (1834), see Lhamon, *Jump Jim Crow*, 73–92; and W. T. Lhamon Jr., "Introduction," in Rice, *Jim Crow, American*, vii–xxiv.

57 Rice, *Otello*, 117.

58 Shakespeare, *Othello*, 1.3.165.

59 Rice, *Otello*, 120.

60 Rice, *Otello*, 120.

61 On this debate, see Daileader's discussion of "offstage sex and female desire" in *Eroticism on the Renaissance Stage: Transcendence, Desire, and the Limits of the Visible* (Cambridge: Cambridge University Press, 1998), 24–49. See also Stephen Greenblatt on "the unrepresented consummations of unrepresented marriages" in *Shakespearian Negotiations: The Circulation of Social Energy in Renaissance England* (Berkeley: University of California Press, 1988), 89.

62 Rice, *Otello*, 123.

63 For Lhamon's argument about this possible moment of conception, see Rice, *Otello*, 175n29.

64 See Rice, *Otello,* 176n37; and Lhamon, "Introduction," xxi, note to figure 1.

65 Rice, *Otello,* 158.

66 *Othello; A Burlesque* [1866?] and *Desdemonum: An Ethiopian Burlesque, in Three Scenes* [1874?], both in *This Grotesque Essence: Plays from the American Minstrel Stage,* edited by Gary D. Engle (Baton Rouge: Louisiana State University Press, 1978). Gary D. Engle holds that Griffin and Christy's *Othello* was probably first performed in 1866, while it is possible that *Desdemonum* was performed earlier than 1874. See Engle, *This Grotesque Essence,* 69.

67 Kris Collins, "White-Washing the Black-a-Moor: Othello, Negro Minstrelsy and Parodies of Blackness," *Journal of American Culture* 19, no. 3 (1996): 87.

68 Nyong'o, *Amalgamation Waltz,* 104.

69 Nyong'o, *Amalgamation Waltz,* 108.

70 Ania Loomba refers to Desdemona as becoming an "honorary black" in her supposed infidelity. See Ania Loomba, *Gender, Race, Renaissance Drama* (New York: Oxford University Press, 1992), 59.

71 William J. Mahar notes the "interchangeability of costumes, props, dialects, and settings" that would alter depictions of race and ethnicity. Mahar, "Ethiopian Skits and Sketches: Contents and Contexts of Blackface Minstrelsy, 1840–1890," in *Inside the Minstrel Mask: Readings in Nineteenth-Century Blackface Minstrelsy,* edited by Annemarie Bean, James V. Hatch, and Brooks McNamara (Middletown, CT: Wesleyan University Press 1996), 184–85.

72 Most literary critics (ranging from George Philip Krapp in the 1920s to Eric Lott and Michael North in the 1990s) have agreed that representations of dialect do more complex work than simply presenting phonetic representations of speech. Lott, also notes "the ease with which the blackface mask accommodated a variety of dialects." Lott, *Love and Theft,* 264n6.

73 On the possibilities of white identification with blackface characters, see Lott, *Love and Theft*; and W. T. Lhamon Jr., *Raising Cain: Blackface Performance from Jim Crow to Hip Hop* (Cambridge, MA: Harvard University Press, 1998).

74 *Othello; A Burlesque,* 71.

75 *Othello; A Burlesque,* 71.

76 Adams, "Misconceptions of Shakespeare," 226.

77 *Desdemonum: An Ethiopian Burlesque,* 63.

78 *Desdemonum: An Ethiopian Burlesque,* 65.

79 *Desdemonum: An Ethiopian Burlesque,* 65.

80 Gross notes the irony of Desdemona's "blacked up" appearance. Gross, *Shakespeare's Noise,* 103.

81 Joyce Green MacDonald, "Acting Black: *Othello, Othello* Burlesques, and the Performance of Blackness," *Theatre Journal* 46, no. 2 (1994): 243. Annmarie Bean discusses George Christy and other blackface minstrel female impersonators in "Transgressing the Gender Divide: The Female Impersonator in Nineteenth-Century Blackface Minstrelsy," in *Inside the Minstrel Mask: Readings in Nineteenth-Century Blackface Minstrelsy,* edited by Annemarie Bean, James V.

Hatch, and Brooks McNamara (Middletown, CT: Wesleyan University Press, 1996), 245–56.

82 *Desdemonum: An Ethiopian Burlesque*, 63.

83 Callaghan, *Shakespeare without Women*, 76.

84 Gross, *Shakespeare's Noise*, 103. For other adaptations casting men as Desdemona, see George C. D. Odell, *Annals of the New York Stage*, 15 vols. (New York: Columbia University Press, 1927), vol. 6, 430, 519, 520, 596, and vol. 10, 363. On would-be president Ulysses S. Grant's short run as Desdemona, see Lawrence W. Levine, *Highbrow/Lowbrow: The Emergence of Cultural Hierarchy in America* (Cambridge: Harvard University Press, 1988), 37; Michael Dobson, *Shakespeare and Amateur Performance: A Cultural History* (Cambridge: Cambridge University Press, 2011), 131; and Shapiro, *Shakespeare in America*, xix.

85 See Odell's index entries for Desdemona in *Annals of the New York Stage*. Odell also notes instances of the same actor playing Desdemona in both original and burlesque productions in the same theater. Odell, *Annals of the New York Stage*, vol. 4, 87, 166–67, and vol. 5, 458. On Rice's *Otello*, see Lhamon, "Introduction," xx–xxi; Lhamon, *Jump Jim Crow*, 440–41n1; and Odell, *Annals of the New York Stage*, vol. 5, 157, 458, 551.

86 Sheila Rose Bland, "How I Would Direct Othello," in *Othello: New Essays by Black Writers*, edited by Mythili Kaul (Washington, DC: Howard University Press, 1997), 38.

87 An all-female production of *Othello*, by the Los Angeles Women's Shakespeare Company in March 2008, raises additional questions about how we might differently understand the play when gender is recast.

88 Bland, "How I Would Direct *Othello*," 31.

89 Andrew Carlson, "Oteller and Desdemonum: Defining Nineteenth-Century Blackness," *Theatre History Studies* 30 (2010): 177.

90 Carlson, "Oteller and Desdemonum," 180.

91 Frederick Warde's account of Louis James's Othello in the 1890s describes one blackened Desdemona as both comic and masculinized, as James "took some of the dark color of his make-up and marked a moustache and imperial [pointed beard] on the face of the sleeping figure." Frederick Warde, *Fifty Years of Make-Believe* (New York: International Press Syndicate, 1920), 248.

92 Carlson, "Oteller and Desdemonum," 179.

93 Paraic Finnerty suggests the possibility of a nineteenth-century white woman's cross-gender, cross-racial identification, arguing that Emily Dickinson's letters suggest that "she actually identified with Othello as the personification of extreme possessiveness and jealousy, despite, and perhaps because of, the racial and sexual controversy that surrounded the play." Finnerty, *Emily Dickinson's Shakespeare*, 174.

94 Lott, *Love and Theft*, 159.

95 Lott, *Love and Theft*, 161.

96 Lott, *Love and Theft*, 166.

97 Toni Morrison, *Desdemona* (London: Oberon Books, 2011), 13.

98 Although this name appears as "Barbary" in authoritative editions of *Othello*, in most nineteenth-century American editions I have examined, Desdemona calls this woman "Barbara." While the translation of Barba**ry** into Barba**ra** may seem to de-emphasize readings of this servant as Black, the name Barbara means "foreign," and that racialized meaning registered in the American nineteenth century. Sarah C. Carter correlates Barbara's signification of "stranger" with loneliness, a resonance in line with Desdemona's reminiscences. See Sarah C. Carter, *Lexicon of Ladies' Names: With Their Floral Emblems* (Boston: G. W. Cotrell, 1865). Associations of Africa and "Barbary" with excessive sexuality also signify. See Hall, *Things of Darkness*, 33; and Iyengar, "Moorish Dancing in *The Two Noble Kinsmen*," *Medieval and Renaissance Drama in England* 20 (2007): 90.

99 Richard Grant White, *Studies in Shakespeare* (Boston: Houghton, Mifflin and Company, 1886), 101.

100 English translation by Thomas Massnick. The original German reads "Mit Geschichten seiner Abenteuer hatte Othello einmal Desdemona verführt. Von einer Afrikanerin aufgezogen, fühlte Desdemona sich mit Othello vertraut und verwandt." "The Desdemona Project" Theater Akzent. (https://www .akzent.at/home/spielplan/archiv/243/the-Desdemona-project).

101 Cindy Warner, "Peter Sellars Starts Rehearsal on the Desdemona Project, update of Otello," *San Francisco Opera Examiner*, April 27, 2011 (http://www .examiner.com/opera-in-san-francisco/peter-sellars-starts-rehearsal).

102 Erin Russell Thiessen, "Toni Morrison's Desdemona Delivers a Haunting, Powerful 'Re-Membering,'" *Expatica*, May 26, 2011 (www.expatica.com/be /leisure/arts_culture/ Desdemona-project_17437.html).

103 Morrison, *Desdemona*, 45.

104 MacDonald, "Black Ram, White Ewe," 194.

105 MacDonald, "Black Ram, White Ewe," 194.

106 Morrison, *Desdemona*, 45.

107 Morrison, *Desdemona*, 48.

108 Morrison, *Desdemona*, 49.

109 Daileader, *Racism, Misogyny, and the Othello Myth*, 13.

110 Hall, *Things of Darkness*, 9.

111 Adams, "Misconceptions of Shakespeare," 225.

Chapter Two. "Almost Eliza"

Portions of this material were previously published in "'Almost Eliza': Reading Mary King as the Mixed-Race Heroine of William Allen's *The American Prejudice Against Color*," *Studies in American Fiction*, 40, no. 1 (2013), 1–25, © 2013 by the Johns Hopkins University Press.

1 I refer to this person as "Mary King" because this is what she is called throughout Allen's narrative, which discusses events primarily before the couple's marriage and any assumed change of her name.

2 William G. Allen, *The American Prejudice against Color* [1853], in William G. Allen, Mary King, and Louisa May Alcott, *The American Prejudice against Color*, edited with an introduction by Sarah Elbert (Boston: Northeastern University Press, 2002), 87. All subsequent quotations are from this edition of Allen's text.

3 For more on William G. Allen's biography, see Richard J. Blackett, "William G. Allen, the Forgotten Professor," *Civil War History* 26, no. 1 (1980): 39–52; and Sarah Elbert, "Introduction," in William G. Allen, Mary King, and Louisa May Alcott, *The American Prejudice against Color*, edited by Sarah Elbert (Boston: Northeastern University Press, 2002). Elbert's edited edition includes both of Allen's personal narratives, *The American Prejudice Against Color: An Authentic Narrative, Showing How Easily the Nation Got into An Uproar* (1853) and *A Personal Narrative* (1860).

4 I stipulate here that King and Allen's kinship ties are implied by their intent to marry, at which time their familial relationship to one another would be taken for granted based on their legal marriage relation, the assumption that they would then share a "family" name, and—importantly—the probability that they would produce children together. The implied (though supposedly future) sexual relation in their engagement is therefore the basis for King and Allen's entrance into interracial kinship. I will discuss the particular implications of Mary King as the potential mother of children who are differently raced from herself below.

5 Mark Twain, *Pudd'nhead Wilson* [1894] edited by Sidney E. Berger (New York: Norton, 2005), 9. I discuss the case of Roxy further in chapter 3.

6 For a discussion of the similar uses of sentimentality in the captivity narrative and antislavery literature, see Michelle Burnham, *Captivity and Sentiment: Cultural Exchange in American Literature, 1682–1861* (Hanover, NH: University Press of New England, 1997), 122–26.

7 At the heart of anti-miscegenation law is not simply the belief that racial sexual mixing was "unnatural," but that white supremacist ideologies were also highly invested in preserving "white" property and inheritance. Peggy Pascoe argues this point in *What Comes Naturally*. However, the case of William Allen and Mary King's marriage does not directly concern this body of law, as interracial marriage was never illegal in the state of New York, where they lived. For a clear picture of where, when, and to whom interracial sexual relations were illegal in the United States between 1662 and 1967, see the extremely useful interactive legal map for interracial relationships at the Loving Day website (accessed January 28, 2020, http://lovingday.org/legal-map). Loving Day is an organization dedicated to celebrating interracial relationships, and draws its name from the Supreme Court case *Loving v. Virginia*, , 388 US 1 (1967), which decided that state laws barring interracial marriage were unconstitutional. For more on the legality of interracial marriage in the United States, see Eva Saks, "Representing *Miscegenation* Law," *Raritan* 8, no. 2 (1988): 39–69. I discuss this mapping of interracial marriage and its implications for national scales of racialization in chapter 6.

8 See Harriet E. Wilson, *Our Nig; or, Sketches in the Life of a Free Black* [1859], edited by Henry Louis Gates Jr. and Richard J. Ellis (New York: Vintage, 2011);

and Frank J. Webb, *The Garies and Their Friends* (Baltimore: Johns Hopkins University Press, 1997). Martha Hodes offers a case-study history of relationships between Black men and white women in the South, a relation she argues shifts from the antebellum to the post–Civil War period, in *White Women, Black Men*. Other texts that discuss accounts of interracial sexual relations in the nineteenth-century United States include Hodes, *Sex, Love, Race*, and *The Sea Captain's Wife: A True Story of Love, Race, and War in the Nineteenth Century* (New York: Norton, 2007); Rothman, *Notorious in the Neighborhood*; and Jackson, *Barriers Between Us*.

9 Allen, *American Prejudice*, 56. It seems most reasonable to surmise that castration or some other sexual violence is implied in this passage, indicating that the "threat" Allen is assumed to pose and from which Mary King must ostensibly be "rescued" is also sexual in nature.

10 Burnham, *Captivity and Sentiment*, 63.

11 What I am calling "anti-amalgamation" literature is also closely connected to a broader, overlapping genre of anti-abolition literature. I will discuss these connections further below.

12 Christopher Castiglia discusses the larger implications of the white male presence in the captivity narrative in *Bound and Determined: Captivity, Culture-Crossing, and White Womanhood from Mary Rowlandson to Patty Hearst* (Chicago: University of Chicago Press, 1996), 8–9, 20–25, and 37–38.

13 June Namias and Christopher Castiglia both note the difficulty of placing Jemison generically in the captivity narrative tradition. See Namias, *White Captives* (Chapel Hill: University of North Carolina Press, 1993); and Castiglia, *Bound and Determined*.

14 Allen, *American Prejudice*, 75, 63, and 62 respectively. These references are also meant to satirize the "Jerry Rescue" of October 1, 1851. During the antislavery Liberty Party convention in Syracuse, New York, a group of local abolitionists and activists in the Underground Railroad illegally freed William "Jerry" Henry, who had been arrested and held under the 1850 Fugitive Slave Law, and ultimately helped him escape to Canada. At the climax of this rescue, a crowd of approximately 2,500 people stormed the police justice offices, where Jerry was being held.

15 Later examples of this discourse include Thomas Dixon's novel *The Clansman: An Historical Romance of the Ku Klux Klan* (New York: Doubleday and Page, 1905), the epic depiction of which was D. W. Griffith's film *The Birth of a Nation* (1915), and the letter of Rebecca Latimer Felton, the would-be US senator from Georgia, to the *Atlanta Constitution* in August 1897, in which she argues, "if it needs lynching to protect woman's dearest possession from the ravening human beasts—then I say lynch, a thousand times a week if necessary." The letter is reprinted in Charles Chesnutt, *The Marrow of Tradition* [1901], edited by Nancy Bentley and Sandra Gunning (New York: Bedford/St. Martin's Press, 2002), 409–11.

16 Elise Lemire discusses the history of this imagined racial "preference," linking it with an "aesthetic hierarchy of the races" in *Miscegenation*, 5.

17 Eric Lott discusses a white working-class male concern with Black masculinity as central to the minstrel tradition in *Love and Theft*, 9. This is not, of course, an

explicitly nineteenth-century phenomenon. The phenomenon of white men's obsession with Black men's sexuality can be seen in twentieth century texts such as Normal Mailer's *White Negro* (San Francisco: City Lights Books, 1957), John Howard Griffin's *Black Like Me* (Boston: Houghton Mifflin, 1961) and is critiqued in texts such as Frantz Fanon's *Black Skin, White Masks* [1952] (New York: Grove Press, 1967), and various writings by James Baldwin.

18 Lemire, *Miscegenation*, 4.

19 Allen, *American Prejudice*, 64–65.

20 For extensive discussions of the social, material, and legal benefits of white privilege, see George Lipsitz, *The Possessive Investment in Whiteness: How White People Profit from Identity Politics* (Philadelphia: Temple University Press, 2006); Cheryl Harris, "Whiteness as Property," *Harvard Law Review* 106, no. 8 (1993): 1707–91; and Ian Haney-López, *White by Law: The Legal Construction of Race* (New York: New York University Press, 2006).

21 Sarah Elbert acknowledges that Allen centers his narrative on the problem of American racism rather than the supposed "problem" his marriage to Mary King represented. Here she also describes Allen and King in terms of fugitivity, remarking that, though William Allen was never enslaved, "he and his white bride, Mary King Allen, were indeed fugitives [when they fled the United States to England in 1853], fleeing for their lives from 'the American Prejudice Against Color.'" See Allen, *American Prejudice*, 4. I will discuss how this position of fugitivity is expressly depicted in their narrative below.

22 Lydia Maria Child, a prominent abolitionist, presents her own radical support of interracial marriage in *An Appeal*, 196. For other examples of this argument, see her letter to the *New York Daily Tribune*, September 3, 1852, reprinted in *A Lydia Maria Child Reader*, edited by Carolyn L. Karcher (Durham, NC: Duke University Press, 1997), 262–66. William Lloyd Garrison also supports interracial marriage in "The Marriage Law," *The Liberator*, May 7 and 21, 1831.

23 For example, in the account of Mrs. Bird, the senator's wife, Stowe asks the reader directly to think of their own children as they contemplate the flight of Eliza and her son, Harry. See Harriet Beecher Stowe, *Uncle Tom's Cabin; or, Life Among the Lowly* [1852], edited by Elizabeth Ammons (New York: Norton, 1994), 67–80. A common critique of the way on which Stowe's "whitewashed" sympathetic depiction of mixed-race (and visually white) characters are used to garner abolitionist sympathy (as was a common trope in abolitionist writing) can be seen in James Baldwin's well-known piece "Everybody's Protest Novel," in *Notes of a Native Son* [1955] (Boston: Beacon Press, 1984), 13-23.

24 This is true, to some extent, in *Uncle Tom's Cabin*, where Eliza's story spans a greater part of the novel than does that of Little Eva. The prioritization of mixed-race heroines is more emphatically the case in texts such as Lydia Maria Child's "The Quadroons" [1842], in *Fact and Fiction: A Collection of Stories* (New York: C. S. Francis, 1846), 61–76, and *A Romance of the Republic* [1867], edited by Dana D. Nelson (Lexington: University of Kentucky Press, 1997), and William

Wells Brown's *Clotel; or, The President's Daughter* [1853], edited by Robert S. Levine (Boston: Bedford/St. Martin's Press, 2000).

25 Examples of white male adversaries seem available enough. Simon Legree is, of course, at the head of this list. In the latter group, I am thinking of characters such as Henry Morton in Brown's *Clotel*, and each of Cassy's lovers in Stowe's *Uncle Tom's Cabin*: the "young lawyer" who is Henry and Elise's father, and Captain Stewart.

26 This conflation explains, in part, the similarities of various genres of captivity narrative, including those of Barbary captivity.

27 Allen, *American Prejudice*, 64

28 Karen Woods Weierman, *One Nation, One Blood: Interracial Marriage in American Fiction, Scandal, and Law, 1820–1870* (Amherst: University of Massachusetts Press, 2005), 102.

29 Croly and Wakeman, *Miscegenation*; Seaman, *What Miscegenation Is!*

30 See Abraham Lincoln, *Speeches and Writings, 1832–1858*, edited by Don E. Fehrenbacher (New York: Library of America, 1989), 397–98, original emphasis. Elise Lemire discusses Lincoln's stance on "miscegenation" in *Miscegenation*, esp. 116–23 and 138–42.

31 For a discussion of mid-century Democrats' fear and hatred of "black Republicanism" (implicating supposed support for racial equality), see McPherson, *Battle Cry of Freedom*, 159–60. Karen Woods Weierman writes about links between abolition and intermarriage in light of Allen's narrative in *One Nation, One Blood*. For a discussion of literary connections between abolitionism and interracial intermarriage, see her discussion of Allen, and of works by Child, Webb, and Harper, in *One Nation, One Blood*, 101–24 and 145–70.

32 See Stephen P. Knadler, *The Fugitive Race: Minority Writers Resisting Whiteness* (Jackson: University Press of Mississippi, 2009), ix. For a further discussion of fugitivity, see Michael Chaney's discussion of the August 11, 1854, issue of *Frederick Douglass' Paper*, in which an anonymous writer critiques the contrast between the "icon of fugitivity" in advertisements for self-emancipated people and the image of so-called "permanence" in the happy nuclear family within Uncle Tom and Aunt Chloe's cabin, in *Fugitive Vision: Slave Image and Black Identity in Antebellum Narrative* (Bloomington: Indiana University Press, 2009), 1–2.

33 Allen, *American Prejudice*, 89.

34 The long history of using imagery of enslavement to describe the condition of women (particularly related to their legal state of coverture in marriage and to the "competition" between Black men and white women for civil rights) is also worth mentioning here. Though these implications are not central to Sarah and John Porter's encouragement to Mary King, they resonate as we think about the conditions that create King as a potentially unfree subject with regard to her marriage's existence within the same white paternalistic system that puts Allen in danger of enslavement.

35 Karen Woods Weierman illustrates this kind of legal racial marking in reference to a 1723 Virginia law specifying that the wives of Black or Indian men would be

tithable according to the rules taxing the labor of nonwhite women, regardless of the wife's race. White women, regarded as dependent, were not subject to this tax. See *One Nation, One Blood*, 126.

36 Allen, *American Prejudice*, 89–90.

37 Stowe, *Uncle Tom's Cabin*, 121.

38 Stowe, *Uncle Tom's Cabin*, 121.

39 Stowe, *Uncle Tom's Cabin*, 161.

40 Burnham, *Captivity and Sentiment*, 136.

41 William Allen, Letter from Wm. Allen, *Frederick Douglass' Paper*, May 20, 1852, original emphasis.

42 Although Stowe fails to mention Hildreth's *The Slave* in *A Key to Uncle Tom's Cabin* (Boston: John P. Jewett, 1853), Charles Nichols argues convincingly that this text was a probable source (i.e., "the real source") for her novel. See Charles Nichols, "The Origins of *Uncle Tom's Cabin*," *Phylon Quarterly* 19, no. 3 (1958): 328–34.

43 Leslie Fiedler, *Love and Death in the American Novel* (New York: Anchor/Doubleday, 1992), 265; Carolyn Vellenga Berman, "Creole Family Politics in *Uncle Tom's Cabin* and *Incidents in the Life of a Slave Girl*," *Novel* 33, no. 3 (2000): 329.

44 Martin Delany, letter, *Frederick Douglass' Paper*, May 6, 1853.

45 Allen, *American Prejudice*, 77.

46 Allen, *American Prejudice*, 59.

47 Allen, *American Prejudice*, 74.

48 Allen, *American Prejudice*, 75.

49 Allen, *American Prejudice*, 86.

50 Shakespeare, *Othello*, 1.2.65.

51 Allen, *American Prejudice*, 43.

52 Allen, *American Prejudice*, 76–77, 90.

53 Allen, *American Prejudice*, 77.

54 Allen, *American Prejudice*, 79.

55 Barbara J. Fields cites the concept of "interracial" motherhood in her discussion of the absurdity of biologically construed race, referring to "the well-known anomaly of American racial convention that considers a white woman capable of giving birth to a black child but denies that a black woman can give birth to a white child." See Fields, "Ideology and Race in American History," in *Region, Race, and Reconstruction*, edited by J. Morgan Kousser and James M. McPherson (New York: Oxford University Press, 1982), 149. I will discuss interracial motherhood at length in the next chapter.

56 See Harriet Jacobs, *Incidents in the Life of a Slave Girl* [1861], edited by Nellie Y. McKay and Frances Smith Foster (New York: Norton, 2001), 135.

57 Allen, *American Prejudice*, 81–82.

58 Allen, *American Prejudice*, 90.

59 Sarah Elbert argues that Alcott's "M. L." must have been based on the popular Allen-King controversy, which Alcott probably learned about through her uncle, the Reverend Samuel May, who was in correspondence with Allen. See Elbert,

"Introduction," and "An Inter-Racial Love Story in Fact and Fiction: William and Mary King Allen's Marriage and Louisa May Alcott's Tale, 'M. L.,'" *History Workshop Journal* 53 (2002): 17–42.

60 Sarah Elbert, *Louisa May Alcott on Race, Sex, and Slavery* (Boston: Northeastern University Press, 1997), xl.

61 Elbert, *Louisa May Alcott*, xl.

62 Louisa May Alcott, "M. L.," in William G. Allen, Mary King, and Louisa May Alcott, *The American Prejudice against Color*, edited by Sarah Elbert (Boston: Northeastern University Press, 2002), 142. Further citations of "M. L." are taken from this edition.

63 Alcott, "M. L.," 126.

64 Alcott, "M. L.," 142–43.

65 Alcott, "M. L.," 141.

66 Alcott, "M. L.," 142, 144.

67 Alcott, "M. L.," 152.

68 Alcott also conveys this sentiment of national interracial brotherhood in her better-known short story "The Brothers," which I discuss in the next chapter.

69 Alcott, "M. L.," 140.

70 Elise Lemire rightly argues that interracial "brotherly" kinship is also closely related to the notion and acceptance of sexual kinship, writing that "the only way that Paul, or any other 'black' person for that matter, can claim the political and social status of 'brother' . . . would be through his full acceptance by 'whites' as a lover and a husband as well." While I agree, I am interested here in the prioritization or prominence of an ironically desexualized kinship in Alcott's story. As Lemire herself notes, "Alcott . . . avoids depicting racial blackness as attractive." See Lemire, *Miscegenation*, 9, and her further discussion of "M. L.," 133–36, in which she contrasts Alcott's desexualized depiction of interracial romance with the more "pornographic" depictions of anti-amalgamationists such as Edward Williams Clay and Jerome Holgate.

71 Burnham, *Captivity and Sentiment*, 7.

Chapter Three. Mothers and Mammies

1 The story originally appeared in *Atlantic Monthly* 12, no. 73 (November 1863) as "The Brothers" despite Alcott's preference for the title "My Contraband." The story was reprinted as "My Contraband; or the Brothers" in *Hospital Sketches, and Camp and Fireside Stories* (Boston: Roberts Brothers, 1869). For further discussion of the publication history of this story and the significance of the changing title, see Sarah Elbert's *Louisa May Alcott*, xli.

2 Elbert, *Louisa May Alcott*, xli.

3 Alcott, *Hospital Sketches*, 172.

4 Elbert, *Louisa May Alcott*, xlii.

5 Daniel P. Moynihan, "The Moynihan Report" [1965]. In *The Moynihan Report and the Politics of Controversy: A Transaction Social Science and Public Policy*

Report, edited by Lee Rainwater and William L. Yancey (Cambridge, MA: MIT Press, 1967), 47–94.

6 Fields, "Ideology and Race in American History," 149.

7 Sterling Brown, "The Muted South" [1945], *Callaloo* 21, no. 4 (1998): 768.

8 Thomas Nelson Page, "The Old-Time Negro," *Scribner's Magazine* 36 (July–December 1904): 525.

9 Sarah Morgan Bryan Piatt, "The Black Princess (A True Fable of My Old Kentucky Nurse)" [1872], in *Palace-Burner: The Selected Poetry of Sarah Piatt*, edited by Paula Bernat Bennett (Urbana: University of Illinois Press, 2001), 38.

10 As Robin Bernstein has noted, white childhood has not, historically, been "innocent" of perpetuating racism. See Bernstein, *Racial Innocence.*

11 *Oxford English Dictionary*, s.v. "mammy" (accessed January 30, 2020, https://www.lexico.com/definition/mammy).

12 See Brown, "The Muted South," 768.

13 One example of this use of the mammy figure is the Daughters of the Confederacy's attempt to erect a National Mammy memorial on the National Mall in Washington, DC, in 1923.

14 Page, "The Old-Time Negro," 525.

15 Patricia Hill Collins, *Black Feminist Thought: Knowledge, Consciousness, and the Politics of Empowerment* (New York: Routledge, 2000), 81.

16 Collins, *Black Feminist Thought*, 83.

17 Mary Niall Mitchell, *Raising Freedom's Children: Black Children and Visions of the Future after Slavery* (New York: New York University Press, 2008), 180.

18 David Macrae, *The Americans at Home: Pen-and-Ink Sketches of American Men, Manners and Institutions*, vol. 2 (Edinburgh: Edmonston and Couglas, 1870), 45. See also the discussion of this scene in Mitchell, *Raising Freedom's Children*, 180–81.

19 Macrae, *Americans at Home*, 44.

20 Virginia Common Law, 1662, act XII.

21 Writers such as Catherine Clinton and Patricia A. Turner argue that the iconic cultural version of the mammy is more a product of mythic depictions of the American South following the Civil War than of the reality of enslaved Black women during the antebellum period. They indicate that only the wealthiest white people could afford to keep house servants and point to the fact that the majority of house servants were racially mixed people who did not resemble the dark-skinned caricature of the mammy. See Catherine Clinton, *The Plantation Mistress: Woman's World in the Old South* (New York: Pantheon Books, 1982), 201–2; Patricia A. Turner, *Ceramic Uncles and Celluloid Mammies: Black Images and Their Influence on Culture* (New York: Anchor Books, 1994), 44.

22 I owe special thanks to Kelly Cobb and Kendra Hebel for helping me obtain an image of Scott's sculpture.

23 See Kimberly Wallace-Sanders, *Mammy: A Century of Race, Gender, and Southern Memory* (Ann Arbor: University of Michigan Press, 2008), 8. I am more interested in the ways that racial and kinship identifications converge in the texts

I discuss, which tend to prioritize biological kinship relations, even while these are complicated by instances of "interracial" kinship that are often articulated through bonds of maternity.

24 Like the other texts I discuss in this chapter and the next, Charles Chesnutt's "Her Virginia Mammy" is best defined, perhaps, against what it is not: the plantation nostalgia genre, a Southern strand of what David Blight calls the diverse "literature of reunion," which emerges at the closing of the Civil War and builds with the failure of Reconstruction to produce a unified nation. The pastoral vein of this largely sentimental literature employs the historical fiction of antebellum white Southern benevolence and loyal enslaved people to promote national regional and/or racial reconciliation (and often to argue for postbellum white supremacy). See David W. Blight's discussion of Southern plantation nostalgia and other postwar literature in *Race and Reunion: The Civil War in American Memory* (Cambridge, MA: Belknap Press, 2001).

25 Charles Chesnutt, "Her Virginia Mammy" [1899], in *The Northern Stories of Charles W. Chesnutt*, edited by Charles Duncan (Athens: Ohio University Press, 2004), 93.

26 Chesnutt, "Her Virginia Mammy," 94–95.

27 Chesnutt, "Her Virginia Mammy," 93.

28 Chesnutt, "Her Virginia Mammy," 82.

29 Wallace-Sanders, *Mammy*, 8.

30 For a case study of nineteenth-century assumptions about racial essentialism in a race-based system of slavery, see Walter Johnson, "The Slave-Trader, the White Slave, and the Politics of Racial Determination in the 1850s," *Journal of American History* 87, no. 1 (2000): 13–38.

31 Chesnutt, "Her Virginia Mammy," 85.

32 Chesnutt, "Her Virginia Mammy," 92.

33 Eric Sundquist, *To Wake the Nations: Race in the Making of American Literature* (Cambridge, MA: Belknap Press, 1993), 401.

34 Any clear distinction between the mother and mammy figures is admittedly confused by the affectionate usages of "mammy" to denote African American mothers. I will discuss one such ambiguous use in *Pudd'nhead Wilson*, below. I am also thinking here of the use of "mammy" in Frances Ellen Watkins Harper's *Iola Leroy*, which I discuss in the next chapter.

35 See Wallace-Sanders, *Mammy*, 73.

36 Mark Twain, *Pudd'nhead Wilson* [1894], edited by Sidney E. Berger (New York: Norton, 2005), 9.

37 Omi and Winant, *Racial Formation*.

38 Wallace-Sanders, *Mammy*, 17.

39 Wallace-Sanders, *Mammy*, 73.

40 Twain, *Pudd'nhead Wilson*, 9.

41 Besides her marked speech, Roxy's performance is also evident in her clothing—in the checkered handkerchief that hides her "white" hair and the clothes that class her as a Black. It is her clothes through which Roxy later performs

gender as well as race. Linda A. Morris discusses this in "Beneath the Veil: Clothing, Race, and Gender in Mark Twain's *Pudd'nhead Wilson*" *Studies in American Fiction* 27, no. 1 (1999): 37–52.

42 Twain, *Pudd'nhead Wilson*, 9.

43 Twain, *Pudd'nhead Wilson*, 8.

44 Barbara Chellis, "Those Extraordinary Twins: Negroes and Whites," *American Quarterly* 21, no. 1 (1969): 103.

45 Leslie Fiedler, "As Free as Any Cretur . . ." in *Pudd'nhead Wilson*, edited by Sidney E. Berger (New York: Norton, 2005), 254.

46 See Michael Rogin, "Francis Galton and Mark Twain: The Natal Autograph in *Pudd'nhead Wilson*," in *Mark Twain's* Pudd'nhead Wilson: *Race, Conflict and Culture*, edited by Susan Gillman and Forrest G. Robinson (Durham, NC: Duke University Press, 1990), 78.

47 Fiedler, "As Free as Any Cretur," 254.

48 Twain, *Pudd'nhead Wilson*, 5.

49 Barbara Ladd, in her discussion of *Pudd'nhead Wilson*, goes to great pains in an attempt to prove that Tom Driscoll, by virtue of a Missouri law of 1855, would have been deemed "legally white," having "less than one-fourth African ancestry." Glaringly missing from her consideration, however, is the fact that Roxy, as a legally enslaved person, would have been unable to prove the paternity by which her son's apparent percentage of "African ancestry" or "white ancestry" might be determined. See Ladd, *Nationalism and the Color Line in George W. Cable, Mark Twain, and William Faulkner* (Baton Rouge: Louisiana State University Press, 1996), 117–19. What I refer to here by calling Chambers "fatherless" dovetails with Hortense Spillers' notion of "kinlessness," which I will discuss at length in the next chapter.

50 Chellis, "Those Extraordinary Twins," 107.

51 Chellis, "Those Extraordinary Twins," 102–3.

52 See Myra Jehlen, "The Ties that Bind: Race and Sex in *Pudd'nhead Wilson*," *American Literary History* 2, no. 1 (1990), 47. Carolyn Porter, though, regards this as not a reversal of the mammy figure, but as "Satirizing the southern ideology that exalted the mammy's devotion to her white owner's children as well as theirs to her." See Carolyn Porter, "Roxana's Plot," *Cultural Critique* 15 (1990): 161.

53 Twain, *Pudd'nhead Wilson*, 17.

54 There is some debate among scholars whether Twain's text presents Tom's bad character as a result of his innate "Blackness" or his upbringing. See Chellis's discussion of this debate in "Those Extraordinary Twins," 101.

55 Chellis denies that Roxy's motives here are maternal at all, reading her aspirations for her son only as the sublimation of her own desire for (legitimized) whiteness. This ignores Roxy's initial thoughts of infanticide and suicide, however, as whiteness does not figure in her plan to accompany her son to Heaven. See Chellis, "Those Extraordinary Twins," 108–9.

56 Twain, *Pudd'nhead Wilson*, 10.

57 Twain, *Pudd'nhead Wilson*, 16.

58 Twain, *Pudd'nhead Wilson*, 14, original emphasis.

59 James Grove, "Mark Twain and the Endangered Family," *American Literature* 57, no. 3 (1985): 381.

60 Porter, "Roxana's Plot," 165.

61 Porter notes that "mother" can be regarded as a social—not a natural—identity when discussing the status and agency of enslaved mothers, that "the slave mother is specifically positioned in and by that economy [of social death] in *Pudd'nhead Wilson*." Porter also notes the sexual and maternal dualism in Black female figures in the simultaneous hypersexualization and desexualization of a "Jezebel/Mammy." See Porter, "Roxana's Plot," 148, 154, 148.

62 Twain, *Pudd'nhead Wilson*, 21.

63 Twain, *Pudd'nhead Wilson*, 18–19.

64 Jehlen, "The Ties that Bind," 50.

65 Porter cites Roxy's removal of "Driscoll" from "Tom's" name as one iteration of her imitation of the enslaver, made ironic by the fact that the body of the enslaved mother itself negates paternity. See Porter, "Roxana's Plot," 156–57.

66 Twain, *Pudd'nhead Wilson*, 43.

67 Twain, *Pudd'nhead Wilson*, 39.

68 Twain, *Pudd'nhead Wilson*, 45. The problem of naming the interchanged children presents some confusion in the text, which the narration itself recognizes. I will discuss this problem further, below.

69 Mark R. Patterson, "Surrogacy and Slavery: The Problematics of Consent in Baby M, *Romance of the Republic* and *Pudd'nhead Wilson*," *American Literary History* 8, no. 3 (1996): 464.

70 Twain, *Pudd'nhead Wilson*, 86.

71 Patterson, "Surrogacy and Slavery," 463.

72 That Twain's story takes up science in a text invested in questions of racial difference is unsurprising. But this use of a science of individual identification rather than one of racialization sets him against other uses of science by which racism was explained and justified in the mid- to late-nineteenth century. Melville's *Moby-Dick* comes most obviously to mind as another text in clear engagement with the science of racialization and racism. Herman Melville, *Moby-Dick* [1851], (New York: W. W. Norton, 1967).

73 Susan Gillman suggests that "Siamese twins" and "mulattoes" are presented as equally "freakish [and] monstrous" in the postwar context of Twain's novel, and Eric Sundquist notes the parallel in these entities "that are meant to be separated but have become freakishly, uncannily merged." See Susan Gillman, "'Sure Identifyers': Race, Science, and the Law in *Pudd'nhead Wilson*," in *Mark Twain's Pudd'nhead Wilson: Race, Conflict and Culture*, edited by Susan Gillman and Forrest G. Robinson (Durham, NC: Duke University Press, 1990), 88; and Sundquist, *To Wake the Nations*, 259. This pairing of conjoined twins and mixed-race people both suggest the discourse of kinship at work in Twain's text. Gillman also argues that the themes of twinning and mistaken identity in

Pudd'nhead Wilson and *Those Extraordinary Twins* "must be understood against the context of turn-of-the-century racism: legal discourse on issues of blood, race and sex, miscegenation; Jim Crow laws and Negrophobic mob violence; the ideologies of imperial and racial Darwinism." Susan Gillman, *Dark Twins: Imposture and Identity in Mark Twain's America* (Chicago: University of Chicago Press, 1989), 9.

74 Barbara Ladd notes the centrality of Wilson for contemporary readers of Twain, and the story's end as implicating Northern whites in the perpetuation of slavery and its postwar effects. See Ladd, *Nationalism and the Color Line*, 110–11.

75 Forrest Robinson, discussing the "happily distracting conclusion" of the "bad faith narrative" of Pudd'nhead Wilson's court trial, cites Wilson and the deceptively happy ending he produces as distracting everyone (including the reader) from the wrongs of slavery. See Forrest G. Robinson, "The Sense of Disorder in *Pudd'nhead Wilson*," in *Mark Twain's* Pudd'nhead Wilson: *Race, Conflict and Culture*, edited by Susan Gillman and Forrest G. Robinson (Durham, NC: Duke University Press, 1990), 28 and 44.

76 The rationalization of Twain's conclusion aligns with the perpetuation of slavery in the United States' carceral system following abolition, as the Thirteenth Amendment to the US Constitution (ratified in 1865) abolishes slavery or involuntary servitude "except as a punishment for crime whereof the party shall have been duly convicted." US Const. amend. XIII, § 1.

77 In one version of this, Lawrence Howe discusses the reader's potential points of identification in the story, wondering whether he can identify with the detective or the criminal. Howe does not suspect that his reader might identify with Roxy. See Lawrence Howe, "Race, Genealogy and Genre in Mark Twain's *Pudd'nhead Wilson*," *Nineteenth-Century Literature* 46, no. 4 (1992): 502.

78 James Cox, "*Pudd'nhead Wilson* Revisited," in *Mark Twain's* Pudd'nhead Wilson: *Race, Conflict and Culture*, edited by Susan Gillman and Forrest G. Robinson (Durham, NC: Duke University Press, 1990), 13 and 16.

79 See Wallace-Sanders, *Mammy*, 75. In her role as mother, Roxy might also be figured as the character who gives life to the story, sharing the role of author with Twain. Jehlen argues that Roxy's "sovereignty over the children extends naturally to the story of which she is a sort of author." See Jehlen, "The Ties that Bind," 43. Similarly, Ladd notes Twain's "paternal distance" from the text and its raced characters, painting him as a "symbolic mulatto," in *Nationalism and the Color Line*, 137; while Sundquist calls Twain "(black) mother as well as (white) father to his illegitimate mulatto heir" in *To Wake the Nations*, 257. These constructions present Roxy as an appropriate parallel for Twain, and this is an appropriate text in which to match Twain with one of his characters, as its composition is caught up with concepts of twins and twinning.

80 We see a similar discussion of fingerprints at the end of Edgar Rice Burroughs's *Tarzan of the Apes*, in which characters state that fingerprints, while useful for determining continuity of identity, cannot determine whether someone is white or Black. See Burroughs, *Tarzan of the Apes* [1914] (New York: Penguin, 1990), 251.

81 Mark Twain, *Those Extraordinary Twins* [1894], edited by Sidney E. Berger (New York: Norton, 2005), 125.

82 See Ladd, *Nationalism and the Color Line*, 106.

83 Wallace-Sanders, 75, original emphasis.

Chapter Four. Kinfullness

1 John Anderson Collins, "The Slave-Mother" (Philadelphia: [Pennsylvania Anti-slavery Fair], 1855). The end of the poem makes a connection between enslaved Black women in the United States and Virginia, whose father killed her himself rather than see her enslaved. The relation between Verginia and Virginia here is a radical one, as the allusion explains, even if it does not justify, infanticide for the most desperate enslaved mothers. In this way, the poem alludes to the Roman origin of *Partus sequitur ventrem*, which was a departure from English patriarchal law when adopted in the Virginia colony in 1662.

2 Hortense J. Spillers, "Mama's Baby, Papa's Maybe: An American Grammar Book," *Diacritics* 17, no. 2 (1987): 74–75; Saidiya Hartman, *Lose Your Mother: A Journey along the Atlantic Slave Route* (New York: Farrar, Straus and Giroux, 2007), 155–57.

3 Frances Ellen Watkins Harper, [1854], "The Slave Mother," in *A Brighter Coming Day: A Frances Ellen Watkins Reader,* edited by Frances Smith Foster (New York: Feminist Press, City University of New York, 1990), 59.

4 Sojourner Truth, *The Narrative of Sojourner Truth* [1850], edited by Margaret Washington (New York: Vintage, 1993), 31.

5 See Nancy Bentley, "The Fourth Dimension: Kinlessness and African American Narrative," *Critical Inquiry* 35, no. 2 (2009): 271.

6 Zora Neale Hurston, *Dust Tracks on a Road: An Autobiography* (Philadelphia: Lippincott, 1942), 239.

7 Collins, "The Slave-Mother," 9-10.

8 Collins, "The Slave-Mother," 11.

9 Christina Sharpe, *In the Wake: On Blackness and Being* (Durham, NC: Duke University Press, 2016), 27.

10 Twain, *Pudd'nhead Wilson*, 11.

11 The patriarchal plantation system is also one in which kinship ties between enslaver and enslaved were suppressed, reduced to a paternalism by which all enslaved people were rendered "children," but by which they could not claim any rights of inheritance from the fathers.

12 See Carol Stack, *All Our Kin: Strategies for Survival in a Black Community* (New York: Harper and Row, 1974).

13 Ira Berlin and Leslie S. Rowland, *Families and Freedom: A Documentary History of African-American Kinship in the Civil War Era* (New York: New Press, 1997), 225.

14 Brown, *Clotel* (2000 ed.), 47–48.

15 Butler, *Undoing Gender*, 5.

16 Peggy Pascoe shows that race and gender are inextricable in anti-miscegenation law, which "channeled property, propriety, personal choice, and legitimate procreation into one very particular kind of monogamous pair: couples that were made up of one White man and one White woman, whose sameness of race was required by law and whose difference in sex was taken entirely for granted." Pascoe, *What Comes Naturally*, 3.

17 Pascoe, *What Comes Naturally*, 2.

18 Katherine M. Franke, "Becoming a Citizen: Reconstruction Era Regulation of African American Marriages," *Yale Journal of Law and the Humanities* 11, no. 2 (1999): 252.

19 Ferguson, *Aberrations in Black*, 86.

20 Cathy Cohen, "Punks, Bulldaggers, and Welfare Queens: The Radical Potential of Queer Politics?" GLQ: *A Journal of Lesbian and Gay Studies* 3, no. 4 (1997): 453–55.

21 Moynihan, "Moynihan Report"; See also Cohen, "Punks, Bulldaggers, and Welfare Queens," 457.

22 Collins, *Black Feminist Thought*, 77.

23 Rosalie Riegle Troester, "Turbulence and Tenderness: Mothers, Daughters, and 'Othermothers' in Paule Marshall's *Brown Girl, Brownstones*," *Sage: A Scholarly Journal on Black Women* 1, no. 2 (1984): 13–16.

24 Collins, *Black Feminist Thought*, 192.

25 Benjamin, "Black AfterLives Matter," 56.

26 Frances Ellen Watkins Harper, *Iola Leroy, or Shadows Uplifted* [1892], edited by Koritha Mitchell (Peterborough, ON: Broadview Press, 2018), 76, 79.

27 Annette Gordon-Reed argues for complexity that might allow for complex relations of affection while also acknowledging disparate positions of power in her discussions of Sally Hemings and Thomas Jefferson. See Gordon-Reed, *Thomas Jefferson and Sally Hemings: An American Controversy* (Charlottesville: University Press of Virginia, 1997).

28 Harper, *Iola Leroy*, 67.

29 Harper, *Iola Leroy*, 67.

30 Harper, *Iola Leroy*, 67.

31 Harper, *Iola Leroy*, 74.

32 Harper, *Iola Leroy*, 164.

33 Harper, *Iola Leroy*, 188.

34 See Jourdan Anderson, "Letter from a Freedman to his Old Master" [1865], in *The Freedman's Book*, edited by Lydia Maria Child (Boston: Ticknor and Fields, 1865), 266, emphasis added.

35 On Harper's various uses of respectability in her fiction and the importance of Black origins for respect, see Brigitte Fielder, "Radical Respectability," in *African American Literature in Transition*, edited by Eric Gardner (Cambridge: Cambridge University Press), forthcoming.

36 Harper, *Iola Leroy*, 83. This prioritization of family over freedom is not unique to Harper's novel. Another example of this sentiment can be seen in Charles Chesnutt's anti-plantation-nostalgia tale, "The Passing of Grandison" [1899], in

The Northern Stories of Charles W. Chesnutt, edited by Charles Duncan (Athens: Ohio University Press, 2004), 1–21. Frances Smith Foster and Annette Gordon-Reed discuss enslaved people as taking relations of family and community into account when considering their own self-emancipation. See Foster, 'Til Death or Distance Do Us Part: Love and Marriage in African America (Oxford: Oxford University Press, 2010); and Gordon-Reed, The Hemingses of Monticello: An American Family (New York: Norton, 2008).

37 This refusal of white, enslaving fathers to acknowledge their children by enslaved mothers is not, of course, uncommon. This choice also makes for an emphatic rejection of the white father in Richard Hildreth's 1836 novel, The Slave: or Memoirs of Archy Moore, republished with an extended second-half as The White Slave; or, Memoirs of a Fugitive (Boston: Tappan and Whittemore, 1852). In The Slave, both Archy and his would-be wife, Cassy, are the children of their enslaver, Colonel Moore, but have different (enslaved) mothers. Archy not only rejects kinship with his enslaver and (legitimate, white) brother in this narrative, but refuses to acknowledge his relation to Cassy through the Colonel, rejecting the notion that their siblinghood ought to prevent their marriage. He notes that the Colonel's wife "discovered in it no impediment to my marriage with Cassy. Nor did I;—for how could that same regard for the *decencies of life*—such is the soft phrase which justifies the most unnatural cruelty—that refused to acknowledge our paternity, or to recognize any relationship between us, pretend at the same time, and on the sole ground of relationship, to forbid our union?" Hildreth, The Slave, (Boston: John H. Eastburn, 48–49).

38 Harper, Iola Leroy, cover.

39 P. Gabrielle Foreman, "Who's Your Mama? 'White' Mulatta Genealogies, Early Photography, and Anti-Passing Narratives of Slavery and Freedom," American Literary History 14, no. 3 (2002): 507.

40 Bentley, "The Fourth Dimension," 271.

41 Foreman, "Who's Your Mama?," 507.

42 Harper, Iola Leroy, 142.

43 Spillers, "Mama's Baby, Papa's Maybe," 75.

44 For further discussion of the workings of patriarchy in the system of American plantation slavery, see Russ Castronovo, Fathering the Nation: American Genealogies of Slavery and Freedom (Berkeley: University of California Press, 1995).

45 Harper, Iola Leroy, 128.

46 While Harper emphasizes the relevance of biological kinship in Iola Leroy, Alice Rutkowski discusses the trope of interracial adoption in Harper's poetry in "Leaving the Good Mother: Frances E. W. Harper, Lydia Maria Child, and the Literary Politics of Reconstruction," Legacy 25, no. 1 (2008): 83–104.

47 Harper, Iola Leroy, 176.

48 Foundational, that is, but definitely not "seminal."

49 Harper, Iola Leroy, 182.

50 Harper, Iola Leroy, 183.

51 Minnie Blake, "Information Wanted of my mother, Jane Ross," *Christian Recorder*, June 10, 1886, 3.

52 Frances Smith Foster and Heather Andrea Williams discuss such advertisements at length. See Foster, *'Til Death or Distance Do Us Part*; and Williams, *Help Me to Find My People: The African American Search for Family Lost in Slavery* (Chapel Hill: University of North Carolina Press, 2012). Advertisements of this kind can be viewed via the digital project "Last Seen: Finding Family after Slavery," a collaboration between the Villanova University's graduate history program and Philadelphia's Mother Bethel African Methodist Episcopal Church (accessed February 4, 2020, http://informationwanted.org/).

53 Harper, *Iola Leroy*, 138, 141.

54 Harper, *Iola Leroy*, 141.

55 Harper, *Iola Leroy*, 141.

56 Harper, *Iola Leroy*, 222.

57 Harper, *Iola Leroy*, 195.

58 Vashti Lewis, "The Near-White Female in Frances Ellen Harper's *Iola Leroy*," *Phylon* 45, no. 4 (1984): 321. Further, as the 1965 Moynihan Report indicates, the view of African American motherhood as a "pathology" is long lived. See Moynihan, "Moynihan Report." Spillers's discussion of this "pathology" questions these assumptions about differences between the "white" and "Negro" family. See Spillers, "Mama's Baby, Papa's Maybe," 65–69.

59 Harper, *Iola Leroy*, 232.

60 William Andrews, *The Literary Career of Charles W. Chesnutt* (Baton Rouge: Louisiana State University Press, 1980), 202.

61 Andrews, *Literary Career of Charles W. Chesnutt*, 205.

62 Charles W. Chesnutt, *The Marrow of Tradition* [1901], edited by Nancy Bentley and Sandra Gunning (Boston: Bedford/St. Martin's Press, 2002), 45.

63 Chesnutt, *Marrow of Tradition*, 69.

64 Chesnutt, *Marrow of Tradition*, 71.

65 Chesnutt, *Marrow of Tradition*, 69.

66 In contrast to Mammy Jane and Jerry, as well as middle-class Black people such as the Millers, are those involved in the race riot at the novel's climax. Matthew Wilson discusses "Silly Milly," Josh Green's mother, who suffers from the terror of having witnessed the murder of her husband. Matthew Wilson notes that Chesnutt writes this Black woman's "personal experience of white terror" in the context of anxieties about protecting white women from the threat of rape by Black men. See Wilson, *Whiteness in the Novels of Charles Chesnutt* (Jackson: University Press of Mississippi, 2004), 115.

67 Chesnutt, *Marrow of Tradition*, 70.

68 Chesnutt, *Marrow of Tradition*, 70.

69 Chesnutt, *Marrow of Tradition*, 45.

70 Chesnutt, *Marrow of Tradition*, 49.

71 Chesnutt, *Marrow of Tradition*, 85.

72 Chesnutt, *Marrow of Tradition*, 203.

73 See Pascoe, *What Comes Naturally.*

74 Sundquist, *To Wake the Nations,* 397.

75 Chesnutt, *Marrow of Tradition,* 123.

76 In this vein, Samina Najmi argues that "Chesnutt parallels lynching hysteria with its counterpart: the sexual exploitation of black women" in Janet and Olivia's family drama. See Najmi, "Janet, Polly, and Olivia: Constructs of Blackness and White Femininity in Charles Chesnutt's *The Marrow of Tradition,*" *Southern Literary Journal* 32, no. 1 (1999): 9.

77 Chesnutt, *Marrow of Tradition,* 124, 128.

78 Chesnutt, *Marrow of Tradition,* 124, 128. Polly Ochiltree's vehemence in this scene makes clear the fact that white women, like white men, could be violent enslavers. On this point, see Stephanie E. Jones-Rogers, *They Were Her Property: White Women as Slave Owners in the American South* (New Haven: Yale University Press, 2019).

79 Chesnutt, *Marrow of Tradition,* 85, original emphasis.

80 Chesnutt, *Marrow of Tradition,* 245.

81 Chesnutt, *Marrow of Tradition,* 85.

82 Chesnutt, *Marrow of Tradition,* 245.

83 Stephen P. Knadler, "Untragic Mulatto: Charles Chesnutt and the Discourse of Whiteness," *American Literary History* 8, no. 3 (1996): 441, original emphasis.

84 Najmi, "Janet, Polly, and Olivia," 15.

85 Knadler, "Untragic Mulatto," 437.

86 Chesnutt, *Marrow of Tradition,* 245.

87 Elizabeth Ammons, "Stowe's Dream of the Mother-Savior: *Uncle Tom's Cabin* and American Women Writers before the 1920s," in *New Essays on Uncle Tom' Cabin,* edited by Eric Sundquist (New York: Cambridge University Press, 1986), 176.

88 Knadler, "Untragic Mulatto," 438, 443.

89 Elizabeth Maddock Dillon, "Reassembling the Novel: Kinlessness and the Novel of the Haitian Revolution," *Novel* 47, no. 1 (2014): 179.

90 Dillon, "Reassembling the Novel," 172.

91 Frances Ellen Watkins [Harper], "The Slave Mother, A Tale of the Ohio," in *Poems on Miscellaneous Subjects* (Philadelphia: Merrihew and Tompson, 1857), 42.

92 Toni Morrison, *Margaret Garner: Opera in Two Acts,* composed by Richard Danielpour (New York: Associated Music, 2004), (act 1, scene 1). All citations come from the libretto. See also the piano and vocal score, Richard Danielpour, *Margaret Garner: Opera in Two Acts,* libretto by Toni Morrison (New York: Associated Music, 2016). First performed at the Detroit Opera House, May 7, 2005.

93 Morrison, *Margaret Garner,* (act 1, scene 1).

94 Morrison, *Margaret Garner,* (act 1, scene 2).

95 Morrison, *Margaret Garner,* (act 2, scene 1).

96 Morrison, *Margaret Garner,* (act 2, scene 2).

97 Morrison, *Margaret Garner,* (act 2, scene 2).

98 Morrison, *Margaret Garner,* (act 2, scene 2).

99 Morrison, *Margaret Garner,* (act 2, scene 2).

100 Morrison, *Margaret Garner*, (act 2, intermezzo).

101 Morrison, *Margaret Garner*, (act 2, intermezzo).

102 Morrison, *Margaret Garner*, (act 2, scene 4).

103 Morrison, *Margaret Garner*, (act 2, scene 4).

104 Morrison, *Margaret Garner*, (act 2, scene 4), original emphasis.

105 Morrison, *Margaret Garner*, (epilogue).

106 Frederick Douglass, *Narrative of the Life of Frederick Douglass* [1845], edited by William L. Andrews and William S. McFeely (New York: Norton, 1996).

107 Cited in Mark Reinhardt, *Who Speaks for Margaret Garner?* (Minneapolis: University of Minnesota Press, 2010), 40–41.

108 Harper, "Slave Mother, A Tale of the Ohio" 40.

109 Sarah Remond, "Lecture on American Slavery by a Colored Lady," *Warrington Times*, January 29, 1859.

110 Neither Noble's original painting nor the engraving of it in *Harper's Weekly* make any visual gesture toward the family's mixed-race genealogies. The painting, in particular, depicts Garner and her children with dark skin that contrasts with that of the other adults. On the difficulties of representing mixed-race Black people using engraving technologies, see Senchyne, "Bottles of Ink."

111 Leslie Furth, "'The Modern Medea' and Race Matters: Thomas Satterwhite Noble's 'Margaret Garner'," *American Art* 12, no. 2 (1998): 39.

112 Elizabeth Livermore, "The Fugitives," *Independent Highway*, February 2, 1856, 7.

113 Dillon, "Reassembling the Novel," 168.

114 See Hartman, *Lose Your Mother*; Toni Morrison, *Beloved* (New York: Knopf, 1987); Octavia Butler, *Kindred* [1979] (Boston: Beacon Press, 2003).

115 *Liberator*, March 11, 1856.

116 Furth muses on the additional child here, reading them both as boys killed by Garner, perhaps more likely to be rendered valuable by Noble's viewers. See Furth, "'The Modern Medea'," 40.

Chapter Five. Mary Jemison's Cabin

1 For reasons similar to why I chose to represent another racial epithet as "n[—]" I have chosen to represent the word "squaw" as "s[—]" in my main text. Even as I note the relevance of this word's historical uses in racist representations of Native people, I wish to resist unnecessarily repeating this term myself, even in quotation.

2 On the difficulty of separating Jemison's voice from Seaver's in this text, see Karen Oakes, "We Planted, Tended, and Harvested Our Corn: Gender, Ethnicity, and Transculturation in A Narrative of the Life of Mrs. Mary Jemison," *Women and Language* 18, no. 1 (1995) 45–51; Michelle Burnham, "However Extravagant the Pretention: Bivocalism and US Nation-Building in *A Narrative of the Life of Mrs. Mary Jemison*," *Nineteenth-Century Contexts* 23, no. 3 (2001): 327–33; and Elena Ortells Montón, "*A Narrative of the Life of Mrs. Mary Jemison*:

Rhetorical Drag and the Defiance of Hegemonic Cultural Models," *Atlantis* 32, no. 1 (2010): 73–86. Because my focus here is on readings of Seaver's 1824 narrative, I refer to Mary Jemison by the name ascribed in his title, rather than her Seneca name, Dehgewanus (spelled Dickewamis in the first edition of Jemison's narrative, Deh-he-wä-mis in some later editions, and variously elsewhere). I mean here, in part, to acknowledge the settler colonialist perspective of Seaver's framing and recounting of Jemison's autobiography, even as I seek to glean how the woman's life that Seaver recounts resists that settler colonialist perspective.

3 See Lisa Brooks, *Our Beloved Kin*, 5; Pauline Turner Strong, *Captivating Selves, Captivating Others: The Politics and Poetics of Colonial American Captivity Narratives* (Boulder, CO: Westview Press, 1999), 12; and Margaret Ellen Newell, *Brethren by Nature: New England Indians, Colonists, and the Origins of American Slavery* (Ithaca, NY: Cornell University Press, 2015), 4.

4 June Namias discusses the genre of the white woman's captivity narrative, characterizing the most prominent female types as "the Survivor, the Amazon, and the Frail Flower," the last of these being most prominent after 1820. Jemison differs from Namias's "Frail Flower," who rarely recovers from the trauma of her captivity. See *White Captives*, 24, 37. Namias regards Jemison's story as an evolving one, charting it through the various editions of Seaver's narrative, noting that the figure of Jemison is remade throughout literary retellings. Christopher Castiglia also discusses the difficulty of placing Jemison among representations of the white woman captive. See *Bound and Determined*, 9.

5 This derogatory word does not simply characterize race but refers directly to interracial sexual kinship. Theresa Gaul discusses white people's similar use of the pejorative "s[—]" to designate all Cherokee wives, regardless of these women's races. See Gaul, *To Marry an Indian: The Marriage of Harriett Gold and Elias Boudinot in Letters, 1823–1839* (Chapel Hill: University of North Carolina Press, 2005), 51.

6 James E. Seaver, *A Narrative of the Life of Mrs. Mary Jemison* [1824], edited by June Namias (Norman: University of Oklahoma Press, 1995), 104. All further references are to this edition.

7 Seaver, *Narrative*, 105.

8 Seaver, *Narrative*, 105.

9 Seaver, *Narrative*, 105.

10 During the Revolutionary War, the Sullivan Expedition waged an offensive attack against the Iroquois Confederacy. In western New York, George Washington ordered Sullivan's army to carry out a scorched-earth campaign, destroying Indian villages as part of a genocidal attack on the Iroquois tribes who had aligned themselves with the British.

11 *An Authentic Narrative of the Seminole War; and of the Miraculous Escape of Mrs. Mary Godfrey, and her Four Female Children* (Providence, RI: D. F. Blanchard, 1836), 8.

12 *Authentic Narrative of the Seminole War*, 9.

13 *Authentic Narrative of the Seminole War*, 10.

14 *Authentic Narrative of the Seminole War*, 10.

15 Burnham, *Captivity and Sentiment*, 124.

16 Tiffany Lethabo King, *The Black Shoals: Offshore Formations of Black and Native Studies* (Durham, NC: Duke University Press, 2019), xi.

17 *Authentic Narrative of the Seminole War*, 12.

18 Rifkin, *Erotics of Sovereignty*, 35.

19 Seaver, *Narrative*, 105–6.

20 Seaver, *Narrative*, 106.

21 G. Peter Jemison, "Epilogue," in Rayna M. Gangi, *Mary Jemison: White Woman of the Seneca* (Santa Fe, NM: Clear Light Publications, 1996), 152. Particular focus on this episode in Jemison's narrative appears in Gangi's and Deborah Larsen's novelizations of Mary Jemison's life. See Gangi, *Mary Jemison*, 71–80; and Deborah Larsen, *The White* (New York: Random House, 2002), 152–61, 165.

22 Laura Romero, *Home Fronts: Domesticity and its Critics in the Antebellum United States* (Durham, NC: Duke University Press, 1997), 6–7.

23 Rifkin, *Erotics of Sovereignty*, 29.

24 Rifkin, *Erotics of Sovereignty*, 33.

25 Castiglia, *Bound and Determined*, 36.

26 Seaver, *Narrative*, 80.

27 Seaver, *Narrative*, 93.

28 Seaver, *Narrative*, 93.

29 Seaver, *Narrative*, 93.

30 Seaver, *Narrative*, 120.

31 Seaver, *Narrative*, 83.

32 On the very different circumstances of the (usually temporary) adoption of native children into white families, see Dawn Peterson, *Indians in the Family: Adoption and the Politics of Antebellum Expansion* (Cambridge, MA: Harvard University Press, 2017).

33 Jemison, "Epilogue," 151.

34 Seaver, *Narrative*, 78.

35 Seaver, *Narrative*, 77. The spellings of all Indian names I use are from Seaver's first edition of Jemison's narrative, published in 1824 (and on which June Namias's scholarly edition is based), unless otherwise indicated. The English spellings of these names vary across other historical documents, as does the last name of Mary Jemison and her descendants. I keep Seaver's original spellings merely for consistency with the narrative about which I am most concerned here.

36 Elias Johnson, *Legends, Traditions and Laws, of the Iroquois, or Six Nations, and History of the Tuscarora Indians* (Lockport, NY: Union Printing and Publishing Co., 1881), 26.

37 Seaver, *Narrative*, 89.

38 See *United States v. Rogers*, 45 U.S. 573 (1846).

39 Cheyfitz, "(Post)Colonial Construction of Indian Country," 23.

40 *Rogers*, 45 U.S. at 573.

41 Cheyfitz, "(Post)Colonial Construction of Indian Country," 22.

42 *Rogers*, 45 U.S. at 568.

43 *Rogers*, 45 U.S. at 571, 570.

44 *Rogers*, 45 U.S. at 570.

45 The pairing of blood quantum measures and tribal enrollment as requirements for federal recognition of Indian status illuminates the continued political and social importance of bio-logic for determining Native identity.

46 Oakes. "We Planted, Tended, and Harvested Our Corn," 50.

47 Rifkin, *Beyond Settler Time: Temporal Sovereignty and Indigenous Self-Determination*, (Durham, NC: Duke University Press, 2017), xii.

48 Kimberly TallBear, "Making Love and Relations beyond Settler Sex and Family," in *Making Kin, Not Population*, edited by Adele E. Clarke and Donna Haraway (Chicago: Prickly Paradigm Press, 2018), 145.

49 For examples of such discussions, see Castiglia, *Bound and Determined*, 34–48; Oakes, "We Planted, Tended, and Harvested Our Corn," 45–51; Pauline Turner Strong, *Captive Selves, Captivating Others*, 2, 145; and Hilary Wyss, "Captivity and Conversion," *American Indian Quarterly* 23, nos. 3/4 (1999): 64–65.

50 On this text's relevance for the genre of the frontier romance, see Harry Brown, "'The Horrid Alternative': Miscegenation and Madness in the Frontier Romance," *Journal of American Culture* 24, nos. 3/4 (2001): 137–51; Annette Kolodny, "Among the Indians: The Uses of Captivity," *Women's Studies Quarterly* 21, nos. 3/4 (1993): 184–95; and Ezra F. Tawil, *The Making of Racial Sentiment: Slavery and the Birth of the Frontier Romance* (Cambridge: Cambridge University Press, 2006). On Jemison's narrative as Native autobiography, see Susan Walsh, "'With Them Was My Home': Native American Autobiography and *A Narrative of the Life of Mrs. Mary Jemison*," *American Literature* 64, no. 1 (1992): 49–70; and Laura L. Mielke, *Moving Encounters: Sympathy and the Indian Question in Antebellum Literature* (Amherst: University of Massachusetts Press, 2008), 78–85.

51 TallBear, "Making Love," 147.

52 See Pascoe, *What Comes Naturally*, 10, 95. Karen Woods Weierman also emphasizes that interracial marriage is tied closely to land possession. See especially her discussion of Cooper's *The Pioneers* and *Johnson v. M'Intosh* in *One Nation, One Blood*, 87.

53 Pascoe, *What Comes Naturally*, 96.

54 Namias, *White Captives*, 99. See also Pascoe, *What Comes Naturally*, 94–95.

55 Namias, *White Captives*, 99.

56 Seaver, *Narrative*, 82.

57 Gaul, *To Marry an Indian*, 11.

58 See Gaul, *To Marry an Indian*, 3.

59 James Fenimore Cooper, *The Last of the Mohicans* [1826], edited by John McWilliams (New York: Oxford University Press, 1998), 125.

60 Cooper, *Last of the Mohicans*, 180.

61 Cooper, *Last of the Mohicans*, 180.

62 Jackson, *Barriers Between Us*, 7, 9.

63 Cooper, *Last of the Mohicans*, 387.

64 Catharine Maria Sedgwick, *Hope Leslie* [1827], edited by Mary Kelley (New Brunswick, NJ: Rutgers University Press, 2003), 338.

65 Sedgwick, *Hope Leslie*, 188.

66 Seaver, *Narrative*, 19–20.

67 Linda Kerber, *Women of the Republic: Intellect and Ideology in Revolutionary America* (New York: Norton, 1986), 228–29.

68 Lydia Maria Child, *Hobomok* [1824], edited by Carolyn L. Karcher (New Brunswick, NJ: Rutgers University Press, 1999), 137.

69 Child, *Hobomok*, 150.

70 Jefferson, *Notes on the State of Virginia*, 181. The irony of Jefferson's public claims against "amalgamation" between white people and Black people has, of course, been revealed by scholars such as Annette Gordon-Reed. See Gordon-Reed, *Thomas Jefferson and Sally Hemings*.

71 Lydia Fisher, "The Savage in the House," *Arizona Quarterly* 64, no. 1 (2008): 50.

72 Seaver, *Narrative*, 106.

73 Namias, *White Captives*, 185.

74 *Johnson v. M'Intosh*, 21 U.S. 543 (1823) at 572.

75 It is interesting that Mary Jemison signed treaties as a Seneca signatory with the federal government or other land dealers after she became a US citizen—a century before the Indian Citizen Act. This is another way in which her mode of identification becomes necessarily transcultural as she negotiates her position within the Seneca community and in relation to the US government.

76 Namias, *White Captives*, 186.

77 Seaver, *Narrative*, 54.

78 Seaver, *Narrative*, 54.

79 Seaver, *Narrative*, 54.

80 Castiglia, *Bound and Determined*, 36.

81 See "The Jemison Cabin," Letchworth Park History (accessed February 10, 2020, http://www.letchworthparkhistory.com/jemcab.html).

82 *Authentic Narrative of the Seminole War*, 8.

83 Philip J. Deloria, *Playing Indian* (New Haven, CT: Yale University Press, 1998), 167.

Chapter Six. Racial Re(Construction)

1 Jefferson, *Notes on the State of Virginia*, 176.

2 Jefferson, *Notes on the State of Virginia*, 181.

3 Ralina L. Joseph, *Transcending Blackness: From the New Millennium Mulatta to the Exceptional Multiracial* (Durham, NC: Duke University Press, 2013), 7.

4 For a discussion of these metaphors of color, see Richard Dyer, *White: Essays on Race and Culture* (New York: Routledge, 1997), 42.

5 W. E. B. Du Bois, *Dusk of Dawn: An Essay Toward an Autobiography of a Race Concept* [1940] (New Brunswick, NJ: Transaction Publishers, 2011), 153.

6 Du Bois, *Dusk of Dawn*, 152–53.

7 Du Bois, *Dusk of Dawn*, xxix–xxx.

8 Pascoe, *What Comes Naturally*, 94–95.

9 The maps were created with data from the LovingDay website (http://lovingday.org/legal-map), which celebrates the 1967 Supreme Court case of *Loving v. Virginia,* in which anti-miscegenation laws were deemed unconstitutional. See *Loving v. Virginia,* 388 US 1 (1967). The site's interactive map presents the history of anti-miscegenation law in what would become the United States between 1662 and 1967.

10 *Loving v. Virginia.*

11 Joseph, *Transcending Blackness*, 7.

12 *Oxford English Dictionary*, online ed., s.v. "amalgamation" (accessed October 13, 2018, http://www.oed.com.ezproxy.library.wisc.edu/view/Entry/5979?redirectedFrom=amalgamation).

13 Jerome Holgate [Oliver Bolokitten, pseud.], *A Sojourn in the City of Amalgamation, in the Year of Our Lord 19—* (New York: privately published, 1835).

14 Holgate, *Sojourn*, 31, 41.

15 The subheading of this section alludes to one anti-miscegenation pamphlet I mention in chapter 1: Seaman, *What Miscegenation Is!* The cover of this publication illustrates a Black man and a white woman kissing (see figure 1.1). This attention to interracial sexuality, of course, was misleading, as my aim has been to show how anxieties about interracial mixture expanded well beyond sexual kinship. Holgate's text illustrates how even the seeming obsession with interracial sex in racist anti-miscegenation literature was directly connected to anxieties about larger scales of racial reproduction.

16 Lemire notes that the premise of Holgate's dystopian *Sojourn* is "much [like the] . . . fabricated advertisements during the July riots of 1834" during which "abolitionism was perceived as linked to amalgamation and deserving of violent opposition on that count." Lemire, *Miscegenation*, 68.

17 See David Walker, *Appeal in Four Articles; Together with a Preamble, to the Coloured Citizens of the World, but in Particular and Very Expressly, to Those of the United States of America* [1829], edited by Sean Wilentz (New York: Hill and Wang, 1995), 9–10.

18 Alexis de Tocqueville, *Democracy in America* [1835], translated by Gerald E. Bevan (New York: Penguin Books, 2003), 417.

19 Tocqueville, *Democracy in America*, 417.

20 Jerome Holgate, *American Genealogy: Being a History of Some of the Early Settlers of North America and Their Descendants* (New York: George P. Putnam, 1851), 5.

21 On nineteenth-century African American contributions to scientific thought, which flew in the face of such dehumanization, see Rusert, *Fugitive Science.*

22 See Louis Menand, "Morton, Agassiz, and the Origins of Scientific Racism in the United States," *The Journal of Blacks in Higher Education* 34 (Winter 2001–2002): 111.

23 See Rush, "Observations"; and Nott, "The Mulatto."

24 Jefferson, *Notes on the State of Virginia*, 180.

25 See Lemire's discussion of Holgate in *Miscegenation*, 68, 70–71.

26 Holgate, *Sojourn*, 71.

27 Holgate, *Sojourn*, 69.

28 Nott, "The Mulatto."

29 Holgate, *Sojourn*, 95.

30 Lydia Maria Child, *A Romance of the Republic* [1867], edited by Dana D. Nelson (Lexington: University of Kentucky Press, 1997).

31 Child, *Romance*, 32.

32 Child's use of plant imagery counters racist scientific discourses of nonwhite people as animals, presenting a multi-scaled argument about racial amalgamation that departs from the most prominent framings of hybridity and species. In her use of floral imagery, Child deliberately avoids comparisons that would use human-animal relations as racist metaphors, as plants do not carry the same cultural baggage that animals do in US cultures of racial discourse. Racially mixed bodies are thereby naturalized in the floral imagery of the novel. Debra Rosenthal makes this argument, describing *Romance of the Republic*'s use of "uplifting floral counterdiscourse of botanical hybridity to counteract the postbellum prejudice that viewed African Americans and mixed-race peoples as animals." See Rosenthal, *Race Mixture in Nineteenth-Century US and Spanish American Fictions: Gender, Culture, and Nation Building* (Chapel Hill: University of North Carolina Press, 2004), 95–96.

33 Carter, *The United States of the United Races*, 2.

34 Jefferson, *Notes on the State of Virginia*, 151.

35 Jefferson, *Notes on the State of Virginia*, 149.

36 Jefferson, *Notes on the State of Virginia*, 148.

37 Child, *Romance*, 352.

38 Child, *Romance*, 352.

39 Child, *Romance*, 362.

40 Child, *Romance*, 364.

41 Child, *Romance*, 364. Gerald's only complaint about this new abundance of kin is that, before his birth had been revealed to him, he had fallen in love with Eulalia, Rosa and Alfred King's daughter—and Gerald's half-sister. Rosa's revelation about the switched babies is also, then, meant to prevent incest. The threat of endogamy outweighs that of exogamy, as marrying too closely within the family is shown as a legitimate worry, while interracial romance poses no threat for the novel's nonracist characters.

42 Child, *Romance*, 386.

43 Child, *Romance*, 420.

44 Child, *Romance*, 394.

45 Child, *Romance*, 436, 437.

46 Child, *Romance*, 438.

47 For a discussion of how the national story of the family also implicates women in issues of violence via their marriage and reproduction, see Shirley Samuels, "Women, Blood, and Contract," *American Literary History* 20, nos. 1/2 (2008): 57–75.

48 Theresa C. Zackodnik, *The Mulatta and the Politics of Race* (Jackson: University Press of Mississippi, 2004), xvi.

49 Foreman, "Who's Your Mama?" 506.

50 Clarence E. Walker, *Mongrel Nation: The America Begotten by Thomas Jefferson and Sally Hemings* (Charlottesville: University Press of Virginia, 2009), 2, 29.

51 On Frances Harper's and Julia Collins's revision of mixed-race heroines, see Brigitte Fielder, "Radical Respectability," in *African American Literature in Transition, 1865–1880*, edited by Eric Gardner (Cambridge: Cambridge University Press, forthcoming).

52 William Wells Brown, *Clotel; or, The President's Daughter* [1853], edited by Robert S. Levine (Boston: Bedford/St. Martin's Press, 2000).

53 For a comparison of the various editions of *Clotel*, see Samantha Marie Sommers, "A Tangled Text: William Wells Brown's *Clotel* (1853, 1860, 1864, 1867)" (BA diss., Wesleyan University, 2009). The University Press of Virginia's Rotunda scholarly edition of these texts facilitates such comparative work. See William Wells Brown, *Clotel: An Electronic Scholarly Edition*, edited by Christopher Mulvey (University Press of Virginia, 2006, https://www.upress.virginia.edu/content/clotel-william-wells-brown-electronic-scholarly-edition).

54 Julia C. Collins, *The Curse of Caste; or the Slave Bride* (New York: Oxford University Press, 2006).

55 On the development of the mixed-race heroine from the early nineteenth-century forward, see my discussions in Brigitte Fielder, "*The Woman of Colour* and Black Atlantic Movement," in *Women's Narratives of the Early Americas and the Formation of Empire*, edited by Mary Balkun and Susan Imbarrato (New York: Palgrave, 2016), 171–85; and Brigitte Fielder, "'Theresa' and the Transatlantic Mixed-Race Heroine," in *African American Literature in Transition, 1800–1830*, edited by Jasmine Cobb (Cambridge: Cambridge University Press, forthcoming).

56 William Wells Brown, *Miralda; or, the Beautiful Quadroon*, 226; William Wells Brown, *Clotelle, a Tale of the Southern States*, 176; William Wells Brown, *Clotelle; or The Colored Heroine, A Tale of the Southern States*, 178, all in Brown, *Clotel: An Electronic Scholarly Edition*. All subsequent page numbers for these texts are from this edition.

57 Brown, *Miralda*, 205, 234; Brown, *Clotelle, a Tale of the Southern States*, 160, 178; *Clotelle; or The Colored Heroine*, 162, 180.

58 On Clotel's racialization and legibility in print media, see Senchyne, "Bottles of Ink," 140–58.

59 See Gordon-Reed, *Thomas Jefferson and Sally Hemings*, 15.

60 See Gordon-Reed, *Thomas Jefferson and Sally Hemings*, 234–35.

Conclusion

1 Frances Ellen Watkins Harper, "We Are All Bound Up Together" [1866], in *We Must Be Up and Doing: A Reader in Early African American Feminisms*, edited by Teresa Zackodnik (Toronto, ON: Broadview Press, 2010), 303.

2 Lott, *Love and Theft*.

3 Johnny Pratter, email message to author and others, January 7, 2017.

4 Croly and Wakeman, *Miscegenation,* 24.

5 Walker, *Appeal*, 10, original emphasis.

6 Walker, *Appeal*, 13.

7 On African American engagement with white-dominated scientific fields and interrogation of white-supremacist scientific theory, see Rusert, *Fugitive Science*.

8 Toni Morrison, *A Mercy* (New York: Knopf, 2008), 155–56.

9 Morrison, *A Mercy*, 58.

10 Morrison, *A Mercy*, 58.

11 Morrison, *A Mercy*, 63.

12 Morrison, *A Mercy*, 59.

13 Morrison, *A Mercy*, 165.

14 Sharpe, "Lose Your Kin."

15 I owe thanks to Shirleen Robinson and Liz Swenson for making additional information available to me and to pointing out to me the necessary logistics of this act, as my initial writing about the incident did not take into account the hat's size, which makes the deliberately planned nature of its placement apparent.

16 Nicole Moore, (thehotnessgrrrl), Instagram photo, January 21, 2018, https://www.instagram.com/p/BeOHqaejj-8/?utm_source=ig_embed.

Adams, Abigail. Letter to William Stephens Smith, 18 September 1785. Adams Papers, Digital Edition, Adams Family Correspondence, Vol. 6, Massachusetts Historical Society. http://www.masshist.org/publications/adams-papers /index.php/view/ADMS-04-06-02-0116.

Adams, John Quincy. "The Character of Desdemona" [1836]. In *Notes and Comments upon Certain Plays and Actors of Shakespeare, with Criticism and Correspondence*, edited by James Henry Hackett, 3rd ed., 234–49. New York: Carleton, 1864.

Adams, John Quincy. "Misconceptions of Shakespeare upon the Stage" [1835]. In *Notes and Comments upon Certain Plays and Actors of Shakespeare, with Criticism and Correspondence*, edited by James Henry Hackett, 3rd ed., 217–28. New York: Carleton, 1864.

Albanese, Denise. "Black and White, and Dread All Over: The Shakespeare Theater's 'Photonegative' *Othello* and the Body of Desdemona." In *A Feminist Companion to Shakespeare*, edited by Dympna Callaghan, 226–49. Oxford: Blackwell, 2000.

Alcott, Louisa May. "The Brothers." *Atlantic Monthly* 12, no. 73 (1863): 48–59.

Alcott, Louisa May. *Hospital Sketches, and Camp and Fireside Stories*. Boston: Roberts Brothers, 1869.

Alcott, Louisa May. "M.L." In William G. Allen, Mary King, and Louisa May Alcott, *The American Prejudice against Color*, edited by Sarah Elbert, 121–53. Boston: Northeastern University Press, 2002.

Allen, William G. *The American Prejudice against Color: An Authentic Narrative, Showing How Easily the Nation Got into an Uproar*. London: W. and F. G. Cash, 1853.

Allen, William G. *The American Prejudice against Color*. In William G. Allen, Mary King, and Louisa May Alcott, *The American Prejudice against Color*, edited by Sarah Elbert, 35–92. Boston: Northeastern University Press, 2002.

Allen, William G. "Letter from Wm. Allen." *Frederick Douglass' Paper*, May 20, 1852.

Allen, William G. *A Short Personal Narrative*. Dublin: William Curry and Co., 1860.

Ammons, Elizabeth. "Stowe's Dream of the Mother-Savior: *Uncle Tom's Cabin* and American Women Writers before the 1920s." In *New Essays on Uncle Tom's Cabin*, edited by Eric Sundquist, 155–95. New York: Cambridge University Press, 1986.

Anderson, Jordan. "Letter from a Freedman to His Old Master" [1865]. In *The Freedman's Book*, edited by Lydia Maria Child, 265–67. Boston: Ticknor and Fields, 1865.

Andreas, James. "Othello's African-American Progeny." *South Atlantic Review* 57, no. 4 (1992): 39–57.

Andrews, William. *The Literary Career of Charles W. Chesnutt*. Baton Rouge: Louisiana State University Press, 1980.

An Authentic Narrative of the Seminole War; and of the Miraculous Escape of Mrs. Mary Godfrey, and her Four Female Children. Providence, RI: D. F. Blanchard, 1836.

Baldwin, James. "Everybody's Protest Novel" [1955]. In *Notes of a Native Son*, 13–23. Boston: Beacon Press, 1984.

Bean, Annmarie. "Transgressing the Gender Divide: The Female Impersonator in Nineteenth-Century Blackface Minstrelsy." In *Inside the Minstrel Mask: Readings in Nineteenth-Century Blackface Minstrelsy*, edited by Annemarie Bean, James V. Hatch, and Brooks McNamara, 245–56. Middletown, CT: Wesleyan University Press 1996.

Belson, M. [Mary Elliot?]. "My Mammy." In *Grateful Tributes; or, Recollections of Infancy*. New York: Shaw & Shoemaker, 1819.

Benjamin, Ruha. "Black AfterLives Matter: Cultivating Kinfulness as Reproductive Justice." In *Making Kin, Not Population*, edited by Adele Clarke and Donna Haraway, 41–66. Chicago: Prickly Paradigm Press, 2018.

Bentley, Nancy. "The Fourth Dimension: Kinlessness and African American Narrative." *Critical Inquiry* 35, no. 2 (2009): 2270–92.

Berlin, Ira, and Leslie S. Rowland. *Families and Freedom: A Documentary History of African-American Kinship in the Civil War Era*. New York: New Press, 1997.

Berman, Carolyn Vellenga. "Creole Family Politics in *Uncle Tom's Cabin* and *Incidents in the Life of a Slave Girl*." *Novel* 33, no. 3 (2000): 328–52.

Bernstein, Robin. *Racial Innocence: Performing American Childhood from Slavery to Civil Rights*. New York: New York University Press, 2011.

Blackett, Richard J. "William G. Allen, the Forgotten Professor." *Civil War History* 26, no. 1 (1980): 39–52.

Bland, Sheila Rose. "How I Would Direct Othello." In *Othello: New Essays by Black Writers*, edited by Mythili Kaul, 29–41. Washington, DC: Howard University Press, 1997.

Blight, David W. *Race and Reunion: The Civil War in American Memory*. Cambridge, MA: Belknap Press, 2001.

Brown, Harry. "'The Horrid Alternative': Miscegenation and Madness in the Frontier Romance." *Journal of American Culture* 24, nos. 3/4 (2001): 137–51.

Brown, Sterling. "The Muted South" [1945]. *Callaloo* 21, no. 4 (1998): 767–78.

Brown, William Wells. *Clotel: An Electronic Scholarly Edition*, edited by Christopher Mulvey. University Press of Virginia, 2006. https://www.upress.virginia.edu /content/clotel-william-wells-brown-electronic-scholarly-edition.

Brown, William Wells. *Clotel; or, The President's Daughter* [1853], edited by Robert S. Levine. Boston: Bedford/St. Martin's Press, 2000.

Brown, William Wells. *Clotelle, a Tale of the Southern States*. In *Clotel: An Electronic Scholarly Edition*, edited by Christopher Mulvey. University Press of Virginia, 2006. https://www.upress.virginia.edu/content/clotel-william-wells-brown-electronic-scholarly-edition.

Brown, William Wells. *Clotelle; or The Colored Heroine. A Tale of the Southern States*. In *Clotel: An Electronic Scholarly Edition*, edited by Christopher Mulvey. University Press of Virginia, 2006. https://www.upress.virginia.edu/content /clotel-william-wells-brown-electronic-scholarly-edition.

Brown, William Wells. *Miralda; or, the Beautiful Quadroon*. In *Clotel: An Electronic Scholarly Edition*, edited by Christopher Mulvey. University Press of Virginia, 2006. https://www.upress.virginia.edu/content/clotel-william-wells-brown-electronic-scholarly-edition.

Burnham, Michelle. *Captivity and Sentiment: Cultural Exchange in American Literature, 1682–1861*. Hanover, NH: University Press of New England, 1997.

Burnham, Michelle. "However Extravagant the Pretention: Bivocalism and US Nation-Building in *A Narrative of the Life of Mrs. Mary Jemison*." *Nineteenth-Century Contexts* 23, no. 3 (2001): 327–33.

Burroughs, Edgar Rice. *Tarzan of the Apes* [1914]. New York: Penguin, 1990.

Butler, Judith. *Undoing Gender*. New York: Routledge, 2004.

Butler, Octavia. *Kindred* [1979]. Boston: Beacon Press, 2003.

Byrd, Jodi. *The Transit of Empire: Indigenous Critiques of Colonialism*. Minneapolis: University of Minnesota Press, 2011.

Callaghan, Dympna. *Shakespeare without Women*. New York: Routledge, 2000.

Carlson, Andrew. "Oteller and Desdemonum: Defining Nineteenth-Century Blackness." *Theatre History Studies* 30 (2010): 176–86.

Carter, Greg. *The United States of the United Races: A Utopian History of Racial Mixing*. New York: New York University Press, 2013.

Carter, Sarah C. *Lexicon of Ladies' Names: With Their Floral Emblems*. Boston: G. W. Cotrell, 1865.

Castiglia, Christopher. *Bound and Determined: Captivity, Culture-Crossing, and White Womanhood from Mary Rowlandson to Patty Hearst*. Chicago: University of Chicago Press, 1996.

Castronovo, Russ. *Fathering the Nation: American Genealogies of Slavery and Freedom*. Berkeley: University of California Press, 1995.

Chaney, Michael. *Fugitive Vision: Slave Image and Black Identity in Antebellum Narrative*. Bloomington: Indiana University Press, 2009.

Chellis, Barbara. "Those Extraordinary Twins: Negroes and Whites." *American Quarterly* 21, no. 1 (1969): 100–112.

Chesnutt, Charles. "Her Virginia Mammy" [1899]. In *The Northern Stories of Charles W. Chesnutt*, edited by Charles Duncan, 76–95. Athens: Ohio University Press, 2004.

Chesnutt, Charles. *The Marrow of Tradition* [1901], edited by Nancy Bentley and Sandra Gunning. New York: Bedford/St. Martin's Press, 2002.

Chesnutt, Charles. "The Passing of Grandison" [1899]. In *The Northern Stories of Charles W. Chesnutt*, edited by Charles Duncan, 1–21. Athens: Ohio University Press, 2004.

Cheyfitz, Eric. "The (Post)Colonial Construction of Indian Country." In *The Columbia Guide to American Indian Literatures of the United States since 1945*, edited by Eric Cheyfitz, 1–124. New York: Columbia University Press, 2006.

Child, Lydia Maria. *An Appeal in Favor of Americans Called Africans* [1833]. New York: Arno Press, 1968.

Child, Lydia Maria. *Hobomok* [1824], edited by Carolyn L. Karcher. New Brunswick, NJ: Rutgers University Press, 1999.

Child, Lydia Maria. "Letter to the *New York Daily Tribune*, 3 September, 1852." In *A Lydia Maria Child Reader*, edited by Carolyn L. Karcher, 262–66. Durham, NC: Duke University Press, 1997.

Child, Lydia Maria. "The Quadroons" [1842]. In *Fact and Fiction: A Collection of Stories*. New York: C. S. Francis, 1846.

Child, Lydia Maria. *A Romance of the Republic* [1867], edited by Dana D. Nelson. Lexington: University of Kentucky Press, 1997.

Chiles, Katy L. *Transformable Race: Surprising Metamorphoses in the Literature of Early America*. New York: Oxford University Press, 2014.

Chopin, Kate. "Désirée's Baby" [1893]. In *Bayou Folk*. Cambridge, MA: Riverside Press, 1895.

Christian, Barbara. "The Race for Theory," *Feminist Studies* 14, no. 1 (Spring, 1988): 67–79.

Clinton, Catherine. *The Plantation Mistress: Woman's World in the Old South*. New York: Pantheon Books, 1982.

Cohen, Cathy. "Punks, Bulldaggers, and Welfare Queens: The Radical Potential of Queer Politics?" *GLQ: A Journal of Lesbian and Gay Studies* 3, no. 4 (1997): 453–55.

Collins, John Anderson. "The Slave Mother." Philadelphia: Pennsylvania Anti-Slavery Fair, 1855.

Collins, Julia C. *The Curse of Caste; or the Slave Bride* [1865], edited by William L. Andrews and Mitch Kachun. New York: Oxford University Press, 2006.

Collins, Kris. "White-Washing the Black-a-Moor: Othello, Negro Minstrelsy and Parodies of Blackness." *Journal of American Culture* 19, no. 3 (1996): 87–101.

Collins, Patricia Hill. *Black Feminist Thought: Knowledge, Consciousness, and the Politics of Empowerment*. New York: Routledge, 2000.

Cooper, James Fenimore. *The Last of the Mohicans* [1826], edited by John McWilliams. New York: Oxford University Press, 1998.

Cox, James. "*Pudd'nhead Wilson* Revisited." In *Mark Twain's* Pudd'nhead Wilson: *Race, Conflict and Culture*, edited by Susan Gillman and Forrest G. Robinson, 1–21. Durham, NC: Duke University Press, 1990.

Croly, David, and George Wakeman. *The Theory of the Blending of the Races, Applied to the American White Man and Negro*. New York: H. Dexter Hamilton, 1864.

Daileader, Celia. *Eroticism on the Renaissance Stage: Transcendence, Desire, and the Limits of the Visible*. Cambridge: Cambridge University Press, 1998.

Daileader, Celia. *Racism, Misogyny, and the Othello Myth: Interracial Couples from Shakespeare to Spike Lee*. New York: Cambridge University Press, 2005.

Danielpour, Richard. *Margaret Garner: Opera in Two Acts*. Libretto by Toni Morrison. New York: Associated Music Publishers, 2016.

Dayan, Colin. *The Law is a White Dog: How Legal Rituals Make and Unmake Persons*. Princeton, NJ: Princeton University Press, 2013.

Delany, Martin. "Letter." *Frederick Douglass' Paper*, May 6, 1853.

Deloria, Philip J. *Playing Indian*. New Haven, CT: Yale University Press, 1998.

Desdemonum: An Ethiopian Burlesque, in Three Scenes [1874], in *This Grotesque Essence: Plays from the American Minstrel Stage*, edited by Gary D. Engle, 62–67. Baton Rouge: Louisiana State University Press, 1978.

Dillon, Elizabeth Maddock. "Reassembling the Novel: Kinlessness and the Novel of the Haitian Revolution." *Novel* 47, no. 1 (2014): 167–85.

Dixon, Thomas. *The Clansman: An Historical Romance of the Ku Klux Klan*. New York: Doubleday, Page & Company, 1905.

Dobson, Michael. *Shakespeare and Amateur Performance: A Cultural History*. Cambridge: Cambridge University Press, 2011.

Dormon, James H. *Theater in the Antebellum South, 1815–1861*. Chapel Hill: University of North Carolina Press, 1967.

Douglass, Frederick. *Narrative of the Life of Frederick Douglass* [1845], edited by William L. Andrews and William S. McFeely. New York: Norton, 1996.

Du Bois, W. E. B. *Dusk of Dawn: An Essay Toward an Autobiography of a Race Concept* [1940]. New Brunswick, NJ: Transaction Publishers, 2011.

Dyer, Richard. *White: Essays on Race and Culture*. New York: Routledge, 1997.

Edelman, Lee. *No Future: Queer Theory and the Death Drive*. Durham, NC: Duke University Press, 2004.

Edelstein, Tilden G. "*Othello* in America: The Drama of Racial Intermarriage." In *Region, Race, and Reconstruction: Essays in Honor of C. Vann Woodward*, edited by J. Morgan Kousser and James M. McPherson, 179–97. New York: Oxford University Press, 1982.

Elbert, Sarah. "An Inter-Racial Love Story in Fact and Fiction: William and Mary King Allen's Marriage and Louisa May Alcott's Tale, 'M.L.'" *History Workshop Journal* 53 (2002): 17–42.

Elbert, Sarah. "Introduction." In William G. Allen, Mary King, and Louisa May Alcott, *The American Prejudice against Color*, edited by Sarah Elbert, 1–34. Boston: Northeastern University Press, 2002.

Elbert, Sarah. *Louisa May Alcott on Race, Sex, and Slavery*. Boston: Northeastern University Press, 1997.

Elfenbein, Anna Shannon. *Women on the Color Line: Evolving Stereotypes and the Writings of George Washington Cable, Grace King, Kate Chopin*. Charlottesville: University Press of Virginia, 1989.

Engle, Gary D. (ed.). *This Grotesque Essence: Plays from the American Minstrel Stage*. Baton Rouge: Louisiana State University Press, 1978.

Ernest, John. *Chaotic Justice: Rethinking African American Literary History*. Chapel Hill: University of North Carolina Press, 2009.

Fanon, Frantz. *Black Skin, White Masks*. New York: Grove Press, 1967.

Ferguson, Roderick. *Aberrations in Black: Toward a Queer of Color Critique*. Minneapolis: University of Minnesota Press, 2003.

Fiedler, Leslie. "As Free as Any Cretur . . ." In Mark Twain, *Pudd'nhead Wilson*, edited by Sidney E. Berger, 248–57. New York: Norton, 2005.

Fiedler, Leslie. *Love and Death in the American Novel*. New York: Anchor/Doubleday, 1992.

Fielder, Brigitte. "Radical Respectability." In *African American Literature in Transition, 1865–1880*, edited by Eric Gardner. Cambridge: Cambridge University Press, forthcoming.

Fielder, Brigitte. "'Theresa' and the Transatlantic Mixed-Race Heroine." In *African American Literature in Transition, 1800–1830*, edited by Jasmine Cobb. Cambridge: Cambridge University Press, forthcoming.

Fielder, Brigitte. "*The Woman of Colour* and Black Atlantic Movement." In *Women's Narratives of the Early Americas and the Formation of Empire*, edited by Mary Balkun and Susan Imbarrato, 171–85. London: Palgrave, 2016.

Fields, Barbara J. "Ideology and Race in American History." In *Region, Race, and Reconstruction*, edited by J. Morgan Kousser and James M. McPherson, 143–78. New York: Oxford University Press, 1982.

Finnerty, Paraic. *Emily Dickinson's Shakespeare*. Amherst: University of Massachusetts Press, 2006.

Fisher, Lydia. "The Savage in the House." *Arizona Quarterly* 64, no. 1 (2008): 49–75.

Foner, Eric. *Reconstruction: America's Unfinished Revolution, 1863–1877*. New York: Harper and Row, 1988.

Foreman, P. Gabrielle. "'Who's Your Mama?' 'White' Mulatta Genealogies, Early Photography, and Anti-Passing Narratives of Slavery and Freedom." *American Literary History* 14, no. 3 (2002): 505–39.

Foster, Frances Smith. *'Til Death or Distance Do Us Part: Love and Marriage in African America*. Oxford: Oxford University Press, 2010.

Franke, Katherine M. "Becoming a Citizen: Reconstruction Era Regulation of African American Marriages." *Yale Journal of Law and the Humanities* 11, no. 2 (1999): 251–309.

Freeman, Elizabeth. *Time Binds: Queer Temporalities, Queer Histories*. Durham, NC: Duke University Press, 2010.

Furth, Leslie. "'The Modern Medea' and Race Matters: Thomas Satterwhite Noble's 'Margaret Garner.'" *American Art* 12, no. 2 (1998): 36–57.

Gaines, Alisha. *Black for a Day: White Fantasies of Race and Empathy*. Chapel Hill: University of North Carolina Press, 2017.

Gangi, Rayna M. *Mary Jemison: White Woman of the Seneca*. Santa Fe, NM: Clear Light Publications, 1996.

Garrison, William Lloyd. "The Marriage Law." *The Liberator*, May 7 and May 21, 1831.

Gaul, Theresa Strouth. *To Marry an Indian: The Marriage of Harriett Gold and Elias Boudinot in Letters, 1823–1839*. Chapel Hill: University of North Carolina Press, 2005.

Gillman, Susan. *Dark Twins: Imposture and Identity in Mark Twain's America*. Chicago: University of Chicago Press, 1989.

Gillman, Susan. "'Sure Identifyers': Race, Science, and the Law in *Pudd'nhead Wilson*." In *Mark Twain's* Pudd'nhead Wilson: *Race, Conflict and Culture*, edited by Susan Gillman and Forrest G. Robinson, 86–104. Durham, NC: Duke University Press, 1990.

Gill-Peterson, Julian, Rebekah Sheldon, Kathryn Bond Stockton. "What Is the Now, Even of Then?" GLQ: *A Journal of Lesbian and Gay Studies* 22, no. 4 (2016): 495–503.

Gniadek, Melissa. "Mary Howard's Mark: Children's Literature and the Scales of Reading the Pacific." *Early American Literature* 50, no. 3 (2015): 797–826.

Gordon-Reed, Annette. *The Hemingses of Monticello: An American Family*. New York: Norton, 2008.

Gordon-Reed, Annette. *Thomas Jefferson and Sally Hemings: An American Controversy*. Charlottesville: University Press of Virginia, 1997.

Greenblatt, Stephen. *Shakespearian Negotiations: The Circulation of Social Energy in Renaissance England*. Berkeley: University of California Press, 1988.

Griffin, John Howard. *Black Like Me*. Boston: Houghton Mifflin, 1961.

Gross, Kenneth. *Shakespeare's Noise*. Chicago: University of Chicago Press, 2001.

Grove, James. "Mark Twain and the Endangered Family." *American Literature* 57, no. 3 (1985): 377–94.

Gumbs, Alexis Pauline. "Nobody Mean More: Black Feminist Pedagogy and Solidariry." In *Imperial University: Academic Repression and Scholarly Dissent*, edited by Piya Chatterjee and Sunaina Maira, 237–60. Minneapolis: University of Minnesota Press, 2014.

Hall, Kim F. *Things of Darkness: Economies of Race and Gender in Early Modern Europe*. Ithaca, NY: Cornell University Press, 1995.

Haney-López, Ian. *White by Law: The Legal Construction of Race*. New York: New York University Press, 2006.

Harper, Frances Ellen Watkins. *A Brighter Coming Day: A Frances Ellen Watkins Harper Reader*, edited by Frances Smith Foster. New York: Feminist Press, City University of New York, 1990.

Harper, Frances Ellen Watkins. *Iola Leroy, or Shadows Uplifted* [1892], edited by Koritha Mitchell. Peterborough, ON: Broadview Press, 2018.

Harper, Frances Ellen Watkins. *Minnie's Sacrifice* [1869]. In *Three Rediscovered Novels by Frances E. W. Harper,* edited by Frances Smith Foster, 1–92. Boston: Beacon Press, 1994.

Harper, Frances Ellen Watkins. "The Slave Mother" [1854]. In *A Brighter Coming Day: A Frances Ellen Watkins Harper Reader,* edited by Frances Smith Foster, 59. New York: Feminist Press, City University of New York, 1990.

Harper, Frances Ellen Watkins. "The Slave Mother, A Tale of Ohio." In *Poems on Miscellaneous Subjects.* Philadelphia: Merrihew and Thompson, 1857.

Harper, Frances Ellen Watkins. "We Are All Bound Up Together" [1866]. In *We Must Be Up and Doing: A Reader in Early African American Feminisms,* edited by Teresa Zackodnik, 300–303. Toronto, ON: Broadview Press, 2010.

Harris, Cheryl. "Whiteness as Property." *Harvard Law Review* 106, no. 8 (1993): 1707–91.

Hartman, Saidiya. *Lose Your Mother: A Journey along the Atlantic Slave Route.* New York: Farrar, Straus and Giroux, 2007.

Hartnett, Stephen H. *Democratic Dissent and the Cultural Fictions of Antebellum America.* Urbana: University of Illinois Press, 2002.

Hildreth, Richard. *The Slave: or Memoirs of Archy Moore.* Boston: John H. Eastburn, 1836.

Hildreth, Richard. *The White Slave; or, Memoirs of a Fugitive.* Boston: Tappan and Whittemore, 1852.

Hodes, Martha. *The Sea Captain's Wife: A True Story of Love, Race, and War in the Nineteenth Century.* New York: Norton, 2007.

Hodes, Martha. *Sex, Love, Race: Crossing Boundaries in North American History.* New York: New York University Press, 1995.

Hodes, Martha. *White Women, Black Men: Illicit Sex in the Nineteenth-Century South.* New Haven, CT: Yale University Press, 1997.

Holbein, Woodrow L. "Shakespeare in Charleston, 1800–1860." In *Shakespeare in the South: Essays on Performance,* edited by Philip C. Kolin, 88–111. Jackson: University Press of Mississippi, 1983.

Holgate, Jerome. *American Genealogy: Being a History of Some of the Early Settlers of North America and Their Descendants.* New York: George P. Putnam, 1851.

Holgate, Jerome [Oliver Bolokitten, pseud.]. *Sojourn in the City of Amalgamation, in the Year of Our Lord 19—.* New York: privately published, 1835.

Hopkins, Pauline. "Talma Gordon" [1900]. In *The American 1890s,* edited by Susan Harris Smith and Melanie Dawson, 105–16. Durham, NC: Duke University Press, 2000.

Howe, Lawrence. "Race, Genealogy and Genre in Mark Twain's Pudd'nhead Wilson." *Nineteenth-Century Literature* 46, no. 4 (1992): 495–516.

Hsu, Hsuan L. *Sitting in Darkness: Mark Twain, Asia, and Comparative Racialization.* New York: New York University Press, 2015.

Hurston, Zora Neale. *Dust Tracks on a Road: An Autobiography.* Philadelphia: Lippincott, 1942.

Iyengar, Sujata. "Moorish Dancing in *The Two Noble Kinsmen.*" *Medieval and Renaissance Drama in England* 20 (2007): 85–107.

Iyengar, Sujata. *Shades of Difference: Mythologies of Skin Color in Early Modern England*. Philadelphia: University of Pennsylvania Press, 2005.

Iyengar, Sujata. "White Faces, Blackface: The Production of 'Race' in Othello." In *Othello: New Critical Essays*, edited by Philip C. Kolin, 103–31. New York: Routledge, 2002.

Jackson, Cassandra. *Barriers Between Us: Interracial Sex in Nineteenth-Century American Literature*. Bloomington: Indiana University Press, 2004.

Jackson, Holly. *American Blood: The Ends of Family in American Literature, 1850–1900*. New York: Oxford University Press, 2014.

Jacobs, Harriet. *Incidents in the Life of a Slave Girl*, edited by Nellie Y. McKay and Frances Smith Foster. New York: Norton, 2001.

Jameson, Mrs. (Anna). "Desdemona" [1832]. In *Characteristics of Women, Moral, Poetical, and Historical*, 155–65. New York: John Wiley, 1848.

Jefferson, Thomas. *Notes on the State of Virginia* [1785], edited by David Waldstreicher. Boston: Bedford/St. Martin's Press, 2002.

Jehlen, Myra. "The Ties that Bind: Race and Sex in *Pudd'nhead Wilson*." *American Literary History* 2, no.1 (1990): 39–55.

Jemison, G. Peter. "Epilogue." In Rayna M. Gangi, *Mary Jemison: White Woman of the Seneca–A Novel*, 151–52. Santa Fe, NM: Clear Light Publications, 1996.

Johnson, Elias. *Legends, Traditions and Laws, of the Iroquois, or Six Nations, and History of the Tuscarora Indians*. Lockport, NY: Union Printing and Publishing Co., 1881.

Johnson, Walter. "The Slave-Trader, the White Slave, and the Politics of Racial Determination in the 1850s." *Journal of American History* 87, no. 1 (2000): 13–38.

Jones-Rogers, Stephanie. *They Were Her Property: White Women as Slave Owners in the American South*. New Haven: Yale University Press, 2019.

Jordan, Winthrop D. *White Over Black: American Attitudes toward the Negro, 1550–1812*. Chapel Hill: University of North Carolina Press, 1968.

Joseph, Ralina L. *Transcending Blackness: From the New Millennium Mulatta to the Exceptional Multiracial*. Durham, NC: Duke University Press, 2013.

Kahn, Edward. "Desdemona and the Role of Women in the Antebellum North." *Theatre Journal* 60, no. 2 (2008): 235–55.

Kauanui, J. Kēhaulani. *Hawaiian Blood: Colonialism and the Politics of Sovereignty and Indigeneity*. Durham, NC: Duke University Press, 2008.

Kerber, Linda. *Women of the Republic: Intellect and Ideology in Revolutionary America*. New York: Norton, 1986.

King, Tiffany Lethabo. *The Black Shoals: Offshore Formations of Black and Native Studies*. Durham, NC: Duke University Press, 2019.

Knadler, Stephen P. *The Fugitive Race: Minority Writers Resisting Whiteness*. Jackson: University Press of Mississippi, 2009.

Knadler, Stephen P. "Untragic Mulatto: Charles Chesnutt and the Discourse of Whiteness." *American Literary History* 8, no. 3 (1996): 426–48.

Kolodny, Annette. "Among the Indians: The Uses of Captivity." *Women's Studies Quarterly* 21, nos. 3/4 (1993): 184–95.

Ladd, Barbara. *Nationalism and the Color Line in George W. Cable, Mark Twain, and William Faulkner*. Baton Rouge: Louisiana State University Press, 1996.

Larsen, Deborah. *The White*. New York: Random House, 2002.

Lee, Julia H. *Interracial Encounters: Reciprocal Representations in African and Asian American Literatures, 1896–1937*. New York: New York University Press, 2011.

Lemcke, Julius Augustus. *Reminiscences of an Indianian*. Indianapolis: Hollenbeck Press, 1905.

Lemire, Elise. *Miscegenation: Making Race in America*. Philadelphia: University of Pennsylvania Press, 2002.

Levine, Lawrence W. *Highbrow/Lowbrow: The Emergence of Cultural Hierarchy in America*. Cambridge, MA: Harvard University Press, 1988.

Lewis, Vashti. "The Near-White Female in Frances Ellen Harper's *Iola Leroy*." *Phylon* 45, no. 4 (1984): 314–22.

Lhamon, W. T., Jr. "Introduction." In T. D. Rice, *Jim Crow, American: Selected Songs and Plays*, edited by W. T. Lhamon Jr., vii–xxiv. Cambridge, MA: Harvard University Press 2009.

Lhamon, W. T., Jr. *Jump Jim Crow: Lost Plays, Lyrics, and Street Prose of the First Atlantic Popular Culture*. Cambridge, MA: Harvard University Press, 2003.

Lhamon, W. T., Jr. *Raising Cain: Blackface Performance from Jim Crow to Hip Hop*. Cambridge, MA: Harvard University Press, 1998.

Lincoln, Abraham. *Speeches and Writings, 1832–1858*, edited by Don E. Fehrenbacher. New York: Library of America, 1989.

Lipsitz, George. *The Possessive Investment in Whiteness: How White People Profit from Identity Politics*. Philadelphia: Temple University Press, 2006.

Livermore, Elizabeth. "The Fugitives." *Independent Highway*, February 2, 1856, 6–22.

Loomba, Ania. *Gender, Race, Renaissance Drama*. New York: Oxford University Press, 1992.

Loomba, Ania. *Shakespeare, Race, and Colonialism*. New York: Oxford University Press, 2002.

Lott, Eric. *Love and Theft: Blackface Minstrelsy and the American Working Class*. New York: Oxford University Press, 1995.

Lower, Charles B. "Othello as Black on Southern Stages, Then and Now." In *Shakespeare in the South: Essays on Performance*, edited by Philip C. Kolin, 199–228. Jackson: University Press of Mississippi, 1983.

MacDonald, Joyce Green. "Acting Black: *Othello*, *Othello* Burlesques, and the Performance of Blackness." *Theatre Journal* 46, no. 2 (1994): 231–49.

MacDonald, Joyce Green. "Black Ram, White Ewe: Shakespeare, Race, and Women." In *A Feminist Companion to Shakespeare*, edited by Dympna Callaghan, 188–207. Malden, MA: Blackwell, 2000.

MacDonald, Joyce Green. "Border Crossings: Women, Race, and *Othello* in Gayl Jones's *Mosquito*." *Tulsa Studies in Women's Literature* 28, no. 2 (2009): 315–36.

Macrae, David. *The Americans at Home: Pen-and-Ink Sketches of American Men, Manners and Institutions*, vol. 2. Edinburgh: Edmonston and Couglas, 1870.

Mahar, William J. "Ethiopian Skits and Sketches: Contents and Contexts of Blackface Minstrelsy, 1840–1890." In *Inside the Minstrel Mask: Readings in Nineteenth- Century Blackface Minstrelsy,* edited by Annemarie Bean, James V. Hatch, and Brooks McNamara, 179–222. Middletown, CT: Wesleyan University Press, 1996.

Mailer, Norman. *White Negro.* San Francisco: City Lights Books, 1957.

McAllister, Marvin. *White People Do Not Know How to Behave at Entertainments Designed for Ladies and Gentlemen of Color: William Brown's African and American Theater.* Chapel Hill: University of North Carolina Press, 2003.

McKittrick, Katherine. *Demonic Grounds: Black Women and the Cartographies of Struggle.* Minneapolis: University of Minnesota Press, 2006.

McPherson, James M. *Battle Cry of Freedom: The Civil War Era, 1848–1865.* New York: Ballantine Books, 1988.

Melville, Herman. *Moby-Dick* [1851]. New York: W. W. Norton, 1967.

Mielke, Laura L. *Moving Encounters: Sympathy and the Indian Question in Antebellum Literature.* Amherst: University of Massachusetts Press, 2008.

Mitchell, Koritha. "The N-Word in the Classroom: Just Say NO," March 4, 2019, in *C19 Podcast.* Produced by Xine Yao, Paul Kotheimer, and Koritha Mitchell, MP3 audio, https://podcasts.apple.com/us/podcast/s2e6-the-n-word-in-the-classroom-just-say-no/id1275235064?i=1000431046556.

Mitchell, Koritha. "Teaching & the N-word: Questions to Consider." Koritha Mitchell's Official Website. Accessed April 16, 2020. http://www.korithamitchell.com/teaching-and-the-n-word/.

Mitchell, Mary Niall. *Raising Freedom's Children: Black Children and Visions of the Future after Slavery.* New York: New York University Press, 2008.

Moore, Nicole. (thehotnessgrrrl). Instagram photo, January 21, 2018. https://www.instagram.com/p/BeOHqaejj-8/?utm_source=ig_embed.

Montón, Elena Ortells. "*A Narrative of the Life of Mrs. Mary Jemison*: Rhetorical Drag and the Defiance of Hegemonic Cultural Models." *Atlantis* 32, no. 1 (2010): 73–86.

Morgan, Jennifer. *Laboring Women: Reproduction and Gender in New World Slavery.* Philadelphia: University of Pennsylvania Press, 2004.

Morris, Linda A. "Beneath the Veil: Clothing, Race, and Gender in Mark Twain's *Pudd'nhead Wilson.*" *Studies in American Fiction* 27, no. 1 (1999): 37–52.

Morrison, Toni. *Beloved.* New York: Knopf, 1987.

Morrison, Toni. *Desdemona.* London: Oberon Books 2011.

Morrison, Toni. *Margaret Garner: Opera in Two Acts.* Composed by Richard Danielpour. Revised edition. New York: Associated Music, 2004.

Morrison, Toni. *A Mercy.* New York: Knopf, 2008.

Morrison, Toni. *Playing In the Dark: Whiteness and the Literary Imagination.* New York: Vintage, 1992.

Morton, Samuel. *Crania Aegyptiaca; or, Observations on Egyptian Ethnography, Derived from Anatomy, History, and the Monuments.* Philadelphia: J. Penington, 1844.

Morton, Samuel. *Crania Americana; or, A Comparative View of the Skulls of Various Aboriginal Nations of North and South America, to Which Is Prefixed an Essay on the Varieties of the Human Species.* Philadelphia: J. Dobson, 1839.

Moynihan, Daniel P. "The Moynihan Report" [1965], in *The Moynihan Report and the Politics of Controversy: A Transaction Social Science and Public Policy Report,* edited by Lee Rainwater and William L. Yancey, 47–94. Cambridge: MIT Press, 1967.

Najmi, Samina. "Janet, Polly, and Olivia: Constructs of Blackness and White Femininity in Charles Chesnutt's *The Marrow of Tradition.*" *Southern Literary Journal* 32, no.1 (1999): 1–19.

Namias, June. *White Captives.* Chapel Hill: University of North Carolina Press, 1993.

Newell, Margaret Ellen. *Brethren by Nature: New England Indians, Colonists, and the Origins of American Slavery.* Ithaca, NY: Cornell University Press, 2015.

Nichols, Charles. "The Origins of *Uncle Tom's Cabin.*" *Phylon Quarterly* 19, no. 3 (1958): 328–34.

Nott, Josiah C. "The Mulatto, a Hybrid—Probable Extermination of the Two Races if the Whites and Blacks Are Allowed to Intermarry." *American Journal of the Medical Sciences* 6 (1843): 252–56.

Nyong'o, Tavia. *The Amalgamation Waltz: Race, Performance, and the Ruses of Memory.* Minneapolis: University of Minnesota Press, 2009.

Oakes, Karen. "We Planted, Tended, and Harvested Our Corn: Gender, Ethnicity, and Transculturation in *A Narrative of the Life of Mrs. Mary Jemison.*" *Women and Language* 18, no. 1 (1995) 45–51.

O'Brien, Jean. *Firsting and Lasting: Writing Indians Out of Existence in New England.* Minneapolis: University of Minnesota Press, 2010.

Odell, George C. D. *Annals of the New York Stage,* 15 volumes. New York: Columbia University Press, 1927.

Omi, Michael, and Howard Winant. *Racial Formation in the United States from the 1960s to the 1990s.* New York: Routledge, 1994.

Othello; A Burlesque [1866?], in *This Grotesque Essence: Plays from the American Minstrel Stage,* edited by Gary D. Engle, 68–77. Baton Rouge: Louisiana State University Press, 1978.

"Othello's Costume," *Once a Week,* September 8, 1866, 274.

Page, Thomas Nelson. "The Old-Time Negro." *Scribner's Magazine,* July–December 1904, 522–32.

Pao, Angela C. "Ocular Revisions: Re-Casting *Othello* in Text and Performance." In *Colorblind Shakespeare: New Perspectives on Race and Performance,* edited by Ayanna Thompson, 37–45. New York: Routledge, 2006.

Pascoe, Peggy. *What Comes Naturally: Miscegenation Law and the Making of Race in America.* Oxford: Oxford University Press, 2009.

Patterson, Mark R. "Surrogacy and Slavery: The Problematics of Consent in Baby M, *Romance of the Republic* and *Pudd'nhead Wilson.*" *American Literary History* 8, no. 3 (1996): 449–70.

Peterson, Dawn. *Indians in the Family: Adoption and the Politics of Antebellum Expansion.* Cambridge, MA: Harvard University Press, 2017.

Piatt, Sarah Morgan Bryan. "The Black Princess (A True Fable of My Old Kentucky Nurse)" [1872]. In *Palace-Burner: The Selected Poetry of Sarah Piatt,* edited by Paula Bernat Bennett, 38. Urbana: University of Illinois Press, 2001.

Porter, Carolyn. "Roxana's Plot." *Cultural Critique* 15 (1990): 145–65.

Potter, Lois. *Othello.* Manchester: Manchester University Press, 2002.

Preston, Mary. *Studies in Shakespeare: A Book of Essays.* Philadelphia: Claxton, Remsen, and Haffelfinger, 1869.

Rawley, James A. *Race and Politics: "Bleeding Kansas" and the Coming of the Civil War.* Philadelphia: Lippincott, 1969.

Reinhardt, Mark. *Who Speaks for Margaret Garner?* Minneapolis: University of Minnesota Press, 2010.

Remond, Sarah. "Lecture on American Slavery by a Colored Lady." *Warrington Times,* January 29, 1859.

Rifkin, Mark. *Beyond Settler Time: Temporal Sovereignty and Indigenous Self-Determination.* Durham, NC: Duke University Press, 2017.

Rifkin, Mark. *The Erotics of Sovereignty: Queer Native Writing in the Era of Self-Determination.* Minneapolis: University of Minnesota Press, 2012.

Rifkin, Mark. *When Did Indians Become Straight? Kinship, the History of Sexuality, and Native Sovereignty.* New York: Oxford University Press, 2011.

Rice, T. D. *Otello, a Burlesque Opera* [1853]. In *Jim Crow, American: Selected Songs and Plays,* edited by W. T. Lhamon Jr., 110–58. Cambridge, MA: Harvard University Press, 2009.

Richards, Jeffrey H. "Chastity and the Stage in Mowatt's 'Stella.'" *Studies in American Fiction* 24, no. 1 (1996): 87–100.

Ritchie, Anna Cora Ogden Mowatt. *Mimic Life; or, Before and behind the Curtain. A Series of Narratives.* Boston: Ticknor and Fields, 1856.

Roberts, Dorothy. *Killing the Black Body: Race, Reproduction, and the Meaning of Liberty.* New York: Pantheon Books, 1997.

Robinson, Forrest G. "The Sense of Disorder in *Pudd'nhead Wilson.*" In *Mark Twain's* Pudd'nhead Wilson: *Race, Conflict and Culture,* edited by Susan Gillman and Forrest G. Robinson, 28–44. Durham, NC: Duke University Press, 1990.

Rogin, Michael. "Frances Galton and Mark Twain: The Native Autograph in *Pudd'nhead Wilson.*" In *Mark Twain's* Pudd'nhead Wilson: *Race, Conflict and Culture,* edited by Susan Gillman and Forrest G. Robinson, 73–85. Durham, NC: Duke University Press, 1990.

Romero, Laura. *Home Fronts: Domesticity and Its Critics in the Antebellum United States.* Durham, NC: Duke University Press, 1997.

Rosenthal, Debra J. *Race Mixture in Nineteenth-Century US and Spanish American Fictions: Gender, Culture, and Nation Building.* Chapel Hill: University of North Carolina Press, 2004.

Rothman, Joshua D. *Notorious in the Neighborhood: Sex and Families across the Color Line in Virginia, 1787–1861*. Chapel Hill: University of North Carolina Press, 2003.

Royster, Francesca T. "Playing with (a) Difference: Early Black Shakespearean Actors, Blackface and Whiteface." In *Shakespeare in America*, edited by Alden T. Vaughan and Virginia Mason Vaughan, 35–47. Washington, DC: Folger Shakespeare Library, 2007.

Rusert, Britt. *Fugitive Science: Empiricism and Freedom in Early African American Culture*. New York: New York University Press, 2017.

Rush, Benjamin. "Observations Intended to Favour a Supposition that the Black Color (as it is called) of the Negroes is Derived from Leprosy." *Transactions of the American Philosophical Society* 4 (1799): 289–97.

Rutkowski, Alice. "Leaving the Good Mother: Frances E. W. Harper, Lydia Maria Child, and the Literary Politics of Reconstruction." *Legacy* 25, no. 1 (2008): 83–104.

Saks, Eva. "Representing Miscegenation Law." *Raritan* 8, no. 2 (1988): 39–69.

Samuels, Shirley. "Women, Blood, and Contract." *American Literary History* 20, nos. 1/2 (2008): 57–75.

Scott, Darieck. *Extravagant Abjection: Blackness, Power, and Sexuality in the African American Literary Imagination*. New York: New York University Press, 2010.

Seaman, L. *What Miscegenation Is! And What We Are to Expect Now that Mr. Lincoln is Re-Elected*. New York: Waller and Willetts, 1865.

Seaver, James E. *A Narrative of the Life of Mrs. Mary Jemison* [1824], edited by June Namias Norman: University of Oklahoma Press, 1995.

Seaver, James E. *A Narrative of the Life of Mary Jemison, Deh-he-wä-mis*, 6th ed. New York: G. P. Putnam, 1898.

Sedgwick, Catharine Maria. *Hope Leslie* [1827], edited by Mary Kelley. New Brunswick, NJ: Rutgers University Press, 2003.

Senchyne, Jonathan. "Bottles of Ink and Reams of Paper: *Clotel*, Racialization, and the Material Culture of Print." In *Early African American Print Culture*, edited by Lara L. Cohen and Jordan A. Stein, 140–58. Philadelphia: University of Pennsylvania Press, 2012.

Shakespeare, William. *Othello: The Moor of Venice*, edited by Kim F. Hall. Boston: Bedford/St. Martin's Press, 2007.

Shapiro, James (ed.). *Shakespeare in America: An Anthology from the Revolution to Now*. New York: Library of America, 2014.

Sharpe, Christina. *In the Wake: On Blackness and Being*. Durham, NC: Duke University Press, 2016.

Shattuck, Charles H. *Shakespeare on the American Stage: From Booth and Barrett to Sothern and Marlowe*. Cranbury, NJ: Associated University Presses, 1987.

Sommers, Samantha Marie. "A Tangled Text: William Wells Brown's *Clotel* (1853, 1860, 1864, 1867)." BA diss., Wesleyan University, 2009.

Spillers, Hortense J. "Mama's Baby, Papa's Maybe: An American Grammar Book." *Diacritics* 17, no. 2 (1987): 65–85.

Spires, Derrick. *The Practices of Citizenship: Black Politics and Print Culture in the Early United States*. Philadelphia: University of Pennsylvania Press, 2019.

Stack, Carol. *All Our Kin: Strategies for Survival in a Black Community.* New York: Harper and Row, 1974.

Stanton, William. *The Leopard's Spots.* Chicago: University of Chicago Press, 1960.

Stowe, Harriet Beecher. *A Key to Uncle Tom's Cabin.* Boston: John P. Jewett, 1853.

Stowe, Harriet Beecher. *Uncle Tom's Cabin; or, Life Among the Lowly* [1852], edited by Elizabeth Ammons. New York: Norton, 1994.

Strong, Pauline Turner. *Captive Selves, Captivating Others: The Politics and Poetics of Colonial American Captivity Narratives.* Boulder, CO: Westview Press, 1999.

Sturgess, Kim C. *Shakespeare and the American Nation.* New York: Cambridge University Press, 2004.

Sundquist, Eric. *To Wake the Nations: Race in the Making of American Literature.* Cambridge, MA: Belknap Press, 1993.

TallBear, Kimberly. "Making Love and Relations beyond Settler Sex and Family." In *Making Kin, Not Population,* edited by Adele E. Clarke and Donna Haraway, 145–66. Chicago: Prickly Paradigm Press, 2018.

TallBear, Kimberly. "Narratives of Race and Indigeneity in the Genographic Project." *Journal of Law, Medicine and Ethics* 35, no. 3 (2007): 412–24.

TallBear, Kimberly. *Native American DNA: Tribal Belonging and the False Promise of Genetic Science.* Minneapolis: University of Minnesota Press, 2013.

Tawil, Ezra F. *The Making of Racial Sentiment: Slavery and the Birth of the Frontier Romance.* Cambridge: Cambridge University Press, 2006.

Terry, Ellen. *Ellen Terry's Memoirs,* edited by Edith Craig and Christopher St. John. New York: G. P. Putnam, 1932.

Thompson, Ayanna. *Passing Strange: Shakespeare, Race, and Contemporary America.* New York: Oxford University Press, 2011.

Tocqueville, Alexis de. *Democracy in America* [1835], translated by Gerald E. Bevan. New York: Penguin Books, 2003.

Toll, Robert. *Blacking Up: The Minstrel Show in Nineteenth-Century America.* New York: Oxford University Press, 1974.

Troester, Rosalie Riegle. "Turbulence and Tenderness: Mothers, Daughters, and 'Othermothers' in Paule Marshall's *Brown Girl, Brownstones.*" *Sage: A Scholarly Journal on Black Women* 1, no. 2 (1984): 13–16.

Truth, Sojourner. *Narrative of Sojourner Truth* [1850], edited by Margaret Washington. New York: Vintage, 1993.

Turner, Patricia A. *Ceramic Uncles and Celluloid Mammies: Black Images and Their Influence on Culture.* New York: Anchor Books, 1994.

Twain, Mark. *Pudd'nhead Wilson* [1894], edited by Sidney E. Berger. New York: Norton, 2005.

Vaughan, Alden T., and Virginia Mason Vaughan, eds. *Shakespeare in American Life.* Washington, DC: Folger Shakespeare Library, 2007.

Vaughan, Virginia Mason. "Making Shakespeare American: Shakespeare's Dissemination in Nineteenth-Century America." In *Shakespeare in American Life,* edited by Alden T. Vaughan and Virginia Mason Vaughan, 23–34. Washington, DC: Folger Shakespeare Library, 2007.

Vaughan, Virginia Mason. *Othello: A Contextual History*. New York: Cambridge University Press, 1994.

Walker, Clarence E. *Mongrel Nation: The America Begotten by Thomas Jefferson and Sally Hemings*. Charlottesville: University Press of Virginia, 2009.

Walker, David. *Appeal in Four Articles; Together with a Preamble, to the Coloured Citizens of the World, but in Particular and Very Expressly, to Those of the United States of America* [1829], edited by Sean Wilentz. New York: Hill and Wang, 1995.

Wallace-Sanders, Kimberly. *Mammy: A Century of Race, Gender, and Southern Memory*. Ann Arbor: University of Michigan Press, 2008.

Walsh, Susan. "'With Them Was My Home': Native American Autobiography and *A Narrative of the Life of Mrs. Mary Jemison*." *American Literature* 64, no. 1 (1992): 49–70.

Warde, Frederick. *Fifty Years of Make-Believe*. New York: International Press Syndicate, 1920.

Webb, Frank J. *The Garies and Their Friends*. Baltimore: Johns Hopkins University Press, 1997.

Weierman, Karen Woods. *One Nation, One Blood: Interracial Marriage in American Fiction, Scandal, and Law, 1820–1870*. Amherst: University of Massachusetts Press, 2005.

Weinbaum, Alys Eve. *Wayward Reproductions: Genealogies of Race and Nation in Transatlantic Modern Thought*. Durham, NC: Duke University Press, 2004.

White, Richard Grant. *Studies in Shakespeare*. New York: Houghton, Mifflin and Company, 1886.

Williams, Heather Andrea. *Help Me to Find My People: The African American Search for Family Lost in Slavery*. Chapel Hill: University of North Carolina Press, 2012.

Wilson, Harriet E. *Our Nig; or, Sketches in the Life of a Free Black* [1859], edited by Henry Louis Gates Jr. and Richard J. Ellis. New York: Vintage, 2011.

Wilson, Matthew. *Whiteness in the Novels of Charles Chesnutt*. Jackson: University Press of Mississippi, 2004.

Wyss, Hilary. "Captivity and Conversion." *American Indian Quarterly* 23, nos. 3/4 (1999): 63–82.

Zackodnik, Theresa C. *The Mulatta and the Politics of Race*. Jackson: University Press of Mississippi, 2004.

INDEX

King, Mary: as captive "damsel," 57–64, 66, 68, 75–76; fugitivity of, 20, 57, 67–77, 173–74, 260n21; marriage to William Allen 22, 54–82, 157, 174, 206; as mixed-race heroine, 20–21, 55–58, 64–72, 74, 81; as mother, 72, 77, 88–89; racial vulnerability of, 105

King, Tiffany Lethabo, 170

Kindred (Butler), 155

kinfullness, 123–26, 130, 135–36, 148, 157, 249n44

kinlessness, 6, 106, 118–26, 135, 150–53, 238–39, 249n44

kinship: aunts, 99–100, 125–27, 133, 148; as behavioral, 165, 170, 177, 186, 193, 215; brothers, 81; 85–89, 97, 115–17, 226–28, 234, 263n1; as cultural, 89; 176; ersatz kinship, 89–93, 97–98, 101, 131, 137–38; fathers, 5–6, 15, 125, 129, 132, 136; "fictive" kinship, 82, 90, 104, 125–35; sexual kinship, 4, 14–20, 31–54, 86–88, 182–86, 237; uncles, 125–27, 131, 133. *See also* children; kinfullness; kinlessness; mothers; sisters

Knadler, Stephen, 70, 146–47

Knowland, Thomas, 76

Kolodny, Annette, 181

language: blackface dialect, 40, 46–47; of kinship, 125–30, 171; as metaphor for race, 211–16; Native languages, 176, 180, 215; "polyglot" multilingualism, 211–17, 220; of race and racialization, 9–10, 204–5, 224; racist, 162, 247n28, 274n1; racialized relationships and, 133, 196–97

Last of the Mohicans, The (Cooper) 105, 175, 181, 185–87

law: coverture, 190; Federal Indian law, 166, 178, 181; Fugitive Slave Law, 66, 70–71, 77, 151; inheritance of slavery and, 6, 94, 119, 269n1. *See also* anti-miscegenation law; individual cases

Lemire, Elise, 13, 17, 41, 65, 68–69, 206, 248n29, 263n70

Letchworth State Park (New York), 162–63, 193–94

"Letter from a Freedman to his Old Master" (Anderson), 134

Lewis, Vashti, 142

Lhamon, W. T., 43

Liberator, The, 155

Lincoln, Abraham, 35, 64, 69–70

"Little Black Boy, The" (Blake), 106

Livermore, Elizabeth, 155

Lott, Eric, 31, 49, 232, 259n17

Love and Theft (Lott), 31, 232

Loving v. Virginia (1967), 201–4, 252n24, 258n7, 279n9

Luciano, Dana, 16

lynching, 259n15, 273n76

"M. L." (Alcott), 78–81

MacDonald, Joyce Green, 19, 48, 52

Macrae, David, 94, 113

Madison, Wisconsin, 226

mammy: as alternate name for mother, 92, 94, 117, 130–31, 265n34; as ambiguous kinship term, 113, 130

mammy trope: blackface and, 93; distinguished from Black mothers 131, 137–38, 141–42, 148; Margaret Garner and, 153–55; in *Iola Leroy*, 130–31, 143–44, 147, 149; "mammy-mother" / "mother-mammy" role, 89–119, 125–26, 130–31; "mulatto mammy" variation 109, 116–17; national monument to, 264n13; and nostalgia, 51–52, 143, 149, 264n21; in *Othello*, 51–52; in Sarah Piatt's "The Black Princess," 91–92, 95; in *Pudd'nhead Wilson*, 102–19

manifest domesticity, 165–66

Margaret Garner: A New American Opera in Two Acts (Morrison and Danielpour), 150–55, 198

Marrow of Tradition, The (Chesnutt), 125, 142–50

Mary Jemison: White Woman of the Seneca (Gangi), 161, 172

McDaniel, Hattie, 94

McKittrick, Katherine, 24

Mercy, A (Morrison), 25, 229, 237–40, 242

Mielke, Laura, 181

Minnie's Sacrifice (Harper), 73, 136, 212, 222, 225

Miralda; or the Beautiful Quadroon (Brown), 212, 224–26